Scheduling Algorithms

Peter Brucker

Scheduling Algorithms

Fifth Edition

With 77 Figures and 32 Tables

 Springer

Professor Dr. Peter Brucker
Universität Osnabrück
Fachbereich Mathematik/Informatik
Albrechtstraße 28a
49069 Osnabrück
Germany
pbrucker@uni-osnabrueck.de

Library of Congress Control Number: 2006940721

ISBN 978-3-540-69515-8 Springer Berlin Heidelberg New York
ISBN 978-3-540-20524-1 4th ed. Springer Berlin Heidelberg New York

Springer is part of Springer Science+Business Media

springer.com

© Springer-Verlag Berlin Heidelberg 2001, 2004, 2007

Production: LE-TEX Jelonek, Schmidt & Vöckler GbR, Leipzig
Cover-design: WMX Design GmbH, Heidelberg

SPIN 11970705   42/3100YL - 5 4 3 2 1 0   Printed on acid-free paper

Preface of the Fifth and Fourth Edition

In these editions new results have been added to the complexity columns. Furthermore, the bibliographies have been updated.

Again many thanks go to Marianne Gausmann for the typesetting and to Dr. Sigrid Knust for taking care of the complexity columns which can be found under the www-address

http://www.mathematik.uni-osnabrueck.de/research/OR/class.

Osnabrück, October 2006   Peter Brucker

Preface of the Third Edition

In this edition again the complexity columns at the end of each chapter and the corresponding references have been updated. I would like to express may gratitude to Dr. Sigrid Knust for taking care of a corresponding documentation of complexity results for scheduling problems in the Internet. These pages can be found under the world-wide-web address http://www.mathematik.uni-osnabrueck.de/research/OR/class.

In addition to the material of the second edition some new results on scheduling problems with release times and constant processing times and on multiprocessor task problems in which each task needs a certain number of processors have been included.

The new edition has been rewritten in LATEX 2$_\varepsilon$. Many thanks go to Marianne Gausmann for the new typesetting and to Christian Strotmann for creating the bibliography database files.

Osnabrück, March 2001   Peter Brucker

Preface of the Second Edition

In this revised edition new material has been added. In particular, the chapters on batching problems and multiprocessor task scheduling have been augmented. Also the complexity columns at the end of each chapter have been updated. In this connection I would like thank Jan Karel Lenstra for providing the current results of the program MSPCLASS. I am grateful for the constructive comments of Jacek Blazewicz, Johann Hurink, Sigrid Knust, Svetlana Kravchenko, Erwin Pesch, Maurice Queyranne, Vadim Timkowsky, Jürgen Zimmermann which helped to improve the first edition.

Finally, again special thanks go to Marianne Gausmann and Teresa Gehrs for the TEX typesetting and for improving the English.

Osnabrück, November 1997   Peter Brucker

Preface

This is a book about scheduling algorithms. The first such algorithms were formulated in the mid fifties. Since then there has been a growing interest in scheduling. During the seventies, computer scientists discovered scheduling as a tool for improving the performance of computer systems. Furthermore, scheduling problems have been investigated and classified with respect to their computational complexity. During the last few years, new and interesting scheduling problems have been formulated in connection with flexible manufacturing.

Most parts of the book are devoted to the discussion of polynomial algorithms. In addition, enumerative procedures based on branch & bound concepts and dynamic programming, as well as local search algorithms, are presented.

The book can be viewed as consisting of three parts. The first part, Chapters 1 through 3, covers basics like an introduction to and classification of scheduling problems, methods of combinatorial optimization that are relevant for the solution procedures, and computational complexity theory.

The second part, Chapters 4 through 6, covers classical scheduling algorithms for solving single machine problems, parallel machine problems, and shop scheduling problems.

The third and final part, Chapters 7 through 11, is devoted to problems discussed in the more recent literature in connection with flexible manufacturing, such as scheduling problems with due dates and batching. Also, multiprocessor task scheduling is discussed.

Since it is not possible to cover the whole area of scheduling in one book, some restrictions are imposed. Firstly, in this book only machine or processor scheduling problems are discussed. Secondly, some interesting topics like cyclic scheduling, scheduling problems with finite input and/or output buffers, and general resource constrained scheduling problems are not covered in this book.

I am indebted to many people who have helped me greatly in preparing this book. Students in my courses during the last three years at the University of Osnabrück have given many suggestions for improving earlier versions of this material. The following people read preliminary drafts of all or part of the book and made constructive comments: Johann Hurink, Sigrid Knust, Andreas Krämer, Wieslaw Kubiak, Helmut Mausser.

I am grateful to the Deutsche Forschungsgemeinschaft for supporting the research that underlies much of this book. I am also indebted to the Mathematics and Computer Science Department of the University of Osnabrück, the College of Business, University of Colorado at Boulder, and the Computer Science Department, University of California at Riverside for providing me with an excellent environment for writing this book.

Finally, special thanks go to Marianne Gausmann for her tireless efforts in translating my handwritten hieroglyphics and figures into input for the TEX typesetting system.

Osnabrück, April 1995   Peter Brucker

Contents

Chapter 1

Classification of Scheduling Problems

The theory of scheduling is characterized by a virtually unlimited number of problem types (see, e.g. Baker [12], Blazewicz et al. [27], Coffman [69], Conway et al. [72], French [93], Lenstra [151] , Pinedo [180], Rinnooy Kan [181], Tanaev et al. [193], Tanaev et al. [194]). In this chapter, a basic classification for the scheduling problems covered in the first part of this book will be given. This classification is based on a classification scheme widely used in the literature (see, e.g. Lawler et al. [145]). In later chapters we will extend this classification scheme.

1.1   Scheduling Problems

Suppose that m **machines** $M_j (j = 1, \ldots, m)$ have to process n **jobs** $J_i (i = 1, \ldots, n)$. A **schedule** is for each job an allocation of one or more time intervals to one or more machines. Schedules may be represented by **Gantt charts** as shown in Figure 1.1. Gantt charts may be machine-oriented (Figure 1.1(a)) or job-oriented (Figure 1.1(b)). The corresponding scheduling problem is to find a schedule satisfying certain restrictions.

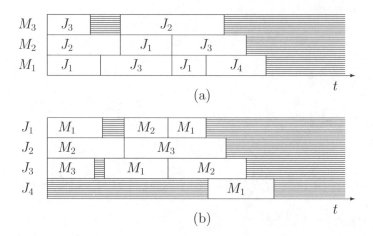

Figure 1.1: Machine- and job-oriented Gantt charts.

1.2   Job Data

A job J_i consists of a **number n_i of operations** $O_{i1}, \ldots, O_{i,n_i}$. Associated with operation O_{ij} is a **processing requirement** p_{ij}. If job J_i consists of only one operation ($n_i = 1$), we then identify J_i with O_{i1} and denote the processing requirement by p_i. Furthermore, a **release date** r_i, on which the first operation of J_i becomes available for processing may be specified. Associated with each operation O_{ij} is a **set of machines** $\mu_{ij} \subseteq \{M_1, \ldots, M_m\}$. O_{ij} may be processed on any of the machines in μ_{ij}. Usually, all μ_{ij} are one element sets or all μ_{ij} are equal to the set of all machines. In the first case we have **dedicated machines**. In the second case the machines are called **parallel**. The general case is introduced here to cover problems in flexible manufacturing where machines are equipped with different tools. This means that an operation can be processed on any machine equipped with the appropriate tool. We call scheduling problems of this type problems with **multi-purpose machines** (MPM).

It is also possible that all machines in the set μ_{ij} are used simultaneously by O_{ij} during the whole processing period. Scheduling problems of this type are called **multiprocessor task scheduling problems**. Scheduling problems with multi-purpose machines and multiprocessor task scheduling problems will be classified in more detail in Chapters 10 and 11.

Finally, there is a **cost function** $f_i(t)$ which measures the cost of completing J_i at time t. A **due date** d_i and a **weight** w_i may be used in defining f_i.

In general, all data $p_i, p_{ij}, r_i, d_i, w_i$ are assumed to be integer. A schedule is **feasible** if no two time intervals overlap on the same machine, if no two time intervals allocated to the same job overlap, and if, in addition, it meets a number of problem-specific characteristics. A schedule is **optimal** if it minimizes a given optimality criterion.

Sometimes it is convenient to identify a job J_i by its index i. We will use this brief notation in later chapters.

We will discuss a large variety of classes of scheduling problems which differ in their complexity. Also the algorithms we will develop are quite different for different classes of scheduling problems. Classes of scheduling problems are specified in terms of a three-field classification $\alpha|\beta|\gamma$ where α specifies the **machine environment**, β specifies the **job characteristics**, and γ denotes the **optimality criterion**. Such a classification scheme was introduced by Graham et al. [108].

1.3 Job Characteristics

The job characteristics are specified by a set β containing at the most six elements $\beta_1, \beta_2, \beta_3, \beta_4, \beta_5$, and β_6.

β_1 indicates whether **preemption** (or job splitting) is allowed. Preemption of a job or operation means that processing may be interrupted and resumed at a later time, even on another machine. A job or operation may be interrupted several times. If preemption is allowed, we set $\beta_1 = pmtn$. Otherwise β_1 does not appear in β.

β_2 describes **precedence relations** between jobs. These precedence relations may be represented by an acyclic directed graph $G = (V, A)$ where $V = \{1, \ldots, n\}$ corresponds with the jobs, and $(i, k) \in A$ iff J_i must be completed before J_k starts. In this case we write $J_i \rightarrow J_k$. If G is an arbitrary acyclic directed graph we set $\beta_2 = \textbf{prec}$. Sometimes we will consider scheduling problems with restricted precedences given by chains, an intree, an outtree, a tree or a series-parallel directed graph. In these cases we set β_2 equal to chains, intree, outtree, and sp-graph.

If $\beta_2 = \textbf{intree}$ (**outtree**), then G is a rooted tree with an outdegree (indegree) for each vertex of at the most one. Thus, in an intree (outtree) all arcs are directed towards (away from) a root. If $\beta_2 = $ **tree**, then G is either an intree or an outtree. A set of **chains** is a tree in which the outdegree and indegree for each vertex is at the most one. If $\beta_2 = $ chains, then G is a set of chains.

Series-parallel graphs are closely related to trees. A graph is called **series-parallel** if it can be built by means of the following rules:

Base graph. Any graph consisting of a single vertex is series-parallel. Let $G_i = (V_i, A_i)$ be series-parallel $(i = 1, 2)$.

Parallel composition. The graph $G = (V_1 \cup V_2, A_1 \cup A_2)$ formed from G_1 and G_2 by joining the vertex sets and arc sets is series parallel.

Series composition. The graph $G = (V_1 \cup V_2, A_1 \cup A_2 \cup T_1 \times S_2)$ formed from G_1 and G_2 by joining the vertex sets and arc sets and adding all arcs (t, s) where t belongs to the set T_1 of sinks of G_1 (i.e. the set of vertices without successors) and s belongs to the set S_2 of sources of G_2 (i.e. the set of vertices without predecessors) is series parallel.

We set $\beta_2 = $ **sp-graph** if G is series parallel. If there are no precedence constraints, then β_2 does not appear in β.

If $\beta_3 = r_i$, then release dates may be specified for each job. If $r_i = 0$ for all jobs, then β_3 does not appear in β.

β_4 specifies restrictions on the processing times or on the number of operations. If β_4 is equal to $p_i = 1(p_{ij} = 1)$, then each job (operation) has a **unit processing requirement**. Similarly, we may write $p_i = p(p_{ij} = p)$. Occasionally, the β_4 field contains additional characteristics with an obvious interpretation such as $p_i \in \{1, 2\}$ or $d_i = d$.

If $\beta_5 = d_i$, then a deadline d_i is specified for each job J_i, i.e. job J_i must finish not later than time d_i.

In some scheduling applications, sets of jobs must be grouped into batches. A batch is a set of jobs which must be processed jointly on a machine. The finishing time of all jobs in a batch is defined as equal to the finishing time of the batch. A batch may consist of a single job up to n jobs. There is a set-up time s for each batch. We assume that this set-up time is the same for all batches and sequence independent. A **batching problem** is to group the jobs into batches and to schedule these batches. There are two types of batching problems, denoted by **p-batching problems**, and **s-batching problems**. For p-batching problems (s batching-problems) the length of a batch is equal to the maximum (sum) of processing times of all jobs in the batch. $\beta_6 = p$-batch or $\beta_6 = s\text{-batch}$ indicates a batching problem. Otherwise β_6 does not appear in β.

1.4 Machine Environment

The machine environment is characterized by a string $\alpha = \alpha_1 \alpha_2$ of two parameters. Possible values of α_1 are $\circ, P, Q, R, PMPM, QMPM, G, X,$ O, J, F. If $\alpha_1 \in \{\circ, P, Q, R, PMPM, QMPM\}$, where $\circ$ denotes the empty symbol (thus, $\alpha = \alpha_2$ if $\alpha_1 = \circ$), then each J_i consists of a single operation.

If $\alpha_1 = \circ$, each job must be processed on a specified **dedicated** machine.

If $\alpha_1 \in \{P, Q, R\}$, then we have parallel machines, i.e. each job can be processed on each of the machines $M_1, \ldots, M_m$. If $\alpha_1 = P$, then there are **identical parallel machines**. Thus, for the processing time p_{ij} of job J_i on M_j we have $p_{ij} = p_i$ for all machines M_j. If $\alpha_1 = Q$, then there are **uniform parallel machines**, i.e. $p_{ij} = p_i/s_j$ where s_j is the speed of machine M_j. Finally, if $\alpha_1 = R$, then there are **unrelated parallel machines**, i.e. $p_{ij} = p_i/s_{ij}$ for job-dependent speeds s_{ij} of M_j.

If $\alpha_1 = PMPM$ and $\alpha_1 = QMPM$, then we have multi-purpose machines with identical and uniform speeds, respectively.

If $\alpha_1 \in \{G, X, O, J, F\}$, we have a multi-operation model, i.e. associated with each job J_i there is a set of operations $O_{i1}, \ldots, O_{i,n_i}$. The machines are dedicated, i.e. all μ_{ij} are one element sets. Furthermore, there are precedence relations between arbitrary operations. This general model is called a **general shop**. We indicate the general shop by setting $\alpha_1 = G$. Job shops, flow shops, open shops, and mixed shops are special cases of the general shop. In a **job shop**, indicated by $\alpha_1 = J$, we have special precedence relations of the form

$$O_{i1} \rightarrow O_{i2} \rightarrow O_{i3} \rightarrow \ldots \rightarrow O_{i,n_i} \quad \text{for } i = 1, \ldots, n.$$

Furthermore, we generally assume that $\mu_{ij} \neq \mu_{i,j+1}$ for $j = 1, \ldots, n_i - 1$. We call a job shop in which $\mu_{ij} = \mu_{i,j+1}$ is possible a **job shop with machine repetition**.

The **flow shop**, indicated by $\alpha_1 = F$, is a special case of the job-shop in which $n_i = m$ for $i = 1, \ldots, n$ and $\mu_{ij} = \{M_j\}$ for each $i = 1, \ldots, n$ and $j = 1, \ldots, m$. The **open shop**, denoted by $\alpha_1 = O$, is defined as the flow shop, with the exception that there are no precedence relations between

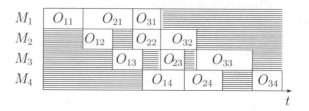

Figure 1.2: Feasible schedule for a permutation flow shop problem.

the operations. A **mixed shop**, indicated by $\alpha_1 = X$, is a combination of a job shop and an open shop.

A **permutation flow shop** is a flow shop in which jobs are processed in the same order on each machine. Figure 1.2 shows a feasible schedule for a permutation flow shop. If we have a job shop problem, we may set β_4 equal to $n_i \leq 2$. In this case all jobs have at the most two operations. If α_2 is equal to a positive integer $1, 2, \ldots$, then α_2 denotes the number of machines. If $\alpha_2 = k$, then k is an arbitrary, but fixed number of machines. If the number of machines is arbitrary, we set $\alpha_2 = \circ$.

1.5 Optimality Criteria

We denote the **finishing time** of job J_i by C_i, and the associated **cost** by $f_i(C_i)$. There are essentially two types of total cost functions

$$f_{\max}(C) := \max\{f_i(C_i)|i = 1, \ldots, n\}$$

and

$$\sum f_i(C) := \sum_{i=1}^{n} f_i(C_i)$$

called **bottleneck objectives** and **sum objectives**, respectively. The **scheduling problem** is to find a feasible schedule which minimizes the total cost function.

If the functions f_i are not specified, we set $\gamma = f_{\max}$ or $\gamma = \sum f_i$. However, in most cases we consider special functions f_i.

The most common objective functions are the **makespan** $\max\{C_i|i = 1, \ldots, n\}$, **total flow time** $\sum_{i=1}^{n} C_i$, and **weighted (total) flow time**

$\sum_{i=1}^{n} w_i C_i$. In these cases we write $\gamma = C_{\max}, \gamma = \sum C_i$, and $\gamma = \sum w_i C_i$, respectively.

Other objective functions depend on due dates d_i which are associated with jobs J_i. We define for each job J_i:

$$L_i := \quad C_i - d_i \qquad\qquad \textbf{lateness}$$

$$E_i := \quad \max\{0, d_i - C_i\} \qquad \textbf{earliness}$$

$$T_i := \quad \max\{0, C_i - d_i\} \qquad \textbf{tardiness}$$

$$D_i := \quad |C_i - d_i| \qquad\qquad \textbf{absolute deviation}$$

$$S_i := \quad (C_i - d_i)^2 \qquad\qquad \textbf{squared deviation}$$

$$U_i := \quad \left\{ \begin{array}{ll} 0 & \text{if } C_i \le d_i \\ 1 & \text{otherwise} \end{array} \right. \qquad \textbf{unit penalty}.$$

With each of these functions G_i we get four possible objectives $\gamma = \max G_i, \max w_i G_i, \sum G_i, \sum w_i G_i$. The most important bottleneck objective besides $C_{\max}$ is **maximum lateness** $L_{\max} := \max_{i=1}^{n} L_i$. Other objective functions which are widely used are $\sum T_i, \sum w_i T_i, \sum U_i, \sum w_i U_i,$ $\sum D_i, \sum w_i D_i, \sum S_i, \sum w_i S_i, \sum E_i, \sum w_i E_i$. Linear combinations of these objective functions are also considered.

An objective function which is nondecreasing with respect to all variables C_i is called **regular**. Functions involving E_i, D_i, S_i are not regular. The other functions defined so far are regular.

A schedule is called **active** if it is not possible to schedule jobs (operations) earlier without violating some constraint. A schedule is called **semiactive** if no job (operation) can be processed earlier without changing the processing order or violating the constraints.

1.6 Examples

To illustrate the three-field notation $\alpha | \beta | \gamma$ we present some examples. In each case we will describe the problem. Furthermore, we will specify an instance and present a feasible schedule for the instance in the form of a Gantt chart.

Example 1.1 $P|prec; p_i = 1|C_{max}$ is the problem of scheduling jobs with unit processing times and arbitrary precedence constraints on m identical machines such that the makespan is minimized.

An instance is given by a directed graph with n vertices and the number of machines.

Figure 1.3 shows an instance of this problem and a corresponding feasible schedule.

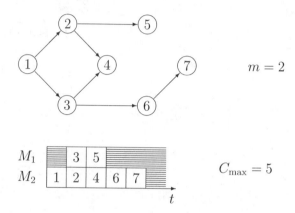

Figure 1.3: Instance for $P \mid prec; p_i = 1 \mid C_{max}$.

Example 1.2 $1|s\text{-batch}| \sum w_i C_i$ is the problem of splitting a set of jobs into batches and scheduling these batches on one machine such that the weighted flow time is minimized. The processing time of a batch is the sum of processing times of the jobs in the batch.

Figure 1.4 shows a schedule with three batches for the following instance of this problem:

i	1	2	3	4	5	6	
p_i	3	2	2	3	1	1	$s = 1$
w_i	1	2	1	1	4	4	

The objective value for the schedule is

$$\sum w_i C_i = 2 \cdot 3 + (1 + 1 + 4) \cdot 10 + (1 + 4)15.$$

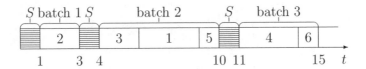

Figure 1.4: Schedule with three batches.

Example 1.3 $1|r_i; pmtn|L_{max}$ is the problem of finding a preemptive schedule on one machine for a set of jobs with given release times $r_i \neq 0$ such that the maximum lateness is minimized. An instance is presented in Figure 1.5

i	1	2	3	4
p_i	2	1	2	2
r_i	1	2	2	7
d_i	2	3	4	8

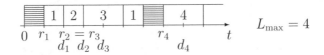

$L_{max} = 4$

Figure 1.5: Instance for $1 \mid r_i; pmtn \mid L_{max}$.

Example 1.4 $J3|p_{ij} = 1|C_{max}$ is the problem of minimizing maximum completion time in a three-machine job shop with unit processing times. An instance is presented in Figure 1.6. The table contains the machines μ_{ij} associated with the operations O_{ij}.

i/j	1	2	3	4
1	M_1	M_3	M_2	M_1
2	M_2	M_3	–	–
3	M_3	M_1	–	–
4	M_1	M_3	M_1	–
5	M_3	M_1	M_2	M_3

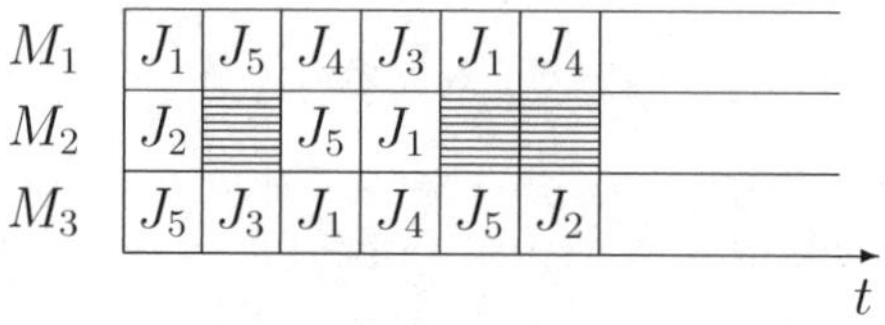

M_1 | J_1 | J_5 | J_4 | J_3 | J_1 | J_4 |

M_2 | J_2 | | J_5 | J_1 | | |

M_3 | J_5 | J_3 | J_1 | J_4 | J_5 | J_2 |

t

Figure 1.6: Instance for $J_3 \mid p_{ij} = 1 \mid C_{\max}$.

Chapter 2

Some Problems in Combinatorial Optimization

Some scheduling problems can be solved efficiently by reducing them to well-known combinatorial optimization problems, such as linear programs, maximum flow problems, or transportation problems. Others can be solved by using standard techniques, such as dynamic programming and branch-and-bound methods. In this chapter we will give a brief survey of these combinatorial optimization problems. We will also discuss some of the methods.

2.1 Linear and Integer Programming

A **linear program** is an optimization problem of the form

$$
\begin{aligned}
\text{minimize } z(x) \quad = \quad & c_1 x_1 + \ldots + c_n x_n & (2.1) \\
& \text{subject to (s.t.)} \\
& a_{11} x_1 + \ldots + a_{1n} x_n \geq b_1 \\
& \quad \vdots & (2.2) \\
& a_{m1} x_1 + \ldots + a_{mn} x_n \geq b_m \\
& x_i \geq 0 \text{ for } i = 1, \ldots, n.
\end{aligned}
$$

A vector $x = (x_1, \ldots, x_n)$ satisfying (2.2) is called a **feasible solution**. The problem is to find a feasible solution which minimizes (2.1). A linear program that has a feasible solution is called **feasible**. A linear program may also be **unbounded**, which means that for each real number K there exists a feasible solution x with $z(x) < K$. Linear programs which have a feasible solution and are not unbounded always have an optimal solution.

The most popular method for solving linear programs is the simplex algorithm. It is an iterative procedure which finds an optimal solution or detects infeasibility or unboundedness after a finite number of steps. Although the number of iteration steps may be exponential, the simplex algorithm is very efficient in practice.

An **integer linear program** is a linear program in which all variables x_i are restricted to integers. If the variables x_i can only take the values 0 or 1, then the corresponding integer linear program is called a **binary linear program**. If in a linear program only some variables are restricted to integers, then we have a **mixed integer linear program**.

Many books exist on linear and integer programming. The interested reader is referred to the more recent books by Chvátal [67], Nemhauser & Wolsey [175], and Schrijver [182].

2.2 Transshipment Problems

The transshipment problem is a special linear program. Let $G = (V, A)$ be a directed graph with vertex set $V = \{1, \ldots, n\}$ and arc set A. Arcs are denoted by (i, j) with $i, j \in V$. A **transshipment problem** is given by

$$\text{minimize} \sum_{(i,j) \in A} c_{ij} x_{ij}$$
$$\text{s.t.}$$
$$\sum_{\substack{j \\ (j,i) \in A}} x_{ji} - \sum_{\substack{j \\ (i,j) \in A}} x_{ij} = b_i \text{ for all } i \in V \tag{2.3}$$
$$l_{ij} \le x_{ij} \le u_{ij} \text{ for all } (i, j) \in A. \tag{2.4}$$

Graph G may be interpreted as a transportation network. The b_i-value is the demand for or the supply of some goods in vertex i. If $b_i > 0$, we have a demand of b_i units. If $b_i < 0$, we have a supply of $-b_i$ units.

Notice that either the demand in i or the supply in i may be zero. The goods may be transported along the arcs. c_{ij} are the costs of shipping one unit of the goods along arc (i, j). x_{ij} denotes the number of units to be shipped from vertex i to vertex j. Equations (2.3) are balancing equations: in each vertex i, the amount shipped to i plus the supply in i must be equal to the amount shipped away from i, or the amount shipped to i must be equal to the demand plus the amount shipped away. By (2.4) the amount shipped along (i, j) is bounded from below by l_{ij} and from above by u_{ij}. We may set $l_{ij} = -\infty$ or $u_{ij} = \infty$, which means that there are no bounds. A vector $x = (x_{ij})$ satisfying (2.3) and (2.4) is called a feasible flow. The problem is to find a feasible flow which minimizes the total transportation costs. We assume that

$$\sum_{i=1}^{n} b_i = 0, \tag{2.5}$$

i.e. the total supply is equal to the total demand. A transshipment problem with $b_i = 0$ for all $i \in V$ is called a **circulation problem** .

Standard algorithms for the transshipment problem are the network simplex method (Dantzig [74]), and the out-of-kilter algorithm, which was developed independently by Yakovleva [207], Minty [168], and Fulkerson [94]. Both methods have the property of calculating an integral flow if all finite b_i, l_{ij}, and u_{ij} are integers. These algorithms and other more recent algorithms can be found in a book by Ahuja et al. [6]. Complexity results for the transshipment problem and the equivalent circulation problem will be discussed in Chapter 3. In the next two sections we discuss special transshipment problems.

2.3   The Maximum Flow Problem

A **flow graph** $G = (V, A, s, t)$ is a directed graph (V, A) with a **source vertex** s, and a **sink vertex** t. Associated with each arc $(i, j) \in A$ is a nonnegative capacity u_{ij}, which may also be ∞. The maximum flow problem is to send as much flow as possible from the source to the sink without violating capacity constraints in the arcs. For this problem, we have the linear programming formulation

$$\text{maximize } v$$
$$\text{s.t.}$$
$$\sum_{\substack{j \\ (j,i) \in A}} x_{ji} - \sum_{\substack{j \\ (i,j) \in A}} x_{ij} = \begin{cases} -v & \text{for } i = s \\ v & \text{for } i = t \\ 0 & \text{otherwise} \end{cases}$$
$$0 \leq x_{ij} \leq u_{ij} \text{ for all } \quad (i,j) \in A.$$

The maximum flow problem may be interpreted as a transshipment problem with exactly one supply vertex s and exactly one demand vertex t, and variable supply (demand) v which should be as large as possible. It can be formulated as a minimum cost circulation problem by adding an arc (t, s) with $u_{ts} = \infty$ and cost $c_{ts} = -1$. The cost of all other arcs $(i, j) \in A$ should be equal to zero.

The first algorithm for the maximum flow problem was the augmenting path algorithm of Ford and Fulkerson [91]. Other algorithms and their complexity are listed in Chapter 3. All these algorithms provide an optimal solution which is integral if all capacities are integers.

2.4   Bipartite Matching Problems

The **bipartite maximum cardinality matching problem** is a special maximum flow problem which can be formulated as follows:

Consider a **bipartite graph**, i.e. a graph $G = (V_1 \cup V_2, A)$ where the vertex set V is the union of two disjoint sets V_1 and V_2, and $A \subseteq V_1 \times V_2$. A **matching** is a set $M \subseteq A$ of arcs such that no two arcs in M have a common vertex, i.e. if $(i, j), (i', j') \in M$ with $(i, j) \neq (i', j')$, then $i \neq i'$ and $j \neq j'$. The problem is to find a matching M with maximal cardinality.

The maximum cardinality bipartite matching problem may be reduced to a maximum flow problem by adding a source s with arcs $(s, i), i \in V_1$ and a sink t with arcs $(j, t), j \in V_2$ to the bipartite graph. Furthermore, we associate unit capacities with all arcs in the augmented network. It is not difficult to see that a maximal integer flow from s to t corresponds with a maximum cardinality matching M. This matching is given by all arcs $(i, j) \in A$ carrying unit flow.

The maximum cardinality bipartite matching problem can be solved in

$O(\min\{|V_1|, |V_2|\} \cdot |A|)$ steps by maximum flow calculations. Hopcroft and Karp [114] developed an $O(n^{\frac{1}{2}}r)$ (see Section 3.1 for a definition of this O-notation) algorithm for the case $n = |V_1| \leq |V_2|$ and $r = |A|$.

Now, consider a bipartite graph $G = (V_1 \cup V_2, A)$ with $|V_1| \geq |V_2| = m$. For each $j \in V_2$ let $P(j)$ be the set of predecessors of j, i.e. $P(j) = \{i \in V_1 \mid (i, j) \in A\}$. Clearly, m is an upper bound for the cardinality of a maximal cardinality matching in G. The following theorem due to Hall [110] gives necessary and sufficient conditions for the existence of a matching with cardinality m.

Theorem 2.1 Let $G = (V_1 \cup V_2, A)$ be a bipartite graph with $|V_1| \geq |V_2| = m$. Then there exists in G a matching with cardinality m if and only if

$$\left| \bigcup_{i \in N} P(i) \right| \geq |N| \quad \text{for all } N \subseteq V_2.$$

□

Next we will show how to use this theorem and network flow theory to solve an open shop problem.

$O \mid \text{pmtn} \mid C_{\max}$

This preemptive open shop problem can be formulated in the following way: n jobs $J_1, \ldots, J_n$ are given to be processed on m machines $M_1, \ldots, M_m$. Each job J_i consists of m operations O_{ij} $(j = 1, \ldots, m)$ where O_{ij} must be processed on machine M_j for p_{ij} time units. Preemption is allowed and the order in which the operations of J_i are processed is arbitrary. The only restriction is that a machine cannot process two jobs simultaneously and a job cannot be processed by two machines at the same time. We have to find a schedule with minimal makespan.

For each machine $M_j(j = 1, \ldots, m)$ and each job $J_i(i = 1, \ldots, n)$ define

$$T_j := \sum_{i=1}^{n} p_{ij} \quad \text{and} \quad L_i := \sum_{j=1}^{m} p_{ij}.$$

T_j is the total time needed on machine M_j, and L_i is the length of job J_i.

Clearly,

$$T = \max\{\max_{i=1}^{n} L_i, \max_{j=1}^{m} T_j\} \tag{2.6}$$

is a lower bound for the $C_{\max}$-value.

A schedule which achieves this bound must be optimal. We construct such a schedule step by step using the following ideas.

First, we add m dummy jobs J_{n+j} $(j = 1, \ldots, m)$ and n dummy machines M_{m+i} $(i = 1, \ldots, n)$. Then we construct a network N which has the following vertices:

- a source s and a sink t,

- job vertices J_i $(i = 1, \ldots, n + m)$, and

- machine vertices M_j $(j = 1, \ldots, n + m)$.

The arcs in N are

- for each J_i $(i = 1, \ldots, n + m)$ an arc (s, J_i) with capacity T and for each M_j $(j = 1, \ldots, n + m)$ an arc (M_j, t) with capacity T,

- for each job J_i $(i = 1, \ldots, n)$ and each machine M_j $(j = 1, \ldots, m)$ with $p_{ij} > 0$ an arc (J_i, M_j) with capacity p_{ij},

- for each $i = 1, \ldots, n$ with $T - L_i > 0$ an arc (J_i, M_{m+i}) with capacity $T - L_i$ connecting the job J_i with the dummy machine M_{m+i}, and

- for each $j = 1, \ldots, m$ with $T - T_j > 0$ an arc (J_{n+j}, M_j) with capacity $T - T_j$ connecting the dummy job J_{n+j} with machine M_j.

If all arcs defined thus far receive a flow equal to the capacity of the arc, then for each job vertex J_i $(i = 1, \ldots n)$ and each machine vertex M_j $(j = 1, \ldots, m)$ the total flow T into such a vertex is equal to the total flow out of this vertex. This is not true for the dummy vertices. To create a flow balance in these vertices, we send $\sum_{j=1}^{m} T_j = \sum_{i=1}^{n} \sum_{j=1}^{m} p_{ij} = \sum_{i=1}^{n} L_i$ units of flow from the dummy job vertices to the dummy machine vertices. Such a flow (f_{ij}) exists in the complete bipartite graph connecting all dummy jobs with all dummy machines. We complete our network N by adding

- for each $i = 1, \ldots, n$ and $j = 1, \ldots, m$ with $f_{n+j,m+i} > 0$ an arc (J_{n+j}, M_{m+i}) with capacity $f_{n+j,m+i}$.

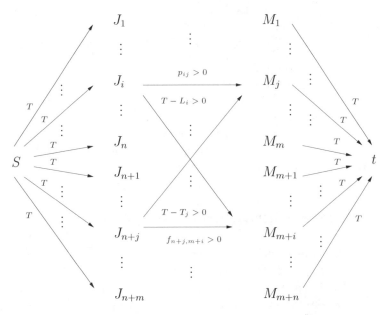

If we now saturate all arcs up to their capacity, we get a flow $x = (x_{ij})$ from s to t with the value $(n+m)T$. For a set $M \subseteq \{M_1, \ldots, M_{n+m}\}$ of machines let $P(M)$ be the set of all predecessors of vertices in M, i.e. all jobs J_i such that $x_{ij} > 0$ for some $M_j \in M$. We have

$$|M|\, T = \sum_{M_j \in M} \sum_{J_i \in P(M_j)} x_{ij} \le |P(M)|\, T$$

which implies $|M| \le |P(M)|$ for all machine sets M. By Theorem 2.1 there exists a matching R with cardinality $n + m$. Let $\triangle_1 := \min\{x_{ij} \mid (J_i, M_j) \in R\}$. Then we construct a partial schedule in the time interval $[0, \triangle_1]$ by

- scheduling J_i in $[0, \triangle_1]$ on M_j if $(J_i, M_j) \in R$,

- scheduling J_i not in $[0, \triangle_1]$ if $(J_i, M_{m+i}) \in R$, and

- leaving M_j idle in $[0, \triangle_1]$ if $(J_{n+j}, M_j) \in R$.

Furthermore, we replace T by $T - \triangle_1$, reduce the capacity of all arcs in R by $\triangle_1$ and eliminate all arcs which now have zero capacity. Finally, we replace the current scheduling time $s = 0$ by $s = \triangle_1$ and repeat the process to schedule the next interval $[s, s+\triangle_2]$, etc. The whole procedure stops if $T = 0$, providing a schedule of length T which is optimal.

After each step at least one arc is eliminated. Thus, if r is the number of operations O_{ij} with $p_{ij} > 0$, then we have at the most $O(r)$ steps (we assume that $r \geq n$ and $r \geq m$). A matching can be calculated in $O(r(n+m)^{0.5})$ steps (Hopcroft and Karp [114]). Thus, the total complexity is $O(r^2(n+m)^{0.5})$. The complexity can be reduced to $O(r^2)$ due to the fact that in each step the matching from the previous step may be used to calculate the new matching.

2.5   The Assignment Problem

Consider the complete bipartite graph, $G = (V_1 \cup V_2, V_1 \times V_2)$ with $V_1 = \{v_1, \ldots, v_n\}$ and $V_2 = \{w_1, \ldots, w_m\}$. Assume w.l.o.g. that $n \leq m$. Associated with each arc (v_i, w_j) there is a real number c_{ij}. An **assignment** is given by a one-to-one mapping $\varphi : V_1 \to V_2$. The **assignment problem** is to find an assignment φ such that

$$\sum_{v \in V_1} c_{v\varphi(v)}$$

is minimized.

We may represent the assignment problem by the $n \times m$-matrix $C = (c_{ij})$ and formulate it as a linear program with 0-1-variables x_{ij}:

$$\text{minimize} \qquad \sum_{i=1}^{n} \sum_{j=1}^{m} c_{ij} x_{ij} \qquad (2.7)$$

s.t.

$$\sum_{j=1}^{m} x_{ij} = 1 \quad i = 1, \ldots, n \qquad (2.8)$$

$$\sum_{i=1}^{n} x_{ij} \leq 1 \quad j = 1, \ldots, m \qquad (2.9)$$

$$x_{ij} \in \{0, 1\} \; i = 1, \ldots, n; \; j = 1, \ldots, m. \qquad (2.10)$$

Here $x_{ij} = 1$ if and only if v_i is assigned to w_j. Due to (2.8) and (2.9) each $v_i \in V_1$ is assigned to a unique element in V_2, and each $w_j \in V_2$ is involved in at the most one assignment.

The assignment problem may be reduced to the transshipment problem by adding a source vertex s with arcs $(s, v_i), v_i \in V_1$ and a sink t with arcs $(w_j, t), w_j \in V_2$ to the bipartite graph. All costs of the new arcs are defined as zero, and the lower and upper capacities are zero and one, respectively. Finally, we let s be the only supply node, and t the only demand node. Both supply and demand are equal to n.

Any integer solution provided by an algorithm which solves this transshipment problem is feasible for (2.7) to (2.10). Thus, we may solve the assignment problem by solving the corresponding transshipment problem. The first algorithm for the assignment problem was the Hungarian method introduced by Kuhn [132]. It solves the assignment problem in $O(n^2 m)$ steps by exploiting its special structure.

Next we show that single machine problems with unit processing times can be reduced to assignment problems.

$1|r_i; p_i = 1| \sum f_i$

To solve problem $1|r_i; p_i = 1| \sum f_i$, where the f_i are monotone functions of the finishing times C_i of jobs $i = 1, \ldots, n$, we have to assign to the jobs n different time slots. If we assign time slot t to job i, the corresponding costs are $f_i(t + 1)$. Next we will show that at the most n time slots are to be considered. Thus, the corresponding assignment problem can be solved in $O(n^3)$ time.

Because functions f_i are monotone nondecreasing, the jobs should be scheduled as early as possible. The n earliest time slots t_i for scheduling all n jobs may be calculated using the following algorithm, in which we assume that the jobs are enumerated in such a way that

$$r_1 \leq r_2 \leq \ldots \leq r_n.$$

Algorithm Time Slots
1. $t_1 := r_1$;
2. FOR $i := 2$ TO n DO
        $t_i := \max\{r_i, t_{i-1} + 1\}$

There exists an optimal schedule which occupies all of the time slots $t_i (i = 1, \ldots, n)$. To see this, consider an optimal schedule S which occupies time slots $t_1, \ldots, t_j$ where $j < n$ is maximal. According to the construction of the t_i-values, t_{j+1} is the next time slot in which a job can be scheduled. If time slot t_{j+1} in S is empty, a job scheduled later in S can be moved to t_{j+1} without increasing the objective value. Thus, the new schedule is optimal, too, and we have a contradiction to the maximality of j. Notice that the schedule created this way defines time intervals I_ν in which the machine is busy. These intervals are separated by idle periods of the machine.

The complete bipartite graph which defines the corresponding assignment problem is given by

$$V_1 = \{1, \ldots, n\}$$
$$V_2 = \{t_1, \ldots, t_n\}.$$

For the c_{ij}-values we choose

$$c_{ij} = \begin{cases} f_i(t_j + 1) & \text{if } r_i \leq t_j \\ \infty & \text{otherwise.} \end{cases}$$

Next we consider an assignment problem which has a very simple solution.

Let $V_1 = \{v_1, \ldots, v_n\}$ and $V_2 = \{w_1, \ldots, w_m\}$ and consider the corresponding complete bipartite graph $G = (V_1 \cup V_2, V_1 \times V_2)$. Then the corresponding assignment problem is specified by a $n \times m$ array $C = (c_{ij})$. C is called a **Monge array** if

$$c_{ik} + c_{jl} \leq c_{il} + c_{jk} \text{ for all } i < j \text{ and } k < l. \tag{2.11}$$

Theorem 2.2 Let (c_{ij}) be a Monge array of dimension $n \times m$ where $n \leq m$. Furthermore, let $c_{ij} \leq c_{ik}$ for all i and $j < k$. Then

$$x_{ij} = \begin{cases} 1 \text{ if } i = j \\ 0 \text{ otherwise} \end{cases}$$

is an optimal solution for the assignment problem.

Proof: Let $y = (y_{ij})$ be an optimal solution of the assignment problem with $y_{\nu\nu} = 1$ for $\nu = 1, \ldots, i$ where i is as large as possible. Assume that $i < n$ (if $i = n$ we have finished). Because $y_{i+1,i+1} = 0$, there exists an index $l > i + 1$ with $y_{i+1,l} = 1$. Now we consider two cases.

Case 1: There exists an index $j > i + 1$ with $y_{j,i+1} = 1$.

(2.11) yields

$$c_{i+1,i+1} + c_{jl} \leq c_{i+1,l} + c_{j,i+1}.$$

Thus, if we set

$$\bar{y}_{rs} = \begin{cases} 1 & \text{if } r = s = i + 1 \text{ or } r = j, s = l \\ 0 & \text{if } r = i + 1, s = l \text{ or } r = j, s = i + 1 \\ y_{rs} & \text{otherwise} \end{cases}$$

then $\bar{y}_{rs}$ is again an optimal solution of the assignment problem, contradicting the maximality of i.

Case 2: $y_{\nu,i+1} = 0$ for all $\nu \geq i+1$.

There exists an $l > i+1$ with $y_{i+1,l} = 1$. Furthermore, $c_{i+1,i+1} \leq c_{i+1,l}$. Thus, $\bar{y}_{rs}$ defined by

$$\bar{y}_{rs} = \begin{cases} 1 & \text{if } r = s = i+1 \\ 0 & \text{if } r = i+1, s = l \\ y_{rs} & \text{otherwise} \end{cases}$$

is again an optimal solution, contradicting the maximality of i. □

Corollary 2.3 Let $C = (c_{ij})$ be a Monge array of dimension $n \times n$. Then

$$x_{ij} = \begin{cases} 1 & \text{if } i = j \\ 0 & \text{otherwise} \end{cases}$$

is an optimal solution for the assignment problem.

Proof: If $m = n$, then all $w_j \in V_2$ must be assigned. Thus, we only have Case 1 and therefore we do not need the rows of C to be monotone.

□

Corollary 2.4 Let (a_i) and (b_j) be arrays of real numbers $a_1 \geq a_2 \geq \dots \geq a_n \geq 0$ and $0 \leq b_1 \leq b_2 \leq \dots \leq b_m$ where $n \leq m$. Then the assignment problem given by the array

$$C = (c_{ij})_{n \times m} \text{ with } c_{ij} = a_i b_j$$

has an optimal solution given by

$$x_{ij} = \begin{cases} 1 & \text{if } i = j \\ 0 & \text{otherwise.} \end{cases}$$

Proof: We have $c_{ij} = a_i b_j \leq a_i b_k = c_{ik}$ for all i and $j < k$. Furthermore, C is a Monge array because if $i < j$ and $k < l$, then $a_i \geq a_j$ and $b_k \leq b_l$. Thus,

$$a_i b_l + a_j b_k - a_i b_k - a_j b_l = (a_i - a_j)(b_l - b_k) \geq 0,$$

i.e.

$$a_i b_k + a_j b_l \leq a_i b_l + a_j b_k.$$

□

Due to Corollary 2.4 we may efficiently solve the following scheduling problem.

$\mathbf{P||\sum C_i}$

n jobs $i = 1, \ldots, n$ with processing times p_i are to be processed on m identical parallel machines $j = 0, \ldots, m-1$ to minimize mean flow time. There are no precedence constraints between the jobs.

A schedule S is given by a partition of the set of jobs into m disjoint sets $I_0, \ldots, I_{m-1}$ and for each I_j, a sequence of the jobs in I_j. Assume that I_j contains n_j elements and that $j(i)(i = 1, \ldots, n_j)$ is the job to be scheduled in position $n_j - i + 1$ on machine M_j. We assume that the jobs in I_j are scheduled on M_j starting at zero time without idle times. Then the value of the objective function is

$$\sum_{i=1}^{n} C_i = \sum_{j=0}^{m-1} \sum_{i=1}^{n_j} i \cdot p_{j(i)}. \tag{2.12}$$

Now consider the assignment problem with $c_{ik} = a_i b_k$ where $a_i = p_i$ for $i = 1, \ldots, n$, and $b_k = \lceil \frac{k}{m} \rceil^1$ for $k = 1, \ldots, n$. A schedule S corresponds with an assignment with objective value (2.12). In this schedule job i is assigned to the b_k-last position on a machine if i is assigned to k.

If we assume that

$$p_1 \geq p_2 \geq \ldots \geq p_n,$$

then we get an optimal assignment by assigning $a_i = p_i$ to $b_i(i = 1, \ldots, n)$. This assignment corresponds with a schedule in which job i is scheduled on machine $(i-1) \, mod(m)$. Furthermore, on each machine the jobs are scheduled according to nondecreasing processing times. Such a schedule can be calculated in $O(n \log n)$-time, which is the time to sort the jobs according to their processing times.

2.6   Arc Coloring of Bipartite Graphs

Consider again a directed bipartite graph $G = (V_1 \cup V_2, A)$ with $V_1 = \{v_1, \ldots, v_n\}$ and $V_2 = \{w_1, \ldots, w_m\}$. **(Arc) coloring** is the assignment of a color to each arc of G such that arcs incident to any vertex (i.e. arcs $(v_i, w_k), (v_i, w_l)$ with $k \neq l$ or arcs $(v_k, w_j), (v_l, w_j)$ with $l \neq k$) have distinct colors. **Minimum coloring** uses as few colors as possible. The problem we address in this section is to find a minimum coloring for a bipartite graph.

---

[1] $\lceil x \rceil$ is the smallest integer greater or equal to x

For each $v \in V_1 \cup V_2$ let $deg(v)$ be the number of arcs incident with v (i.e. arcs of the form (v_i, w_k) if $v = v_i \in V_1$ or arcs of the form (v_k, w_i) if $v = w_i \in V_2$). $deg(v)$ is called the **degree** of node v. The maximum degree

$$\triangle := \max\{deg(v) \mid v \in V_1 \cup V_2\}$$

of G is a lower bound for the number of colors needed for coloring. Next, we describe an algorithm to construct a coloring using $\triangle$ colors.

It is convenient to represent G by its adjacency matrix $A = (a_{ij})$ where

$$a_{ij} = \begin{cases} 1 & \text{if } (v_i, w_j) \in A \\ 0 & \text{otherwise.} \end{cases}$$

By definition of $\triangle$ we have

$$\sum_{j=1}^{m} a_{ij} \le \triangle \text{ for all } i = 1, \ldots, n \tag{2.13}$$

and

$$\sum_{i=1}^{n} a_{ij} \le \triangle \text{ for all } j = 1, \ldots, m. \tag{2.14}$$

Entries (i, j) with $a_{ij} = 1$ are called **occupied cells**. We have to assign colors $c \in \{1, \ldots, \triangle\}$ to the occupied cells in such a way that the same color is not assigned twice in any row or column of A. This is done by visiting the occupied cells of A row by row from left to right. When visiting the occupied cell (i, j) a color c not yet assigned in column j is assigned to (i, j). If c is assigned to another cell in row i, say to (i, j^*), then there exists a color $\bar{c}$ not yet assigned in row i and we can replace the assignment c of (i, j^*) by $\bar{c}$. If again a second cell (i^*, j^*) in column j^* also has the assignment $\bar{c}$, we replace this assignment by c, etc. We stop this process when there is no remaining conflict. If the partial assignment before coloring (i, j) was feasible (i.e. no color appears twice in any row or column) then this conflict resolution procedure ends after at the most n steps with feasible coloring. We will prove this after giving a more precise description of the algorithm.

Algorithm Assignment
1. For $i := 1$ TO n DO
2. While in row i there exists an uncolored occupied cell DO
        BEGIN

3.   Find a first uncolored occupied cell (i, j);
4.   Find a color c not assigned in column j;
5.   Assign c to (i, j);
6.   IF c is assigned twice in row i THEN
               BEGIN
7.   Find a color $\bar{c}$ that is not assigned in row i;
8.   Conflict $(i, j, c, \bar{c})$
               END
        END

Conflict$(i, j, c, \bar{c})$ is a conflict resolution procedure which applies to a situation in which c is assigned to cell (i, j). It is convenient to write Conflict$(i, j, c, \bar{c})$ as a recursive procedure.

Procedure Conflict $(\mathbf{i}, \mathbf{j}, \mathbf{c}, \bar{\mathbf{c}})$
1. IF c is assigned to some cell (i, j^*) with $j^* \neq j$
    THEN assign $\bar{c}$ to (i, j^*)
2. ELSE RETURN;
3. IF $\bar{c}$ is assigned to some cell (i^*, j^*) with $i^* \neq i$ THEN
        BEGIN
4.   Assign c to (i^*, j^*);
5.   Conflict $(i^*, j^*, c, \bar{c})$
        END
6. ELSE RETURN

Due to (2.14), a color c can always be found in Step 4 of Algorithm Assignment. Furthermore, due to (2.13), in Step 7 there exists a color $\bar{c}$ which is not yet assigned to a cell in row i. Next, if there is a $\bar{c}$-conflict in column j^* due to the fact that c is replaced by $\bar{c}$, then c cannot appear in this column again if we assume that previous conflicts have been resolved. Thus, it is correct to resolve the $\bar{c}$-conflict by replacing the other $\bar{c}$-value by c (Step 4 of Procedure Conflict$(i, j, c, \bar{c})$). Similarly, Step 1 of Procedure Conflict$(i^*, j^*, c, \bar{c})$) is correct.

Finally, we claim that the Procedure Conflict terminates after at the most n recursive calls. To prove this, it is sufficient to show that if color c of cell (i, j^*) is replaced by $\bar{c}$, then it is impossible to return to a cell in row i again. The only way to do so is by having a $\bar{c}$-conflict in some column s where $\bar{c}$ is the color of (i, s) and (k, s) with $i \neq k$. Consider a situation where this happens the first time. We must have $s = j^*$ because otherwise $\bar{c}$ is the color of two different cells in row i, which contradicts the correctness of previous steps. Because $s = j^*$ we must have visited column j^* twice, the first time when moving from cell (i, j^*) to some cell (i^*, j^*). (i^*, j^*) cannot be visited a second time due to the assumption that row i is the first row which is revisited. Thus, when visiting column j^* a second time we visit some cell (k, j^*) which is different from (i, j^*) and (i^*, j^*). At that time cells (i^*, j^*) and (k, j^*) are colored c, which again contradicts the fact that the algorithm maintains feasibility.

Next we show that Algorithm Assignment has a running time of $O((n + \triangle)e)$, where e is the number of occupied cells.

We use a data structure with the following components:

- An $n \times \triangle$-array J-INDEX where

$$J\text{-INDEX}(i, l) = \begin{cases} j & \text{if } (i, j) \text{ is the } l\text{-th occupied cell in row } i \\ 0 & \text{if there are less than } l \text{ occupied cells in row } i. \end{cases}$$

- For each column j, a list COLOR(j) containing all color numbers assigned to cells in column j in increasing order.

- For each row i, a double linked list FREE(i) containing all colors not yet assigned to cells in row i. Moreover, we use a $\triangle$-vector of pointers to this list such that deletion of a color can be done in constant time.

- An $\triangle \times m$-array I-INDEX where

$$I\text{-INDEX}(c, j) = \begin{cases} i & \text{if color } c \text{ is assigned to cell } (i, j) \\ 0 & \text{if no cell in column } j \text{ is assigned to } c. \end{cases}$$

Using the array J-INDEX Step 3 of Algorithm Assignment can be done in constant time. In Step 4 color c is found in $O(\triangle)$ time using the list COLOR(j) because this list contains at the most $\triangle$ elements. Step 5 is done by updating COLOR(j), FREE(i), and I-INDEX in $O(\triangle)$ steps. Step 6 is done in $O(\triangle)$-time using the arrays J-INDEX and I-INDEX. Furthermore, the color $\bar{c}$ in Step 7 is found in constant time using FREE(i).

During the recursive processing of the Procedure Conflict, the list FREE is not changed. Moreover, the list COLOR(j) only changes if a column not already containing color $\bar{c}$ is found (in this case Conflict terminates).

A cell (i^*, j^*) already colored by $\bar{c}$ (Step 3 of Conflict) can be found in constant time using the array I-INDEX. Because each change of the array I-INDEX only needs a constant amount of time and Conflict always terminates after n steps, we get an overall complexity of $O((n + \triangle)e)$.

Another more sophisticated algorithm for solving the arc coloring problem for bipartite graphs can be found in Gabow & Kariv [95]. It improves the complexity to $O(e \log^2(n + m))$.

2.7   Shortest Path Problems and Dynamic Programming

Another method for solving certain scheduling problems is dynamic programming, which enumerates in an intelligent way all possible solutions. During the enumeration process, schedules which cannot be optimal are eliminated. We shall explain the method by solving the following scheduling problems:

$1 || \sum \mathbf{w_i U_i}$

Given n jobs $i = 1, \ldots, n$ with processing times p_i and due dates d_i, we have to sequence these jobs such that $\sum\limits_{i=1}^{n} w_i U_i$ is minimized where $w_i \geq 0$ for $i = 1, \ldots, n$. Assume that the jobs are enumerated according to nondecreasing due dates:

$$d_1 \leq d_2 \leq \ldots \leq d_n. \tag{2.15}$$

Then there exists an optimal schedule given by a sequence of the form

$$i_1, i_2, \ldots, i_s, i_{s+1}, \ldots, i_n$$

where jobs $i_1 < i_2 < \ldots < i_s$ are on time and jobs $i_{s+1}, \ldots, i_n$ are late. This can be shown easily by applying the following interchange arguments. If a job i is late, we may put i at the end of the schedule without increasing the objective function. If i and j are early jobs with $d_i \leq d_j$ such that i is not scheduled before j, then we may shift the block of all jobs scheduled between j and i jointly with i to the left by p_j time units and schedule j immediately after this block. Because i was not late and $d_i \leq d_j$ this creates no late job.

To solve the problem, we calculate recursively for $t = 0, 1, \ldots, T := \sum_{i=1}^{n} p_i$ and $j = 1, \ldots, n$ the minimum criterion value $F_j(t)$ for the first j jobs, subject to the constraint that the total processing time of the on-time jobs is at the most t. If $0 \leq t \leq d_j$ and job j is on time in a schedule which corresponds with $F_j(t)$, then $F_j(t) = F_{j-1}(t - p_j)$. Otherwise $F_j(t) = F_{j-1}(t) + w_j$. If $t > d_j$, then $F_j(t) = F_j(d_j)$ because all jobs $1, 2, \ldots, j$ finishing later than $d_j \geq \ldots \geq d_1$ are late. Thus, for $j = 1, \ldots, n$ we have the recursion

$$F_j(t) = \begin{cases} \min\{F_{j-1}(t - p_j), F_{j-1}(t) + w_j\} & \text{for } 0 \leq t \leq d_j \\ F_j(d_j) & \text{for } d_j < t < T \end{cases}$$

with $F_j(t) = \infty$ for $t < 0, j = 0, \ldots, n$ and $F_0(t) = 0$ for $t \geq 0$.

Notice that $F_n(d_n)$ is the optimal solution to the problem.

The following algorithm calculates all values $F_j(t)$ for $j = 1, \ldots, n$ and $t = 0, \ldots, d_j$. We assume that the jobs are enumerated such that (2.15) holds. $p_{\max}$ denotes the largest processing time.

Algorithm 1|| $\sum w_i U_i$
1. FOR $t := -p_{\max}$ TO -1 DO
2.   FOR $j := 0$ TO n DO
        $F_j(t) := \infty$;
3. FOR $t := 0$ TO T DO $F_0(t) := 0$;
4. FOR $j := 1$ TO n DO
   BEGIN
5.   FOR $t := 0$ TO d_j DO
6.   IF $F_{j-1}(t) + w_j < F_{j-1}(t - p_j)$ THEN $F_j(t) := F_{j-1}(t) + w_j$
     ELSE $F_j(t) := F_{j-1}(t - p_j)$;
7.   FOR $t := d_j + 1$ TO T DO
      $F_j(t) := F_j(d_j)$
   END

The computational time of this algorithm is bounded by $O(n \sum_{i=1}^{n} p_i)$.

To calculate an optimal schedule it is sufficient to calculate the set L of late jobs in an optimal schedule. Given all $F_j(t)$-values this can be done by the following algorithm.

Algorithm Backward Calculation

   $t := d_n;\ L := \phi$

   FOR $j := n$ DOWN TO 1 DO

     BEGIN

     $t := \min\{t, d_j\};$

     IF $F_j(t) = F_{j-1}(t) + w_j$ THEN $L := L \cup \{j\}$

     ELSE $t := t - p_j$

     END

$P|| \sum w_i C_i$

n jobs $1, \ldots, n$ are to be processed on m identical parallel machines such that $\sum_{i=1}^{n} w_i C_i$ is minimized. All w_i are assumed to be positive.

We first consider the problem $1|| \sum w_i C_i$. An optimal solution of this one machine problem is obtained if we sequence the jobs according to nondecreasing ratios p_i/w_i. The following interchange argument proves this. Let j be a job which is scheduled immediately before job i. If we interchange i and j, the objective function changes by

$$w_i p_i + w_j(p_i + p_j) - w_j p_j - w_i(p_i + p_j) = w_j p_i - w_i p_j$$

which is nonpositive if and only if $p_i/w_i \leq p_j/w_j$. Thus, the objective function does not increase if i and j are interchanged.

A consequence of this result is that in an optimal solution of problem $P|| \sum w_i C_i$, jobs to be processed on the same machine must be processed in order of nondecreasing ratios p_i/w_i. Therefore we assume that all jobs are indexed such that

$$p_1/w_1 \leq p_2/w_2 \leq \ldots \leq p_n/w_n.$$

Let T be an upper bound on the completion time of any job in an optimal schedule. Define $F_i(t_1, \ldots, t_m)$ to be the minimum cost of a schedule without idle time for jobs $1, \ldots, i$ subject to the constraint that the last job on M_j is completed at time t_j for $j = 1, \ldots, m$. Then

$$F_i(t_1, \ldots, t_m) = \min_{j=1}^{m}\{w_i t_j + F_{i-1}(t_1, \ldots, t_{j-1}, t_j - p_i, t_{j+1}, \ldots, t_m)\}.$$

$$(2.16)$$

The initial conditions are

$$F_0(t_1, \ldots, t_m) = \begin{cases} 0 & \text{if } t_j = 0 \text{ for } j = 1, \ldots, m \\ \infty & \text{otherwise .} \end{cases} \tag{2.17}$$

Starting with (2.17), for $i = 1, 2, \ldots, n$ the $F_i(t)$-values are calculated for all $t \in \{1, 2, \ldots, T\}^m$ in a lexicographic order of the integer vectors t. A $t^* \in \{1, 2, \ldots, T\}^m$ with $F_n(t)$ minimal provides the optimal value of the objective function. The computational complexity of this procedure is $O(mnT^m)$.

Similar techniques may be used to solve problem $Q || \sum w_j C_j$.

A Shortest Path Algorithm

Next we will introduce some shortest path problems and show how these problems can be solved by dynamic programming.

A network $N = (V, A, c)$ is a directed graph (V, A) together with a function c which associates with each arc $(i, j) \in A$ a real number c_{ij}. A **(directed) path** p in N is a sequence of arcs:

$$p : (i_0, i_1), (i_1, i_2,) \ldots, (i_{r-1}, i_r).$$

p is called an **s-t–path** if $i_0 = s$ and $i_r = t$. p is a **cycle** if $i_0 = i_r$. The length $l(p)$ of a path p is defined by

$$l(p) = c_{i_0 i_1} + c_{i_1 i_2} + \ldots + c_{i_{r-1} i_r}.$$

Assume that $N = (V, A, c)$ has no cycles, and $|V| = n$. Then the vertices can be enumerated by numbers $1, \ldots, n$ such that $i < j$ for all $(i, j) \in A$. Such an enumeration is called **topological**. If (i, j) is an arc, then i is the **predecessor** of j, and j is the **successor** of i. Using this notion, an algorithm for calculating a topological enumeration $\alpha(v)(v \in V)$ may be formulated as follows.

Algorithm Topological Enumeration
1. $i := 1$;
2. WHILE there exists a vertex $v \in V$ without predecessor DO
          BEGIN
3. $\alpha(v) := i$;
4.   Eliminate vertex v from V and all arcs (v, j) from A;
5. $i := i + 1$
          END
6. If $V \neq \emptyset$ then (V, A) has a cycle and there exists no topological enumeration.

Using an appropriate data structure this algorithm can be implemented in such a way that the running time is $O(|A|)$.

The problem **shortest paths to s** is to find for each vertex $i \in V$ a shortest i-s–path. We solve this problem for networks without cycles by a dynamic programming approach. Assume that the vertices are enumerated topologically, and that $s = n$. If we denote by $F(i)$ the length of a shortest i-n–path, then we have the recursion

$$F(n) := 0$$
$$F(i) = \min\{c_{ij} + F(j)|(i,j) \in A, j > i\} \text{ for } i = n-1, \ldots, 1. \quad (2.18)$$

This leads to

Algorithm Shortest Path 1
1. $F(n) := 0$;
2. FOR $i := n - 1$ DOWN TO 1 DO
       BEGIN
3. $F(i) := \infty$;
4.   FOR $j := n$ DOWN TO $i + 1$
5.   IF $(i, j) \in A$ AND $c_{ij} + F(j) < F(i)$ THEN
               BEGIN
6. $F(i) := c_{ij} + F(j)$;
7. $SUCC(i) := j$
               END
    END

$SUCC(i)$ is the successor of i on a shortest path from i to n. Thus, shortest paths can be constructed using this successor array. The running time of this algorithm is $O(n^2)$.

A Special Structured Network

Now we consider an even more special situation. Let $N = (V, A, c)$ be a network with

$$V = \{1, \ldots, n\}$$
$$(i, j) \in A \text{ if and only if } i < j \quad (2.19)$$
$$c_{il} - c_{ik} = r(k, l) + f(i)h(k, l) \text{ for } i < k < l$$

where $f(i)$ is nonincreasing, the values $r(k,l)$ are arbitrary, and $h(k,l) \geq 0$ for all k,l. The last property is called the **product property**. It is not difficult to show that an array $C = (c_{ij})$ which satisfies the product property also satisfies the Monge property, i.e. is a Monge array.

Next we will develop an $O(n)$-algorithm for finding shortest paths in a network satisfying (2.19). Later we will apply this algorithm to certain batching problems.

Again we use the recursion formulas (2.18). However, due to the special properties of the c_{ij}-values the computational complexity decreases from $O(n^2)$ to $O(n)$.

As before, let $F(i)$ be the length of a shortest path from i to n and set

$$F(i,k) = c_{ik} + F(k) \quad \text{for } i < k.$$

Thus, we have

$$F(i) = \min_{k=i+1}^{n} F(i,k).$$

First, we assume that $h(k,l) > 0$ for all $k < l$. The relation

$$F(i,k) \leq F(i,l) \quad i < k < l \tag{2.20}$$

stating that k is as good as l as a successor of i is equivalent to

$$F(k) - F(l) \leq c_{il} - c_{ik} = r(k,l) + f(i)h(k,l)$$

or

$$\vartheta(k,l) := \frac{F(k) - F(l) - r(k,l)}{h(k,l)} \leq f(i). \tag{2.21}$$

Lemma 2.5 Assume that $\vartheta(k,l) \leq f(i)$ for some $1 \leq i < k < l \leq n$. Then $F(j,k) \leq F(j,l)$ for all $j = 1, \ldots, i$.

Proof: Because f is monotonic nonincreasing for all $j \leq i$, the inequality $\vartheta(k,l) \leq f(i) \leq f(j)$ holds, which implies $F(j,k) \leq F(j,l)$. $\qquad \square$

Lemma 2.6 Assume that $\vartheta(i,k) \leq \vartheta(k,l)$ for some $1 \leq i < k < l \leq n$. Then for each $j = 1, \ldots, i$ we have $F(j,i) \leq F(j,k)$ or $F(j,l) \leq F(j,k)$.

Proof: Let $1 \leq j \leq i$. If $\vartheta(i,k) \leq f(j)$, then $F(j,i) \leq F(j,k)$. Otherwise we have $f(j) < \vartheta(i,k) \leq \vartheta(k,l)$, which implies $F(j,l) < F(j,k)$. $\qquad \square$

An Efficient Shortest Path Algorithm

As Algorithm Shortest Path 1, the efficient algorithm to be developed next calculates the $F(i)$-values for $i = n$ down to 1. When calculating $F(i)$ all values $F(i+1), \ldots, F(n)$ are known. Furthermore, a queue Q of the form

$$Q : i_r, i_{r-1}, \ldots, i_2, i_1$$

with

$$i_r < i_{r-1} < \ldots < i_2 < i_1 \tag{2.22}$$

is used as a data structure. i_1 is the head and i_r is the tail of this queue. Vertices not contained in the queue are no longer needed as successors on shortest paths from $1, \ldots, i$ to n. Furthermore, the queue satisfies the following invariance property

$$\vartheta(i_r, i_{r-1}) > \vartheta(i_{r-1}, i_{r-2}) > \ldots > \vartheta(i_2, i_1). \tag{2.23}$$

In the general iteration step we have to process vertex i and calculate $F(i)$:

If $f(i) \geq \vartheta(i_2, i_1)$, then by Lemma 2.5 we have $F(j, i_2) \leq F(j, i_1)$ for all $j \leq i$. Thus, vertex i_1 is deleted from Q. We continue with this elimination process until we reach some $t \geq 1$ such that

$$\vartheta(i_r, i_{r-1}) > \ldots > \vartheta(i_{t+1}, i_t) > f(i)$$

which implies

$$F(i, i_{\nu+1}) > F(i, i_\nu) \text{ for } \nu = t, \ldots, r - 1.$$

This implies that i_t must be a successor of i on a shortest path from i to n, i.e. $F(i) = c_{i i_t} + F(i_t)$.

Next we try to append i at the tail of the queue. If $\vartheta(i, i_r) \leq \vartheta(i_r, i_{r-1})$, then by Lemma 2.6 vertex i_r can be eliminated from Q. We continue this elimination process until we reach some ν with $\vartheta(i, i_\nu) > \vartheta(i_\nu, i_{\nu-1})$. When we now add i at the tail of the queue the invariance property (2.23) remains satisfied.

Details are given by the following algorithm. In this algorithm, head(Q) and tail(Q) denote the head and tail of the queue. In $SUCC(i)$ we store the successor of i in a shortest path from i to n. Next(j) and previous(j) are the elements immediately after and immediately before, respectively, the element j in the queue when going from head to tail.

Algorithm Shortest Path 2

1. $Q := \{n\}$; $F(n) := 0$;
2. FOR $i := n - 1$ DOWN TO 1 DO
   BEGIN
3.   WHILE head$(Q) \neq$ tail(Q) and $f(i) \geq \vartheta$ (next(head(Q)), head(Q))
          DO delete head(Q) from the queue;
4. $SUCC(i) :=$ head(Q);
5. $j := SUCC(i)$;
6. $F(i) := c_{ij} + F(j)$;
7.   WHILE head$(Q) \neq$ tail(Q) and $\vartheta(i, \text{tail } (Q)) \leq \vartheta(\text{tail}(Q),$
      previous(tail(Q)))) DO delete tail(Q) from the queue;
8.   Add i to the queue
   END

Each vertex is added and deleted once at the most. Thus, the algorithm runs in $O(n)$ time if the necessary ϑ-values can be computed in total time $O(n)$, which is the case in many applications.

If $h(k, l) = 0$, then $\vartheta(k, l)$ is not defined. Therefore Steps 7 and 8 of the Algorithm Shortest Path 2 must be modified if $h(i, k) = 0$ and $k = tail(Q)$:

For all $j < i$ we have with (2.19) the equations

$$F(j, k) - F(j, i) = c_{jk} - c_{ji} + F(k) - F(i) = F(k) - F(i) + r(i, k).$$

If $F(k) - F(i) + r(i, k) \geq 0$, then $F(j, i) \leq F(j, k)$ for all $j < i$. Thus $k = tail(Q)$ can be deleted from the queue. Otherwise $F(j, i) > F(j, k)$ for all $j < i$, and i is not added to the queue. Furthermore, in Step 3 the condition $f(i) \geq \vartheta(i_{\nu+1}, i_\nu)$ must be replaced by $F(i_{\nu+1}) - F(i_\nu) - r(i_{\nu+1}, i_\nu) \leq 0$.

$1 \mid s - \text{batch} \mid \sum C_i$ and $1 \mid p_i = p$; $s - \text{batch} \mid \sum w_i C_i$

Single machine s-batching problems can be formulated as follows. n jobs J_i are given with processing times p_i ($i = 1, \ldots, n$). Jobs are scheduled in so-called s-batches. Recall that an **s-batch** is a set of jobs which are processed jointly. The length of an s-batch is the sum of the processing time of jobs in the batch. The flow time C_i of a job coincides with the completion time of the last scheduled job in its batch and all jobs in this batch have the same flow time. The production of a batch requires a machine set-up S of $s \geq 0$ time units. We assume that the machine set-ups are both sequence independent and batch independent, i.e. they depend neither on the sequence of batches nor on the number of jobs in a batch. The **single machine s-batching problem** we consider is to find a sequence of jobs and a collection of batches that partitions this sequence of jobs such that the weighted flow time

$$\sum_{i=1}^{n} w_i C_i$$

is minimized. We assume that all weights w_i are non-negative and consider also the case that all $w_i = 1$.

Consider a fixed, but arbitrary job sequence $J_1, J_2, \ldots, J_n$ of the single machine s-batching problem. Any solution is of the form

$$BS : S J_{i(1)} \ldots J_{i(2)-1} S J_{i(2)} \ldots \ldots J_{i(k)-1} S J_{i(k)} \ldots J_n$$

where k is the number of batches and

$$1 = i(1) < i(2) < \ldots < i(k) \leq n.$$

Notice that this solution is completely characterized by the job sequence and a **sequence of batch sizes** $n_1, \ldots, n_k$ with $n_j = i(j+1) - i(j)$ where $i(k+1) := n+1$. We now calculate the $\sum w_i C_i$ value $F(BS)$ for BS. The processing time of the jth batch equals

$$P_j = s + \sum_{\nu=i(j)}^{i(j+1)-1} p_\nu.$$

Thus,

$$F(BS) = \sum_{i=1}^{n} w_i C_i = \sum_{j=1}^{k} \left(\sum_{\nu=i(j)}^{n} w_\nu \right) P_j = \sum_{j=1}^{k} \left(\sum_{\nu=i(j)}^{n} w_\nu \right) \left(s + \sum_{\nu=i(j)}^{i(j+1)-1} p_\nu \right).$$

In order to solve the batch sizing problem, we obviously have to find an integer $1 \leq k \leq n$ and a sequence of indices

$$1 = i(1) < i(2) < \ldots < i(k) < i(k+1) = n+1$$

such that the above objective function value is minimized. This problem can be reduced to the specially structured shortest path problem.

$$\overbrace{SJ_{i(1)}\ldots J_{i(2)-1}}^{c_{i(1),i(2)}}SJ_{i(2)}\ldots J_{i(3)-1}^{c_{i(2),i(3)}}SJ_{i(3)}\ldots^{c_{i(3),i(4)}}\ldots J_{i(k)-1}^{c_{i(k-1),i(k)}}SJ_{i(k)}\ldots J_{n}^{c_{i(k),i(k+1)}}J_{n+1}$$

Every solution BS corresponds to a path of the form

Here J_{n+1} is a dummy job. The length c_{ij} of arc (i,j) is set to

$$c_{ij} = (\sum_{\nu=i}^{n} w_\nu)(s + \sum_{\nu=i}^{j-1} p_\nu).$$

c_{ij} is the "cost" of the batch $J_i, J_{i+1}, \ldots, J_{j-1}$. For $i < k < l$ we have

$$c_{il} - c_{ik} = (\sum_{\nu=i}^{n} w_\nu)(\sum_{\nu=k}^{l-1} p_\nu) = f(i)h(k,l)$$

where $f(i) = \sum_{\nu=i}^{n} w_\nu$ is monotone nonincreasing and $h(k,l) = \sum_{\nu=k}^{l-1} p_\nu \geq 0$.

Thus, we have a network with $n+1$ vertices satisfying conditions (2.19) and we may use Algorithm Shortest Path 2 to solve the problem.

To calculate each $f(i)$-value and $h(k,l)$-value in constant time we first calculate in a preprocessing step the sums $sp_i = \sum_{\nu=1}^{i-1} p_\nu$ and $sw_i = \sum_{\nu=1}^{i} w_\nu$. Then $f(i) = sw_n - sw_{i-1}$ and $h(k,l) = sp_l - sp_k$. The preprocessing can be done in $O(n)$-time. Thus, we have an overall time bound of $O(n)$.

Next we will show that problem $1 \mid s\text{-batch} \mid \sum C_i$ can be solved by sequencing the jobs in a nondecreasing order of processing times and applying the batching procedure to this sequence. Similarly, problem $1 \mid p_i = p; batch \mid \sum w_i C_i$ can be solved by sequencing the jobs in non-increasing order of job weights w_i. In both cases we have an overall computational complexity of $O(n \log n)$.

Lemma 2.7 Any optimal schedule for problem $1 \mid s\text{-batch} \mid \sum C_i$ can be transformed into an optimal schedule in which the jobs are ordered according to nondecreasing processing times.

Proof: Consider an optimal solution of the problem $1 \mid s\text{-batch} \mid \sum C_i$ given by a job sequence S and a sequence $n_1, n_2, \ldots, n_k$ of batch sizes. If J_i and J_k are jobs with $p_k < p_i$ such that in S job J_i is processed before

J_k, then we may swap J_i and J_k and move the block of jobs in S between J_i and J_k by $p_i - p_k$ time units to the left. Furthermore, we keep the sequence of batch sizes unchanged. This does not increase the value of the objective function because the new C_i-value is the old C_k-value, the new C_k-value is less than or equal to the old C_i-value, and the C_j-values of the other jobs are not increased. Iterating such changes leads to an optimal solution with the desired property.   □

Lemma 2.8 Any optimal schedule for problem $1 \mid p_i = p; s\text{-batch} \mid \sum w_i C_i$ can be transformed into an optimal schedule in which the jobs are ordered according to nonincreasing job weights w_i.

Proof: Consider an optimal solution and let J_i and J_k be two jobs with $w_i < w_k$, where J_i is scheduled preceding J_k. Interchanging J_i and J_k does not increase the value of the objective function and iterating such interchanges leads to an optimal solution with the desired property.   □

Chapter 3

Computational Complexity

Practical experience shows that some computational problems are easier to solve than others. Complexity theory provides a mathematical framework in which computational problems are studied so that they can be classified as "easy" or "hard". In this chapter we will describe the main points of such a theory. A more rigorous presentation can be found in the fundamental book of Garey & Johnson [99].

3.1 The Classes $\mathcal{P}$ and $\mathcal{NP}$

A computational problem can be viewed as a function h that maps each input x in some given domain to an output $h(x)$ in some given range. We are interested in algorithms for solving computational problems. Such an algorithm computes $h(x)$ for each input x. For a precise discussion, a Turing machine is commonly used as a mathematical model of an algorithm. For our purposes it will be sufficient to think of a computer program written in some standard programming language as a model of an algorithm. One of the main issues of complexity theory is to measure the performance of algorithms with respect to computational time. To be more precise, for each input x we define the input length $|x|$ as the length of some encoding of x. We measure the efficiency of an algorithm by an upper bound $T(n)$ on the number of steps that the algorithm takes on any input x with $|x| = n$. In most cases it will be difficult to calculate the precise form of T. For these reasons we will replace the precise form of T by its asymptotic order. Therefore, we say that $T(n) \in O(g(n))$ if there exist constants $c > 0$ and a nonnegative integer n_0 such that

$T(n) \leq cg(n)$ for all integers $n \geq n_0$. Thus, rather than saying that the computational complexity is bounded by $7n^3 + 27n^2 + 4$, we say simply that it is $O(n^3)$.

Example 3.1 Consider the problem $1 \parallel \sum w_i C_i$. The input x for this problem is given by the number n of jobs and two n-dimensional vectors (p_i) and (w_i). We may define $|x|$ to be the length of a binary encoded input string for x. The output $f(x)$ for the problems is a schedule minimizing $\sum_{i=1}^{n} w_i C_i$. It can be represented by an n-vector of all C_i-values. The following algorithm calculates these C_i-values (see Section 4.3).

Algorithm $1 \parallel \sum w_i C_i$
1. Enumerate the jobs such that
   $w_1/p_1 \geq w_2/p_2 \geq \ldots \geq w_n/p_n$;
2. $C_0 := 0$;
3. FOR $i := 1$ TO n DO
      $C_i := C_{i-1} + p_i$

The number of computational steps in this algorithm can be bounded as follows. In Step 1 the jobs have to be sorted. This takes $O(n \log n)$ steps. Furthermore, Step 3 can be done in $O(n)$ time. Thus, we have $T(n) \in O(n \log n)$. If we replace n by the input length $|x|$, the bound is still valid because we always have $n \leq |x|$.   □

A problem is called **polynomially solvable** if there exists a polynomial p such that $T(|x|) \in O(p(|x|))$ for all inputs x for the problem, i.e. if there is a k such that $T(|x|) \in O(|x|^k)$. Problem $1 \parallel \sum w_i C_i$ is polynomially solvable, as we have shown in Example 3.1

Important classes of problems which are polynomially solvable are linear programming problems (Khachiyan [125]) and integer linear programming problems with a fixed number of variables (Lenstra [149]).

The fastest currently known algorithms for network flow problems are presented in Tables 3.1 and 3.2. In these tables n and m denote the number of vertices and arcs in the underlying network.

Table 3.1 contains the running times of maximum flow algorithms and corresponding references.

U denotes the maximum of all arc capacities.

Table 3.2 contains running times of algorithms for the minimum-cost circulation problem.

Running time	References
$O(n^3)$	Malhotra, Kumar, Maheshwari [164]
$O(n^2\sqrt{m})$	Cheriyan & Maheshwari [65]
$O(nm\log(\frac{n}{m}\sqrt{\log U}+2))$	Ahuja, Orlin, Tarjan [7]

Table 3.1: Running times of algorithms for the maximum flow problem.

Running time	References
$O(m\log U(m+n\log n))$	Edmonds & Karp [87]
$O(nm\log(n^2/m)\log(nC))$	Goldberg & Tarjan [101]
$O(m(m+n\log n)\log n)$	Orlin [178]
$O(nm\log\log U\log(nC))$	Ahuja, Goldberg, Orlin, Tarjan [5]

Table 3.2: Running times of algorithms for the minimum-cost circulation problem.

C is the maximum of all cost values.

The notion polynomially solvable depends on the encoding. We assume that all numerical data describing the problem are binary encoded. For example, Algorithm $1||\sum w_i U_i$ is not polynomially bounded because the number of steps depends on $\sum_{i=1}^{n} p_i$, which is an exponentially growing function of the length of an input string with a binary encoding. Algorithm $1||\sum w_i U_i$ is called **pseudopolynomial** which means that $T(n)$ is polynomial where n is the input length with respect to unary encoding. With unary encoding all numerical data, which are assumed to be integers, are encoded by strings of ones (more specifically an integer d is represented by a sequence of d ones). A problem is called **pseudopolynomially solvable** if there exists a pseudopolynomial algorithm which solves the problem.

A problem is called a **decision problem** if the output range is {yes, no}. We may associate with each scheduling problem a decision problem by defining a threshold k for the corresponding objective function f. This decision problem is: Does there exist a feasible schedule S such that $f(S) \leq k$?

The class of all decision problems which are polynomially solvable is denoted by $\mathcal{P}$.

When a scheduling problem is formulated as a decision problem there is an important asymmetry between those inputs whose output is "yes" and those whose output is "no". A "yes"-answer can be certified by a small amount of information: the feasible schedule S with $f(S) \leq k$. Given this **certificate**, the "yes"-answer can be verified in polynomial time. This is not the case for the "no"-answer.

In general, let $\mathcal{NP}$ denote the class of decision problems where each "yes" input x has a certificate y, such that $|y|$ is bounded by a polynomial in $|x|$ and there is a polynomial-time algorithm to verify that y is a valid certificate for x.

Example 3.2 Consider the decision version of problem $P|prec|C_{\max}$: Given m machines, n jobs J_i with processing times $p_i (i = 1, \ldots, n)$, precedence relations between the jobs, and a threshold value k. Does there exist a schedule such that the corresponding $C_{\max}$-value is less than or equal to k?

A certificate is given by a vector (C_i) of finishing times and a vector (μ_i) where μ_i is the machine on which J_i is processed. Clearly, (C_i) and (μ_i) have binary encodings which are bounded by polynomials in the input length of the problem. Furthermore, it can be checked in polynomial time whether (C_i) and (μ_i) define a feasible schedule with $C_{\max}$-value $\leq k$. This is done by checking that

- $C_i \leq C_j - p_j$ for all jobs J_i, J_j with $J_i \rightarrow J_j$,

- $\max\limits_{i=1}^{n} C_i \leq k$, and

- the intervals $[C_i - p_i, C_i[, [C_j - p_j, C_j[$ do not overlap for all $i \neq j$ with $\mu_i = \mu_j$.

Thus, problem $P|prec|C_{\max}$ belongs to $\mathcal{NP}$.   □

Similarly, it can be shown that other scheduling problems when considered as decision problems belong to $\mathcal{NP}$.

Every decision problem solvable in polynomial time belongs to $\mathcal{NP}$. If we have such a problem P and an algorithm which calculates for each input x the answer $h(x) \in \{yes, no\}$ in a polynomial number of steps, then this answer $h(x)$ may be used as a certificate. This certificate can be verified by the algorithm. Thus P is also in $\mathcal{NP}$ which implies $\mathcal{P} \subseteq \mathcal{NP}$.

One of the major open problems of modern mathematics is whether $\mathcal{P}$ equals $\mathcal{NP}$. It is generally conjectured that this is not the case. There is a beautiful theory developed by Cook [73], Karp [124], and Levin [159] which provides some strong evidence that $\mathcal{P} \neq \mathcal{NP}$. We will discuss this theory in the next section.

3.2 $\mathcal{NP}$-complete and $\mathcal{NP}$-hard Problems

The principal notion in defining $\mathcal{NP}$-completeness is that of a **reduction**. For two decision problems P and Q, we say that P reduces to Q (denoted $P \propto Q$) if there exists a polynomial-time computable function g that transforms inputs for P into inputs for Q such that x is a 'yes'-input for P if and only if $g(x)$ is a 'yes'-input for Q.

To illustrate these concepts we first introduce some decision problems which play an important role in proving that decision versions of scheduling problems are $\mathcal{NP}$-complete.

PARTITION (PART)

Given n positive integer numbers $s_1, s_2, \ldots, s_n$, is there a subset $J \subseteq I = \{1, \ldots, n\}$ such that

$$\sum_{i \in J} s_i = \sum_{i \in I \setminus J} s_i?$$

3-DIMENSIONAL MATCHING (3DM)

We are given a set $N \subseteq W \times X \times Y$ where $W, X,$ and Y are disjoint sets with the same number of q elements.

Does N contain a **matching**, that is, a subset $M \subseteq N$ with q elements such that no two elements of M agree in any coordinate?

VERTEX COVER (VC)

We are given an undirected graph $G = (V, E)$ and a positive integer $k \leq |V|$.

Is there a **vertex cover** of size k or less for G, that is, a subset $C \subseteq V$ with at the most k elements such that for each edge $\{u, v\} \in E$, at least one of u and v belongs to C?

CLIQUE

We are given an undirected graph $G = (V, E)$ and a positive integer $k \leq |V|$.

Does G contain a **clique** of size k or more, that is, a subset $C \subseteq V$ with at least k elements such that every two vertices in C are joined by an edge in E?

HAMILTON CIRCUIT (HC)

We are given an undirected graph $G = (V, E)$.

Does G contain a **Hamiltonian circuit**, that is, an ordering $v_1, v_2, \ldots, v_n$ of the vertices of G, where $n = |V|$, such that $\{v_n, v_1\} \in E$ and $\{v_i, v_{i+1}\} \in E$ for $i = 1, \ldots, n-1$?

In the following examples we will illustrate some reductions.

Example 3.3 The partitioning problem is reducible to the decision version of problem $F3 \parallel C_{\max}$: PARTITION $\propto F3 \parallel C_{\max}$. To prove this, we consider a 3-machine flow shop problem with $n + 1$ jobs $i = 1, \ldots, n+1$, where the processing times of the operations are of the form

$$p_{i1} = 0, p_{i2} = s_i, p_{i3} = 0 \text{ for } i = 1, \ldots, n$$
$$p_{n+1,1} = p_{n+1,2} = p_{n+1,3} = b := \tfrac{1}{2} \sum_{i=1}^{n} s_i.$$

We choose $k = 3b$ as the threshold for the corresponding decision problem.

If PARTITION has a solution, then there exists an index set $J \subseteq \{1, \ldots, n\}$ such that

$$\sum_{i \in J} s_i = b.$$

In this case the schedule shown in Figure 3.1 solves the decision version of problem $F3 \parallel C_{\max}$.

If, on the other hand, the flow-shop problem has a solution with $C_{\max} \leq 3b$, then job $n+1$ must be scheduled as shown in Figure 3.1. Furthermore, $J = \{i|$ job finishes not later than $b\}$ solves the partitioning problem.

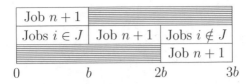

Figure 3.1: Feasible schedule.

Finally, the input of the flow-shop problem can be computed in polynomial time given the input of the partitioning problem. □

Example 3.4 We show that CLIQUE $\propto P2|prec; p_i \in \{1,2\}|C_{\max}$. The input of CLIQUE is given by an undirected graph $G = (V, E)$ with vertices $v_1, \ldots, v_q$ and edges $e_1, \ldots, e_r$, and a threshold value p ($0 < p \leq q$). We must polynomially transform this input into an instance of the $P2|prec; p_i \in \{1,2\}|C_{\max}$-problem such that there is a clique C with $|C| \geq p$ if and only if there is a schedule with $C_{\max} \leq k$ for a suitable value k.

We set $k = q + 2r + (q - p + 1)$ and define the scheduling problem as follows: Consider jobs denoted by

$$v_1, \ldots, v_q, e_1, \ldots, e_r, w_1 \ldots, w_t \text{ with } t = k + (q - p + 1),$$

i.e. we have v-jobs and e-jobs which correspond with the vertices and edges of G and dummy jobs w_i.

Let the processing time of all e-jobs be equal to 2. The processing times of v-jobs and dummy jobs are 1. Furthermore, define $v_i \to e_j$ if and only if v_i is an endpoint of e_j. We only have additional precedence relations between dummy jobs. They are chosen in such a way that, under the assumption that $C_{\max} \leq k$ in each time period, at least one dummy job must be scheduled, say on machine 2, and that on machine 1 free blocks are created, as shown in Figure 3.2.

In the first block there is exactly space for the p vertex jobs and $\frac{1}{2}p(p-1)$ edge jobs which correspond to a clique with p vertices. Thus the length of this block is $p + 2 \cdot \frac{1}{2}p(p-1) = p^2$. In the following $q - p$ unit time blocks which are separated by dummy jobs, there is space for the remaining vertex jobs. In the last block, which starts at time $p^2 + 2(q - p) + 1$ and ends at time k, there is exactly space for the remaining edge jobs.

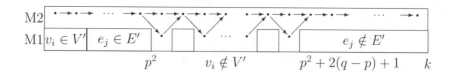

Figure 3.2: Additional precedence relations.

Given the clique problem, this scheduling problem can be constructed in polynomial time.

If G contains a clique (V', E') with p vertices, then the schedule shown in Figure 3.2 is feasible and satisfies $C_{\max} \leq k$. If, on the other hand, there exists a feasible schedule with $C_{\max} \leq k$, then we may assume that the dummy jobs are processed as in Figure 3.2. The blocks created on machine 1 must be completely filled. Thus, in the $q - p$ unit time blocks in the middle, $q - p$ v-jobs must be scheduled. To fill the p^2 units of the first block, the p remaining v-jobs and $\frac{1}{2}p(p - 1)$ e-jobs must be used. The corresponding vertices and edges must build a clique. $\square$

The significance of a polynomial transformation comes from the following lemma:

Lemma 3.1 Let P, Q be decision problems. If $P \propto Q$, then $Q \in \mathcal{P}$ implies $P \in \mathcal{P}$ (and, equivalently, $P \notin \mathcal{P}$ implies $Q \notin \mathcal{P}$).

Furthermore, we have

Lemma 3.2 Let P, Q, R be decision problems. If $P \propto Q$ and $Q \propto R$, then $P \propto R$.

We omit the easy proofs of these two lemmas.

A decision problem Q is called $\mathcal{NP}$-**complete** if $Q \in \mathcal{NP}$ and, for all other decision problems $P \in \mathcal{NP}$, we have $P \propto Q$.

If any single $\mathcal{NP}$-complete problem Q could be solved in polynomial time, then due to Lemma 3.1 all problems in $\mathcal{NP}$ could be solved in polynomial time and we would have $\mathcal{P} = \mathcal{NP}$. This underlines the important role of $\mathcal{NP}$-complete problems in complexity theory.

Cook [73] has proved that there exist $\mathcal{NP}$-complete problems. The first such problem is a decision problem from Boolean logic, which is usually referred to as the satisfiability problem. The terms we shall use in describing it are defined as follows.

Let $U = \{u_1, u_2, \ldots, u_m\}$ be a set of **Boolean variables** . A **truth assignment** for U is a function $t : U \rightarrow \{\text{true, false}\}$. $u \in U$ is true (false) if and only if $t(u) = \text{true (false)}$. If $u \in U$, then u and $\overline{u}$ are **literals** over U, where $\overline{u}$ is true iff u is false.

A **clause** over U is a set of literals over U (such as $\{u_1, \overline{u_2}, u_7\}$). It represents the disjunction of those literals and is **satisfied** by a truth assignment if and only if at least one of its members is true under the assignment. A collection C of clauses over U is **satisfiable** if and only if there exists some truth assignment for U that simultaneously satisfies all the clauses in C. Such a truth assignment is called a **satisfying truth assignment** for C. The satisfiability problem is specified as follows.

SATISFIABILITY (SAT)

We are given a set U of Boolean variables and a collection C of clauses over U.

Is there a satisfying truth assignment for C?

The problem in which each clause contains exactly 3 literals is called the **3-SATISFIABILITY** problem (**3-SAT**).

The important theorem of Cook [73] can now be stated:

Theorem 3.3 (Cook's Theorem) SAT is $\mathcal{NP}$-complete.

For a proof of this theorem we refer to Garey & Johnson [99].

The following lemma gives us a straightforward approach for proving new problems to be $\mathcal{NP}$-complete.

Lemma 3.4 If P and Q belong to $\mathcal{NP}$, P is $\mathcal{NP}$-complete, and $P \propto Q$, then Q is $\mathcal{NP}$-complete.

Proof: Since $Q \in \mathcal{NP}$, all we need to do is to show that, for every $R \in \mathcal{NP}$, $R \propto Q$. However, because P is $\mathcal{NP}$-complete, we have $R \propto P \propto Q$ and thus by Lemma 3.2, $R \propto Q$ for every $R \in \mathcal{NP}$. $\quad\square$

Usually it is an easy task to show that $Q \in \mathcal{NP}$. Therefore, when proving $\mathcal{NP}$-completeness the main task is to find an $\mathcal{NP}$-complete problem P such that $P \propto Q$.

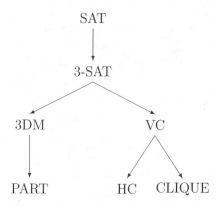

Figure 3.3: Basic polynomial transformations.

The diagram of Figure 3.3 shows some basic polynomial transformations between problems introduced in this section. An arc from P to Q in Figure 3.3 indicates that $P \propto Q$. Because all problems in Figure 3.3 belong to $\mathcal{NP}$ all these problem are $\mathcal{NP}$-complete.

We are dealing with scheduling problems which are not decision problems, but optimization problems. An optimization problem is called $\mathcal{NP}$-**hard** if the corresponding decision problem is $\mathcal{NP}$-complete. Examples 3.3 and 3.4 show that the scheduling problems $F3 \parallel C_{\max}$ and $P2|prec; p_i \in \{1,2\}|C_{\max}$ are $\mathcal{NP}$-hard.

Note that if we could polynomially solve an $\mathcal{NP}$-hard optimization problem, this would imply $\mathcal{P} = \mathcal{NP}$.

Finally, we will introduce the concept of strong NP-completeness which is related to pseudopolynomial algorithms.

Let x be the input of some problem. Then we denote by $|x|_{\mathrm{bin}}$ the length of x with respect to some binary encoding. Furthermore, let $|x|_{\max}$ be the magnitude of the largest number in x. A problem P is **pseudopolynomially solvable** if and only if its time complexity function is bounded above by a polynomial function of the two variables $|x|_{\max}$ and $|x|_{\mathrm{bin}}$.

A decision problem P is a **number problem** if there exists no polynomial p such that $|x|_{\max} \leq p(|x|_{\mathrm{bin}})$ for all inputs x of P. The partition problems PART is a number problem, because $\max\limits_{i=1}^{n} s_i$ is an exponential function of the length of a binary input string which encodes all s_i-values. All other decision problems introduced in this section are not number problems because no numbers are used to define them (in which case we set $|x|_{max} = 1$).

An NP-complete problem P which is not a number problem cannot be solved by a pseudopolynomial algorithm unless $P = NP$. Otherwise, there exists a monotone polynomial function h such that the time complexity is bounded by $h(|x|_{max}, |x|_{bin}) \leq h(p(|x|_{bin}), |x|_{bin})$, i.e. the NP-complete problem P would be polynomially solvable.

For any decision problem P and any polynomial q let P_q denote the subproblem of P obtained by restricting P to those instances satisfying $|x|_{max} \leq q(|x|_{bin})$. Then P_q is not a number problem. A decision problem P is NP-**complete in the strong sense** if P belongs to NP and there exists a polynomial q for which P_q is NP-complete.

Lemma 3.5 If P is NP-complete in the strong sense, then P cannot be solved by a pseudopolynomial time algorithm unless $P = NP$.

Proof: Let q be a polynomial such that P_q is NP-complete. P_q is not a number problem. Thus, the existence of a pseudopolynomial algorithm for P (which is also pseudopolynomial for P_q) would imply $P = NP$. $\square$

This lemma implies that it is very unlikely that problems which are NP-complete in the strong sense can be solved pseudopolynomially.

The most straightforward way to prove that a number problem P is NP-complete in the strong sense is simply to prove for some specific polynomial q that P_q is NP-complete. In this way we conclude that NP-complete problems which do not involve numbers are NP-complete in the strong sense. With the exception of PART, all basic problems introduced in this section are NP-complete in the strong sense for this reason. PART can be proved to be pseudopolynomially solvable (Garey & Johnson [99]). Thus, by Lemma 3.5 it is not NP-complete in the strong sense (unless $P = NP$). Another way to prove NP-completeness in the strong sense is to use pseudopolynomial reductions (Garey & Johnson [99]): P is NP-complete in the strong sense if P belongs to NP and there exists a pseudopolynomial reduction from a problem Q, which is NP-complete in the strong sense, to P.

A **pseudopolynomial reduction** from a problem Q to a problem P uses a pseudopolynomial time computable function g (i.e. $g(x)$ is computable in time polynomial in two variables $|x|_{max}$ and $|x|_{bin}$.) Furthermore, g must satisfy the following two conditions:

- there exists a polynomial q_1 such that $q_1(|g(x)|'_{\text{bin}}) \geq |x|_{\text{bin}}$ for all inputs x of Q, and

- there exists a two-variable polynomial q_2 such that

$$|g(x)|'_{\text{max}} \leq q_2(|x|_{\text{max}}, |x|_{\text{bin}})$$

for all inputs x of Q.

The first condition is almost always satisfied. It requires that g does not cause a substantial decrease in the input length. The second condition ensures that the magnitude of the largest number in $g(x)$ does not blow up exponentially.

3.3 Simple Reductions Between Scheduling Problems

If in a description of a scheduling problem we replace F by J, we get a simple reduction because the flow shop is a special case of a job shop. Similarly, we get a simple reduction if we replace tree by prec. Possible simple reductions are shown by the reduction graphs $G_i (i = 1, \ldots, 8)$ in Figure 3.4.

Note that the reduction of G_8 only holds if the objective function is regular. In this case, s-batching with set-up time $s = 0$ means that we may consider only one-element batches, which is equivalent to having no batches at all.

There are similar relations between objective functions. These relations are shown in Figure 3.5.

$\sum f_j$ reduces to $\sum w_j f_j$ by setting $w_j = 1$ for all j. C_{max}, $\sum C_j$, and $\sum w_j C_j$ reduce to L_{max}, $\sum T_j$, and $\sum w_j T_j$, respectively, by setting $d_j = 0$ for all j. Furthermore, we have

$$
\begin{aligned}
\max L_j \leq k \quad &\Leftrightarrow C_j - d_j \leq k \text{ for all } j \\
&\Leftrightarrow C_j - (d_j + k) \leq 0 \text{ for all } j \\
&\Leftrightarrow \max\{0, C_j - (d_j + k)\} \leq 0 \text{ for all } j \\
&\Leftrightarrow \sum T_j = \sum \max\{0, C_j - (d_j + k)\} \leq 0 \\
&\Leftrightarrow \sum U_j \leq 0.
\end{aligned}
$$

Thus L_{max} reduces to $\sum T_j$ and $\sum U_j$.

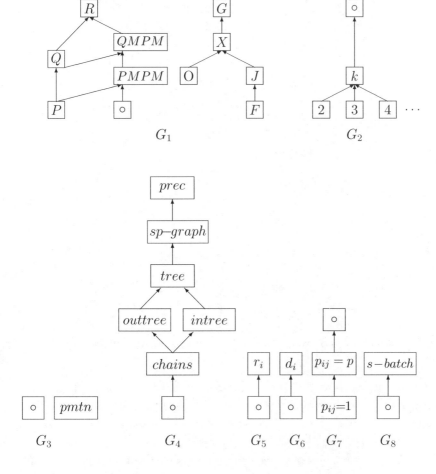

Figure 3.4: Graphs of basic reductions.

Each scheduling problem in the class outlined in Chapter 1 corresponds to a nine-tuple $(v_1, \ldots, v_9)$ where v_i is a vertex of the graph G_i shown in Figures 3.4 and 3.5 ($i = 1, \ldots, 9$). For two problems $P = (v_1, \ldots, v_9)$ and $Q = (w_1, \ldots, w_9)$ we have $P \propto Q$ if either $v_i = w_i$ or G_i contains a directed path from v_i to w_i, for $i = 1, \ldots, 9$.

These types of reductions play an instrumental role in the computer program MSPCLASS developed by Lageweg, Lawler, Lenstra & Rinnooy Kan [134]. The program records the complexity status of scheduling problems on the basis of known results and the use of simple inference

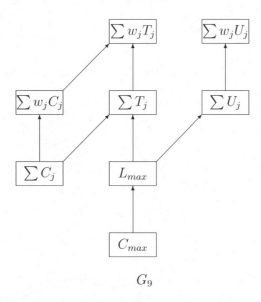

Figure 3.5: Reductions between objective functions.

rules as given above. Of interest are the hardest problems which are known to be polynomially solvable, the simplest problems which are known to be $\mathcal{NP}$-hard, as well as the simplest and hardest problems for which the complexity status is unknown.

For each problem class discussed in this book corresponding updated lists containing the problems which are

- maximal polynomial solvable,

- minimal NP-hard, and

- minimal and maximal open

can be found under our world-wide-web address
http: //www.mathematik.uni-osnabrueck.de/research/OR/class.

3.4 Living with $\mathcal{NP}$-hard Problems

The knowledge that a scheduling problem is $\mathcal{NP}$-hard is little consolation for the algorithm designer who needs to solve the problem. Fortunately, despite theoretical equivalence, not all $\mathcal{NP}$-hard problems are equally hard from a practical perspective. We have seen that some $\mathcal{NP}$-hard problems can be solved pseudopolynomially using dynamic programming. Such an approach may provide satisfactory results if the problems to be solved are not too large. A method related to dynamic programming is branch-and-bound, which will be discussed at the end of this section. The branch-and-bound method is based on the idea of intelligently enumerating all feasible solutions.

Another possibility is to apply approximation algorithms. These algorithms produce solutions that are guaranteed to be within a fixed percentage of the actual optimum. One of the most successful methods of attacking hard combinatorial optimization problems is the discrete analog of "hill climbing", known as local (or neighborhood) search, which will be discussed at the beginning of this section. Local search methods generally only provide feasible solutions which are not guaranteed to be optimal. However, for minimization (maximization) problems, a possible deviation from the optimal objective value can be bounded if a lower (upper) bound is available.

Any approach without formal guarantee of performance can be considered a "heuristic". Such approaches are useful in practical situations if no better methods are available.

3.4.1 Local Search Techniques

In this section we will study local search techniques which are useful tools for solving discrete optimization problems. A **discrete optimization problem** can be described as follows. For a given finite set S and a given function $c : S \to \mathbb{R}$, one has to find a solution $s^* \in S$ with

$$c(s^*) \leq c(s) \text{ for all } s \in S.$$

All nonpreemptive scheduling problems introduced thus far are discrete optimization problems. Local search is an iterative procedure which moves from one solution in S to another as long as necessary. In order to systematically search through S, the possible moves from a solution s

to the next solution should be restricted in some way. To describe such restrictions, we introduce a **neighborhood structure** $N : S \rightarrow 2^S$ on S. For each $s \in S$, $N(s)$ describes the subset of solutions which can be reached in one step by moving from s. The set $N(s)$ is called the neighborhood of s.

A neighborhood structure N may be represented by a directed graph $G = (V, A)$ where $V = S$ and

$$(s, t) \in A \text{ iff } t \in N(s).$$

G is called the **neighborhood graph** of the neighborhood structure.

Usually it is not possible to store the neighborhood graph because S has an exponential size. To overcome this difficulty, a set AM of **allowed modifications** $F : S \rightarrow S$ is introduced. For a given solution s, the neighborhood of s can now be defined by

$$N(s) = \{F(s) \mid F \in AM\}.$$

Using these definitions, a **local search method** may be described as follows. In each iteration we start with a solution $s \in S$ and choose a solution $s' \in N(s)$ (or a modification $F \in AM$ which provides $s' = F(s)$). Based on the values $c(s)$ and $c(s')$, we choose a starting solution of the next iteration. According to different criteria used for the choice of the starting solution of the next iteration, we get different types of local search techniques.

The simplest choice is to take the solution with the smallest value of the cost function. This choice leads to the well-known iterative improvement method which may be formulated as follows.

Algorithm Iterative Improvement
1. Choose an initial solution $s' \in S$;
2. REPEAT
3. $s := s'$
4.   Generate the best solution $s' \in N(s)$;
5. UNTIL $c(s') \geq c(s)$

This algorithm will terminate with some solution s^*. In general, s^* is only a **local minimum** with respect to the neighborhood N (i.e. a solution such that no neighbor is better than this solution) and may differ considerably from the global minimum.

A method which seeks to avoid being trapped in a local minimum is **simulated annealing**. It is a randomized method because

- s' is chosen randomly from $N(s)$, and

- in the i-th step s' is accepted with probability

$$\min\{1, \exp(-\frac{c(s') - c(s)}{c_i})\}$$

where (c_i) is a sequence of positive control parameters with $\lim_{i \to \infty} c_i = 0$.

The interpretation of this probability is as follows. If $c(s') \leq c(s)$, then s is replaced by s' with probability one. If, on the other hand, $c(s') > c(s)$, then s is replaced by s' with some probability. This probability decreases with increasing i. In other words, we can leave a local minimum, but the probability for doing so will be low after a large number of steps. In the following algorithm random $[0, 1]$ denotes a function which yields a uniformly distributed random value between 0 and 1. Furthermore, the sequence (c_i) is created by a function g, i.e. $c_{i+1} = g(c_i)$ for all i.

Algorithm Simulated Annealing
1. $i := 0$;
2. Choose an initial solution $s \in S$;
3. $best := c(s)$;
4. $s^* := s$;
5. REPEAT
6.   Generate randomly a solution $s' \in N(s)$;
7.   IF random $[0, 1] < \min\{1, \exp(-\frac{c(s')-c(s)}{c_i})\}$ THEN $s := s'$;
8.   IF $c(s') < best$ THEN
           BEGIN
9. $s^* := s'$;
10. $best := c(s')$;
           END;
11. $c_{i+1} := g(c_i)$;
12. $i := i + 1$
       UNTIL stop criterion

A detailed discussion of how one should define the control function g and the stop criterion for practical applications is described in Van Laarhoven and Aarts [205]. One possibility is to stop after a given amount of computation time.

A variant of simulated annealing is the **threshold acceptance method**. It differs from simulated annealing only by the acceptance rule for the randomly generated solution $s' \in N(s)$. s' is accepted if the difference $c(s') - c(s)$ is smaller than some non-negative threshold t. t is a positive control parameter which is gradually reduced.

Algorithm Threshold Acceptance
1. $i := 0$;
2. Choose an initial solution $s \in S$;
3. $best := c(s)$;
4. $s^* := s$;
5. REPEAT
6.   Generate randomly a solution $s' \in N(s)$;
7.   IF $c(s') - c(s) < t_i$ THEN $s := s'$;
8.   IF $c(s') < best$ THEN
          BEGIN
9. $s^* := s'$;
10. $best := c(s')$;
          END;
11. $t_{i+1} := g(t_i)$;
12. $i := i + 1$
     UNTIL stop criterion

g is a non-negative function with $g(t) < t$ for all t.

Simulated annealing and the threshold acceptance method have the advantage that they can leave a local minimum. They have the disadvantage that it is possible to get back to solutions already visited. Therefore oscillation around local minima is possible and this may lead to a situation where much computational time is spent on a small part of the solution set. A simple way to avoid such problems is to store all visited solutions in a list called **tabu list** T and to only accept solutions which are not contained in the list. However, storing all visited solutions in a tabu list and testing if a candidate solution belongs to the list is generally too consuming, both in terms of memory and computational time. To make the approach practical, we store attributes which define a set of solutions. The definition of the attributes is done in such a way that for each solution visited recently, the tabu list contains a corresponding attribute. All moves to solutions characterized by these attributes are forbidden (tabu). In this way cycles smaller than a certain length t, where t usually grows with the length of the tabu list, will not occur.

Besides a tabu status, a so-called aspiration criterion is associated with each attribute. If a current move leading to a solution s' is tabu, then this move will be considered admissible if s' satisfies the aspiration criterion associated with the attribute of s'. For example, we may associate with each attribute a threshold k for the objective function and allow a move m to a solution s' if $c(s') \le k$, even though m is tabu.

The following algorithm describes the general framework of tabu search.

Algorithm Tabu Search
1. Choose an initial solution $s \in S$;
2. $best := c(s)$;
3. $s^* := s$;
4. Tabu-list:= ϕ;
   REPEAT
5. $Cand(s) := \{s' \in N(s) \mid$ the move from s to s' is not tabu OR s' satisfies the aspiration criterion $\}$;
6.   Generate a solution $\bar{s} \in Cand(s)$;
7.   Update the tabu list;
8. $s := \bar{s}$;
9.   IF $c(s) <$ best THEN
          BEGIN
10. $s^* := s$;
11. $best := c(s)$
          END
     UNTIL stop criterion

Different stopping criteria and procedures for updating the tabu list T can be developed. We also have the freedom to choose a method for generating a solution $\bar{s} \in Cand(s)$. A simple strategy is to choose the best possible $\bar{s}$ with respect to function c:

$$c(\bar{s}) = \min\{c(s') \mid s' \in Cand(s)\}. \tag{3.1}$$

However, this simple strategy can be much too time-consuming, since the cardinality of the set $Cand(s)$ may be very large. For these reasons we may restrict our choice to a subset $V \subseteq Cand(s)$:

$$c(\bar{s}) = \min\{c(s') \mid s' \in V\}. \tag{3.2}$$

Usually the discrete optimization problem (3.1) or (3.2) is solved heuristically.

3.4.2 Branch-and-Bound Algorithms

Branch-and-bound is another method for solving combinatorial optimization problems. It is based on the idea of intelligently enumerating all feasible solutions.

To explain the details, we assume again that the discrete optimization problem P to be solved is a minimization problem. We also consider subproblems of P which are defined by a subsets S' of the set S of feasible solutions of P. It is convenient to identify P and its subproblems with the corresponding subset $S' \subseteq S$. Two things are needed for a branch-and-bound algorithm.

1. **Branching:** S is replaced by smaller problems $S_i (i = 1, \ldots, r)$ such that $\bigcup_{i=1}^{r} S_i = S$. This process is called **branching**. Branching is a recursive process, i.e. each S_i is the basis of another branching. The whole branching process is represented by a **branching tree**. S is the root of the branching tree, $S_i (i = 1, \ldots, r)$ are the children of S, etc. The discrete optimization problems created by the branching process are called **subproblems**.

2. **Lower bounding:** An algorithm is available for calculating a lower bound for the objective values of all feasible solutions of a subproblem.

3. **Upper bounding:** We calculate an upper bound U of the objective value of P. The objective value of any feasible solution will provide such an upper bound. If the lower bound of a subproblem is greater than or equal to U, then this subproblem cannot yield a better solution for P. Thus, we need not continue to branch from the corresponding node in the branching tree. To stop the

branching process in many nodes of the branching tree, the bound U should be as small as possible. Therefore, at the beginning of the branch-and-bound algorithm we apply some heuristic to find a good feasible solution with small value U. After branching many times we may reach a situation in which the subproblem has only one feasible solution. Then the lower bound LB of the subproblem is set equal to the objective value of this solution and we replace U by LB if $LB < U$.

Algorithm Branch-and-Bound summarizes these basic ideas. In this algorithm, LIST contains all subproblems for which we have to continue the branching process.

Algorithm Branch-and-Bound
1. LIST:=$\{S\}$;
2. $U:=$ value of some heuristic solution;
   currentbest:= heuristic solution;
3. WHILE LIST $\neq \phi$ DO
       BEGIN
4.   Choose a branching node k from LIST;
5.   Remove k from LIST;
6.   Generate children child (i) for $i = 1, \ldots, n_k$ and calculate
       corresponding lower bounds LB_i;
7.   For $i := 1$ TO n_k DO
8.   IF $LB_i < U$ THEN
9.   IF child (i) consists of a single solution THEN
                   BEGIN
10. $U := LB_i$;
11.   currentbest := solution corresponding with
                   child (i)
                   END
12.   ELSE add child (i) to LIST
       END

As an example, we will present a branch-and-bound algorithm for problem $F2||\sum C_i$ which is known to be $\mathcal{NP}$-hard (Garey et al. [100]).

Example 3.5 Problem $F2||\sum C_i$ is defined as follows. We are given n jobs $i = 1, \ldots, n$. Each job has two operations to be performed on one of

Figure 3.6: Different job orders.

two machines. Job i requires a processing time p_{ij} on machine $j(j = 1, 2)$ and each job must complete processing on machine 1 before starting on machine 2. Let C_i be the time at which job i finishes on machine 2. We have to find a schedule which minimizes the sum of finishing times $\sum_{i=1}^{n} C_i$.

The next theorem shows that we may restrict our search to a single permutation that determines the complete schedule.

Theorem 3.6 For the flow-shop problem $F2||\sum C_i$ there exists an optimal schedule in which both machines process the jobs in the same order.

Proof: Consider an optimal schedule in which the processing order on both machines is identical for the first k scheduled jobs, where $k < n$ is maximal. Let i be the k-th job and let j be the job scheduled on machine 2 after the second operation of job i. Then we may have a situation as shown in Figure 3.6.

If on machine 1 we shift job j to the position immediately after job i and move the jobs scheduled previously between job i and job j by p_{j1} time units to the right, we get another optimal schedule. This contradicts the maximality of k.   □

According to Theorem 3.6, an optimal schedule may be represented by a job permutation.

Using this result, a natural way to branch is to choose the first job to be scheduled at the first level of the branching tree, the second job at the next level, and so on. What we need next is a lower bound. Such a bound is derived as follows.

Suppose we are at a node at which the jobs in the set $M \subseteq \{1, \ldots, n\}$ have been scheduled, where $|M| = r$. Let i_k, $k = 1, \ldots, n$, be the index of the k-th job under any schedule which is a descendant of the node under consideration.

The cost of this schedule, which we wish to bound, is

$$S = \sum_{i \in M} C_i + \sum_{i \notin M} C_i. \tag{3.3}$$

For the second sum in (3.3) we will derive two possible lower bounds.

(1) If every job $i \notin M$ could start its processing on machine 2 immediately after completing its processing on machine 1, the second sum in (3.3) would become

$$S_1 = \sum_{k=r+1}^{n} [\sum_{i \in M} p_{i1} + (n - k + 1)p_{i_k 1} + p_{i_k 2}].$$

If that is not possible, then we have

$$\sum_{i \notin M} C_i \geq S_1.$$

The bound S_1 depends on the way the jobs not in M are scheduled. This dependence can be eliminated by noting that S_1 is minimized by scheduling jobs $i \notin M$ in an order of nondecreasing p_{i1}-values (compare to solution of $P \parallel \sum C_i$ in Section 2.5). Call the resulting minimum value S_1^*.

(2) $\max\{C_{i_r}, \sum_{i \in M} p_{i1} + \min_{i \notin M} p_{i1}\}$ is a lower bound on the start of the first job $i \notin M$ on machine 2. Thus, the second sum in (3.3) would be bounded by

$$S_2 = \sum_{k=r+1}^{n} [\max\{C_{i_r}, \sum_{i \in M} p_{i1} + \min_{i \notin M} p_{i1}\} + (n - k + 1)p_{i_k 2}].$$

Again, S_2 is minimized by scheduling jobs $i \notin M$ in an order of nondecreasing p_{i2}-values. Call the resulting minimum value S_2^*.

Combining the two lower bounds we get

$$\sum_{i \in M} C_i + \max\{S_1^*, S_2^*\} \tag{3.4}$$

which is an easily computed lower bound.

Algorithm Branch-and-Bound may be implemented using lower bound (3.4) and the simple branching rule. This algorithm can be improved by exploiting a natural dominance relation introduced by Ignall and Schrage [117]:

Suppose we have two nodes t and u representing partial sequences $i_1, \ldots, i_r$ and $j_1, \ldots, j_r$ of the same set of jobs, M. Denote by $C_i(t)$ and $C_j(u)$ the corresponding finishing times. If

$$C_{i_r}(t) \leq C_{j_r}(u) \tag{3.5}$$

and if the accumulated cost under the partial schedule t is no more than under u,

$$\sum_{i \in M} C_i(t) \leq \sum_{j \in M} C_j(u) \tag{3.6}$$

then the best completion of schedule t is at least as good as the best completion of u. Checking conditions (3.5) and (3.6) for nodes with identical sets M, nodes may be eliminated from LIST in Algorithm Branch-and-Bound. $\qquad\square$

There are many alternatives to implement a branch-and-bound algorithm. There may be many possibilities to organize the branching. When calculating lower bounds, one often has a choice between bounds that are relatively tight, but require much computation time, and bounds that are not so tight but can be computed quickly. A similar trade-off may exist in choosing a dominance relation. At each branching step, it is necessary to select the branching node. The usual alternatives are least-lower-bound-next, last-in-first-out, or first-in-first-out.

Finally, we should mention that the branch-and-bound algorithm is often terminated before optimality is reached. In this case we have a complete solution with cost U, and the lowest lower bound LB of all nodes in the list provides a lower bound on the optimal cost.

Note that if OPT is the optimal solution value, then $\frac{U-OPT}{OPT} \leq \frac{U-LB}{LB}$, i.e. $\frac{U-LB}{LB}$ is an upper bound for the performance ratio for the heuristic we get by terminating the branch-and-bound procedure before reaching the optimum.

Which design strategy is taken depends very much on the problem and its data. Designing a good branch-and-bound procedure usually requires some computational experience.

Chapter 4

Single Machine Scheduling Problems

The single machine case has been the subject of extensive research ever since the early work of Jackson [118] and Smith [188]. In this chapter, we will present algorithms for single machine scheduling problems which are polynomial or pseudopolynomial. It is useful to note the following general result which holds for single machine problems: if all $r_j = 0$ and if the objective function is a monotone function of the finishing times of the jobs, then only schedules without preemption and without idle time need to be considered. This follows from the fact that the optimal objective value does not improve if preemption is allowed. To see this, consider a schedule in which some job i is preempted, i.e.

- i is scheduled in $[t_1, t_2[$ and $[t_3, t_4[$ where $t_1 < t_2 < t_3 < t_4$, and

- i is neither scheduled in $[t_2, t_3[$ nor immediately before t_1.

If we reschedule so that the part of i occurring in $[t_1, t_2[$ is scheduled between $t_3 - (t_2 - t_1)$ and t_3, and so that anything scheduled between t_2 and t_3 is moved back $t_2 - t_1$ units of time, we eliminate this preemption of i without increasing the objective function. Furthermore, no new preemption is created. Continuing this process, we obtain an optimal solution for the preemptive problem where no preemption is necessary.

Note that this transformation generally creates infeasibility if $r_j \neq 0$ for some jobs j.

4.1   Minimax Criteria

4.1.1   Lawler's Algorithm for 1 | prec | f$_{\max}$

To solve problem $1 \mid prec \mid f_{\max}$ with $f_{\max} = \max\limits_{j=1}^{n} f_j(C_j)$ and f_j monotone for $j = 1, \ldots, n$, it is sufficient to construct an optimal sequence π : $\pi(1), \pi(2), \ldots, \pi(n)$ ($\pi(i)$ denotes the job in position i). Lawler [135] developed a simple algorithm which constructs this sequence in reverse order.

Let $N = \{1, \ldots, n\}$ be the set of all jobs and denote by $S \subseteq N$ the set of unscheduled jobs. Furthermore, define $p(S) = \sum\limits_{j \in S} p_j$. Then the scheduling rule may be formulated as follows: Schedule a job $j \in S$, which has no successor in S and has a minimal $f_j(p(S))$-value, as the last job in S.

To give a precise description of the algorithm, we represent the precedence constraints by the corresponding **adjacency matrix** $A = (a_{ij})$ where $a_{ij} = 1$ if and only if j is a direct successor of i. By $n(i)$ we denote the number of immediate successors of i.

Algorithm 1 | prec | f$_{\max}$

1. FOR $i := 1$ TO n DO $n(i) := \sum\limits_{j=1}^{n} a_{ij}$;

2. $S := \{1, \ldots, n\}$; $p := \sum\limits_{j=1}^{n} p_j$;

3. FOR $k := n$ DOWN TO 1 DO
       BEGIN
4.   Find job $j \in S$ with $n(j) = 0$ and minimal $f_j(p)$-value;
5. $S := S \backslash \{j\}$;
6. $n(j) := \infty$;
7. $\pi(k) := j$;
8. $p := p - p_j$;
9.   FOR $i := 1$ to n DO
             IF $a_{ij} = 1$ THEN $n(i) := n(i) - 1$
           END

The complexity of this algorithm is $O(n^2)$.

Theorem 4.1 Algorithm $1 \mid prec \mid f_{\max}$ constructs an optimal sequence.

Proof: Enumerate the jobs in such a way that $1, 2, \ldots, n$ is the sequence constructed by the algorithm. Let $\sigma : \sigma(1), \ldots, \sigma(n)$ be an optimal sequence with $\sigma(i) = i$ for $i = n, n - 1, \ldots, r$ and $\sigma(r - 1) \neq r - 1$ where r is minimal. We have the following situation

| $\sigma :$ | $\cdots$ | $r-1$ | k | $\cdots$ | j | r | $\cdots$ | | n |

It is possible to schedule $r - 1$ immediately before r. Therefore, $r - 1$ and j have no successor in the set $\{1, \ldots, r - 1\}$. This implies $f_{r-1}(p) \leq f_j(p)$ with $p = \sum_{i=1}^{r-1} p_i$ because $1, \ldots, n$ was constructed by the algorithm. Thus, the schedule we get by shifting the block of jobs between $r - 1$ and r an amount of p_{r-1} units to the left and processing $r - 1$ immediately before r is again optimal. This contradicts the minimality of r. $\qquad\square$

In the next section, we show that the problem can also be solved efficiently if we have release times r_j and either preemption is allowed or all jobs have unit processing times.

4.1.2 $1 \,|\, \mathbf{prec}; \mathbf{p_j} \!=\! 1; \mathbf{r_j} \,|\, \mathbf{f_{max}}$ and $1 \,|\, \mathbf{prec}; \mathbf{pmtn}; \mathbf{r_j} \,|\, \mathbf{f_{max}}$

We assume again that $f_{\max}$ is the maximum of monotone functions. The first step in solving these problems is to modify the release times r_j. If $i \to j$ (i.e. if j is a successor of i) and $r_i + p_i > r_j$, then job j cannot start before $r_j' = r_i + p_i$. Thus, we may replace r_j by r_j'. The release times can be modified in a systematic way using the following algorithm. We assume that the jobs are enumerated topologically (i.e. for all jobs i, j with $i \to j$ we have $i < j$). If this is not the case, we apply the algorithm presented in Section 2.7.

Algorithm Modify r_j
1. FOR $i := 1$ TO $n - 1$ DO
2.   FOR $j := i + 1$ TO n DO
3.   IF $i \to j$ THEN $r_j := \max\{r_j, r_i + p_i\}$

We denote the modified release time by r_j'. Note that if the processing times are nonzero, then we have

$$r_j' > r_i' \text{ if } i \to j. \tag{4.1}$$

Figure 4.1: Schedule with three blocks.

Thus, if we schedule jobs according to nondecreasing release times r'_j such that the release times are respected, we always get a feasible schedule. Such a schedule may consist of several blocks. A **block** is a maximal set of jobs which are processed without any idle time between them (see Fig. 4.1). The following algorithm gives a precise description of blocks B_ν constructed in this way. We assume that all release times are modified and that the jobs are sorted according to these modified release times.

Algorithm Blocks $(\{1, 2, \ldots, n\})$
1. $i := 1; j := 1;$
2. WHILE $i \leq n$ DO
        BEGIN
3. $t := r_i; B_j := \phi;$
4.   WHILE $r_i \leq t$ AND $i \leq n$ DO
                BEGIN
5. $B_j := B_j \cup \{i\};$
6. $t := t + p_i;$
7. $C_i := t$
8. $i := i + 1;$
                END;
9. $j := j + 1;$
        END

The C_i-values calculated by the algorithm define the finishing times of jobs in a feasible nonpreemptive schedule. An example of such a schedule is shown in Figure 4.1. For a block B_j we define

$$s_j := \min_{i \in B_j} r_i$$
$$p(B_j) = \sum_{i \in B_j} p_i$$
$$t_j = t(B_j) := s_j + p(B_j).$$

s_j and t_j are the **starting time** and the **finishing time**, respectively, of B_j.

The discussion thus far is valid for nonpreemptive schedules with jobs having arbitrary processing times.

Now we turn to problem $1 \mid prec; pmtn; r_j \mid f_{\max}$.

Lemma 4.2 For problem $1 \mid prec; pmtn; r_j \mid f_{\max}$ there exists an optimal schedule such that the intervals $[s_j, t_j]$ $(j = 1, \ldots, k)$ constructed by Algorithm Blocks are completely occupied by jobs.

Proof: Consider an optimal schedule with the property that $[s, t]$ is some idle interval contained in some block interval $[s_j, t_j]$. Furthermore, assume that in this schedule $[s, t]$ is the first such interval. We claim that there exists some job i with $r_i \leq s$ which finishes later than time s. Otherwise, for the set T of jobs which are processed in time periods later than time s we would have

$$r = \min\{r_k \mid k \in T\} > s$$

and in the schedule created by Algorithm Blocks interval $[s, r]$ must be an idle interval, which is a contradiction.

We move job i into the idle interval so that either $[s, t]$ is completely filled or job i finishes in $[s, t]$. Continuing this process, after a finite number of steps we get a schedule with the desired properties.   □

Due to Lemma 4.2 we may treat each block separately. The optimal solution value for the whole problem is given by the maximum of the solution values of all blocks.

Let B be such a block. Denote by $f_{\max}^*(B)$ the optimal solution value for the jobs in this block. Furthermore, let $f_{\max}^*(B \backslash \{j\})$ be the optimal solution value for the jobs in $B \backslash \{j\}$. Clearly, $f_{\max}^*(B \backslash \{j\}) \leq f_{\max}^*(B)$ for all j scheduled in B and thus

$$f_{\max}^*(B) \geq \max_{j \in B}\{f_{\max}^*(B \backslash \{j\})\}. \tag{4.2}$$

Furthermore,

$$f_l(t(B)) := \min\{f_j(t(B)) \mid j \in B \text{ without successors in } B\} \leq f_{\max}^*(B) \tag{4.3}$$

because in an optimal schedule one job $k \in B$ without successors in B finishes at time $t(B)$.

A schedule is now constructed as follows. We solve the problem for the set of jobs $B \backslash \{l\}$. The optimal solution of this problem again has a corresponding block structure. Similar to the proof of Lemma 4.2 we can show that job l can be scheduled in the idle periods of this block structure yielding a schedule with objective value of at the most

$$\max\{f^*_{\max}(B\backslash\{l\}), f_l(t(B))\} \leq f^*_{\max}(B)$$

which is the optimal value for B (see (4.2) and (4.3)).

Now we are ready to formulate a recursive procedure which solves problem $1 \mid prec; pmtn; r_j \mid f_{\max}$.

Algorithm 1 | prec; pmtn; r$_j$ | f$_{\max}$

$\quad S \quad := \{1,\ldots,n\};$

$\quad f^*_{\max} \quad := Decompose(S)$

Decompose is a recursive procedure which returns the optimal $f_{\max}$-value for the problem with the job set $S \neq \phi$.

Procedure Decompose (S)
1. If $S = \emptyset$ THEN RETURN $-\infty$;
2. IF $S = \{i\}$ THEN RETURN $f_i(r_i + p_i)$
   ELSE
       BEGIN
3.   Call Blocks (S);
4. $f := -\infty$;
5.   FOR ALL blocks B DO
         BEGIN
6.   Find l with $f_l(t(B)) = \min\{f_j(t(B)) \mid j \in B$
         without successor in $B\}$;
7. $h := Decompose(B\backslash\{l\})$;
8. $f := \max\{f, h, f_l(t(B))\}$
         END;
9.   RETURN f
      END

The procedure Decompose can be easily extended in such a way that the optimal schedule is calculated as well. We have to schedule job l in the idle periods of the schedule for $B\backslash\{l\}$. This is done from left to right respecting r_l. Due to the fact that all release dates are modified, job l will respect the precedence relations.

The complexity of the algorithm is $O(n^2)$. This can be seen as follows. If we exclude the recursive calls in Step 7, the number of steps for the Procedure Decompose is $O(|S|)$. Thus, for the number $f(n)$ of computational steps we have the recursion $f(n) = cn + \sum f(n_i)$ where n_i is the number of jobs in the i-th block and $\sum n_i \leq n$.

The number of preemptions is bounded by $n-1$ because each preemption induces a splitting of blocks.

If all data are integer, then all starting and finishing times of the blocks are also integer. Thus, if we apply the algorithm to a problem with unit processing times, no preemption is necessary. Therefore, our algorithm also solves problem $1 \mid prec; p_j = 1; r_j \mid f_{\max}$.

Finally, we would like to mention that when applying Algorithm 1 $\mid$ $prec; pmtn; r_j \mid f_{\max}$ to problem $1 \mid prec \mid f_{\max}$ Lawler's algorithm is yielded.

4.2 Maximum Lateness and Related Criteria

Problem $1 \mid r_j \mid L_{\max}$ is $\mathcal{NP}$-hard. However, each of the following three special cases is polynomial solvable:

(a) $r_j = r$ for all $j = 1, \ldots, n$.

 We get an optimal schedule by applying Jackson's scheduling rule:

$$\text{Schedule jobs in order of nondecreasing due dates.} \quad (4.4)$$

 This rule is also called the earliest due date (EDD-) rule. It is a consequence of Lawler's algorithm.

(b) $d_j = d$ for all $j = 1, \ldots, n$.

 We get an optimal schedule by applying the following rule:

$$\text{Schedule jobs in order of nondecreasing release dates.} \quad (4.5)$$

(c) $p_j = 1$ for all $j = 1, \ldots, n$.

 For this case Horn [115] formulated the following scheduling rule:

$$\text{At any time schedule an available job with the smallest due date.} \quad (4.6)$$

All of these rules can be implemented in $O(n \log n)$ steps. Furthermore, correctness of all these rules can be proved by using simple interchange arguments.

The results (a), (b) and (c) may be extended to the corresponding problems with precedence relations between jobs. In case (b) we have to modify the release dates before applying rule (4.5). Cases (a) and (c) require a similar modification to the due dates.

If $i \to j$ and $d_i' := d_j - p_j < d_i$, then we replace d_i by the modified due date d_i'. Again, the modification can be done in two steps:

1. Find a topological enumeration;

2. Modify due dates d_j from $j = n$ down to 1.

Here we will present an algorithm which combines both steps. We assume that the precedence relations are represented by the sets $IP(i)$ of **immediate predecessors** of jobs i. Furthermore, n_i denotes the number of immediate successors for job i which have not yet been used, and F is the set of jobs i with $n_i = 0$.

Algorithm Modify d_j
1. FOR $i := 1$ TO n DO $n_i := 0$;
2. FOR $i := 1$ TO n DO
3.   FOR ALL $j \in IP(i)$ DO $n_j := n_j + 1$;
4. $F := \phi$;
5. FOR $i := 1$ TO n DO
6.   IF $n_i = 0$ THEN $F := F \cup \{i\}$;
7. WHILE $F \neq \phi$ DO
8.   BEGIN
9.   Choose $j \in F$;
10.   FOR ALL $i \in IP(j)$ DO
               BEGIN
11. $d_i := \min\{d_i, d_j - p_j\}$;
12. $n_i := n_i - 1$;
13.   IF $n_i = 0$ THEN $F := F \cup \{i\}$
               END;
14. $F := F \backslash \{j\}$
          END

The computational complexity of this algorithm is $O(n + e)$, where e is the number of precedence relations.

Note that if all processing times are positive and all release dates are equal, then a sequence with nondecreasing due dates is compatible with the precedence constraints.

Again, we can prove by exchange arguments that after modifying release times and due dates the scheduling rules (4.4) to (4.6) provide optimal schedules. We will give a proof only for problem $1 \mid prec; r_j; p_j = 1 \mid L_{\max}$. The other proofs are similar.

$1 \mid \mathbf{prec}; \mathbf{r_j}; \mathbf{p_j} = 1 \mid \mathbf{L_{max}}$

Theorem 4.3 A schedule constructed by rule (4.6) is optimal for problem $1 \mid prec; r_j; p_j = 1 \mid L_{\max}$.

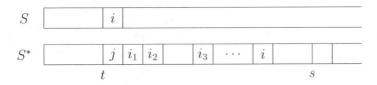

Figure 4.2: Schedules S and S^* for $1 \mid prec; r_j; p_j = 1 \mid L_{\max}$.

Proof: There exists an optimal schedule which is active (i.e. with the property that no job can be moved to the left without violating the constraints). In such an active schedule, each job starts at a release time or at a finishing time of some job. Consider an optimal active schedule S^* which coincides as long as possible with the schedule S constructed by the algorithm (cf. Figure 4.2). Let t be the first time at which a job i of S and a different job j of S^* begin. Because $r_i, r_j \leq t$ we have $d_i \leq d_j$. This follows from the fact that in S job i was scheduled according to rule (4.6). Let $i_1, \ldots, i_l$ be all jobs scheduled in S^* between job j and job i which are (not necessarily immediate) successors of job j. Furthermore, we assume that these jobs are ordered according to their starting times. If we replace i by i_l, i_l by $i_{l-1}, \ldots, i_2$ by i_1, i_1 by j, and j by i, we again have a feasible schedule S'. Furthermore, S' is optimal because $d_i \leq d_j \leq d_{i_\nu}$ for $\nu = 1, \ldots, l$. The last inequality follows from the fact that jobs i_ν are successors of j and we have modified d_j-values. $\square$

1 | prec; pmtn; r$_j$ | L$_{\max}$

This problem is a special case of the problem discussed in 4.1.2 and can be solved using the methods developed in 4.1.2.

A more direct way to solve this problem is to apply the following Earliest Due Date rule (EDD-rule):

> Schedule the jobs starting at the smallest r_j-value. At each decision point t given by a release time or a finishing time of some job, schedule a job j with the following properties: $r_j \leq t$, all its predecessors are scheduled, and it has the smallest modified due date. $\qquad$ (4.7)

Theorem 4.4 A schedule constructed by rule (4.7) is optimal for problem $1 \mid prec; pmtn; r_j \mid L_{\max}$.

Proof: The proof is similar to the proof of Theorem 4.3. Let S be a schedule constructed by applying rule (4.7) and let S^* be an optimal schedule. Assume that both schedules coincide until time t. Then we have a situation as shown in Figure 4.3 where $s > t$ is the earliest time at which job i is processed in S^*. If in S^* we eliminate the part of job

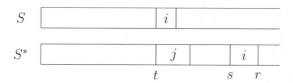

Figure 4.3: Schedules S and S^* for $1 \mid prec; pmtn; r_j \mid L_{\max}$.

i starting at time s, move job j and possible successors of j scheduled between t and s to the right, and reschedule the part of i with length $l = r - s$ in the created empty time slots, then again we have an optimal schedule. Continuing this process we get, after a finite number of steps, an optimal schedule which coincides with S. $\qquad \square$

Optimal schedules for the last two problems can be constructed in $O(n^2)$-time.

If all d_j-values are nonpositive, $L_{\max}$ can be written in the form

$$\max_{j=1}^{n}(C_j - d_j) = \max_{j=1}^{n}(C_j + q_j) \qquad (4.8)$$

where $q_j = -d_j \geq 0$ for all $j = 1, \ldots, n$. q_j is called the **tail** of job j. (4.8) is the finishing time, including post processing times q_j, of all jobs j. Single machine problems with an objective function (4.8) play an important role in connection with job-shop problems, whereby the release times r_j are called **heads**. The **head-tail problem** involves finding a schedule which is feasible with respect to the heads and minimizes (4.8). We have the following result.

Corollary 4.5   (a) A preemptive schedule for the one machine head-tail problem with precedence constraints can be constructed in $O(n^2)$ time using the following rule:

> At each time given by a head t or a finishing time t
> of some job, schedule a precedence feasible job j with   (4.9)
> $r_j \leq t$ which has a largest tail.

(b) If there are no precedence constraints between jobs, then an optimal schedule for the head-tail problem can be found in $O(n \log n)$ time.

Proof: An earliest due date ordering corresponds with a largest tail ordering. Thus, (a) follows from the results in this section.

To get the $O(n \log n)$-algorithm in (b) we first sort the jobs according to nondecreasing heads. In addition to this sorted list, we keep a priority queue with the tails as keys. At each time t this priority queue holds all unfinished jobs j with $r_j \leq t$. It allows us to find an available job with largest tail in constant time. Jobs which become available are inserted into the queue and a job is deleted after finishing. Insertion and deletion of a job takes $O(\log n)$ time.   □

Finally, we will present an efficient algorithm for the problem

$1 \mid \text{prec}; \text{p}_j = 1 \mid \text{L}_{max}$

This problem, which is a special case of problem $1 \mid prec; r_j; p_j = 1 \mid L_{max}$, can be solved more efficiently using an idea of Monma [169].

The first step is to modify the due dates in such a way that they are compatible with the precedence relations. This is done by applying Algorithm Modify d_j. Additionally, we assume that all modified due dates are non-negative. If this is not the case, we subtract the minimum modified due date d_{min} from all modified due dates. This decreases the L_{max}-value by the constant $d_{\min}$. Furthermore, after this second modification we have $L_{\max} \geq 0$.

Using the modified due dates d_j, an optimal schedule can be calculated in $O(n)$ time. The corresponding algorithm is based on two ideas:

- the jobs are processed in $[0, n]$. This implies that no job j with $d_j \geq n$ is late, even if it is processed as the last job. Because $L_{\max} \geq 0$, these jobs have no influence on the $L_{\max}$-value, and

- to sort the jobs we may use a **bucket sorting** method i.e. we construct the sets

$$B_k := \left\{ \begin{array}{l} \{j \mid d_j = k\} \text{ if } 0 \leq k \leq n-1 \\ \{j \mid d_j \geq n\} \text{ if } k = n. \end{array} \right.$$

Note that all due dates are assumed to be integer. If this is not the case, we may replace the due dates by $d'_j = \lfloor d_j \rfloor$ where $\lfloor x \rfloor$ is defined to be the largest integer not greater than x.

An optimal sequence π may be constructed by

Algorithm 1 | prec; $\mathbf{p_j} = 1$ | $\mathbf{L}_{\max}$
1. FOR $k := 0$ TO n DO $B_k := \phi$;
2. FOR $i := 1$ TO n DO
3.   IF $d_i < n$ THEN $B_{d_i} := B_{d_i} \cup \{i\}$
4.   ELSE $B_n := B_n \cup \{i\}$;
5. $i := 1$;
6. FOR $k := 0$ TO n DO
7.   WHILE there exists a $j \in B_k$ DO
           BEGIN
8. $\pi(i) := j$;
9. $B_k := B_k \backslash \{j\}$;
10. $i := i + 1$
           END

A similar approach may be used to solve problem $1 \mid r_j; p_j = 1 \mid L_{\max}$ in $O(n)$ time (see Frederickson [92]).

4.3   Total Weighted Completion Time

We will first discuss problem $1 \mid tree \mid \sum w_j C_j$ and some of its special cases. Problem $1 \mid sp\text{-graph} \mid \sum w_j C_j$ will be discussed in 4.3.2. We allow negative w_j-values. However, in this case all jobs must be scheduled in the time interval $[0, \sum_{j=1}^{n} p_j]$.

4.3.1 $1 \mid tree \mid \sum w_j C_j$

We have to schedule jobs with arbitrary processing times on a single machine so that a weighted sum of completion times is minimized. The processing times are assumed to be positive. Precedence constraints are given by a tree. We first assume that the tree is an outtree (i.e. each node in the tree has at the most one predecessor). Later we will deal with intrees (in which each node has at the most one successor). The algorithms presented are due to Adolphson and Hu [3].

Before presenting an algorithm for outtrees, we will prove some basic properties of optimal schedules, which motivate the algorithm and are useful for the correctness proof.

First we need to introduce some notation. For each job $i = 1, \ldots, n$, define $q_i = w_i/p_i$ and let $S(i)$ be the set of (not necessarily immediate) successors of i including i. For a set of jobs $I \subseteq \{1, \ldots, n\}$ define

$$w(I) := \sum_{i \in I} w_i, \quad p(I) = \sum_{i \in I} p_i, \text{ and } q(I) := w(I)/p(I).$$

Two subsets $I, J \subseteq \{1, \ldots, n\}$ are **parallel** $(I \sim J)$ if, for all $i \in I, j \in J$, neither i is a successor of j nor vice versa. The parallel sets must be disjoint. In the case $\{i\} \sim \{j\}$ we simply write $i \sim j$.

Each schedule is given by a sequence π.

Lemma 4.6 Let π be an optimal sequence and let I, J represent two blocks (sets of jobs to be processed consecutively) of π such that I is scheduled immediately before J. Let π' be the sequence we get from π by swapping I and J. Then

(a) $I \sim J$ implies $q(I) \geq q(J)$,

(b) if $I \sim J$ and $q(I) = q(J)$, then π' is also optimal.

Proof:

(a) Denote by f the objective function $\sum w_j C_j$. We have $f(\pi) \leq f(\pi')$, because π is optimal. Thus

$$0 \leq f(\pi') - f(\pi) = w(I)p(J) - w(J)p(I).$$

Division by $p(I)p(J)$ yields

$$q(I) = w(I)/p(I) \geq w(J)/p(J) = q(J).$$

(b) If $q(I) = q(J)$, then $f(\pi) = f(\pi')$ and π' is also optimal.

$\square$

Theorem 4.7 Let i, j be jobs with $i \to j$ and $q_j = \max\{q_k \mid k \in S(i)\}$. Then there exists an optimal schedule in which i is processed immediately before j.

Proof: Each schedule can be represented by a sequence. Let π be an optimal sequence with the property that the number l of jobs scheduled between i and j is minimal. Assume $l > 0$. Then we have the following situation:

	i	$\cdots$	k	j	

We consider two cases.

Case 1: $k \in S(i)$

j is not a successor of k because otherwise j would have at least two predecessors. Thus, $k \sim j$ and Lemma 4.6 imply $q(k) \geq q(j)$. By definition of j we also have $q(j) \geq q(k)$ which implies $q(j) = q(k)$. Again, by Lemma 4.6, jobs j and k can be interchanged without destroying optimality. This contradicts the minimality of l.

Case 2: $k \notin S(i)$

Let h be the last job scheduled between i and j (i included) which belongs to $S(i)$, i.e. for jobs r in the set K of jobs scheduled between h and j we have $r \notin S(i)$. The outtree structure and $i \to j$ imply that a predecessor of j is also a predecessor of i. Thus, a job in K cannot be a predecessor of j, and we have $K \sim j$. This implies $q(K) \geq q(j)$.

$h \in S(i)$ is not a predecessor of some $r \in K$ because this would imply $r \in S(i)$. Therefore $h \sim K$, which implies $q(h) \geq q(K) \geq q(j)$. By definition of j, we also have $q(j) \geq q(h)$, which implies $q(j) = q(h) = q(K)$. Using Lemma 4.6 we can interchange blocks K and j without destroying optimality. □

The conditions of Theorem 4.7 are satisfied if we choose a job j different from the root with maximal q_j-value, along with its unique father i. Since there exists an optimal schedule in which i is processed immediately before j, we merge nodes i and j and make all sons of j additional sons of i. The new node i, which represents the subsequence $\pi_i : i, j$, will have the label $q(i) := q(J_i)$, with $J_i = \{i, j\}$. Note that for a son of j, its new father i (represented by J_i) can be identified by looking for the set J_i which contains j.

The merging process will be applied recursively.

In the general step, each node i represents a set of jobs J_i and a corresponding sequence π_i of the jobs in J_i, where i is the first job in this sequence. We select a vertex j different from the root with maximal $q(j)$-value. Let f be the unique father of j in the original outtree. Then we have to find a node i of the current tree with $f \in J_i$. We merge j and i, replacing J_i and π_i by $J_i \cup J_j$ and $\pi_i \circ \pi_j$, where $\pi_i \circ \pi_j$ is the concatenation of the sequences π_i and π_j.

Details are given by the following algorithm in which

$E(i)$ denotes the last job of π_i,

$P(i)$ denotes the predecessor of i with respect to the precedence relation, and later a predecessor of i in an optimal sequence.

We assume that $i = 1$ is the root of the tree.

Algorithm 1 | outtree | $\sum w_j C_j$
1. $w(1) := -\infty$;
2. FOR $i := 1$ TO n DO
3. BEGIN $E(i) := i$; $J_i := \{i\}$; $q(i) := w(i)/p(i)$ END;
4. $L := \{1, \ldots, n\}$;
5. WHILE $L \neq \{1\}$ DO
        BEGIN
6.   Find $j \in L$ with largest $q(j)$-value;
7. $f := P(j)$;
8.   Find i such that $f \in J_i$;

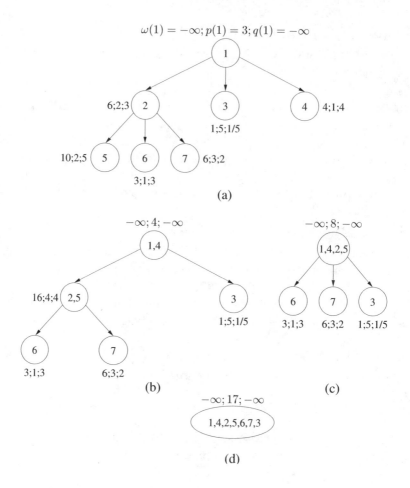

Figure 4.4: Application of Algorithm 1 | *outtree* | $\sum w_j C_j$.

9. $w(i) := w(i) + w(j);$
10. $p(i) := p(i) + p(j);$
11. $q(i) := w(i)/p(i);$
12. $P(j) := E(i);$
13. $E(i) := E(j);$
14. $J_i := J_i \cup J_j;$
15. $L := L \setminus \{j\}$
            END

Initially, we set $w(1) = -\infty$ to avoid choosing the root in Step 6. After termination, the optimal sequence π^* may be constructed using $E(1)$ and the array $P(i)$. This is done by constructing π^* from right to left: $j := E(1)$ is the last job in π^*, $P(j)$ is the predecessor of j in π^*, etc. The example in Figure 4.4 shows how the algorithm works. Fig. 4.4(a) shows a problem with 7 jobs. Fig. 4.4(b) i presents the tree after two iterations. The result after the next operations is shown in Figs 4.4(c) and (d). The optimal sequence is 1,4,2,5,6,7,3.

Algorithm 1 | $outtree$ | $\sum w_j C_j$ can be implemented in $O(n \log n)$-time if a priority queue is used for the $q(i)$-values and an efficient union-find algorithm for sets is used in Steps 8 and 14 (see Aho, Hopcroft, Ullmann [4]). It remains to prove that an optimal sequence is constructed.

Theorem 4.8 Algorithm 1 | $outtree$ | $\sum w_j C_j$ calculates an optimal sequence in $O(n \log n)$-time.

Proof: We prove optimality by induction on the number of jobs.

Clearly the algorithm is correct if we have only one job. Let $\mathcal{P}$ be a problem with n jobs. Assume that i, j are the first jobs merged by the algorithm. Let $\mathcal{P}'$ be the resulting problem with $n - 1$ jobs, where i is replaced by $I := (i, j)$ with $w(I) = w(i) + w(j)$ and $p(I) = p(i) + p(j)$.

Let $\mathcal{R}$ be the set of sequences of the form

$$\pi : \pi(1), \ldots, \pi(k), i, j, \pi(k+3), \ldots, \pi(n)$$

and let $\mathcal{R}'$ be the set of sequences of the form

$$\pi' : \pi(1), \ldots, \pi(k), I, \pi(k+3), \ldots, \pi(n).$$

Note that by Theorem 4.7 set $\mathcal{R}$ contains an optimal schedule. Furthermore, for the corresponding objective function values $f_n(\pi)$ and $f_{n-1}(\pi')$ we have

$$
\begin{aligned}
& f_n(\pi) - f_{n-1}(\pi') \\
& = w(i)p(i) + w(j)(p(i) + p(j)) - (w(i) + w(j))(p(i) + p(j)) \\
& = -w(i)p(j).
\end{aligned}
$$

We conclude that $\pi \in \mathcal{R}$ is optimal if and only if the corresponding $\pi' \in \mathcal{R}'$ is optimal. However, π' has only $n - 1$ jobs. Thus, by the induction hypothesis, the sequence constructed by our algorithm must be optimal. $\square$

To solve a 1 | $intree$ | $\sum w_j C_j$-problem P, we reduce P to a 1 | $outtree$ | $\sum w'_j C_j$-problem P' with

- i is a successor of j in P' if and only if j is a successor of i in P, and

- $w'_j = -w_j$ for $j = 1, \ldots, n$.

Then a sequence $\pi : 1, \ldots, n$ is feasible for P if and only if $\pi' : n, \ldots, 1$ is feasible for P'. Furthermore, we have

$$
\begin{aligned}
f'(\pi') &= \sum_{i=1}^{n}(-w_i)(\sum_{j \geq i} p_j) = \sum_{i=1}^{n}(-w_i)(\sum_{j > i} p_j) - \sum_{i=1}^{n} w_i p_i \\
&= \sum_{i=1}^{n} w_i(\sum_{j \leq i} p_j) - (\sum_{i=1}^{n} w_i)(\sum_{j=1}^{n} p_j) - \sum_{i=1}^{n} w_i p_i \\
&= f(\pi) - a
\end{aligned}
$$

where a does not depend on the sequence π. Thus a sequence π for P is optimal if and only if the reverse sequence π' is optimal for P'.

An instance of problem $1 \mid\mid \sum w_j C_j$ can be reduced to an instance of problem $1 \mid outtree \mid \sum w_j C_j$ by adding a root r with very small processing time as a dummy job. After calculating an optimal sequence, we have to eliminate r to get an optimal sequence for the instance of $1 \mid\mid \sum w_j C_j$. This process leads to

Smith's ratio rule: Put the jobs in order of nondecreasing ratios p_j/w_j, which applies if all $w_j > 0$.

That Smith's ratio rule leads to an optimal sequence can also be shown by a simple interchange argument.

If all weights are equal to one, we have problem $1 \mid\mid \sum C_j$ which is solved by

Smith's rule: Put the jobs in order of nondecreasing processing times ("shortest processing time first" -rule).

A related problem is

$1 \mid r_j; pmtn \mid \sum C_j$

This problem can be solved by constructing a schedule from left to right using:

Modified Smith's rule: At each release time or finishing time of a job, schedule an unfinished job which is available and has the smallest remaining processing time.

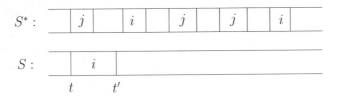

Figure 4.5: Schedules S^* and S for $1 \mid r_j; pmtn \mid \sum C_j$

Theorem 4.9 A schedule constructed by modified Smith's rule is optimal for problem $1 \mid r_j; pmtn \mid \sum C_j$.

Proof: The proof is similar to the proof of Theorem 4.4. Therefore we only discuss the exchange argument which is different.

Assume that an optimal active schedule S^* coincides with a schedule S constructed by modified Smith's rule up to time t. Then we have a situation as shown in Figure 4.5.

Let job i in S which starts at time t be processed up to time t'. Let j be the job in S^* which starts at time t. According to modified Smith's rule, the remaining processing time of j is not smaller than the remaining processing time of job i. Furthermore, we have $r_i, r_j \leq t$. Now in S^* we eliminate all intervals of both jobs i and j which do not start before time t. After this we reschedule these parts in the empty time slots starting at time t by first scheduling the remaining parts of i and then the remaining parts of j. The schedule created in this way is again optimal. We repeat this interchange process until S and the new optimal schedule coincide up to time t'. □

Surprisingly, the problem $1 \mid r_j; pmtn \mid \sum w_j C_j$ is $\mathcal{NP}$-hard.

4.3.2 $1 \mid sp\text{-}graph \mid \sum w_j C_j$

The results of the previous section can be generalized to job systems with series-parallel precedence constraints. Recall that a series-parallel graph can be constructed from singletons (i.e. graphs with one vertex only) by a sequence of series compositions and parallel compositions. A parallel composition joins two directed graphs without adding new arcs. A series composition of two graphs G_1 and G_2 joins G_1 and G_2 and adds all arcs (t, s) where t is a terminal vertex of G_1 and s is an initial vertex of G_2. Note that unlike parallel composition, a series composition is not a symmetric operation.

Figure 4.6(a) shows a series-parallel graph which is constructed by the following operations. First we build G_1 and G_2 by a parallel composition of the singletons 2,3 and 5,6, respectively. Then we construct G_3 and G_4, composing the singleton 1 in series with G_1 and G_3 in series with the singleton 4. Finally, we get the graph shown in Figure 4.6(a) by series composition of G_4 and G_2.

A series-parallel graph may be represented by its decomposition tree, which is a binary tree, with singletons as leaves. Each inner node of the tree represents a composition. Parallel and series composition are labeled P and S, respectively. Figure 4.6(b) shows a decomposition tree for the graph in Figure 4.6(a). The algorithm which solves problem $1 \mid sp\text{-graph} \mid \sum w_j C_j$ works from the bottom of the tree upward, merging sequences of jobs in an appropriate way. These sequences are associated with the leaves of the tree. All sequences are disjoint subsequences of an optimal sequence which can be constructed by concatenating these subsequences. Initially, we associate with a leaf representing job i the one element set $S_i := \{i\}$, consisting of the subsequence i of length 1. In the general step of the algorithm, two leaves with the same father f are merged, creating a new set S_f of subsequences. Furthermore, the father turns into a leaf with subsequences set S_f. The merging process depends on the type of composition represented by the father.

To describe this composition in more detail we need some further notations. Let π be a subsequence. Then $p(\pi)$ and $w(\pi)$ denote the sum of processing times and weights of all jobs in subsequence π. Furthermore, let $q(\pi) = w(\pi)/p(\pi)$. The concatenation of two subsequences π_1 and π_2 is denoted by $\pi_1 \circ \pi_2$.

Let $S_i(S_j)$ be the set of subsequences of the left (right) child of f. Then the following two procedures calculate the set of subsequences of the father f depending on the label of f.

If f is a parallel node, then we simply have

Parallel $(\mathbf{S_i}, \mathbf{S_j})$
1.RETURN $S_i \cup S_j$

The procedure in the case of a series composition is more involved.

Series (S_i, S_j)
1. Find $\pi_i \in S_i$ with $q(\pi_i) = \min\{q(\pi) \mid \pi \in S_i\}$;
2. Find $\pi_j \in S_j$ with $q(\pi_j) = \max\{q(\pi) \mid \pi \in S_j\}$;
3. IF $q(\pi_i) > q(\pi_j)$ THEN RETURN $S_i \cup S_j$
   ELSE
        BEGIN
4. $\pi := \pi_i \circ \pi_j$;
5. $S_i := S_i \setminus \{\pi_i\}$;
6.   Find $\pi_i \in S_i$ with $q(\pi_i) = \min\{q(\pi) \mid \pi \in S_i\}$;
7. $S_j := S_j \setminus \{\pi_j\}$;
8.   Find $\pi_j \in S_j$ with $q(\pi_j) = \max\{q(\pi) \mid \pi \in S_j\}$;
9.   WHILE $q(\pi) \geq q(\pi_i)$ OR $q(\pi_j) \geq q(\pi)$ DO
10.   IF $q(\pi) \geq q(\pi_i)$ THEN
              BEGIN
11. $\pi := \pi_i \circ \pi$; $S_i := S_i \setminus \{\pi_i\}$;
12.   Find $\pi_i \in S_i$ with $q(\pi_i) = \min\{q(\pi) \mid \pi \in S_i\}$
              END
          ELSE
              BEGIN
13. $\pi := \pi \circ \pi_j$; $S_j := S_j \setminus \{\pi_j\}$;
14.   Find $\pi_j \in S_j$ with $q(\pi_j) = \max\{q(\pi) \mid \pi \in S_j\}$
              END;
15.   RETURN $S_i \cup S_j \cup \{\pi\}$
          END

Note that after applying Series (S_i, S_j), for all $\pi_i \in S_i$ and $\pi_j \in S_j$, the inequalities $q(\pi_i) > q(\pi_j)$ or $q(\pi_i) > q(\pi) > q(\pi_j)$ hold. Thus, if a subsequence π_i must be processed before a subsequence π_j, we must have $q(\pi_i) > q(\pi_j)$. The following algorithm calculates an optimal sequence π^* for problem $1 \mid sp\text{-graph} \mid \sum w_j C_j$.

Algorithm $1 \mid$ sp-graph $\mid \sum \mathbf{w_j C_j}$
1. FOR ALL leaves i of the decomposition tree DO $S_i := \{i\}$;
2. WHILE there exists a vertex f with two leaves as children DO
        BEGIN
3. $i := \text{leftchild}(f)$; $j := \text{rightchild}(f)$;
4.   IF f has label P THEN
5. $S_f := \text{Parallel } (S_i, S_j)$
        ELSE

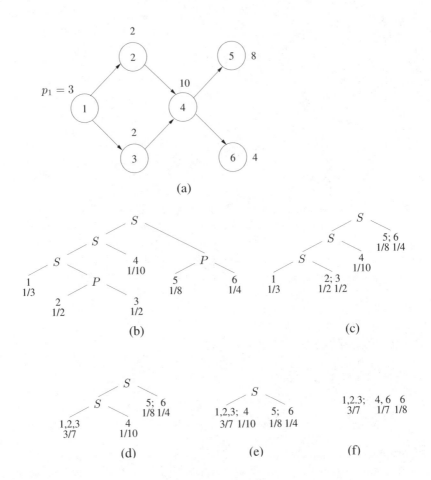

$p_1 = 3$

(a)

(b)

(c)

(d)   (e)   (f)

Figure 4.6: Application of Algorithm $1 \mid sp$-graph $\mid \sum w_j C_j$.

6. $S_f :=$ Series (S_i, S_j);
7.   Eliminate i and j and replace f by a leaf with label S_f
            END;
8. Construct π^* by concatenating all subsequences of the single
   leaf in an order of nonincreasing q-values.

Figure 4.6 demonstrates how the algorithm works if applied to the problem shown in Figure 4.6(a) with $w_i = 1$ for $i = 1, \ldots, 6$. The leaves of
the trees of Figure 4.6(b) to (f) are labeled with the corresponding sets of

sequences. The corresponding $q(\pi)$-value is shown below each sequence π. If we concatenate the three sequences shown in Figure 4.6(f) in such a way that the sequence with the larger q-value is first, we get the optimal sequence $\pi^*: 1, 2, 3, 4, 6, 5$. The algorithm runs in $O(n \log n)$ time if implemented appropriately (Aho et al. [4]).

To prove that Algorithm 1 | sp-graph | $\sum w_j C_j$ is correct, we first show that it satisfies the following invariance property: There exists an optimal solution which can be constructed by concatenating all subsequences associated with the leaves of the current decomposition tree (i.e. all subsequences $\sigma \in \bigcup S_i$).

The invariance property holds initially, when each job corresponds with a one element subsequence associated with some leaf of the decomposition tree. Furthermore, a parallel composition keeps the invariance property satisfied.

Lemma 4.10 The invariance property is satisfied during all steps of Algorithm 1 | sp-graph | $\sum w_j C_j$.

Proof: If the invariance property is violated, it will be violated when concatenating two subsequences. Consider the first concatenation violating the invariance property. We assume that this is a concatenation $\pi_i \circ \pi_j$ done in Step 4 of the procedure Series(S_i, S_j). Concatenations of Steps 11 and 13 are treated similarly. The subsequence $\pi_i \circ \pi_j$ is not contained in an optimal solution σ but all subsequences created previously are contained in some σ. Thus, σ contains π_i with $q(\pi_i) = \min\{q(\pi) \mid \pi \in S_i\}$ and π_j with $q(\pi_j) = \max\{q(\pi) \mid \pi \in S_j\}$. Furthermore, in σ, subsequence π_i is scheduled before π_j and between π_i and π_j we have a sequence $\sigma_1, \sigma_2, \ldots, \sigma_r$. Additionally, $q(\pi_i) \le q(\pi_j)$ holds. We assume that the optimal solution σ is chosen in such a way that the number r of subsequences σ_ν between π_i and π_j is minimal.

If $\sigma_1 \in S_i$, then $q(\sigma_1) \ge \min\{q(\pi) \mid \pi \in S_i\} = q(\pi_i)$ and we can swap σ_1 and π_i without increasing the objective value. This follows from the fact that σ_1 can be processed before π_i because $q(\sigma_1) \ge q(\pi_i)$. Furthermore, according to the proof of Lemma 4.6, the objective function does not increase when swapping σ_1 and π_i. Thus, the new sequence is optimal, contradicting the minimality of r. Similarly, we can swap σ_r and π_j if $\sigma_r \in S_j$. Because $\sigma_s \in S_i$ and $\sigma_t \in S_j$ imply $s < t$, the only cases left are:

Case 1: $\sigma_t \in S_j$ and $\sigma_{t+1}, \ldots, \sigma_r \notin S_i \cup S_j$.

Let $\rho := \sigma_{t+1} \circ \ldots \circ \sigma_r$. If $q(\sigma_t) \le q(\rho)$, we may swap σ_t with ρ, and σ_t

with π_j without increasing the objective function. This follows from the fact that there is no job k in one of the subsequences $\sigma_{t+1}, \ldots, \sigma_r$ which is a successor of a job in $\sigma_t \in S_j$. Otherwise, due to the construction of the series parallel graph, such a job k would also be a successor of a job in $\pi_j \in S_j$, which is impossible. If $q(\rho) \leq q(\pi_j)$, we may swap ρ with π_j and then σ_t with π_j. The remaining case $q(\sigma_t) > q(\rho) > q(\pi_j)$ contradicts the definition of π_j.

Case 2: $\sigma_1, \ldots, \sigma_{s-1} \notin S_i \cup S_j$ and $\sigma_s \in S_i$ is symmetric to Case 1.

Case 3: $\sigma_1, \ldots, \sigma_r \notin S_i \cup S_j$.

Let $\rho := \sigma_1 \circ \ldots \circ \sigma_r$. If $q(\rho) \geq q(\pi_i)$, then we may swap ρ and π_i without increasing the objective function. If $q(\rho) < q(\pi_i) \leq q(\pi_j)$, then we may swap ρ and π_j. $\qquad\square$

Theorem 4.11 Algorithm $1 \mid sp\text{-graph} \mid \sum w_j C_j$ is correct.

Proof: Due to Lemma 4.10 there exists an optimal sequence σ which contains all subsequences created by the algorithm. If, in σ, we permute these subsequences according to nonincreasing q-values, the objective value will not increase. Furthermore, the subsequences are constructed in such a way that the sequence resulting from this permutation is compatible with the precedence constraints. Hence, it must be optimal. $\qquad\square$

4.4   Weighted Number of Late Jobs

In this section we will discuss problems with objective function $\sum w_j U_j$. Karp [124] has shown that problem $1 \mid\mid \sum w_j U_j$ is $\mathcal{NP}$-hard. In Section 2.7 we presented a pseudopolynomial algorithm based on dynamic programming for this problem. In connection with this algorithm, we have shown that an optimal schedule is defined by the set of early jobs scheduled in order of nondecreasing due dates. In this section we will consider special cases of problem $1 \mid\mid \sum w_j U_j$. Furthermore, we will discuss preemptive versions of the problem.

4.4.1 $1 \mid r_j; p_j = 1 \mid \sum w_j U_j$

In Section 2.5 we showed that problem $1 \mid r_j; p_j = 1 \mid \sum w_j U_j$ can be reduced to an assignment problem that can be solved in time $O(n^3)$. In this section we will show that the problems $1 \mid p_j = 1 \mid \sum w_j U_j$ and $1 \mid p_j = 1 \mid \sum U_j$ can be solved more efficiently.

4.4.2 $1 \mid p_j = 1 \mid \sum w_j U_j$

The following algorithm constructs an optimal set S of early jobs. To get an optimal schedule, we schedule the jobs in S according to nondecreasing due dates. All jobs which do not belong to S are late and will be scheduled in an arbitrary order after the jobs in S. The idea of the algorithm is to try to schedule the jobs in earliest due date order. If a job i to be scheduled next is late, then i is scheduled and a job k with smallest w_k-value is deleted from the set of scheduled jobs.

In the following algorithm we assume that $1 \leq d_1 \leq d_2 \leq \ldots \leq d_n$. t denotes the current time.

Algorithm $1 \mid p_j = 1 \mid \sum w_j U_j$
1. $t := 1$; $S := \phi$;
2. FOR $i := 1$ TO n DO
        BEGIN
3.   IF $d_i \geq t$ THEN
4.   BEGIN Add i to S; $t := t + 1$ END
        ELSE
5.   IF there exists a job $k \in S$ with $w_k < w_i$ THEN
            BEGIN
6.   Delete job k from S where k is the largest index such that
            the value w_k is minimal;
7.   Add i to S
            END
        END

To see that this algorithm constructs a feasible schedule, consider the first job i with $d_i < t$. Because the previous job l was scheduled on time we have $t - 1 \leq d_l \leq d_i$. Furthermore, job i is scheduled to finish at time $t - 1$ because k is deleted. Thus, i is on time.

The complexity of the algorithm is $O(n \log n)$ if the scheduled jobs are organized in a priority queue with respect to the w_j-values. For a correctness proof we refer to Section 5.1 where $P \mid p_j = 1 \mid w_j U_j$ is solved by a generalized version of the algorithm.

When solving problem $1 \mid p_j = 1 \mid \sum U_j$, we need only the first four steps of Algorithm $1 \mid p_j = 1 \mid \sum w_j U_j$. Furthermore, all jobs j with $d_j \geq n$ are on time in any schedule. Therefore, we put these jobs at the end of any schedule. To sort the other jobs according to nondecreasing due dates, we use bucket sorting (see Section 4.2): Calculate for $k = 1, \ldots, n - 1$ the sets

$$S_k := \{j \mid d_j = k\}$$

and order the jobs according to the set sequence $S_1, S_2, \ldots, S_{n-1}$. This can be done in $O(n)$ time. Thus, problem $1 \mid p_j = 1 \mid \sum U_j$ can be solved in $O(n)$ time.

4.4.3 $1 \mid\mid \sum U_j$

To generate an optimal schedule, it is sufficient to construct a maximal set S of jobs which are on time. The optimal schedule then consists of the sequence of jobs in S ordered according to nondecreasing d_j-values followed by the late jobs in any order.

An optimal set S is constructed by the following rule.

Add jobs to S in order of nondecreasing due dates. If the addition of job j results in this job being completed after d_j, then a job in S with the largest processing time is marked to be late and removed from S.

The following algorithm, in which t denotes the current schedule time, implements this rule.

Algorithm $1 \mid\mid \sum U_j$
1. Enumerate jobs such that $d_1 \leq d_2 \leq \ldots \leq d_n$;
2. $S := \phi; t := 0$;
3. FOR $i := 1$ to n DO
       BEGIN
4. $S := S \cup \{i\}$;
5. $t := t + p_i$;
6.   IF $t > d_i$ THEN
           BEGIN
7.   Find job j in S with a largest p_j-value;
8. $S := S \backslash \{j\}$;
9. $t := t - p_j$
           END
       END

Theorem 4.12 Algorithm 1 $|| \sum U_j$ constructs the set S of early jobs in an optimal schedule.

Proof: We denote a schedule by $P = (S, F)$, where S is the set of early jobs and F is the set of the late jobs.

Let j be the first job which, in Step 8 of the algorithm, is deleted from set S. We first prove that there exists an optimal schedule $P = (S, F)$ with $j \in F$. Denote by k the job which was added to S in the preceding Step 4. Then

$$p_j = \max_{i=1}^{k} p_i.$$

Furthermore, when scheduling the partial sequence $1, 2, \ldots, j - 1, j + 1, \ldots, k$ no job is late. This follows from the fact that in $1, 2, \ldots, k - 1$ no job is late and $p_k \leq p_j$. We replace j by k and reorder jobs according to nondecreasing due dates.

Now consider an optimal schedule $P' = (S', F')$ with $j \in S'$. There exists a sequence

$$\pi : \pi(1), \ldots, \pi(m), \ldots, \pi(r), \pi(r + 1), \ldots, \pi(n)$$

with

$$F' = \{\pi(r + 1), \ldots, \pi(n)\} \tag{4.10}$$
$$d_{\pi(1)} \leq \ldots \leq d_{\pi(r)} \tag{4.11}$$
$$\{\pi(1), \ldots, \pi(m)\} \subseteq \{1, \ldots, k\} \tag{4.12}$$
$$\{\pi(m + 1), \ldots, \pi(r)\} \subseteq \{k + 1, \ldots, n\} \tag{4.13}$$
$$j \in \{\pi(1), \ldots, \pi(m)\}. \tag{4.14}$$

Since $d_1 \leq d_2 \leq \ldots \leq d_n$, there always exists m such that (4.12) and (4.13) are satisfied. Furthermore, (4.14) holds because $j \in S' \cap \{1, \ldots, k\}$. Since $\{\pi(1), \ldots, \pi(m)\} \subseteq S'$, no job in $\{\pi(1), \ldots, \pi(m)\}$ is late. On the other hand, there is a late job in $\{1, \ldots, k\}$ in any schedule. Thus we have

$$\{\pi(1), \ldots, \pi(m)\} \subsetneq \{1, \ldots, k\},$$

which implies that we have a job $h(1 \leq h \leq k)$ with $h \notin \{\pi(1), \ldots, \pi(m)\}$. We delete job j from $\{\pi(1), \ldots, \pi(m)\}$ and replace it by h. If we order all jobs in $\{\pi(1), \ldots, \pi(m)\} \cup \{h\} \setminus \{j\} \subseteq \{1, \ldots, k\} \setminus \{j\}$ according to nondecreasing due dates, all jobs are on time because $\{1, \ldots, k\} \setminus \{j\}$

has this property. If we add the jobs $\pi(m+1), \ldots, \pi(r)$ to the set $\{\pi(1), \ldots, \pi(m)\} \cup \{h\} \backslash \{j\}$ and sort all jobs according to nondecreasing due dates, all jobs are on time because $p_h \leq p_j$ implies

$$\sum_{i=1}^{m} p_{\pi(i)} - p_j + p_h \leq \sum_{i=1}^{m} p_{\pi(i)}.$$

Thus we get an optimal schedule $P = (S, F)$ with $j \in F$.

Now it is not difficult to prove the theorem by induction on the number n of jobs. Clearly the algorithm is correct if $n = 1$. Assume the algorithm is correct for all problems with $n-1$ jobs. Let $P = (S, F)$ be the schedule constructed by the algorithm and let $P' = (S', F')$, an optimal schedule with $j \in F'$.

Then, by optimality, we have $\mid S \mid \leq \mid S' \mid$.

If we apply the algorithm to the set of jobs $\{1, \ldots, j-1, j+1, \ldots, n\}$ we get an optimal schedule of the form $(S, F \backslash \{j\})$. Because $(S', F' \backslash \{j\})$ is feasible for the reduced problem, we have $\mid S' \mid \leq \mid S \mid$. Thus $\mid S' \mid = \mid S \mid$ and P is optimal. $\square$

4.4.4 $1 \mid r_j; pmtn \mid \sum w_j U_j$

Karp [124] has shown that problem $1 \parallel \sum w_j U_j$ is $\mathcal{NP}$-hard. At the beginning of this chapter, we saw that a preemptive schedule for a one machine problem with monotone objective function and $r_j = 0$ for all jobs j can be polynomially transformed into a nonpreemptive schedule without increasing the objective function. This implies that $1 \mid pmtn \mid \sum w_j U_j$ is $\mathcal{NP}$-hard as well. In this section we present an $O(nk^2W^2)$-algorithm for problem $1 \mid r_j; pmtn \mid \sum w_j U_j$ where k is the number of distinct release dates and $W = \sum_{j=1}^{n} w_j$. This gives an $O(n^5)$-algorithm for problem $1 \mid r_j; pmtn \mid \sum U_j$.

We assume that all data are integer and that $w_j > 0$ for $j = 1, \ldots, n$.

A set of jobs S is **feasible** if there exists a schedule for S in which all jobs are completed on time. To check whether a set is feasible, we may apply the following simplified version of the EDD rule (see 4.7):

> Schedule the jobs in time starting with the smallest r_j-value.
> At each decision point given by a release time or a finish time   (4.15)
> of some job, schedule a job with smallest due date.

S is feasible if and only if there are no late jobs in the EDD schedule for S. This is an immediate consequence of Theorem 4.4. If S has n jobs, the corresponding EDD schedule can be constructed in $O(n \log n)$ time. Our problem reduces to that of finding a maximum-weight feasible set S.

For a given nonempty feasible set S define

$$r(S) = \min_{j \in S} r_j \; ; \; p(S) = \sum_{j \in S} p_j \; ; \; w(S) = \sum_{j \in S} w_j.$$

Furthermore, let $C(S)$ be the completion time of the last job in S in an EDD schedule.

An EDD schedule consists of periods of continuous processing, separated by periods of idle time during which no job is available for processing. This means that S can be partitioned into subsets $S_1, S_2, \ldots, S_l$ with $C(S_i) = r(S_i) + p(S_i) < r(S_{i+1})$ for $i = 1, \ldots, l-1$. A feasible subset S is a **block** if S is processed continuously from start to finish and S cannot be decomposed into subsets that are schedule-disjoint, i.e. $C(S) = r(S) + p(S)$, and S is not the union of subsets S_1, S_2 such that $C(S_1) < r(S_2)$.

Next we will present a dynamic programming solution for problem $1 \mid r_j; pmtn \mid \sum w_j U_j$. Again, we assume that

$$d_1 \leq d_2 \leq \ldots \leq d_n.$$

Let k denote the number of distinct release dates.

For a release date r and an integer w with $0 \leq w \leq W$ define

$$C_j(r, w) := \min\{C(S) \mid S \subseteq \{1, \ldots, j\} \text{ is feasible}; \, r(S) \geq r; w(S) \geq w\}$$

if there exists a feasible set $S \subseteq \{1, \ldots, j\}$ with $r(S) \geq r$, $w(S) \geq w$ and $C_j(r, w) = \infty$ otherwise.

The maximum weight of a feasible set is given by the largest value of w such that $C_n(r_{\min}, w)$ is finite, where $r_{\min} := \min_{j=1}^{n} r_j$.

We compute the values $C_j(r, w)$ in n iterations, $j = 1, 2, \ldots, n$, starting with the initial conditions

$$C_0(r, 0) = r \qquad \text{for all } r,$$
$$C_0(r, w) = \infty \qquad \text{for all } r \text{ and } w > 0.$$

j cannot be contained in a feasible set S with $r(S) > r_j$. Hence,

$$C_j(r, w) \begin{cases} = C_{j-1}(r, w) & \text{if } r > r_j \\ \leq C_{j-1}(r, w) & \text{otherwise .} \end{cases}$$

It follows that at iteration j we have only to compute the value of $C_j(r, w)$ for which $r \leq r_j$.

Let $S \subseteq \{1, 2, \ldots, j\}$ with $C_j(r, w) = C(S)$. If $j \notin S$, then we have $C_j(r, w) = C_{j-1}(r, w)$. If $j \in S$, we consider two cases.

Case 1: Job j starts after $C(S \backslash \{j\})$.

Either $C(S \backslash \{j\}) \leq r_j$, or $C(S \backslash \{j\}) > r_j$. In the first case, we have $C(S) = r_j + p_j$. In the second case, jobs in $S \backslash \{j\}$ are processed continuously in the interval $[r_j, C(S \backslash \{j\})]$ because otherwise j would start before $C(S \backslash \{j\})$. We conclude that

$$C_j(r, w) = \max\{r_j, C(S \backslash \{j\})\} + p_j.$$

We may assume that $S \backslash \{j\}$ is such that

$$C(S \backslash \{j\}) = C_{j-1}(r, w - w_j).$$

If this is not so, replace $S \backslash \{j\}$ by a feasible subset of $\{1, 2, \ldots, j-1\}$ for which this is satisfied.

It follows that

$$C_j(r, w) = \max\{r_j, C_{j-1}(r, w - w_j)\} + p_j.$$

Case 2: Job j starts before $C(S \backslash \{j\})$.

In this case there is idle time in the EDD schedule for the set $S \backslash \{j\}$ after r_j. Let S' be the last block in $S \backslash \{j\}$, i.e. $r(S') = \max\{r(B) \mid B$ is a block of $S \backslash \{j\}\}$. Then $r(S') \geq r_j$, and it must be the case that $C(S') = C_{j-1}(r(S'), w(S'))$, otherwise S is not optimal.

Also, we may assume that the total amount of processing done on jobs in $(S \backslash \{j\}) \backslash S'$ in the interval $[r_j, r(S')]$ is minimal, with respect to all feasible sets $S'' \subseteq \{1, 2, \ldots, j-1\}$ with $r(S'') \geq r, C(S'') \leq r(S'), w(S'') \geq w - w_j - w(S')$.

Let r, r' be release dates with $r \leq r_j < r'$, and w'' be an integer with $0 \leq w'' < W$. Define $P_{j-1}(r, r', w'')$ to be the minimum amount of processing done in the interval $[r_j, r']$ with respect to feasible sets $S'' \subseteq$

$\{1, 2, \ldots, j-1\}$ with $r(S'') \geq r, C(S'') \leq r', w(S'') \geq w''$. If there is no such feasible set S'', then let $P_{j-1}(r, r', w'') = \infty$.

Using this notation, the amount of time available for processing job j in the interval $[r_j, r(S')]$ is

$$(r(S') - r_j) - P_{j-1}(r, r(S'), w - w_j - w(S')).$$

The amount of processing done on j after time $r(S')$ is

$$\max\{0, p_j - (r(S') - r_j) + P_{j-1}(r, r(S'), w - w_j - w(S'))\}$$

and the completion time of the last job in S is

$$C_j(r, w) = \min_{r', w'}\{C_{j-1}(r', w')$$
$$+ \max\{0, p_j - r' + r_j + P_{j-1}(r, r', w - w_j - w')\}\}. \quad (4.16)$$

Putting all of the above observations together, we obtain the recurrence relation

$$C_j(r, w) = \min \begin{cases} C_{j-1}(r, w) \\ \max\{r_j, C_{j-1}(r, w - w_j)\} + p_j \\ \min_{r', w'}\{C_{j-1}(r', w') + \max\{0, p_j - r' + r_j \\ \qquad + P_{j-1}(r, r', w - w_j - w')\}\}, \end{cases} \quad (4.17)$$

where the inner minimization is taken over all distinct release dates $r' > r_j$ such that $r' = r(S') \in \{r_1, \ldots, r_{j-1}\}$ and all integers $w', 0 \leq w' < w - w_j$. It is important to note that (4.17) is valid only if the right-hand side does not exceed d_j; if this is not so we set $C_j(r, w) = \infty$.

Now we have to consider how to compute the values $P_{j-1}(r, r', w'')$ for $r \leq r_j < r'$ and $0 \leq w'' < W$. If $w'' = 0$, then $P_{j-1}(r, r', w'') = 0$. If $w'' > 0$, then $P_{j-1}(r, r', w'')$ is realized by a nonempty set $S'' \subseteq \{1, \ldots, j-1\}$. If $r(S'') > r$, then $P_{j-1}(r, r', w'') = P_{j-1}(r(S''), r', w'')$. Also, in general, we observe that

$$P_{j-1}(r, r', w'') \leq P_{j-1}(r^+, r', w'')$$

where r^+ is the smallest distinct release date, if any, larger than r.

If $r(S'') = r$, then let $S' \subseteq S''$ be the block of S'' such that $r(S') = r$. We may assume that $C(S') = C_{j-1}(r, w(S'))$. Hence, the total amount of processing done on S' in the interval $[r_j, r']$ is

$$\max\{0, C_{j-1}(r, w(S')) - r_j\}.$$

Let r'' be the smallest release date greater than or equal to $C_{j-1}(r, w(S'))$. Then the total amount of processing done on $S'' \backslash S'$ in the interval $[r_j, r']$ is $P_{j-1}(r'', r', w'' - w(S'))$. Hence, the total amount of processing done on S'' in the interval $[r_j, r']$ is

$$\max\{0, C_{j-1}(r, w(S')) - r_j\} + P_{j-1}(r'', r', w'' - w(S')). \qquad (4.18)$$

The right-hand side of (4.18) must be minimal with respect to sets $S', S'' \backslash S'$, with $r(S') = r, C(S') \leq r(S'' \backslash S') = r'', w(S') + w(S'' \backslash S') = w''$. It follows that we now have

$$P_{j-1}(r, r', w'') = \min \begin{cases} P_{j-1}(r^+, r', w'') \\ \min_{0 < w' \leq w''} \{\max\{0, C_{j-1}(r, w') - r_j\} \\ \qquad + P_{j-1}(r'', r', w'' - w')\} \end{cases} \qquad (4.19)$$

with the initial conditions

$P_{j-1}(r, r', 0) = 0 \qquad$ for $j = 1, \ldots, n$

$P_0(r, r', w'') = \infty \qquad$ for $w'' > 0$.

We now analyze the time complexity of the dynamic programming computation.

At each of n iterations $j = 1, \ldots, n$, there are $O(k^2 W)$ of the $P_{j-1}(r, r', w'')$ values to compute, one for each combination of r, r', w''. By (4.19), each $P_{j-1}(r, r', w'')$ is found by minimization over $O(W)$ choices of $w' \leq w''$. Hence, the time required to compute the $P_{j-1}(r, r', w'')$ values at each iteration is bounded by $O(k^2 W^2)$. There are $O(kW)$ of the $C_j(r, w)$ values to compute, one for each combination of r and w. By (4.17), each $C_j(r, w)$ is found by minimization over $O(kW)$ choices of r', w'. Hence, the time required to compute the $C_j(r, w)$ values at each iteration is bounded by $O(k^2 W^2)$. The maximum weight of a feasible subset can be obtained by finding the maximum value w such that $C_n(r_{\min}, w)$ is finite. This takes $O(W)$ time. It follows that the overall time bound is $O(nk^2 W^2)$.

To construct a maximum-weight feasible set, we compute an incidence vector of the set realizing each $P_{j-1}(r, r', w'')$ and $C_j(r, w)$ value. The computation of these incidence vectors can be carried out in $O(n^2 k^2 W)$ time, which is dominated by the $O(nk^2 W^2)$ time bound obtained above.

Finally, we will discuss some special cases. When release dates and due dates are similarly ordered, i.e. when

$$r_1 \leq r_2 \leq \ldots \leq r_n \text{ and } d_1 \leq d_2 \leq \ldots \leq d_n,$$

then Case 2 never applies. In such a situation the recurrence relations (4.17) simplify to

$$C_j(r,w) = \min \begin{cases} C_{j-1}(r,w) \\ \max\{r_j, C_{j-1}(r, w - w_j)\} + p_j \end{cases}$$

or, if we set $C_j(w) := C_j(r_{\min}, w)$, to

$$C_j(w) = \min \begin{cases} C_{j-1}(w) \\ \max\{r_j, C_{j-1}(w - w_j)\} + p_j. \end{cases}$$

This means that we have an $O(nW)$ computation for this special case, with the maximum weight of a feasible set being given by the largest w such that $C_n(w)$ is finite. When all job weights are equal, the time bound becomes $O(n^2)$.

When all release dates are equal to zero, the recurrence further simplifies to

$$C_j(w) = \min\{C_{j-1}(w), C_{j-1}(w - w_j) + p_j\}$$

which, due to the fact that preemption does not improve the optimal solution value, leads to an alternative algorithm for the $1 \parallel \sum w_j U_j$-problem which has complexity $O(n \sum w_j)$ (compare Algorithm $1 \parallel \sum w_j U_j$ in Section 2.7 with complexity $O(n \sum p_j)$).

4.5 Total Weighted Tardiness

In this section we consider the problem of scheduling n jobs $j = 1, \ldots, n$ on one machine such that $\sum_{j=1}^{n} w_j T_j$ is minimized, where $T_j = \max\{0, C_j - d_j\}$ is the tardiness of job j. As before, d_j denotes the due date of job j. If we have arbitrary processing times, then there is no hope of finding polynomial algorithms because problem $1 \parallel \sum T_j$ is $\mathcal{NP}$-hard. This has been shown by Du & Leung [81]. Due to the remark at the beginning of this chapter, this implies that $1 \mid pmtn \mid \sum T_j$ is $\mathcal{NP}$-hard as well.

On the other hand problem $1 \mid r_j; p_j = 1 \mid \sum w_j T_j$ can be solved in $O(n^3)$ time using the matching model we introduced for solving the more general problem $1 \mid r_j; p_j = 1 \mid \sum f_j$ with monotone functions f_j. However, $1 \mid prec; p_j = 1 \mid \sum T_j$ has been shown to be $\mathcal{NP}$-hard (Lenstra & Rinnooy Kan [152]).

Finally, we will present a pseudopolynomial algorithm for problem $1 \parallel \sum T_j$ which is due to Lawler [136]. This algorithm is also applicable to the problem $1 \parallel \sum w_j T_j$ if the *weights w_j are agreeable with the processing times p_j* (i.e. if $p_i < p_j$ implies $w_i \geq w_j$ for $j = 1, \ldots, n$), which are assumed to be integer. Clearly the weights $w_j = 1$ are agreeable.

The algorithm is based on the following results.

Lemma 4.13 Let the jobs have arbitrary weights. Let π be any sequence which is optimal with respect to given due dates $d_1, d_2, \ldots, d_n$, and let C_j be the completion time of job $j(j = 1, \ldots, n)$ for this sequence. Let d'_j be chosen such that

$$\min\{d_j, C_j\} \leq d'_j \leq \max\{d_j, C_j\}.$$

Then any sequence π' which is optimal with respect to the due dates $d'_1, d'_2, \ldots, d'_n$ is also optimal with respect to $d_1, d_2, \ldots, d_n$.

Proof: Let T denote total weighted tardiness with respect to $d_1, d_2, \ldots, d_n$ and let T' denote total weighted tardiness with respect to $d'_1, d'_2, \ldots, d'_n$. Let π' be any sequence which is optimal with respect to $d'_1, d'_2, \ldots, d'_n$ and let C'_j be the completion time of job j for this sequence. We have

$$T(\pi) = T'(\pi) + \sum_{j=1}^{n} A_j \tag{4.20}$$

$$T(\pi') = T'(\pi') + \sum_{j=1}^{n} B_j \tag{4.21}$$

where, if $C_j \leq d_j$

$$A_j = 0$$
$$B_j = -w_j \max\{0, \min\{C'_j, d_j\} - d'_j\}$$

and if $C_j \geq d_j$

$$A_j = w_j(d'_j - d_j)$$
$$B_j = w_j \max\{0, \min\{C'_j, d'_j\} - d_j\}.$$

(4.20) holds, because if $C_j \leq d_j$, then

$$C_j = \min\{d_j, C_j\} \leq d'_j \leq \max\{d_j, C_j\} = d_j$$

which implies

$$w_j \max\{0, C_j - d_j\} = w_j \max\{0, C_j - d'_j\} = 0.$$

If, on the other hand, $d_j \leq C_j$, then

$$d_j = \min\{d_j, C_j\} \leq d'_j \leq \max\{d_j, C_j\} = C_j$$

which implies

$$w_j \max\{0, C_j - d_j\} = w_j \max\{0, C_j - d'_j\} + w_j(d'_j - d_j).$$

(4.21) holds because if $C_j \leq d_j$, then $C_j \leq d'_j \leq d_j$ and, by considering the cases $C'_j \leq d'_j$, $d'_j \leq C'_j \leq d_j$, and $d_j \leq C'_j$, we verify

$$w_j \max\{0, C'_j - d_j\} = w_j \max\{0, C'_j - d'_j\} - w_j \max\{0, \min\{C'_j, d_j\} - d'_j\}.$$

If $d_j \leq C_j$, then $d_j \leq d'_j \leq C_j$ and we have

$$w_j \max\{0, C'_j - d_j\} = w_j \max\{0, C'_j - d'_j\} + w_j \max\{0, \min\{C'_j, d'_j\} - d_j\}.$$

Clearly, $A_j \geq B_j$ for all j and therefore $\sum_{j=1}^{n} A_j \geq \sum_{j=1}^{n} B_j$. Moreover, $T'(\pi) \geq T'(\pi')$ because π' minimizes T'. Therefore, the right-hand side of (4.20) dominates the right-hand side of (4.21). It follows that $T(\pi) \geq T(\pi')$ and π' is optimal with respect to $d_1, d_2, \ldots, d_n$. $\quad\square$

Lemma 4.14 Suppose the jobs are agreeably weighted. Then there exists an optimal sequence π in which job i precedes job j if $d_i \leq d_j$ and $p_i < p_j$, and in which all on time jobs are in nondecreasing due date order.

Proof: Let π be an optimal sequence. Suppose that i follows j in π, where $d_i \leq d_j$ and $p_i < p_j$. Because the jobs are agreeably weighted, $p_i < p_j$ implies $w_j \leq w_i$. Therefore, $w_j \max\{0, T - d_j\} \leq w_i \max\{0, T - d_i\}$ holds for all T. Thus, if we shift job j to the position immediately after job i, then this new schedule must also be optimal.

Furthermore, if job i follows job j where $d_i \leq d_j$ and i and j are both on time, then moving j to the position immediately following i keeps j on time. Thus, we get a sequence for which the total weighted tardiness does not increase.

Repeated application of these two rules yields an optimal sequence satisfying the conditions of the lemma.   □

In order to simplify exposition somewhat, let us assume that all processing times are distinct. If this is not the case, then they may be perturbed infinitesimally without violating the assumption of agreeable weighting and without changing the problem significantly.

Theorem 4.15 Let $j = 1, \ldots, n$ be jobs with $d_1 \leq d_2 \leq \ldots \leq d_n$ and with agreeable weights. Let k be a job with a largest processing time. Then there exists a job $j^* \geq k$ such that in an optimal schedule all jobs $\nu = 1, \ldots, j^*$ with $\nu \neq k$ are scheduled before k and the remaining jobs are scheduled after k.

Proof: Let C'_k be the latest possible completion time of job k in any sequence which is optimal with respect to due dates $d_1, d_2, \ldots, d_n$. Let π be a sequence which is optimal with respect to the due dates

$$d_1, d_2, \ldots, d_{k-1}, d'_k = \max\{C'_k, d_k\}, d_{k+1}, \ldots, d_n$$

and which satisfies the conditions of Lemma 4.15. Let C_k be the completion time of job k for π. By Lemma 4.13, the sequence π is optimal with respect to the original due dates $d_1, d_2, \ldots, d_n$. Thus, by definition of C'_k, we have $C_k \leq C'_k \leq \max\{C'_k, d_k\} = d'_k$.

Therefore, job k cannot be preceded by any job j such that $d_j > d'_k$. Otherwise, job j would also be on time, in violation of the conditions of Lemma 4.15. On the other hand, job k must be preceded by all jobs $j \neq k$ such that $d_j \leq d'_k$ because $p_j < p_k$. If we choose j^* to be the largest integer such that $d_{j^*} \leq d'_k = \max\{C'_k, d_k\}$, then $j^* \geq k$ because $d_k \leq d'_k$ and j^* has the desired properties.   □

The algorithm calculates, for each $j \geq k$, an optimal schedule in which the job set $I_1 = \{1, \ldots, j\} \backslash \{k\}$ is scheduled before k and the set $I_2 = \{j + 1, \ldots, n\}$ is scheduled after k. Thus, for each j, the problem splits into two subproblems. In the first problem, jobs in I_1 are to be scheduled

Sequence $(\mathbf{t}, \mathbf{I})$
1. IF $I = \phi$ THEN $\sigma^* :=$ empty sequence
   ELSE
         BEGIN
2.   Let $i_1 < i_2 < \ldots < i_r$ be the jobs in I;
3.   Find i_k with $p_{i_k} := \max\{p_i \mid i \in I\}$;

4. $f^* := \infty;$
5.   FOR $j = k$ TO r DO
      BEGIN
6. $I_1 := \{i_\nu \mid 1 \le \nu \le j; \ \nu \ne k\}; \ t_1 := t;$
7. $\sigma_1 := $ Sequence $(t_1, I_1);$
8. $I_2 := \{i_\nu \mid j < \nu \le r\}; \ t_2 := t + \sum_{\nu=1}^{j} p_{i_\nu};$
9. $\sigma_2 := $ Sequence $(t_2, I_2);$
10. $\sigma := \sigma_1 \circ i_k \circ \sigma_2;$
11.   Calculate the objective value $f(\sigma, t)$ for $\sigma;$
12.   IF $f(\sigma, t) < f^*$ THEN
           BEGIN
13. $\sigma^* := \sigma;$
14. $f^* := f(\sigma, t)$
           END
         END
      END;
15. RETURN (σ^*)

optimally starting at time $t_1 = 0$. In the second problem, jobs in I_2 are to be scheduled optimally starting at time $t_2 = \sum_{i=1}^{j} p_i$. This suggests the recursive procedure Sequence (t, I), which calculates an optimal sequence σ^* for the job set I starting at time t.

Algorithm 1 $\| \sum w_j T_j$
$\sigma^* := $ Sequence $(0, \{1, \ldots, n\})$

calculates an optimal sequence σ^* if the weights are agreeable with the processing times.

Assume that all processing times are different. Then it is easy to establish a time bound for this algorithm. The sets I which appear in the arguments of the recursive procedure are of the form

$$I_{i,j,k} := \{\nu \mid i \le \nu \le j; \ p_\nu < p_k\},$$

i.e. they are completely characterized by the index triples i, j, k. We also have at the most $p := \sum_{j=1}^{n} p_j$ different t-values. Thus, we need to call procedure Sequence (t, I) at the most $O(n^3 p)$ times. Furthermore, for fixed k, all values $\max\{p_\nu \mid \nu \in I_{ijk}\}$ for $i, j = 1, \ldots, n, i < j$ can be calculated in $O(n^2)$ time. Thus, the computational complexity for all Steps 3 is $O(n^3)$. For each call of the recursive procedure the other steps can be done in constant time. Thus, we have an $O(n^3p)$-algorithm or $O(n^4 p_{\max})$-algorithm where $p_{\max} = \max\limits_{i=1}^{n} p_i$.

4.6   Problems with Release Times and Identical Processing Times

In this section we consider the problem of scheduling jobs j with integer release times r_j and $p_j = p$ for all j where p is an arbitrary integer. If the release times are not multiples of p such problems are in general more complex than problems with unit processing times $p_j = 1$.

4.6.1 $1 \mid r_j; p_j = p \mid \sum w_j U_j$

A schedule for a subset X of jobs is said to be **feasible** if and only if

- all jobs in X start after or at their release date and are completed before or at their due date, and

- jobs do not overlap in time.

We have to find a feasible set X of jobs such that the total weight $\sum\limits_{j \in X} w_j$ is maximal.

This problem can be solved by a dynamic programming algorithm. For this algorithm we assume that jobs are indexed in an non-decreasing order of due dates. The following lemma shows that the starting times of all jobs can be restricted to a set of at most n^2 values.

Lemma 4.16 An optimal schedule exists in which each job starts at a time belonging to the set

$$T := \{r_j + lp \mid j = 1, \ldots, n; \; l = 0, \ldots, n - 1\}$$

Proof: Consider an optimal schedule S. Let $j_1, j_2, \ldots, j_n$ be the corresponding processing order of the jobs in S. By the following procedure S

can be transformed into a feasible schedule which has the desired properties. The first job j_1 can be shifted to the left until its starting time and the release date of j_1 coincide. Then j_2 is shifted to the left until it hits its release date or the finishing time of j_1. In the general step j_ν is left-shifted such that its starting time is equal to the maximum of its release date and the finishing time of the (shifted) job $j_{\nu-1}$.   □

For any integer $k \leq n$ and $s, e \in T$ with $s \leq e$ let $U_k(s, e)$ be the set of jobs $j \leq k$ with $s \leq r_j < e$. Furthermore, let $W_k^*(s, e)$ be the maximal total weight of a subset of $U_k(s, e)$ such that there is a feasible schedule S for the jobs in the subset with

- S is idle before time $s + p$ and after time e, and

- the starting times of jobs on S belong to T.

$W_k^*(s, e)$ is set equal to 0 if no subset providing a feasible schedule exists. To solve problem $1 \mid r_j; p_j = p \mid \sum w_j U_j$ we apply the following algorithm.

Algorithm 1 $\mid$ r$_j$; p$_j$ = p $\mid$ $\sum$ w$_j$U$_j$
1. Enumerate the jobs such that $d_1 \leq d_2 \leq \ldots \leq d_n$;
2. FOR ALL $s, e \in T$ with $s \leq e$ DO $W_0(s, e) := 0$;
3. FOR $k := 1$ TO n DO
4.   FOR ALL $s, e \in T$ with $s \leq e$ DO

$$W_k(s, e) := \begin{cases} W_{k-1}(s, e) & \text{if } r_k \notin [s, e) \\ \max\{W_{k-1}(s, e), W_k'(s, e)\} & \text{otherwise} \end{cases}$$

where

$$W_k'(s, e) := \max\{w_k + W_{k-1}(s, s') + W_{k-1}(s', e) | s' \in T_j;$$
$$\max\{r_k, s + p\} \leq s' \leq \min\{d_k, e\} - p\};$$

5. Calculate $W_n(\min_{t \in T} t - p, \max_{t \in T} t)$

Note, that $W_k'(s, e)$ corresponds to a feasible schedule in which job k starts at time s'. Furthermore, the maximum over the empty set is defined to be equal to zero. Due to the fact that T contains $O(n^2)$ elements the time complexity of this algorithm is $O(n^7)$.

Next we will show the values $W_k(s, e)$ calculated by the algorithm are equal to $W_k^*(s, e)$. Thus, in Step 5 of the algorithm the optimal solution value is calculated.

Theorem 4.17 For $k = 0, \ldots, n$ and all $s, e \in T$ with $s \leq e$ the equality

$$W_k(s, e) = W_k^*(s, e) \tag{4.22}$$

holds.

Proof: We prove (4.22) by the induction on k. Clearly, the assertion is true for $k = 0$. Assume that (4.22) holds for $k - 1$.

If $r_k \notin [s, e)$ then $U_k(s, e) = U_{k-1}(s, e)$ which implies $W_k(s, e) = W_{k-1}(s, e) = W_{k-1}^*(s, e) = W_k^*(s, e)$. It remains to show that

$$\max\{W_{k-1}(s, e), W_k'(s, e)\} = W_k^*(s, e) \text{ if } r_k \in [s, e). \tag{4.23}$$

This is accomplished in two steps by showing that each side of (4.23) is smaller or equal than the other side.

We first prove

$$\max\{\mathbf{W_{k-1}(s, e)}, \mathbf{W_k'(s, e)}\} \leq \mathbf{W_k^*(s, e)}.$$

We have $W_{k-1}(s, e) = W_{k-1}^*(s, e) \leq W_k^*(s, e)$ because $U_{k-1}(s, e) \subseteq U_k(s, e)$. Furthermore, if $W_k'(s, e) > 0$ then there exists some s' with

$$\max\{r_k, s + p\} \leq s' \leq \min\{d_k, e\} - p$$

such that

$$
\begin{aligned}
W_k'(s, e) &= w_k + W_{k-1}(s, s') + W_{k-1}(s', e) \\
&= w_k + W_{k-1}^*(s, s') + W_{k-1}^*(s', e) \\
&\leq W_k^*(s, s').
\end{aligned}
$$

The inequality holds because $w_k + W_{k-1}^*(s, s') + W_{k-1}^*(s', e)$ is the total weight of a schedule of

- job k scheduled in $[s', s' + p]$,

- a subset of jobs of $U_{k-1}(s, s')$ scheduled in $[s + p, s']$, and

- a subset of jobs of $U_{k-1}(s', e)$ scheduled in $[s' + p, e]$.

Finally, we prove

$$\mathbf{W_k^*(s,e) \le \max\{W_{k-1}(s,e), W_k'(s,e)\}}.$$

Let Z be a subset of $U_k(s,e)$ corresponding with $W_k^*(s,e)$. If $k \notin Z$ then $W_k^*(s,e) = W_{k-1}^*(s,e) = W_{k-1}(s,e)$ and we finished the proof. Otherwise, let S^* be the schedule realizing $W_k^*(s,e)$ and let s' be the starting time of job k. We must have $\max\{r_k, s+p\} \le s' \le \min\{d_k, e\} - p$.

We denote by Z^b and Z^a the subset of jobs in Z which in S^* are scheduled before and after job k, respectively. We may assume that the release dates of all jobs in Z^a are greater than the starting time s' of job k. Otherwise let i be a job in Z^a with $r_i \le s'$. Because the jobs are ordered according to non-decreasing due-dates we have $d_i \le d_k$. Thus, by swapping jobs i and k in S^* the total weight does not change. We continue this process until the new schedule S^* has the desired property. We now have

$$W_k^*(s,e) = \sum_{j \in Z} w_j = \sum_{j \in Z^b} w_j + w_k + \sum_{j \in Z^a} w_j \le W_{k-1}^*(s,s') + w_k + W_{k-1}^*(s',e)$$

$$= W_{k-1}(s,s') + w_k + W_{k-1}(s',e) \le W_k'(s,e) \quad (4.24)$$

because clearly $Z^b \subseteq U_{k-1}(s,s')$ and, due to our assumption, $Z^a \subseteq U_{k-1}(s',e)$. holds. $\qquad \square$

The ideas of this section can be extended to the preemptive case. Baptiste [15] has shown that the corresponding problem $1 \mid r_j; p_j = p; pmtn \mid \sum w_j U_j$ can be solved in time $O(n^{10})$.

4.6.2 $\quad 1 \mid r_j; p_j = p \mid \sum w_j C_j$ and $1 \mid r_j; p_j = p \mid \sum T_j$

To derive polynomial algorithms for the problems $1 \mid r_j; p_j = p \mid \gamma$ with $\gamma \in \{\sum w_j C_j, \sum T_j\}$ where $w_j \ge 0$ for all jobs j we use techniques similar to those derived in the previous section. We apply these techniques to a more general objective function $\sum f_j(C_j)$ where the functions $f_1, \ldots, f_n$ have the following properties:

- f_j is non-decreasing for $j = 1, \ldots, n$ $\qquad\qquad$ (4.25)
- $f_i - f_j$ is non-decreasing for all $i, j = 1, \ldots, n$ with $i < j$. (4.26)

$\sum w_j C_j$ and $\sum T_j = \sum \max\{0, C_j - d_j\}$ are functions of the form $\sum f_j(C_j)$ satisfying (4.25) and (4.26) if the jobs are enumerated in such a way that $w_1 \ge w_2 \ge \ldots \ge w_n$ and $d_1 \le d_2 \le \ldots \le d_n$, respectively.

Due to the fact that the functions f_j satisfy (4.25), for problem $1 \mid r_j; p_j = p \mid \sum f_j$ there exists an optimal schedule in which each job starts at a time belonging to the set

$$T := \{r_j + lp \mid j = 1, \ldots, n; l = 0, \ldots, n - 1\}$$

The proof of this claim is identical with the proof of Lemma 4.16.

For any integer $k \leq n$ and $s, e \in T$ with $s \leq e$ let $U_k(s, e)$ be the set of jobs $j \leq k$ with $s \leq r_j < e$. Furthermore, let $F_k^*(s, e)$ be the minimal value that the function

$$\sum_{j \in U_k(s-p,e)} f_j(C_j)$$

can take among the feasible schedules S of all jobs in $U_k(s - p, e)$ such that

- S is idle before time s and after time e, and

- the starting times of jobs on S belong to T.

If non such schedule S exists then we define $F_k^*(s, e) := \infty$.

The following dynamic programming algorithm which solves problem $1 \mid r_j; p_j = p \mid \sum f_j$ is similar to the algorithm formulated in Section 4.6.1.

Algorithm $1 \mid r_j; p_j = p \mid \sum f_j$
1. Enumerate the jobs such that condition (4.26) holds;
2. FOR ALL $s, e \in T$ with $s \leq e$ DO $F_0(s, e) := 0$;
3. FOR $k := 1$ TO n DO
4.   FOR ALL $s, e \in T$ with $s \leq e$ DO

$$F_k(s, e) = \begin{cases} F_{k-1}(s, e) & \text{if } r_k \notin [s - p, e) \\ F_k'(s, e) & \text{otherwise} \end{cases}$$

where

$$F_k'(s, e) = \min \{F_{k-1}(s, t_k) + F_{k-1}(t_k + p, e) + f_k(t_k + p) \mid t_k \in T;$$
$$\max\{s, r_k\} \leq t_k \leq e - p\};$$

5. Calculate $F_n \left(\min_{i=1}^{n} r_i, \max_{t \in T} t + p \right)$

The time complexity of this algorithm which calculates the optimal solution value in Step 5 is $O(n^7)$.

The next theorem shows that the algorithm is correct.

Theorem 4.18 For $k = 0, \ldots, n$ and all $s, e \in T$ with $s \leq e$

$$F_k(s, e) = F_k^*(s, e) \tag{4.27}$$

holds.

Proof: The proof is similar to the proof of Theorem 4.17. Assume that (4.27) is true for $k - 1$ (clearly (4.27) is true for $k = 0$).

If $r_k \notin [s-p, e)$ then $U_k(s-p, e) = U_{k-1}(s-p, e)$ which implies (4.27). It remains to show that (a) $F_k^*(s, e) \leq F_k'(s, e)$ and (b) $F_k'(s, e) \leq F_k^*(s, e)$ when $r_k \in [s - p, e)$.

(a) Assume that $F_k'(s, e)$ is finite. Then some $t_k \in T$ with $\max\{s, t_k\} \leq t_k \leq e - p$ exists such that

$$
\begin{aligned}
F_k'(s, e) &= F_{k-1}(s, t_k) + F_{k-1}(t_k + p, e) + f_k(t_k + p) \\
&= F_{k-1}^*(s, t_k) + F_{k-1}^*(t_k + p, e) + f_k(t_k + p) \geq F_k^*(s, e).
\end{aligned}
$$

(b) Assume that $F_k^*(s, e)$ is finite. Among all feasible schedules providing the value $F_k^*(s, e)$ we choose a schedule S such that the corresponding vector $(C_{i_1}, C_{i_2}, \ldots, C_{i_l})$ of finishing times where $i_1 < i_2 < \ldots < i_l$ is lexicographic minimal. Let $t_k \in T$ be the starting time of job k in S. Then

$$
\begin{aligned}
F_k^*(s, e) &= \sum_{j \in U_k(s-p, e)} f_j(C_j) \\
&= \sum_{j \in U_k(s-p, t_k)} f_j(C_j) + \sum_{j \in U_k(t_k, e)} f_j(C_j) + f_k(t_k + p) \\
&\geq F_{k-1}(s, t_k) + F_{k-1}(t_k + p, e) + f_k(t_k + p) \\
&\geq F_k'(s, e).
\end{aligned}
$$

To prove that the first inequality holds we have to show that all jobs of $U_{k-1}(s - p, t_k)$ are scheduled in S in the interval $[s, t_k]$ and all jobs of $U_{k-1}(t_k, e)$ are scheduled in S in the interval $[t_k + p, e]$. We prove the first assertion (the second follows similarly).

Assume there is a job j with $s - p \leq r_j < t_k$ starting in S at a time $t_j > t_k$, i.e. starting after job k. By swapping k and j we get a feasible schedule S' with

$$\vartheta := \text{objective value of } S' - \text{objective value of } S$$
$$= f_j(t_k + p) + f_k(t_j + p) - f_j(t_j + p) - f_k(t_k + p)$$
$$= (f_j - f_k)(t_k + p) - (f_j - f_k)(t_j + p).$$

Now $j < k$ implies $\vartheta \leq 0$ because $f_j - f_k$ is non-decreasing. Thus, S' is optimal too. However, this contradicts the lexicographic minimality of S. $\square$

4.7   Complexity of Single Machine Problems

The results of this chapter are summarized in Tables 4.1 and 4.2. The processing and release times are assumed to be integer. In Table 4.1 we list problems which are polynomially solvable and their complexity bounds. In addition to the problems discussed in Section 4.6, we listed two other problems with $p_j = p$. $1 \mid prec; r_j; p_j = p \mid \sum C_i$ can be solved by constructing blocks as for $1 \mid prec; r_j; p_j = 1 \mid f_{\max}$ in Section 4.1.2. $1 \mid prec; r_j; p_j = p \mid L_{\max}$ is a special case of a problem with identical parallel machines which will be discussed in Section 5.1. Table 4.2 summarizes some problems which are pseudopolynomially solvable.

Table 4.3 contains the easiest problems which are $\mathcal{NP}$-hard if we consider the elementary reductions of Figures 3.5 and 4.7.

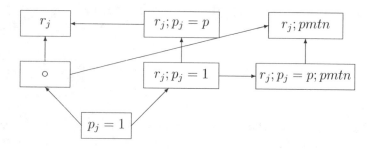

Figure 4.7: Elementary reductions for single machine problems.

Some of the reductions in Figure 4.7 are based on the fact that only schedules without preemption have to be considered in the following cases:

$1 \mid prec; r_j \mid C_{\max}$	4.2	Lawler [135]	$O(n^2)$
$1 \mid prec; r_j; p_j = p \mid L_{\max}$	5.1	Simons [185]	$O(n^3 \log \log n)$
$1 \mid prec \mid f_{\max}$	4.1.1	Lawler [135]	$O(n^2)$
$1 \mid prec; r_j; p_j = 1 \mid f_{\max}$	4.1.2		$O(n^2)$
$1 \mid prec; r_j; pmtn \mid f_{\max}$	4.1.2	Baker et al. [13]	$O(n^2)$
$1 \mid r_j; pmtn \mid \sum C_j$	4.3.1	Baker [12]	$O(n \log n)$
$1 \mid prec; r_j; p_j = p \mid \sum C_j$	4.1.2		$O(n^2)$
$1 \mid prec; r_j; p_j = p, pmtn \mid \sum C_j$		Baptiste et al. [21]	$O(n^2)$
$1 \mid r_j; p_j = p \mid \sum w_j C_j$	4.6.2	Baptiste [18]	$O(n^7)$
$1 \mid sp\text{-graph} \mid \sum w_j C_j$	4.3.2	Lawler [137]	$O(n \log n)$
$1 \parallel \sum U_j$	4.4.2	Moore [171]	$O(n \log n)$
$1 \mid r_j; pmtn \mid \sum U_j$	4.4.3	Lawler [141]	$O(n^5)$
		Baptiste [14]	$O(n^4)$
$1 \mid r_j; p_j = p \mid \sum w_j U_j$	4.6.1	Baptiste [15]	$O(n^7)$
$1 \mid r_j; p_j = p; pmtn \mid \sum w_j U_j$		Baptiste [15]	$O(n^{10})$
$1 \mid r_j; p_j = p \mid \sum T_j$	4.6.2	Baptiste [18]	$O(n^7)$
$1 \mid r_j; p_j = 1 \mid \sum f_j$	2.5		$O(n^3)$
$1 \mid r_j; p; pmtn \mid \sum T_j$		Tian et al. [197]	$O(n^2)$

Table 4.1: Polynomially solvable single machine problems.

$1 \parallel \sum w_j U_j$	2.7	Lawler & Moore [147]
$1 \mid r_j; pmtn \mid \sum w_j U_j$	4.4.3	Lawler [141]
$1 \parallel \sum T_j$	4.5	Lawler [136]

Table 4.2: Pseudopolynomially solvable single machine problems.

- All release times are zero and the objective function is monotone.
- All release times are integer, the objective function is monotone, and we have unit processing times.

Problems which are $\mathcal{NP}$-hard in the strong sense are marked with "$*$". Also, references for the corresponding $\mathcal{NP}$-hardness proofs are given. In the objective functions $f_{\max} = \max f_j$ and $\sum f_j$, the functions f_j are

$*1 \mid r_j \mid L_{\max}$	Lenstra et al. [155]
$*1 \mid r_j \mid \sum C_j$	Lenstra et al. [155]
$*1 \mid prec \mid \sum C_j$	Lenstra & Rinnooy Kan [152]
$*1 \mid chains; r_j; pmtn \mid \sum C_j$	Lenstra [150]
$*1 \mid prec; p_j = 1 \mid \sum w_j C_j$	Lenstra & Rinnooy Kan [152]
$*1 \mid chains; r_j; p_j = 1 \mid \sum w_j C_j$	Lenstra & Rinnooy Kan [154]
$*1 \mid r_j; pmtn \mid \sum w_j C_j$	Labetoulle et al. [133]
$*1 \mid chains; p_j = 1 \mid \sum U_j$	Lenstra & Rinnooy Kan [154]
$1 \parallel \sum w_j U_j$	Karp [124]
$1 \parallel \sum T_j$	Lawler [136]
	Du & Leung [81]
$*1 \mid chains; p_j = 1 \mid \sum T_j$	Leung & Young [157]
$*1 \parallel \sum w_j T_j$	Lawler [136]
	Lenstra et al. [155]

Table 4.3: $\mathcal{NP}$-hard single machine problems.

assumed to be monotone.

Chapter 5

Parallel Machines

In this chapter, we discuss the problem of scheduling jobs on parallel machines. Problem $P \parallel \sum C_i$ and, more generally, problem $R \parallel \sum C_i$ are the only nonpreemptive problems with arbitrary processing times known to be known polynomially solvable. Problems $P2 \parallel C_{\max}$ and $P2 \parallel \sum w_i C_i$ are $\mathcal{NP}$-hard. For these reasons, we essentially discuss problems in which preemption is possible or in which all jobs have unit processing times. In the first section of this chapter, problems with independent jobs are discussed. In the second section, we permit precedence relations between jobs.

5.1 Independent Jobs

In the following three sections, problems with identical, uniform, and unrelated parallel machines are discussed separately.

5.1.1 Identical Machines

Consider n jobs $J_i(i = 1, \ldots, n)$ with processing times p_i $(i = 1, \ldots, n)$ to be processed on m identical parallel machines $M_1, \ldots, M_m$. Then the following problem can be solved polynomially.

$$m = 3 \quad \begin{array}{c|ccccc} i & 1 & 2 & 3 & 4 & 5 \\ \hline p_i & 4 & 5 & 3 & 5 & 4 \end{array}$$

$$0 \hspace{6cm} LB = 7$$

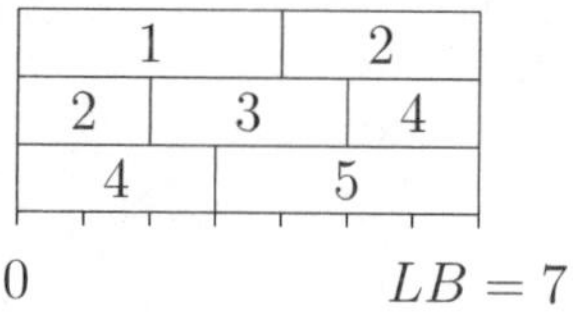

Figure 5.1: Optimal schedule for an instance of $P \mid pmtn \mid C_{\max}$.

P | pmtn | C$_{\max}$

A lower bound for this problem is

$$LB := \max\{\max_i p_i, (\sum_{i=1}^{n} p_i)/m\}.$$

A schedule meeting this bound can be constructed in $O(n)$ time: fill the machines successively, scheduling the jobs in any order and splitting jobs into two parts whenever the above time bound is met. Schedule the second part of a preempted job on the next machine at zero time. Figure 5.1 shows a schedule constructed in this way. Due to the fact that $p_i \leq LB$ for all i, the two parts of a preempted job do not overlap.

P | pmtn; r$_i$ | C$_{\max}$ and P | pmtn | L$_{\max}$

We will show in Section 5.1.2 that the corresponding problems with uniform machines $Q \mid pmtn; r_i \mid C_{\max}$ and $Q \mid pmtn \mid L_{\max}$, which are special cases of $Q \mid pmtn; r_i \mid L_{\max}$, can be solved in time $O(n \log n + mn)$. Thus, the problem with identical machines can be solved with the same time bound.

P | pmtn; r$_i$ | L$_{\max}$

Associated with each job J_i there is a release time r_i and a due date d_i with $r_i \leq d_i$. We have to find a preemptive schedule on m identical machines such that the maximum lateness $\max_{i=1}^{n}\{C_i - d_i\}$ is minimized. To this end, we first consider the decision version of this problem: Given some threshold value L does there exist a schedule such that

$$\max_{i=1}^{n} L_i = \max_{i=1}^{n}\{C_i - d_i\} \leq L? \tag{5.1}$$

In addition, we want to find such a schedule if it exists. (5.1) holds if and only if

$$C_i \leq d_i^L := L + d_i \text{ for all } i = 1, \ldots, n.$$

Thus, all jobs i must finish before the modified due dates d_i^L and cannot start before the release times r_i, i.e. each job J_i must be processed in an interval $[r_i, d_i^L]$ associated with J_i. We call these intervals **time windows**.

Next we address the general problem of finding a preemptive schedule for jobs $J_i(i = 1, \ldots, n)$ on m identical machines such that all jobs J_i are processed within their time windows $[r_i, d_i]$. This problem may be reduced to a maximum flow problem in a network constructed as follows. Let

$$t_1 < t_2 < \ldots < t_r$$

be the ordered sequence of all different r_i-values and d_i-values. Consider the intervals

$$I_K := [t_K, t_{K+1}] \text{ of length } T_K = t_{K+1} - t_K \text{ for } K = 1, \ldots, r - 1.$$

We associate a job vertex with each job J_i and an interval vertex with each interval I_K. Furthermore, we add two dummy vertices s and t. Between these vertices, arcs and capacities for these arcs are defined as follows. From s we have an arc to each job vertex J_i with capacity p_i and from each interval vertex I_K we have an arc to t with capacity mT_K. There exists an arc from J_i to I_K iff job J_i can be processed in I_K, i.e. iff $r_i \leq t_K$ and $t_{K+1} \leq d_i$. The capacity of this arc is T_K. Denote this network, which is shown in Figure 5.2, by $N = (V, A, c)$.

It is not difficult to prove that there exists a schedule respecting all time windows if and only if the maximum flow in N has the value $\sum_{i=1}^{n} p_i$. If this is the case, the flow x_{iK} on the arc (J_i, I_K) corresponds with the time period in which job J_i is processed in the time interval I_K and we have

$$\sum_{K=1}^{r-1} x_{iK} = p_i \quad \text{for } i = 1, \ldots, n \tag{5.2}$$

and

$$\sum_{i=1}^{n} x_{iK} \leq mT_K \quad \text{for } K = 1, \ldots, r - 1. \tag{5.3}$$

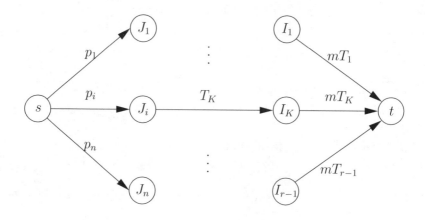

Figure 5.2: A network for problem $P \mid pmtn; r_i \mid L_{\max}$.

Then each job is completely processed and the total amount of processing time in I_K is at the most mT_K, which is the capacity of m machines. Furthermore,

$$x_{iK} \leq T_K \quad \text{for all } (J_i, I_K) \in A. \tag{5.4}$$

If there exists a maximal flow satisfying (5.2) to (5.4), a feasible solution for the scheduling problem with time windows is constructed by scheduling partial jobs J_{iK} with processing times $x_{iK} > 0$ in the intervals I_K on m identical machines. For each K, this is essentially a $P \mid pmtn \mid C_{\max}$-problem, which has a solution with $C_{\max} \leq T_K$ because of (5.3) and (5.4).

Because network N has at the most $O(n)$ vertices, the maximum flow problem can be solved in $O(n^3)$ time. Furthermore, the schedule respecting the windows can be constructed in $O(n^2)$ time. Thus, the window problem can be solved in $O(n^3)$ steps.

To solve problem $P \mid pmtn; r_i \mid L_{\max}$, we apply binary search on different L-values. We assume $d_i \leq r_i + n \max_{j=1}^{n} p_j$, which implies $-n \max_{j=1}^{n} p_j \leq L_{\max} \leq n \max_{j=1}^{n} p_j$. This yields an algorithm which approximates the value of the solutions with absolute error ε in at the most $O(n^3(\log n + \log(\frac{1}{\varepsilon}) + \log(\max_{j=1}^{n} p_j)))$ steps.

P | $p_i = 1; r_i$ | L_{max}

It is convenient to assume that the jobs are indexed in such a way that

$$r_1 \leq r_2 \leq \ldots \leq r_n.$$

The problem has an easy solution if all release times r_i are integer. In this case, we get an optimal schedule by scheduling available jobs in the order of nondecreasing due dates. More specifically, if at the current time t not all machines are occupied and there is an unscheduled job J_i with $r_i \leq t$, we schedule such a job with the smallest due date. Technical details are given by the following algorithm in which K counts the number of machines occupied immediately after Step 7 at current time t, m is the number of machines, M is the set of unscheduled jobs available at time t, and j is a counter for the number of scheduled jobs.

Algorithm P | $p_i = 1; r_i$ integer | L_{max}
1. $j := 1$;
2.   WHILE $j \leq n$ DO
         BEGIN
3. $t := r_j; M := \{J_i \mid J_i$ is not scheduled; $r_i \leq t\}; K := 1$;
4.   WHILE $M \neq \phi$ DO
               BEGIN
5.   Find job J_i in M with smallest due date;
6. $M := M \backslash \{J_i\}$;
7.   Schedule J_i at time t;
8. $j := j + 1$;
9.   IF $K + 1 \leq m$ THEN $K := K + 1$
               ELSE
                   BEGIN
10. $t := t + 1$;
11. $K := 1$;
12. $M := M \cup \{J_i \mid J_i$ in not scheduled; $r_i \leq t\}$
                   END
               END
         END

The inner "while"-loop creates **blocks** of jobs which are processed without idle time on the machines between the scheduled jobs. After finishing such a block, the current r_j-value is the starting time of the next block.

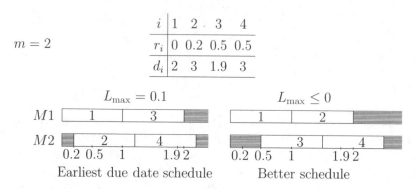

Figure 5.3: Earliest due date schedule is not optimal for problem $P \mid p_i = 1; r_i \mid L_{\max}$.

The algorithm runs in $O(n \log n)$ time if a priority queue data structure is used for M.

Correctness of the algorithm may be proved as follows. Let S be a schedule constructed by the algorithm and denote by S^* an optimal schedule with the following properties:

- the first $r - 1$ jobs scheduled in S are scheduled at the same time in both schedules S and S^*, and

- $r - 1$ is maximal.

Thus, the job J_r is scheduled in S at some time t while J_r is scheduled in S^* at some later time. If some machine is idle in S^* at time t, J_r may be moved to that machine and processed at time t. Otherwise, there exists a Job J_k with $d_r \leq d_k$ which is processed in S^* at time t but not processed in S at time t. Then we interchange J_k and J_r in S^*. In both cases S^* remains optimal, which contradicts the maximality of $r - 1$.

Scheduling available jobs with smallest due dates fails to provide an optimal schedule if the release times are arbitrary rational numbers, as shown in Figure 5.3.

Next we consider the more complicated case in which all release times are rational or even real numbers. To simplify the notation we denote the jobs by $1, \ldots, n$ instead of $J_1, \ldots, J_n$.

First we introduce the notion of a list schedule. A **list** is a permutation $\pi : \pi(1), \pi(2), \ldots, \pi(n)$ of all jobs. A corresponding **cyclic list schedule** is constructed by the following algorithm. In connection with this algorithm, it is convenient to number the machines from 0 to $m-1$. The starting time of job i in this schedule is denoted by $x(i)$, $h(i)$ denotes the machine on which i is to be processed, and $t(j)$ is the finishing time of the last job on machine j.

Algorithm cyclic list schedule
1. FOR $j := 0$ TO $m-1$ DO $t(j) := 0$;
2. FOR $i := 1$ TO n DO
        BEGIN
3.   Schedule job i on machine $h(i) := i(mod\ m)$ at time
            $x(i) := \max\{t(h(i)), r_i\}$;
4. $t(h(i)) := x(i) + 1$
        END

The following lemma shows that we only need to consider cyclic list schedules if we want to solve a problem of the form $P \mid p_i = 1; r_i; d_i \mid f$ with regular objective function f.

Lemma 5.1 Let f be a regular objective function and assume that $P \mid p_i = 1; r_i; d_i \mid f$ has a feasible solution. Then there always exists a cyclic list schedule which is optimal.

Proof: We will show that any feasible solution $(x(i), h(i))$ can be transformed into a feasible cyclic list schedule without increasing the objective function value. Such a transformation is done in two steps. The first step changes the machine on which the jobs are scheduled as follows.
Consider a permutation π with

$$x(\pi(1)) \le x(\pi(2)) \le \ldots \le x(\pi(n)).$$

Then we schedule job $\pi(k)$ on machine $k(mod\ m)$. The corresponding schedule has no overlapping jobs on the same machine. This can be seen as follows. Assume that two jobs $\pi(i_0)$ and $\pi(i_1)$, with $i_0 = jm + k$ and $i_1 = lm + k$ where $l > j$, overlap in an interval I. We have $x(\pi(i_0)) \le x(\pi(i)) \le x(\pi(i_1))$ for all $i_0 \le i \le i_1$ and the processing time of all jobs is equal to one. Therefore, all jobs $\pi(i)$ ($i_0 \le i \le i_1$) are processed during the interval I. This contradicts the feasibility of $(x(i), h(i))$ because there are at least $m + 1$ jobs $\pi(i)$ ($i_0 \le i \le i_1$).

In the second step, the new schedule is transformed into the list schedule which corresponds to π by decreasing the starting times $x(\pi(i))$ of all jobs. Thus, the regular objective function does not increase during the transformation.   □

We will present an algorithm which constructs a schedule $(x(i), h(i))$ respecting all time windows $[r_i, d_i]$ (i.e. with $r_i \leq x(i) < x(i) + 1 \leq d_i$ for $i = 1, \ldots, n$) or finds that such a schedule does not exist. If such a schedule exists, then the schedule constructed by the algorithm minimizes $\sum C_i$ as well as $C_{\max}$.

The idea of the algorithm is to construct an optimal list $\pi(1), \pi(2), \ldots, \pi(n)$. This is done by trying to schedule at the current time t an available job i with the smallest deadline. However, this is not always correct, as we have seen in Figure 5.3. For these reasons, if $d_i < t + 1$ (i.e. if job i is late) we have to call a **crisis subroutine**. The crisis subroutine backtracks over the current partial schedule $\pi(1), \ldots, \pi(k-1)$ searching for a job $\pi(j)$ with a highest position j that has a deadline greater than that of the **crisis job** i. If such a job $\pi(j)$ does not exist, the subroutine concludes that there is no feasible schedule and halts. Otherwise, we call job $\pi(j)$ a **pull job** and the set of all jobs in the partial schedule with positions greater than j a **restricted set**. The subroutine determines the minimum release time r of all jobs in the restricted set and creates a **barrier** (j, r). This barrier is an additional restriction to the starting time of jobs scheduled in positions $k \geq j$. It is added to a barrier list which is used to calculate the current scheduling time. Finally, $\pi(j)$ and all jobs in the restricted set are eliminated from the partial schedule and we continue with the partial schedule $\pi(1), \ldots, \pi(j-1)$.

If $d_i \geq t+1$, then job i is scheduled at time t on machine $h(i) = i (mod\ m)$.

Details are given below. U is the set of unscheduled jobs, the barrier list

Algorithm P $|\ p_i = 1; r_i; d_i\ |\ \sum C_i, C_{\max}$
1. **Initialize;**
2. WHILE there are unscheduled jobs DO
           BEGIN
3.   **Calculate current time t;**
4.   Find unscheduled job i available at time t
              with smallest due date;
5.   If $d_i \geq t + 1$ THEN **schedule job i**
              ELSE
6.   **crisis (i)**
           END

contains all barriers, and $\pi(j)$ denotes the j-th job currently scheduled for $j = 1, 2, \ldots, k - 1$.

We now describe the **initialize, calculate current time t, schedule job i** and **crisis (i)** modules.

The most important module is **crisis (i)**, which resolves a crisis with job i.

Crisis (i)
IF there exists an index $1 \leq \nu \leq k - 1$ with $d_{\pi(\nu)} > d_i$ THEN
    BEGIN
    Calculate largest index $1 \leq j \leq k - 1$ with $d_{\pi(j)} > d_i$;
    $r := \min(\{r_{\pi(\nu)} \mid \nu = j + 1, \ldots, k - 1\} \cup \{r_i\})$;
    Add (j, r) to $barrierlist$;
    Add jobs $\pi(j), \pi(j + 1), \ldots, \pi(k - 1)$ to U;
    $k := j$
    END
ELSE HALT (There exists no feasible schedule)

Initialize
$barrierlist := \phi; k := 1; U := \{1, \ldots, n\}$

Schedule job i
$x(i) := t$;
$h(i) := k(mod\ m)$;
$U := U \backslash \{i\}$;
$t(h(i)) := t + 1$;
$\pi(k) := i$;
$k := k + 1$

Calculate current time t
IF $1 \leq k \leq m$ THEN $t_1 := 0$ ELSE $t_1 := t(k\ (mod\ m))$;
$t_2 := \min\{r_j \mid j$ is an unscheduled job $\}$;
$t_3 := \max(\{r \mid (j, r)$ is a barrier $; 1 \leq j \leq k\} \cup \{0\})$;
$t := \max\{t_1, t_2, t_3\}$

A barrier (j, r) is **correct** for a problem instance if, in all feasible schedules, the job in position j can start no earlier than r. To demonstrate the correctness of the algorithm, we shall prove that each barrier is correct and that if the algorithm does not provide a feasible schedule, then none exists.

Let B be a barrier list. A **feasible B-schedule** is a cyclic list schedule for $P \mid p_i = 1; r_i; d_i \mid \sum C_i, C_{\max}$ with the property that if $(j, r) \in B$, then the job in position j does not begin processing before time r.

We obtain Algorithm (B) by replacing the initialization statement "*barrierlist* := ϕ" by "*barrierlist* := B".

Let $\pi(1), \ldots, \pi(k-1)$ be the current sequence and denote by B the corresponding set of barriers at some stage of the Algorithm $P \mid p_i = 1; r_i; d_i \mid \sum C_i, C_{\max}$. Then we have the following property. If Algorithm (B) is applied to the set of jobs $\{\pi(i) \mid i = 1, \ldots, k-1\}$, then it constructs the sequence $\pi(1), \ldots, \pi(k-1)$ without any call of the crisis subroutine.

Lemma 5.2 Let B be a set of barriers. Assume that Algorithm (B) has scheduled the first jobs $\pi(1), \ldots, \pi(k-1)$ with starting times $t_1, \ldots, t_{k-1}$ and calculates time t as a possible starting time for job $\pi(k)$. Then the following holds:

(i) There is no feasible B-schedule in which any of the jobs $\pi(\nu)$ ($\nu = 1, \ldots, k-1$) is scheduled before time t_ν.

(ii) There is no feasible B-schedule in which $\pi(k)$ starts before t.

Proof: We prove this lemma by induction on k. If (ii) holds for all $\nu \leq k-1$, then (i) holds. Thus, it remains to prove (ii) for $\nu = k$. Let t be the current time after jobs $\pi(1), \ldots, \pi(k-1)$ are scheduled.

If $t = t_1$, then either $t = 0$ or $t = t(k \ (mod \ m))$. In the former case, $\pi(k)$ trivially cannot be started earlier. In the latter case, by assumption $t(k \ (mod \ m))$ is the earliest possible time at which job $\pi(k-m+1)$ can finish. Furthermore, the jobs $\pi(\nu)$ ($\nu = k-m+1, \ldots, k-1$) occupy m different machines. None of these jobs can be finished earlier than time $t(k \ (mod \ m))$. This follows from the fact that all jobs have unit processing times and are scheduled in nonincreasing order of release times and barrier values. $\pi(k)$ cannot be scheduled before any of these m jobs because this would contradict the algorithm. Furthermore, by induction assumption each of these m jobs is scheduled as early as possible. Therefore, $t(k \ (mod \ m))$ is the earliest possible starting time of $\pi(k)$ in any feasible schedule.

If $t = t_2$, then $\pi(k)$ is started at the minimum release time of the unscheduled jobs. Thus, t_2 must be the release time of $\pi(k)$.

If $t = t_3$, then a barrier constraint is preventing $\pi(k)$ from starting earlier. $\qquad \square$

Theorem 5.3 Each barrier created by the algorithm is correct.

Proof: Assume the first $i - 1$ barriers are correct, that the algorithm has constructed a partial schedule $\pi(1), \ldots, \pi(k - 1)$ at the time of the ith crisis, and that (j, r) is the ith barrier to be created. Denote by B the set of the first $i - 1$ barriers.

Suppose to the contrary that there is a feasible schedule in which $\pi(j)$ is scheduled before time r. Since r is the minimum release time of all jobs in the restricted set, all jobs in the restricted set must be scheduled in positions greater than j. Thus, at least one job in the restricted set must be scheduled in a position greater than $k - 1$.

Let t be the current time after jobs $\pi(1), \ldots, \pi(k - 1)$ are scheduled and let l be the crisis job. Thus, $d_l < t + 1$. Furthermore, for each job h in the restricted set we have $d_h \leq d_l < t + 1$. By applying Lemma 5.2 using the set B defined previously, we conclude that a job in position k (and in position $\nu > k$) cannot start before time t.

Thus, a feasible schedule in which $\pi(j)$ is scheduled before time r cannot exist. $\qquad\square$

Lemma 5.4 If the crisis subroutine does not find a pull job, then there is no feasible schedule.

Proof: Let i be a crisis job for which no pull job is found. It follows from the definition of a pull job that all jobs in the current partial schedule $\pi(1), \ldots, \pi(k - 1)$ have a deadline not greater than d_i. Due to the fact that $d_i < t + 1$ and t is the earliest scheduling time of i, if all jobs $\pi(1), \ldots, \pi(k - 1)$ are scheduled as early as possible, then there exists no feasible schedule. $\qquad\square$

Theorem 5.5 If a feasible schedule exists, then the barrier algorithm produces a feasible schedule minimizing $C_{\max}$ and $\sum C_i$ in at the most $O(n^3 \log \log n)$ time.

Proof: There are at the most n distinct release times and n positions. Thus, n^2 is an upper bound on the number of barriers which the algorithm can create. If one uses a standard priority queue, the cost of scheduling each job is $O(\log n)$, but using a stratified binary tree the cost is only $O(\log \log n)$ (see Boas [30]). Since at the most n jobs can be scheduled before a new barrier is created, we have a running time of $O(n^3 \log \log n)$.

Let B be the set of all barriers created by the algorithm. If we apply Lemma 5.2 with this set B, we conclude that the algorithm minimizes C_{max} as well as $\sum C_i$.   □

We may replace the restrictions that $p_i = 1$ and that r_i, d_i are rational by the equivalent restrictions that $p_i = p$ and r_i, d_i are integers. Thus, we have shown that $P \mid p_i = p; r_i; d_i \mid f$ with $f \in \{C_{max}, \sum C_i\}$ can be solved in $O(n^3 \log \log n)$ time.

Problem $P \mid p_i = p; r_i \mid L_{max}$ can be solved using binary search.

$P \mid p_i = 1 \mid \sum w_i U_i$

An optimal schedule for $P \mid p_i = 1 \mid \sum w_i U_i$ is given by a set S of jobs which are early. The late job can be scheduled at the end in an arbitrary order. Furthermore, we may assume that the early jobs are scheduled in the following way: Sort the jobs according to nondecreasing due dates and schedule the jobs in this order, i.e. schedule the first m jobs in S at time 0, the next m jobs at time 1, etc.

To calculate an optimal set S of early jobs we add jobs to S in nondecreasing order of their due dates (and try to schedule them) and as soon as some job appears late we delete from S a job with minimal w_i-value.

More specifically, assume that we have jobs $1, \ldots, n$ with $d_1 \leq d_2 \leq \ldots \leq d_n$. Then the following algorithm calculates an optimal set S of early jobs.

Algorithm $P \mid p_i = 1 \mid \sum w_i U_i$
1. $S := \phi$;
2. FOR $i := 1$ TO n DO
3. IF i is late when scheduled in the earliest empty time slot on a machine
    THEN
          BEGIN
4.   Find a job i^* with $w_{i^*} = \min_{i \in S} w_i$;
5.   IF $w_{i^*} < w_i$ THEN replace i^* by i in the schedule and in S
          END
6. ELSE add i to S and schedule i in the earliest time slot.

Clearly, this algorithm can be implemented in $O(n \log n)$ time if appropriate data structures are used.

Theorem 5.6 Algorithm $P \mid p_i = 1 \mid \sum w_i U_i$ is correct.

Proof: Let S be the set of the jobs calculated by the algorithm. Then all jobs in S are early because if job i replaces an early job k then i must be early as well. This follows from the fact that $d_k \leq d_i$. Let S^* be the set of early jobs of an optimal schedule with the following properties:

- l is the first job in S with $l \notin S^*$, and

- k is the first job in S^* with $k \notin S$.

We may assume that such jobs l and k exist because

- $S \subset S^*$ would lead to a contradiction to the construction of S, and

- if $S^* \subseteq S$ then S must be optimal too and the theorem is proven.

We show that in S^* job k can be replaced by l without increasing the objective function which is a contradiction to the definition of S^*. There are two cases to be considered.

Case 1: $l < k$

The job which eliminates k in S must be considered later than job l. Thus, we must have $w_l \geq w_k$. Due to the definition of k all jobs $i \in S^*$ with $i < k$ must belong to S. Therefore, S^* remains feasible if l replaces k.

Case 2: $k < l$

If in S^* job k is replaced by l then l is on time because k is on time and $d_k \leq d_l$. Therefore, all we have to prove is that $w_l \geq w_k$ holds.

Let $k_{i_0} := k$ be eliminated by i_0 and let $k_{i_1}, \ldots, k_{i_r}$ be the sequence of jobs which are eliminated afterwards from S, where k_{i_ν} is eliminated by i_ν $(\nu = 1, \ldots, r)$. Then $i_0 < i_1 < \ldots < i_r$. We say "i_ν dominates i_μ" $(\mu < \nu)$ if $k_{i_\nu} \leq i_\mu$. In this case the inequality $w_{k_{i_\nu}} \geq w_{k_{i_\mu}}$ holds (Figure 5.4).

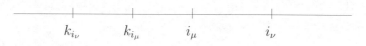

Figure 5.4: i_ν dominates i_μ.

If a subsequence $j_0 = i_0 < j_1 < \ldots j_s$ of $i_0 < i_1 < \ldots < i_r$ exists which has the properties

- $j_{\nu+1}$ dominates j_ν for $\nu = 0, 1, \ldots, s - 1$, and

- $j_{s-1} < l \leq j_s$

then

$$w_l \geq w_{k_{j_s}} \geq \ldots \geq w_{k_{j_0}} = w_k$$

and the theorem is proven.

Otherwise a job i_t with smallest index t exists which is not dominated by a job i_ν with $\nu > t$ and $i_t < l$. Thus, after i_t is added to S no job $i \leq i_t$ will be deleted from S. Because $i_t < l$ all jobs which belong to S when i_t is added must also belong to S^*. This contradicts the fact that $k \in S^*$ and S^* contains no late jobs.

To derive such a contradiction let S_t be set S after deleting k_{i_t} and adding i_t. We consider two cases.

If $k' := k_{i_t} > k$, i.e. $d_{k'} \geq d_k$ then we may replace k by k' in S^* without providing late jobs. Thus, $S_t \cup \{k'\}$ has no late jobs which contradicts the construction of S. Otherwise, $k' < k$. Then all jobs in $S_t \cup \{k\}$ can be scheduled early. Furthermore, all jobs in $\{j \in S_t \mid j < k\} \cup \{k'\}$ can be scheduled early. This implies that all jobs in $S_t \cup \{k'\}$ can be scheduled early which again is a contradiction. $\square$

$P \parallel \sum C_i$

We will show in the next section that the corresponding problem with uniform machines can be solved by a polynomial algorithm, which provides the complexity bound $O(n \log n)$ for problem $P \parallel \sum C_i$.

$P \mid p_i = 1 \mid \sum w_i C_i$ and $P \mid p_i = 1; pmtn \mid \sum w_i C_i$

We get an optimal schedule for problem $P \mid p_i = 1 \mid \sum w_i C_i$ by scheduling the jobs in order of nonincreasing weights w_i. To give a more precise description of such an optimal schedule S, it is convenient to represent the jobs by numbers $0, \ldots, n - 1$ such that

$$w_0 \geq w_1 \geq \ldots \geq w_{n-1}$$

and to denote the machines by $0, \ldots, m - 1$. In S, job i is scheduled at time $\lfloor i/m \rfloor$ on machine $i (mod\ m)$. It can be shown by simple interchange arguments that S is an optimal schedule.

The following theorem shows that an optimal schedule for $P \mid p_i = 1 \mid \sum w_i C_i$ is optimal even if preemption is allowed.

Theorem 5.7 For $P \mid pmtn \mid \sum w_i C_i$ there exists an optimal schedule without preemption.

Proof: It is sufficient to show that an arbitrary schedule with a finite number of preemptions can be transformed into a nonpreemptive schedule without increasing the value of the objective function.

By preemption, a job i may be split at some time s, i.e. processing job i at some machine is stopped and either continued at time s on a different machine or at some time $s' > s$ on the same or a different machine.

Consider an optimal preemptive schedule S with a minimal number l of preemption times. If $l = 0$, we have finished. Otherwise, let $t' < t$ be the two greatest splitting times of S (if $l = 1$, we set $t' = 0$).

We show that by transforming S into a schedule S', all preemptions at time t can be eliminated without creating new preemptions. Furthermore, the objective value for S' is not greater than the objective value for S which contradicts the fact that S is an optimal schedule with a minimal number of preemptions.

If a job i processed on machine M_j is preempted at time t and continued at time t on a different machine M_k, then we may interchange the schedule after time t on M_j and the schedule after t on M_k. This reduces the number of preemptions at time t of this type.

Therefore, we may assume that all jobs $i_\nu (\nu = 1, \ldots, r)$ preempted at time t are continued at some time $t_\nu > t$ on some machine until completed. We assume w.l.o.g. that i_ν is preempted at time t on machine M_ν $(\nu = 1, \ldots, r)$. Now we consider two cases.

Case 1: Each job preemption at time t is continued on a machine which is different to the first r machines $M_1, \ldots, M_r$.

Let M_k, $k > r$ be one of the machines having at least one of the jobs $i_1, \ldots, i_r$ scheduled on it . Suppose that i_l $(1 \leq l \leq r)$ is the earliest such job to be scheduled on M_k after time t. Then i_l is scheduled on M_l between time q and t where $q \geq t'$(if i_l is processed from time $q < t'$ to time t on M_l we preempt i_l at time t') and on M_k between times u and u' where $t \leq u < u'$. Let $c = t - q$, $d = u' - u$, and $e = u - t$ (see Figure 5.5(a)).

Let S_1 be like S, except that i_l is not scheduled on M_l at all after time

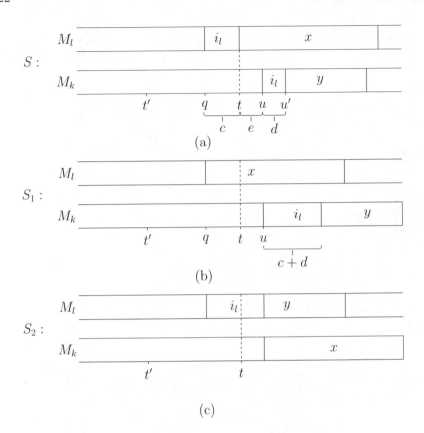

Figure 5.5: Transformation into a non-preemptive schedule: Case 1.

q but is scheduled from u to $u' + c$ on M_k, all the other jobs scheduled after t on M_l in S are moved ahead c units of time, and all jobs scheduled after u' on M_k in S are delayed c units of time (Figure 5.5(b)). S_1 is a feasible schedule because

- jobs which are delayed on M_k are processed only on M_k after time t because there is no preemption after time t, and

- jobs moved ahead on M_l are not preempted after time q because if so, such a job must be preempted at time t on a machine $M_{l'}$ $(1 \leq l' \leq r)$ and continued on M_l which is not possible according to the assumptions of Case 1.

Let S_2 be obtained from S by interchanging the schedule M_l after time t

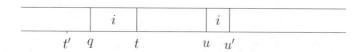

Figure 5.6: Transformation into a non-preemptive schedule: Case 2.

with the schedule of M_k after time u (Figure 5.5(c)). Again, S_2 is feasible because all jobs moved are scheduled after time t.

For $\nu = 1, 2$, the transformation of S into S_ν removes the preemption of i_l at time t and adds no new preemption. To get a contradiction we have to show that for S_1 or S_2 the objective value is not greater than the objective value of S.

Let X be the sum of all weights w_i of jobs scheduled in S after t on M_l. Let Y be the sum of all weights of jobs scheduled in S after time u on M_k (it will include i_l). Going from S to S_ν, the objective value changes by L_ν ($\nu = 1, 2$), where

$$L_1 = cY - cX = c(Y - X)$$
$$L_2 = eX - eY = -e(Y - X).$$

Since both c and e are positive, either L_1 or L_2 is non-positive, i.e. with at least one of the two transformations the objective function does not increase.

Case 2: There exists at least one job preemption at time t and placed on a machine M_j ($1 \leq j \leq r$).

In this case, we partition the set C of jobs split at time t into sets A and B. A is the set of jobs i in C which occur on some M_j, $1 \leq j \leq r$ after time t and there is no other job i' of this type scheduled on M_j after t and before the last part of job i. B is the set of jobs i in C that occur either on M_k, $k > r$ or on some M_j, $1 \leq j \leq r$ after the last part of a job in A has been completed on M_j.

We may assume that each job $i \in A$ preempted on machine M_j finishes on M_j as well (if this is not the case, we have to interchange final blocks of jobs which are scheduled on the same machine from time t). Thus, a job $i \in A$ is processed on machine M_j between q and t, $q \geq t'$, and between u and u' where $t < u$. Furthermore, all jobs scheduled in the intervals $[t', q]$ and $[t, u]$ are different from i (see Figure 5.6).

If we reschedule i to occur between $u - (t - q)$ and u instead of between q

and t and move ahead $t - q$ units of time all that has occurred between in $[t, u]$, we get a feasible schedule with an objective value not greater than before (note that jobs scheduled in $[t, u]$ can be moved ahead because these jobs are not preempted at time t).

By such a rescheduling procedure, jobs in A are eliminated. On the other hand, jobs in C finished after a job in A must be added to A. The rescheduling process ends after a finite number of steps with a Case 1 situation. $\square$

$P \mid p_i = 1; r_i \mid \sum f_i$ can be solved by a network flow algorithm. $P2 \mid p_i = p; pmtn; r_i \mid \sum C_i$ has been solved polynomially by Herrbach & Leung [111].

The following problems are $\mathcal{NP}$-hard:
$P2 \parallel C_{max}$, $P2 \parallel \sum w_i C_i$, $P2 \mid pmtn; r_i \mid \sum C_i$, $P2 \mid pmtn \mid \sum w_i C_i$, $P2 \mid pmtn; r_i \mid \sum U_i$, $P \mid pmtn \mid \sum U_i$.

5.1.2 Uniform Machines

In this section we consider n jobs $J_i(i = 1, \ldots, n)$ to be processed on m **parallel uniform machines** $M_j(j = 1, \ldots, m)$. The machines have different **speeds** $s_j(j = 1, \ldots, m)$. Each job J_i has a **processing requirement** $p_i(i = 1, \ldots, n)$. Execution of job J_i on machine M_j requires p_i/s_j time units. If we set $s_j = 1$ for $j = 1, \ldots, m$, we have m parallel identical machines. All problems with parallel identical machines which are $\mathcal{NP}$-hard are also $\mathcal{NP}$-hard if we replace the machines by uniform machines. Therefore, we first consider problems with preemptions. We also assume that $1 = s_1 \geq s_2 \geq \ldots \geq s_m$ and $p_1 \geq p_2 \geq \ldots \geq p_n$.

$Q \mid pmtn \mid C_{max}$

We will present a lower bound w for the objective value of problem $Q \mid pmtn \mid C_{max}$. In a second step, we will give an algorithm which constructs a schedule of length w (i.e. an optimal schedule). Let

$$P_i = p_1 + \ldots + p_i \quad \text{and} \quad S_j = s_1 + \ldots + s_j$$

for $i = 1, \ldots, n$ and $j = 1, \ldots, m$. Furthermore, we assume that $n \geq m$. If $n < m$, we only have to consider the n fastest machines. A necessary condition for processing all jobs in the interval $[0, T]$ is

$$P_n = p_1 + \ldots + p_n \leq s_1 T + \ldots + s_m T = S_m T$$

or
$$P_n/S_m \leq T.$$

Similarly, we must have $P_j/S_j \leq T$ for $j = 1, \ldots, m-1$ because P_j/S_j is a lower bound on the length of a schedule for the jobs $J_1, \ldots, J_j$. Thus,

$$w := \max\{\max_{j=1}^{m-1} P_j/S_j, \; P_n/S_m\} \qquad (5.5)$$

is a lower bound for the $C_{\max}$-values.

Next we will construct a schedule which achieves this bound. The corresponding algorithm is called the level algorithm. Given a partial schedule up to time t, the **level** $p_i(t)$ of job i at time t is the portion of p_i not processed before t. At time t, the level algorithm calls a procedure **assign** (t) which assigns jobs to machines. The machines are run with this assignment until some time $s > t$. A new assignment is done at time s, and the process is repeated.

Algorithm level
1. $t := 0$;
2. WHILE there exist jobs with positive level DO
        BEGIN
3.   Assign(t);
4. $t_1 := \min\{s > t \mid$ a job completes at time $s\}$;
5. $t_2 := \min\{s > t \mid$ there are jobs i, j with $p_i(t) > p_j(t)$ and $p_i(s) = p_j(s)\}$;
6. $t := \min\{t_1, t_2\}$
        END
7. Construct the schedule.

The procedure assign(t) is given by

Assign (t)
1. $J := \{i \mid p_i(t) > 0\}$;
2. $M := \{M_1, \ldots, M_m\}$;
3. WHILE $J \neq \emptyset$ and $M \neq \emptyset$ DO
        BEGIN
4.   Find the set $I \subseteq J$ of jobs with highest level;
5. $r := \min\{|M|, |I|\}$;
6.   Assign jobs in I to be processed jointly on the r fastest machines in M;

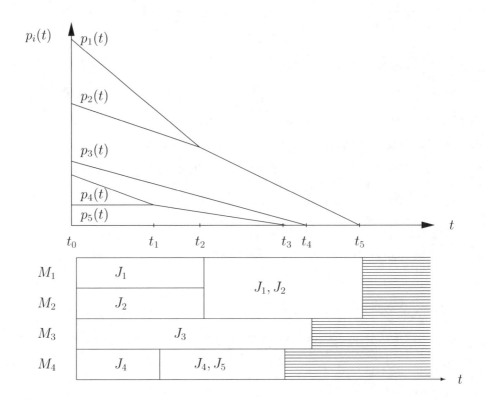

Figure 5.7: Application of the level algorithm.

7. $J := J\backslash I$;
8.   Eliminate the r fastest machines in M from M
            END

The example with 5 jobs to be processed on 4 machines presented in Figure 5.7 shows how the algorithm works.

Initially, the four jobs 1,2,3,4 with the largest processing times are processed on machines M_1, M_2, M_3, M_4, respectively. At time t_1 job 4 has a level which is equal to the processing time of job 5. Thus, from time t_1 jobs 4 and 5 are processed jointly on machine M_4. Due to the fact that job 1 is processed on a faster machine than job 2 at time t_2, we reach the situation that $p_1(t_2) = p_2(t_2)$. Therefore, jobs 1 and 2 are processed jointly on both M_1 and M_2.

1	2	3	4	5	6
6	1	2	3	4	5
5	6	1	2	3	4

Figure 5.8: Processing 6 jobs jointly on 3 machines.

To process r jobs $1, \ldots, r$ jointly on l machines $M_1, \ldots, M_l$ ($r \geq l$) during some time period T, we process each job during a period of T/r time units on each of the machines. A corresponding schedule is shown in Figure 5.8 for the case $r = 6$ and $l = 3$.

Using these ideas, the schedule may be constructed in Step 7 of the algorithm.

Theorem 5.8 Algorithm level constructs an optimal schedule for problem $Q \mid pmtn \mid C_{\max}$.

Proof: Because

$$w := \max\{\max_{j=1}^{m} P_j/S_j, \ P_n/S_m\}$$

is a lower bound for the schedule length, it is sufficient to show that the schedule constructed achieves this bound.

Assume that at the beginning of the level algorithm we have $p_1(0) \geq p_2(0) \geq \ldots \geq p_n(0)$. This order does not change during the algorithm, i.e. we have

$$p_1(t) \geq p_2(t) \geq \ldots \quad \geq p_n(t) \text{ for all } t. \tag{5.6}$$

We assume that the algorithm always assigns jobs to machines in this order.

To prove the desired property, we first assume that no machine is idle before all jobs are finished, say at time T. Then

$$T(s_1 + \ldots + s_m) = p_1 + p_2 + \ldots + p_n \text{ or } T = P_n/S_m.$$

Thus bound w is achieved by the algorithm.

If a machine is idle before the last job finishes, then for the finishing times $f_1, \ldots, f_m$ of machines $M_1, \ldots, M_m$ we have

$$f_1 \geq f_2 \geq \ldots \geq f_m. \tag{5.7}$$

Otherwise, if $f_i < f_{i+1}$ for some $1 \leq i \leq m - 1$, the level of the last job processed on M_i at some time $f_i - \varepsilon$, where $\varepsilon > 0$ is sufficiently small, is smaller than the level of the last job on M_{i+1} at the same time. This is a contradiction. Furthermore, in (5.7) we have at least one strict inequality.

Assume that $T := f_1 = f_2 = \ldots = f_j > f_{j+1}$ with $j < m$. The jobs finishing at time T must have been started at time 0. If this is not the case, then we have a job i which starts at time $t > 0$ and finishes at time T. This implies that at time 0 at least m jobs, say jobs $1, \ldots, m$, are started and processed together on all machines. We have $p_1(0) \geq \ldots \geq p_m(0) \geq p_i(0)$, which implies $p_1(T - \varepsilon) \geq \ldots \geq p_m(T - \varepsilon) \geq p_i(T - \varepsilon) > 0$ for all ε with $0 \leq \varepsilon < T - t$. Thus, until time T no machine is idle, which is a contradiction. We conclude $T = P_j/S_j$. $\qquad\square$

The level algorithm calls the procedure assign(t) at the most $O(n)$ times. The computational effort for assigning jobs to machines after each call is bounded by $O(nm)$. Thus, we get a total complexity of $O(n^2 m)$ (the total work for calculating all t-values is dominated by this).

Unfortunately, the algorithm generates schedules with an excessive number of preemptions. Also the complexity can be improved. This has been shown by Gonzalez & Sahni [106], who developed an algorithm which needs $O(n + m \log n)$ steps to construct an optimal schedule with at the most $2(m - 1)$ preemptions.

Problem $Q \mid pmtn; chains \mid C_{\max}$ which is equivalent to $Q \mid pmtn \mid C_{\max}$ can be solved with the same complexity.

Next we will derive necessary and sufficient conditions for scheduling a set of jobs in a time interval of length T which will be used in the next section.

We have seen that jobs $1, 2, \ldots, n$ with processing times $p_1 \geq p_2 \geq \ldots \geq p_n$ can be scheduled on machines $M_1, \ldots, M_m$ with speeds $s_1 \geq s_2 \geq \ldots \geq s_m$ within an interval of length T if and only if the following inequalities hold:

$$\sum_{i=1}^{j} p_i \leq T \sum_{i=1}^{j} s_i = TS_j \quad \text{for } j = 1, \ldots, \min\{n, m\}$$
$$\sum_{i=1}^{n} p_i \leq T \sum_{i=1}^{m} s_i = TS_m \quad \text{if } n > m.$$

Due to the monotonicity of the p_i-values, for an arbitrary subset $A \subseteq$

$\{1, \ldots, n\}$, we have

$$\sum_{i \in A} p_i \leq \sum_{i=1}^{|A|} p_i \leq Th(A)$$

where

$$h(A) = \begin{cases} S_{|A|} & \text{if } |A| \leq m \\ S_m & \text{otherwise} . \end{cases}$$

Thus, jobs $1, \ldots, n$ with processing requirements $p_1, \ldots, p_n$ can be scheduled within an interval of length T if and only if

$$\sum_{i \in A} p_i \leq Th(A) \text{ for all } A \subseteq \{1, \ldots, n\}. \tag{5.8}$$

Finally, we would like to mention that $Q \mid pmtn; r_i \mid C_{\max}$ and $Q \mid p_i = 1; r_i \mid C_{\max}$ has been solved polynomially by Labetoulle et al. [133] and Dessouky et al. [76], respectively.

$Q \mid pmtn; r_i \mid L_{\max}$

Again, we first consider the problem of finding a schedule with the property that each job i is processed in the time window $[r_i, d_i]$ defined by a release time r_i and a deadline d_i of job i. We call such a schedule **feasible with respect to the time windows** $[r_i, d_i]$. In a second step, we apply binary search to solve the general problem.

As in Section 5.1.1 for identical machines, we solve the feasibility problem by reducing it to a network flow problem. Again, let

$$t_1 < t_2 < \ldots < t_r$$

be the ordered sequence of all different r_i-values and d_i-values and define $I_K := [t_{K-1}, t_K]$, $T_K = t_K - t_{K-1}$ for $K = 2, \ldots, r$. Next we expand the network shown in Figure 5.2 in the following way.

Let I_K be an arbitrary interval node in Figure 5.2 and denote by $J_{i_1}, J_{i_2}, \ldots, J_{i_s}$ the set of predecessors of node I_K. Then we replace the subnetwork defined by $I_K, J_{i_1}, J_{i_2}, \ldots, J_{i_s}$ which is shown in Figure 5.9(a) by the expanded network shown in Figure 5.9(b).

Again, we assume that the machines are indexed in nonincreasing order of speeds

$$s_1 \geq s_2 \geq \ldots \geq s_m.$$

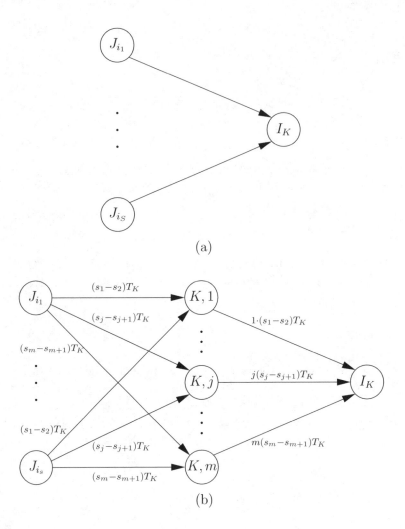

Figure 5.9: Expanded network.

Furthermore, we define $s_{m+1} = 0$. The expanded subnetwork is constructed by adding to vertices $I_K, J_{i_1}, J_{i_2}, \ldots, J_{i_s}$ vertices $(K,1), (K,2),$ $\ldots, (K,m)$. For $j = 1, \ldots, m$, there is an arc from (K,j) to I_K with capacity $j(s_j - s_{j+1})T_K$ and for all $\nu = 1, \ldots, s$ and $j = 1, \ldots, m$ there is an arc from J_{i_ν} to (K,j) with capacity $(s_j - s_{j+1})T_K$. For each I_K we have such an expansion. Furthermore, we keep the arcs from s to J_i with capacity p_i and the arcs from I_K to t with capacity $S_m T_K$ (see

Figure 5.2). The network constructed in this way is called an **expanded network**.

The following theorem shows that we can check feasibility by solving a maximum flow problem in the expanded network.

Theorem 5.9 The following properties are equivalent:

(a) There exists a feasible schedule.

(b) In the expanded network there exists a flow from s to t with value $\sum_{i=1}^{n} p_i$.

Proof: (b) $\Rightarrow$ (a): Consider a flow with value $\sum_{i=1}^{n} p_i$ in the expanded network. Denote by x_{iK} the total flow which goes from J_i to I_K. Then $\sum_{i=1}^{n} \sum_{K=2}^{r} x_{iK} = \sum_{i=1}^{n} p_i$. It is sufficient to show that for each subset $A \subseteq \{1, \ldots, n\}$ we have

$$\sum_{i \in A} x_{iK} \le T_K h(A).$$

This means that condition (5.8) holds and the processing requirements $x_{1K}, \ldots, x_{nK}$ can be scheduled in I_K for $K = 2, \ldots, r$.

Consider in the expanded network the subnetwork induced by A and the corresponding partial flow. The portion of this partial flow which goes through (K, j) is bounded by

$$\min\{j(s_j - s_{j+1})T_K, |A|(s_j - s_{j+1})T_K\} = T_K(s_j - s_{j+1})\min\{j, |A|\}.$$

Thus, we have

$$\sum_{i \in A} x_{iK} \le T_K \sum_{j=1}^{m}(s_j - s_{j+1})\min\{j, |A|\} = T_K h(A). \qquad (5.9)$$

That the equality in (5.9) holds can be seen as follows. If $|A| > m$, we have

$$\sum_{j=1}^{m} \min\{j, |A|\}(s_j - s_{j+1}) = s_1 - s_2 + 2s_2 - 2s_3 + 3s_3 - 3s_4$$
$$+ \ldots + ms_m - ms_{m+1}$$
$$= S_m = h(A).$$

Otherwise

$$\sum_{j=1}^{m} \min\{j, |A|\}(s_j - s_{j+1})$$

$$= s_1 - s_2 + 2s_2 - 2s_3 + 3s_3 - \ldots + (|A| - 1)s_{|A|-1}$$
$$-(|A| - 1)s_{|A|} + |A|(s_{|A|} - s_{|A|+1} + s_{|A|+1} - \ldots - s_m + s_m - s_{m+1})$$
$$= S_{|A|} = h(A).$$

(a) $\Rightarrow$ (b): Assume that a feasible schedule exists. For $i = 1, \ldots, n$ and $K = 2, \ldots, r$ let x_{iK} be the "amount of work" to be performed on job i in the interval I_K according to this feasible schedule. Then for all $K = 2, \ldots, r$ and arbitrary sets $A \subseteq \{1, \ldots, n\}$, the inequality

$$\sum_{i \in A} x_{iK} \leq T_K h(A) \tag{5.10}$$

holds. Furthermore, for $i = 1, \ldots, n$ we have $p_i = \sum_{K=2}^{r} x_{iK}$. It remains to show that it is possible to send x_{iK} units of flow from J_i to I_K ($i = 1, \ldots, n$; $K = 2, \ldots, r$) in the expanded network. A sufficient condition for the existence of such a flow is that for arbitrary $A \subseteq \{1, \ldots, n\}$ and $K = 2, \ldots, r$ the value $\sum_{i \in A} x_{iK}$ is bounded by the value of a minimum cut in the partial network with sources $J_i (i \in A)$ and sink I_K. However, this value is

$$T_K \sum_{j=1}^{m} \min\{j, |A|\}(s_j - s_{j+1}).$$

Using (5.10) and the right-hand side of (5.9), we get

$$\sum_{i \in A} x_{iK} \leq T_K h(A) = T_K \sum_{j=1}^{m} \min\{j, |A|\}(s_j - s_{j+1})$$

which is the desired inequality. $\square$

Because a maximal flow in the expanded network can be calculated in $O(mn^3)$ steps, a feasibility check can be done with the same complexity. To solve problem $Q \mid pmtn; \ r_i \mid L_{\max}$ we do binary search. This yields an ε-approximation algorithm with complexity $O(mn^3(\log n + \log(1/\varepsilon) + \log(\max_{i=1}^{n} p_i))$ because $L_{\max}$ is certainly bounded by $n \max_{i=1}^{n} p_i$ if $s_1 = 1$. Because (5.10) holds for all K, the partial jobs with processing requirements x_{iK} can be scheduled in I_K with the level algorithm. Problem

$Q \mid pmtn; \ r_i \mid C_{\max}$, which is a special case of $Q \mid pmtn; \ r_i \mid L_{\max}$, can be solved more efficiently. Labetoulle, Lawler, Lenstra, and Rinnooy Kan [133] have developed an $O(n \log n + mn)$-algorithm for this special case. Also problem $Q \mid pmtn \mid L_{\max}$ can be solved in $O(n \log n + mn)$ steps. This is a consequence of the following considerations.

Problem $Q \mid pmtn; r_i \mid C_{\max}$ is equivalent to finding a smallest $T \geq 0$ such that the problem with time windows $[r_i, T]$ $(i = 1, \ldots, n)$ has a feasible solution. On the other hand, problem $Q \mid pmtn \mid L_{\max}$ is equivalent to finding a smallest $T \geq 0$ such that the problem with time windows $[0, d_i + T]$ or with time windows $[-T, d_i]$ has a feasible solution. Thus, the problems $Q \mid pmtn; r_i \mid C_{\max}$ and $Q \mid pmtn \mid L_{\max}$ are symmetrical.

$Q \parallel \sum C_i$

Assume that $i_1, i_2, \ldots, i_r$ is the sequence of jobs to be processed on machine M_j. Then the contribution of these jobs on machine M_j in the objective function is given by

$$p_{i_1} \frac{r}{s_j} + p_{i_2} \frac{r-1}{s_j} + \ldots + p_{i_r} \frac{1}{s_j}.$$

This implies that in an optimal schedule the jobs on machine M_j are sequenced according to nondecreasing processing requirements p_i.

To find an optimal distribution of jobs to machines we may proceed as follows. Let $t_1, \ldots, t_n$ be a nondecreasing sequence of the n smallest numbers in the set $\{\frac{1}{s_1}, \frac{1}{s_2}, \ldots, \frac{1}{s_m}, \frac{2}{s_1}, \frac{2}{s_2}, \ldots, \frac{2}{s_m}, \frac{3}{s_1}, \ldots\}$. If $t_i = \frac{k}{s_j}$, then schedule job i on M_j as the k-th last job because we assume $p_1 \geq p_2 \geq \ldots \geq p_n$. Optimality of this strategy is a consequence of the results in Section 2.5.

These ideas lead to the following algorithm in which, for $j = 1, \ldots, m$, we denote by Π_j the sequence of jobs currently scheduled at machine M_j.

Each minimal w-value can be calculated in $O(\log m)$ time if we use a priority queue. Thus, the overall complexity is $O(n \log m)$ if the p_i-values are sorted. Otherwise, we have a total complexity of $O(n \log n)$ if $n > m$. Next we will consider the preemptive version of this problem.

Algorithm $Q \parallel \sum C_i$
1. FOR $j = 1$ TO m DO
2.   BEGIN $\Pi_j := \phi$; $w_j := \frac{1}{s_j}$ END;

3. FOR $i := 1$ TO n DO
      BEGIN
4.   Find the largest index j with $w_j := \min\limits_{\nu=1}^{m} w_\nu$;
5. $\Pi_j := i \circ \Pi_j$;
6. $w_j := w_j + \frac{1}{s_j}$
      END

$Q \mid pmtn \mid \sum C_i$

To solve this problem, we apply an adapted version of the SPT-rule. Order the jobs according to nonincreasing processing requirements, and schedule each successive job preemptively so as to minimize its completion time. In other words, we schedule job n on the fastest machine M_1 until it is completed at time $t_1 = p_n/s_1$. Then we schedule job $n-1$ first on machine M_2 for t_1 time units and then on machine M_1 from time t_1 to time $t_2 \geq t_1$ until it is completed. Job $n-2$ is scheduled on M_3 for t_1 time units, on M_2 for $t_2 - t_1$ time units, and on machine M_1 from time t_2 to time $t_3 \geq t_2$ until it is completed, etc. An example is shown in Figure 5.10. Note the staircase pattern of the schedule.

$$m = 3 \quad s_1 = 3 \quad s_2 = 2 \quad s_3 = 1$$
$$n = 4 \quad p_1 = 10 \quad p_2 = 8 \quad p_3 = 8 \quad p_4 = 3$$

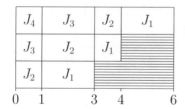

$$\sum C_i = 14$$

Figure 5.10: An optimal schedule for an instance of $Q \mid pmtn \mid \sum C_i$.

A precise description of this procedure is given by the following algorithm which fills the machines simultaneously one time period after the other.

Algorithm $Q \mid pmtn \mid \sum C_i$
1. $a := 0$;
2. WHILE $p_1 > 0$ DO

```
         BEGIN
3.       Find the largest index i with pᵢ > 0;
4.       Δt := pᵢ/s₁;
5.       For ν := i DOWN TO k := max{1, i − m + 1} DO
            BEGIN
6.             Schedule job ν on M₁₊ᵢ₋ᵥ during [a, a + Δt];
7.             pᵥ := pᵥ − Δt · s₁₊ᵢ₋ᵥ
            END
8.       a := a + Δt
         END
```

The computational complexity is $O(n \log n + mn)$. The number of pre-emptions is bounded by $(m-1)n - [1 + 2 + \ldots + (m-1)] = (m-1)(n - \frac{m}{2})$. A simple interchange argument may be used to prove the correctness of the algorithm .

$Q \mid p_i = 1 \mid \sum f_i$ and $Q \mid p_i = 1 \mid f_{max}$

In this section we consider the problem of scheduling n jobs with unit processing requirements on m uniform machines with speeds $s_1, \ldots, s_m$. The objective functions are $\sum_{i=1}^{n} f_i(C_i)$ and $\max_{i=1}^{n} f_i(C_i)$, where $f_i(C_i)$ are monotone nondecreasing functions depending on the finishing times C_i of jobs i. These problems are easily solved in polynomial time. First, observe that there exists an optimal schedule in which the jobs are executed in time periods with the n earliest possible completion times. These completion times can be generated in $O(n \log m)$ time: initialize a priority queue with completion times $1/s_j (j = 1, \ldots, m)$ and, at a general step, remove the smallest completion time from the queue. If this smallest completion time is k/s_j, then $(k+1)/s_j$ is inserted.

Let $t_1, \ldots, t_n$ denote the n smallest completion times in nondecreasing order.

An optimal solution of problem $Q \mid p_i = 1 \mid \sum f_i$ can be found by solving an $n \times n$-assignment problem with cost coefficients $c_{ik} = f_i(t_k)(i, k = 1, \ldots, n)$. The overall complexity is $O(n^3)$.

To solve problem $Q \mid p_i = 1 \mid f_{max}$, Lawler's algorithm can be adapted in the following way.

Algorithm Q | $p_i = 1$ | f_{max}
1. $J := \{1, \ldots, n\}$;
2. FOR $i := n$ DOWN TO 1 DO
      BEGIN
3.   Find a job $j \in J$ with minimal $f_j(t_i)$-value;
4.   Schedule job j finishing at time t_i;
5. $J := J \backslash \{j\}$
      END

The correctness of this algorithm follows in a similar way as for Lawler's algorithm. The overall complexity is $O(n^2)$.

There are several special cases which can be solved more quickly. $Q \mid p_i = 1 \mid \sum w_i C_i$ is solved by assigning the job with the k-th largest weight to t_k, and $Q \mid p_i = 1 \mid \sum T_i$ is solved by assigning the job with the k-th smallest due date to t_k. The time required is $O(n \log n)$.

$Q \mid p_i = 1 \mid L_{max}$ can be solved by simply matching the k-th smallest due date with t_k. Again the complexity is $O(n \log n)$. $Q \mid r_i, p_i = 1 \mid C_{max}$ can be solved symmetrically.

To procedure for calculating the t_k-value can be adapted if we have $p_i = p$ instead of $p_i = 1$ for all jobs i. Thus, also the problems $Q \mid p_i = p \mid L_{max}$ and $Q \mid p_i = p; r_i \mid C_{max}$ can be solved with time complexity $O(n \log n)$.

5.1.3 Unrelated Machines

We have n independent jobs $i = 1, \ldots, n$ to be processed on m machines. The processing time of job i on machine M_j is p_{ij} ($i = 1, \ldots, n; j = 1, \ldots, m$). This model is a generalization of the uniform machine model we get by setting $p_{ij} = p_i/s_j$. In this case, problem $Q \mid\mid \sum C_i$ was the only problem which was polynomially solvable in the case of nonpreemptable jobs with arbitrary processing times. Next we will show that a polynomial algorithm also exists for the corresponding problem with unrelated machines.

R $\mid\mid$ $\sum C_i$

We reduce this problem to an assignment problem. Again, if $i_1, i_2, \ldots, i_r$ is the sequence of jobs processed at machine M_j, then the contribution of these jobs in the objective function is

$$rp_{i_1 j} + (r - 1)p_{i_2 j} + \ldots + 1p_{i_r j}.$$

We define a position of a job on a machine by considering the job processed last on the first position, the job processed second from last on the second position, etc. To solve problem $R \parallel \sum C_i$ we have to assign the jobs i to positions k on machines j. The cost of assigning job i to (k, j) is kp_{ij}. Note that an optimal solution of this assignment problem has the following property: if some job i is assigned to position $k > 1$ on machine j, then there is also a job assigned to position $k - 1$ on machine j. Otherwise, scheduling job i in position $k - 1$ would improve the total assignment cost (provided that $p_{ij} > 0$). Thus, a solution of the assignment problem always yields an optimal solution of our scheduling problem.

$R \mid pmtn \mid C_{\max}$, $R \mid pmtn \mid L_{\max}$ and $R \mid pmtn; r_i \mid L_{\max}$

We solve problem $R \mid pmtn \mid C_{\max}$ in two steps. In the first step we formulate a linear program to calculate for each job i and each machine j the amount of time t_{ij} machine j works on job i in an optimal schedule. In a second step, a corresponding schedule in constructed.

First we give the linear programming formulation. Problem $R \mid pmtn \mid C_{\max}$ is given by nm positive integers p_{ij}, which represents the total processing time of job i on machine M_j. Let t_{ij} be the processing time of that part of job i which is processed on M_j. Then t_{ij}/p_{ij} is the fraction of time that job i spends on machine j, and the equation

$$\sum_{j=1}^{m} \frac{t_{ij}}{p_{ij}} = 1$$

must hold in order for job i to be completed $(i = 1, \ldots, n)$.

This leads to the following formulation of the problem:

minimize $C_{\max}$

subject to

$$\sum_{j=1}^{m} \frac{t_{ij}}{p_{ij}} = 1, \qquad i = 1, \ldots, n \qquad (5.11)$$

$$\sum_{j=1}^{m} t_{ij} \leq C_{\max}, \qquad i = 1, \ldots, n \qquad (5.12)$$

$$\sum_{i=1}^{n} t_{ij} \leq C_{\max}, \qquad j = 1, \ldots, m \qquad (5.13)$$

$$t_{ij} \geq 0, \qquad i = 1, \ldots, n; \ j = 1, \ldots, m.$$

The left-hand side of (5.12) represents the time job i $(i = 1, \ldots, n)$ spends on all machines. The left-hand side of (5.13) represents the total time machine M_j $(j = 1, \ldots, m)$ spends processing jobs. Note that for an optimal solution of this linear program we have

$$C_{\max} = \max\{\max_{i=1}^{n} \sum_{j=1}^{m} t_{ij}, \max_{j=1}^{m} \sum_{i=1}^{n} t_{ij}\}. \qquad (5.14)$$

The problem of finding a corresponding schedule is equivalent to the problem of finding a solution to the preemptive open shop problem with processing times t_{ij} $(i = 1, \ldots, n; \ j = 1, \ldots, m)$ which has a $C_{\max}$-value given by (5.14). In Section 2.4, we presented a polynomial algorithm for solving this problem. We conclude that problem $R \mid pmtn \mid C_{\max}$ is polynomially solvable.

A similar approach may be used to solve $R \mid pmtn \mid L_{\max}$. We formulate a linear programming problem to minimize $L_{\max}$.

Assume that the jobs are numbered in nondecreasing due date order, i.e. $d_1 \leq d_2 \leq \ldots \leq d_n$.

Let $t_{ij}^{(1)}$ be the total amount of time that machine M_j spends on job i in time period $I_1 = [0, d_1 + L_{\max}]$. Furthermore, for $k = 2, \ldots, n$ let $t_{ij}^{(k)}$ be the total amount of time that machine M_j spends on job i within the time period $I_k = [d_{k-1} + L_{\max}, d_k + L_{\max}]$. Then we have to solve minimize $L_{\max}$

subject to

$$\sum_{j=1}^{m}\sum_{k=1}^{i}\frac{t_{ij}^{(k)}}{p_{ij}} = 1, \qquad i = 1,\ldots,n$$

$$\sum_{j=1}^{m} t_{ij}^{(1)} \leq d_1 + L_{\max}, \quad i = 1,\ldots,n$$

$$\sum_{j=1}^{m} t_{ij}^{(k)} \leq d_k - d_{k-1}, \quad i = k,\ldots,n; \quad k = 2,\ldots,n$$

$$\sum_{i=1}^{n} t_{ij}^{(1)} \leq d_1 + L_{\max}, \quad j = 1,\ldots,m$$

$$\sum_{i=k}^{n} t_{ij}^{(k)} \leq d_k - d_{k-1}, \quad j = 1,\ldots,m; \quad k = 2,\ldots,n$$

$$t_{ij}^{(k)} \geq 0, \qquad j = 1,\ldots,m; \; i,k = 1,\ldots,n.$$

Given an optimal solution of this linear programming problem, an $L_{\max}$-optimal schedule can be obtained by constructing for each of the time periods I_k $(k = 1,\ldots,n)$ a corresponding schedule using the data given by the matrix $T_k = (t_{ij}^{(k)})$. We again conclude that problem $R \mid pmtn \mid L_{\max}$ is polynomially solvable.

In a similar way, we may solve problem $R \mid pmtn; r_i \mid L_{\max}$ by considering intervals $[t_k, t_{k+1}]$, $k = 1,\ldots,r-1$, where

$$t_1 < t_2 < \ldots < t_r$$

is the ordered sequence of all r_i-values and $d_i + L_{\max}$ values. In this case, we have the variables $t_{ij}^{(k)}$ and $L_{\max}$ where $t_{ij}^{(k)}$ is the processing time of job i on M_j within the interval $[t_k, t_{k+1}]$.

5.2 Jobs with Precedence Constraints

In this section we consider problems with n jobs $i = 1,\ldots,n$ with precedence constraints between these jobs. We write $i \to j$ if j is an immediate successor of i or, equivalently, i is an immediate predecessor of j. The set $IP(i)$ $(IS(i))$ of all immediate predecessors (successors) of job i is given by

$$IP(i) = \{j \mid j \to i\} \quad (IS(i) = \{j \mid i \to j\}).$$

Besides scheduling problems with arbitrary precedence constraints, we consider intrees (outtrees) which are precedence constraints with the property that each $IS(i)$ $(IP(i))$ contains at the most one job. Given an intree (outtree), we denote by $s(i)$ $(p(i))$ the unique successor (predecessor) of i if such a successor (predecessor) exists. Otherwise we set $s(i) = 0$ $(p(i) = 0)$.

Release times r_i of the jobs are called consistent with the precedence constraints if $r_i + p_i \leq r_j$ whenever $i \to j$. Similarly, due dates d_i are called consistent with the precedence constraints if $d_i \leq d_j - p_j$ whenever $i \to j$.

5.2.1 P | tree; $p_i = 1$ | L_{max}-Problems

We now consider the problem in which unit time jobs with precedence constraints are to be scheduled on identical parallel machines. The precedence constraints are either intrees or outtrees.

P | intree; $p_i = 1$ | L_{max}

The procedure which solves this problem has two steps. In the first step, the due dates of the jobs are modified in such a way that they are consistent with the precedence constraints.

In the second step, jobs are scheduled in an order of nondecreasing modified due dates.

The due date modification procedure is a special case of a corresponding procedure already introduced in the last chapter. The idea is to replace d_i by $\min\{d_i, d_j - 1\}$ whenever $i \to j$. This is done in a systematic way going from the roots (vertices i with $s(i) = 0$) to the leaves (vertices i with $IP(i) = \phi$) of the intree. After modifying the due date d_i, we eliminate i from the intree. T denotes the set of roots in the current tree. Details are described by the following algorithm.

Algorithm Due Date Modification 1
1. $T := \{i \mid i \text{ has no successor}\}$;
2. WHILE $T \neq \phi$ DO
           BEGIN
3.   Choose a job i in T;
4.   FOR ALL $j \in IP(i)$ DO
               BEGIN
5. $d_j := \min\{d_j, d_i - 1\}$;

6. $T := T \cup \{j\}$
                END;
7. $T := T \backslash \{i\}$
           END

Implementing Algorithm Due Date Modification 1 in an appropriate way yields an $O(n)$-algorithm if applied to intrees.

We denote the modified due dates by d'_i. Note that $d'_i < d'_j$ whenever $i \to j$. Furthermore, the following lemma holds.

Lemma 5.10 A schedule has no late jobs with respect to the original due dates d_i if and only if it has no late jobs with respect to the modified due dates.

Proof: Because $d'_i \le d_i$ for all jobs i, a schedule without late jobs with respect to the d'_i-values has no late jobs with respect to the d_i-values.

To prove the other direction, assume w.l.o.g. that $n, n-1, \ldots, 1$ is the order in which the due dates are modified by Algorithm Due Date Modification 1. Consider a schedule with finishing times $C_1, \ldots, C_n$ satisfying $C_i \le d_i$ for $i = 1, \ldots, n$. Then $C_n \le d_n = d'_n$. If for some $1 < r \le n$ we have $C_i \le d'_i$ for $i = r, \ldots, n$, and there exists a job $j \in \{r, \ldots, n\}$ with $s(r-1) = j$ then we have $C_{r-1} \le \min\{d_{r-1}, d'_j - 1\} = d'_{r-1}$. $\square$

In the second step the jobs are scheduled sequentially in order of non-decreasing modified due dates. This is done by scheduling each job at the earliest available starting time, i.e. the earliest time at which less than m tasks are scheduled to start and all predecessors of the job have been completed. A more precise description is given by the following algorithm. We assume that the jobs are numbered in such a way that $d'_1 \le d'_2 \le \ldots, d'_n$. Furthermore, F denotes the earliest time at which a machine is available, and $r(i)$ is the latest finishing time of a predecessor of job i. $n(t)$ counts the number of jobs scheduled at time t and $x(i)$ is the starting time of job i. As before, $s(i)$ is the successor of i.

Algorithm P | intree; $p_i = 1$ | $L_{\max}$
1. $F := 0$;
2. FOR $i := 1$ TO n DO $r(i) := 0$;
3. FOR $t := 0$ TO n DO $n(t) := 0$;
4. FOR $i := 1$ TO n DO

```
        BEGIN
5.          t := max{r(i), F};
6.          x(i) := t;
7.          n(t) := n(t) + 1;
8.          IF n(t) = m THEN F := t + 1;
9.          j := s(i);
10.         r(j) := max{r(j), t + 1}
        END
```

The schedule constructed by this algorithm has the important property that the number of tasks scheduled at any time is never less than the number scheduled at a later time. This can be seen as follows. Suppose k tasks are scheduled to start at a time t and at least $k + 1$ tasks are scheduled to start at time $t + 1$. Since the procedure schedules jobs at the earliest available starting time and less than m jobs are scheduled at time t, the $k+1$ jobs scheduled at time $t+1$ must each have an immediate predecessor scheduled to start at time t. This is impossible because, due to the intree property, each job starting at time t has at the most one successor.

The running time of Algorithm $P \mid intree; p_i = 1 \mid L_{\max}$ is $O(n)$. Thus, problem $P \mid intree; p_i = 1 \mid L_{\max}$ can be solved in $O(n \log n)$ time.

We still have to prove that Algorithm $P \mid intree; p_i = 1 \mid L_{\max}$ is correct.

Lemma 5.11 If there exists a schedule in which no job is late, then a schedule constructed by Algorithm $P \mid intree; p_i = 1 \mid L_{\max}$ has this property.

Proof: Assume that there is a late job in the schedule $x(1), \ldots, x(n)$ constructed by the algorithm. Then there is also a late job with respect to the modified due dates. Consider the smallest i with $x(i) + 1 > d'_i$.

Let $t < d'_i$ be the largest integer with the property that $\mid \{j \mid x(j) = t, d'_j \leq d'_i\} \mid < m$.

Such a t exists because otherwise md'_i jobs j with $d'_j \leq d'_i$ are scheduled before d'_i. Job i does not belong to this set because $x(i) + 1 > d'_i$. This means that at least $md'_i + 1$ jobs must be scheduled in the time interval $[0, d'_i]$ if no job is late. This is a contradiction.

Each job j with $d'_j \leq d'_i$ and $x(j) > t$ must have a (not necessarily immediate) predecessor starting at time t. Now we consider two cases.

Case 1: $t = d'_i - 1$

We have $x(i) > d'_i - 1 = t$. Thus, a predecessor k of i must start at time t and finish at time d'_i. Because $d'_k \leq d'_i - 1 < d'_i = x(k) + 1$, job k is late, too. However, this is a contradiction to the minimality of i.

Case 2: $t < d'_i - 1$

Exactly m jobs j with $d'_j \leq d'_i$ start at time $t + 1$, each of them having a predecessor starting at time t. Due to the intree structure, all these predecessors must be different. Furthermore, if k is such a predecessor of a job j, then $d'_k \leq d'_j - 1 < d'_j \leq d'_i$ which contradicts the definition of t. □

Theorem 5.12 The Algorithm $P \mid intree; p_i = 1 \mid L_{\max}$ is correct.

Proof: Let $L^*_{\max}$ be the optimal solution value. Then there exists a schedule satisfying

$$\max_{i=1}^{n}\{C_i - d_i\} \leq L^*_{\max} \tag{5.15}$$

which is equivalent to

$$C_i \leq d_i + L^*_{\max} \text{ for } i = 1, \ldots, n. \tag{5.16}$$

Due to Lemma 5.10, a schedule S constructed by the algorithm for the due dates $d_i + L^*_{\max}$ satisfies (5.16) or equivalently (5.15). Thus it is optimal. However, S is identical to a schedule constructed by the algorithm for the due dates d_i because $(d_i + L^*_{\max})' = d'_i + L^*_{\max}$ for $i = 1, \ldots, n$. □

If we use the same idea we applied for solving problem $1 \mid prec; p_i = 1 \mid L_{\max}$, the complexity of problem $P \mid intree; p_i = 1 \mid L_{\max}$ can be improved to $O(n)$ as well.

To get this result, we first calculate the modified due dates d'_j using Algorithm Due Date Modification 1. We may assume that the smallest modified due date $d'_{j*} = \min\{d'_j \mid j = 1, \ldots, n\}$ is equal to one. Otherwise, we replace the original due dates by $d_j - d'_{j*} + 1$ which implies that $(d_j - d'_{j*} + 1)' = d'_j - d'_{j*} + 1$. We conclude that

$$L_{\max} = \max_{j=1}^{n}(C_j - d'_j) \geq C_{j*} - d'_{j*} \geq 0$$

for any schedule.

Next we partially sort the jobs according to modified due dates in $O(n)$ time by partitioning the set of jobs into sets S_k, defined by

$$S_k = \begin{cases} \{j \mid d'_j = k\} \text{ if } 1 \le k \le n-1 \\ \{j \mid d'_j \ge n\} \text{ if } k = n. \end{cases}$$

Then we apply Algorithm $P \mid intree; p_i = 1 \mid L_{\max}$ to the job set $\bigcup_{k=1}^{n-1} S_k$ by first scheduling the jobs in S_1 in an arbitrary order, then the jobs in S_2 in an arbitrary order, etc. We extend the partial schedule constructed this way by scheduling the jobs in S_n in an order of nondecreasing d'_j-values according to algorithm $P \mid intree; p_i = 1 \mid L_{\max}$. The resulting schedule must be optimal because all jobs are scheduled in an order of nondecreasing d'_j-values. Denote the corresponding objective value by $L^*_{\max}$.

Unfortunately, the jobs in S_n must be sorted, which takes $O(n \log n)$ time. We can avoid this by ordering the jobs in S_n consistently with the precedence constraints and scheduling them in this order. The resulting schedule must be optimal because

$$\max_{j=1}^{n}\{C_j - d'_j\} = \max(\max\{C_j - d'_j \mid j \in \bigcup_{k=1}^{n-1} S_k\},$$
$$\max\{C_j - d'_j \mid j \in S_n\})$$
$$= \max\{C_j - d'_j \mid j \in \bigcup_{k=1}^{n-1} S_k\} \le L^*_{\max}.$$

The last equality follows from the fact that $C_j \le n \le d'_j$ for all $j \in S_n$.

$P \mid intree; p_i = p \mid L_{\max}$ can be solved with the same complexity because by scaling with factor $1/p$ this problem is transformed into the corresponding equivalent problems with $p_i = 1$. Symmetrically to $P \mid intree; p_i = p \mid L_{\max}$, problem $P \mid outtree; p_i = p; r_i \mid C_{\max}$ can be solved in linear time.

P | tree; $p_i = 1$ | $C_{\max}$

Clearly, $P \mid outtree; p_i = 1 \mid C_{\max}$ can be solved in time $O(n)$ as well. $P \mid intree; p_i = 1 \mid C_{\max}$ has the same complexity because it is symmetrical to $P \mid outtree; p_i = 1 \mid C_{\max}$. Thus, $P \mid tree; p_i = 1 \mid C_{\max}$ can be solved in linear time. However, problem $P \mid outtree; p_i = 1 \mid L_{\max}$ is $\mathcal{NP}$-hard.

P | outtree; $p_i = 1$ | $\sum C_i$

If we specialize algorithm $P \mid intree; p_i = 1 \mid L_{\max}$ to problem $P \mid intree; p_i = 1 \mid C_{\max}$, it may be formulated as follows. Calculate for each job i the number $l(i)$ of jobs on the unique path to the root. Schedule the job according to nonincreasing $l(i)$ values. For problem $P \mid outtree; p_i = 1 \mid C_{\max}$ the same algorithm works if we replace $l(i)$ by the largest number of vertices on a path leaving job i. It can be shown that this algorithm also solves problem $P \mid outtree; p_i = 1 \mid \sum C_i$.

Brucker, Hurink, and Knust [38] have show that $P \mid outtree; p_i = 1; r_i \mid \sum C_i$ can be solved in time $O(n^2)$. Furthermore, they proved that preemption does not help to improve the objective value.

5.2.2   Problem P2 | prec; $p_i = 1$ | $L_{\max}$

As in the last section, we solve this problem by calculating modified due dates and scheduling the jobs in order of nondecreasing modified due dates. However, the due date modification procedure is more sophisticated.

Again, the modified due dates are calculated while going from successors to predecessors. Let $S(i)$ be the set of not necessarily immediate successors of job i. Assume that the modified due dates d'_j are calculated for all $j \in S(i)$. Then we define for each real number d and job i

$$g(i, d) = \mid \{k \mid k \in S(i),\ d'_k \leq d\} \mid,$$

i.e. $g(i, d)$ is the number of successors k of i with $d'_k \leq d$.

If $j \in S(i)$ and all successors of i have to be finished before their modified due dates, then job i must be finished before

$$d'_j - \left\lceil \frac{g(i, d'_j)}{2} \right\rceil$$

where $\lceil x \rceil$ denotes the smallest integer greater or equal to x. This follows from the fact that all successors k of i with $d'_k \leq d'_j$ must be scheduled on two machines in the time period between the finishing time of job i and time d'_j. This leads to the following definition of d'_i

$$d'_i = \min\left\{ d_i, \min\left\{ d'_j - \left\lceil \frac{g(i, d'_j)}{2} \right\rceil \mid j \in S(i) \right\} \right\}. \tag{5.17}$$

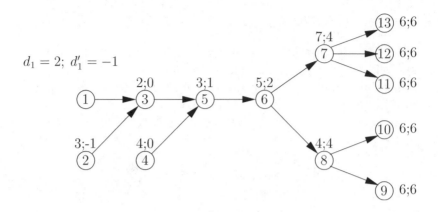

Figure 5.11: Calculation of modified due dates.

Example:

A graph with original and modified due dates is shown in Figure 5.11. For jobs $i = 9, 10, 11, 12, 13$ which have no successors, we have $d_i = d'_i = 6$. Furthermore, we get $d'_8 = \min\{4, 6 - \lceil\frac{2}{2}\rceil\} = 4, d'_7 = \min\{7, 6 - \lceil\frac{3}{2}\rceil\} = 4, d'_6 = \min\{5, 4 - \lceil\frac{2}{2}\rceil, 6 - \lceil\frac{7}{2}\rceil\} = 2$, etc. $\qquad\qquad\square$

If the jobs are ordered topologically, the modified due dates can be calculated by evaluating (5.17) when scanning jobs j in reverse topological order. If we evaluate (5.17) in a straightforward way, we need $O(n^2)$ steps yielding an $O(n^3)$ due date modification algorithm. We will improve the complexity to $O(n^2)$ by keeping a list L in which all jobs are sorted with respect to the current due date. These due dates are either modified or not modified. $L(i)$ is the job in position i of the list and d_i is its current due date. Assume that all successors of job i have been modified and we want to calculate d'_i according to (5.17). Then we scan the list L. If $k = L(j) \in S(i)$, then $g(i, d'_k)$ is the number of successors of i which appear in the list in a position smaller than or equal to j. Thus, by scanning the list L we may evaluate (5.17) in an efficient way. Details are given by Steps 6 to 9 of the following algorithm. As before, $A = (a_{ij})$ is the adjacency matrix associated with the precedence constraints and $n(i)$ is the number of successors not yet treated by the due date modification procedure. S is the set of untreated jobs. The running time of the algorithm is $O(n^2)$ if the successor sets $S(j)$ are known. Otherwise, we may calculate this set by an algorithm of Fischer & Meyer [90] which takes $O(n^{\log 7})$ steps.

Algorithm Due Date Modification 2

1. FOR $i := 1$ TO n DO $n(i) := \sum_{j=1}^{n} a_{ij}$;
2. Calculate a list L of all jobs ordered according to nondecreasing d_i-values;
3. $S := \{1, \ldots, n\}$;
4. WHILE $S \neq \phi$ DO
       BEGIN
5.   Find job $i \in S$ with $n(i) = 0$;
6. $count := 1$;
7.   FOR $j := 1$ TO n DO IF $k := L(j) \in S(i)$ THEN
           BEGIN
8. $d_i := \min\{d_i, d_k - \lceil \frac{count}{2} \rceil\}$;
9. $count := count + 1$;
           END
10.   Eliminate i from L and insert i according to its current d_i-value;
11.   FOR $j := 1$ TO n DO IF $a_{ji} = 1$ THEN $n(j) := n(j) - 1$;
12        $S := S \backslash \{i\}$
       END

The final list L will be input to a second algorithm which constructs an optimal schedule by scheduling jobs in order of nondecreasing modified due dates. Each job is scheduled as early as possible on one of the two

Algorithm P2 | prec; $p_i = 1$ | L_{max}

1. FOR $j := 1$ TO n DO $v(j) = \sum_{i=1}^{n} a_{ij}$;
2. $T := 0$;
3. $M := \phi$;
4. WHILE $L \neq \phi$ DO
       BEGIN
5.   IF $|M| = 2$ OR there is no job in L with $v(j) = 0$ THEN
           BEGIN
6. $T := T + 1$;
7.   WHILE there exists $i \in M$ DO
           BEGIN

8.   FOR $j := 1$ TO n DO

                             IF $a_{ij} = 1$ THEN $v(j) := v(j) - 1$;

9. $M := M \backslash \{i\}$

                    END

              END

10.   Find the first job j in L with $v(j) = 0$;

11. $x(j) := T$;

12. $M := M \cup \{j\}$;

13. $L := L \backslash \{j\}$

              END

machines. The variables used in this algorithm are

- the current time T,

- the number $v(i)$ of predecessors of job i which are not scheduled yet,

- the starting time $x(i)$ of job i in the schedule to be constructed, and

- a set M of at the most two jobs and at least one job to be scheduled at current time T.

The complexity of this algorithm is $O(n^2)$. Thus, the total time for solving problem $P2 \mid prec; p_i = 1 \mid L_{\max}$ is $O(n^2)$ or $O(n^{\log 7})$ if the successor sets $S(j)$ must be calculated.

We still have to prove the correctness of this procedure.

The following lemma is an immediate consequence of the discussions in this section.

Lemma 5.13 A schedule has no late jobs with respect to the original due dates d_i if and only if it has no late jobs with respect to the modified due dates d_i'.   □

Lemma 5.14 If there exists a schedule without late jobs then Algorithm $P2 \mid prec; p_i = 1 \mid L_{\max}$ calculates such a schedule.

Proof: Assume that a schedule $x(1), \ldots, x(n)$ constructed by Algorithm $P2 \mid prec; p_i = 1 \mid L_{\max}$ has a late job with respect to the d-values. By

Lemma 5.13, this schedule also has a job which is late with respect to the d'-values. Let i be a job with the smallest x-value satisfying $d'_i < x(i)+1$. Due to the algorithm, at each time $t < x(i)$ at least one job j with $d'_j \le d'_i$ must be processed. We consider two cases.

Case 1: At some time $t < x(i)$ only one job k with $d'_k \le d'_i$ is processed. We choose a maximal $t < x(i)$ with this property. Then for all jobs j processed in the interval $[t+1, x(i)]$ we have $d'_j \le d'_i$. Furthermore, no machine is idle during this period. All jobs j processed in $[t+1, x(i)]$ and job i must be successors of k, because otherwise such a j must be processed before $t+1$. We have

$$\left\lceil \frac{g(k, d'_i)}{2} \right\rceil \ge \left\lceil \frac{2(x(i) - t) - 1}{2} \right\rceil = x(i) - t$$

which implies

$$d'_k \le d'_i - \left\lceil \frac{g(k, d'_i)}{2} \right\rceil \le d'_i - x(i) + t < x(i) + 1 - x(i) + t = t + 1.$$

We conclude that job k is also late which contradicts the minimality of $x(i)$.

Case 2: At each time $0 \le t < x(i)$, two jobs are scheduled and for all these jobs j the inequality $d'_j \le d'_i$ holds.

Then we have $d'_j \le d'_i < x(i) + 1$ for at least $2x(i) + 1$ jobs, which means that in each schedule there exists a late job. □

The following lemma shows that the schedule constructed by the algorithm will not change if all original due dates are shifted by a constant l.

Lemma 5.15 If $d'_i(i = 1, \ldots, n)$ are the modified due dates for $d_i(i = 1, \ldots, n)$, then $d'_i + l$ are the modified due dates for $d_i + l(i = 1, \ldots, n)$ for any real number l.

Proof: The assertion is clearly true for all jobs without successors. Otherwise, we have by induction

$$(d_i + l)' = \min\{d_i + l, \min\{d'_j + l - \lceil \tfrac{g(i, d'_j)}{2} \rceil \mid j \in S(i)\}$$
$$= d'_i + l$$

because

$$\{k \mid k \in S(i), d'_k + l \le d'_j + l\} = \{k \mid k \in S(i), d'_k \le d'_j\}.$$

□

Theorem 5.16 Algorithm $P2 \mid prec; p_i = 1 \mid L_{\max}$ is correct.

Proof: Similar to proof of Theorem 5.12.

The procedure can be generalized to an $O(n^3 \log n)$-procedure which solves problem $P2 \mid prec; p_i = 1; r_i \mid L_{\max}$ (Garey & Johnson [97]).

$\square$

5.3   Complexity Results

In Tables 5.1 and 5.2 we summarize scheduling problems to be processed without preemption on parallel machines which are polynomially solvable and pseudopolynomially solvable, respectively. In connection with "chains" l denotes the number of chains. In Table 5.3 we will also give a list of related $\mathcal{NP}$-hard problems.

Tables 5.4 to 5.6 summarize the corresponding complexity results for parallel machine problems with preemptions.

Tables 5.1 and 5.6 show that $P \mid p_i = p \mid \sum w_i U_i$ is polynomially solvable but $P \mid p_i = p; pmtn \mid \sum w_i U_i$ is $\mathcal{NP}$-hard. This is very surprising because in the other cases if a problem with $p_i = p$ or $p_i = 1$ is polynomially solvable then the corresponding preemptive problem is also polynomially solvable even with arbitrary processing times. Another result of this type was provided more recently by Sitters [187].

$Q \mid p_i = 1 \mid f_{\max}$	5.2.1 Graham et al. [108]	$O(n^2)$
$P \mid p_i = p; outtree; r_i \mid C_{\max}$ 5.2.1 Brucker et al. [35]		$O(n)$
$P \mid p_i = p; tree \mid C_{max}$	Hu [116]	$O(n)$
$P2 \mid p_i = p; prec \mid C_{max}$	5.2.2 Garey & Johnson [96]	$O(n^{\log^7})$
$Q \mid p_i = 1; r_i \mid C_{max}$	Dessouky et al. [76]	$O(n \log n)$
$Q \mid p_i = p; r_i \mid C_{\max}$	5.1.2	$O(n \log n)$
$Q2 \mid p_i = p; chains \mid C_{max}$	Brucker et al. [39]	$O(l)$
$P \mid p_i = 1; chains; r_i \mid L_{max}$	Dror et al. [78]	
$P \mid p_i = p; intree \mid L_{max}$	5.2.1 Brucker et al. [35],	
	Monma [169]	$O(n)$
$P \mid p_i = p; r_i \mid L_{max}$	5.1.1 Simons [186]	$O(n^3 \log \log n)$
$P2 \mid p_i = 1; prec; r_i \mid L_{max}$	Garey & Johnson [97]	$O(n^3 \log n)$
$P \mid p_i = 1; outtree; r_i \mid \sum C_i$	Brucker et al. [38]	$O(n^2)$
$P \mid p_i = p; outtree \mid \sum C_i$	Hu [116]	$O(n \log n)$
$Pm \mid p_i = p; tree \mid \sum C_i$	Baptiste et al. [22]	$O(n^m)$
$P \mid p_i = p; r_i \mid \sum C_i$	5.1.1 Baptiste & Brucker [20]	$O(n \log n)$
$P2 \mid p_i = p; prec \mid \sum C_i$	Coffman & Graham [70]	$O(n^{\log^7})$
$P2 \mid p_i = 1; prec; r_i \mid \sum C_i$	Baptiste & Timkowski [23]	$O(n^9)$
$Qm \mid p_i = 1; r_i \mid \sum C_i$	Dessouky et al. [76]	$O(mn^{2m+1})$
$R \parallel \sum C_i$	5.1.3 Bruno et al. [58]	$O(mn^3)$
$P \mid p_i = p; r_i \mid \sum w_i C_i$	Brucker & Kravchenko [52]	lin. progr.
$P \mid p_i = p \mid \sum w_i C_i$	5.1.1 McNaughton [165]	$O(n \log n)$
$P \mid p_i = p \mid \sum w_i U_i$	5.1.1 Brucker & Kravchenko [50]	$O(n \log n)$
$P \mid p_i = 1; r_i \mid \sum w_i U_i$	Networkflowproblem	$O(mn^3)$
$Pm \mid p_i = p; r_i \mid \sum w_i U_i$	Baptiste et. al [21]	$O(n^{6m+1})$
$Q \mid p_i = p \mid \sum w_i U_i$	Assignment-problem	$O(n^3)$
$P \mid p_i = p; r_i \mid \sum T_i$	Brucker & Kravchenko [53]	lin. progr.
$P \mid p_i = 1; r_i \mid \sum w_i T_i$	Networkflowproblem	$O(mn^3)$
$Q \mid p_i = p \mid \sum w_i T_i$	Assignment-problem	$O(n^3)$

Table 5.1: Polynomially solvable parallel machine problems without preemption.

	$Qm \mid r_i \mid C_{max}$	Lawler et al. [145]
	$Qm \parallel \sum w_i C_i$	Lawler et al. [145]
	$Qm \parallel \sum w_i U_i$	Lawler et al. [145]

Table 5.2: Pseudopolynomially solvable parallel machine problems without preemption.

	$P2 \parallel C_{max}$	Lenstra et al. [155]
*	$P \parallel C_{max}$	Garey & Johnson [98]
*	$P \mid p_i = 1; intree; r_i \mid C_{max}$	Brucker et al. [35]
*	$P \mid p_i = 1; prec \mid C_{max}$	Ullman [203]
*	$P2 \mid chains \mid C_{max}$	Du et al. [86]
*	$Q \mid p_i = 1; chains \mid C_{max}$	Kubiak [129]
*	$P \mid p_i = 1; outtree \mid L_{max}$	Brucker et al. [35]
*	$P \mid p_i = 1; intree; r_i \mid \sum C_i$	Lenstra [150]
*	$P \mid p_i = 1; prec \mid \sum C_i$	Lenstra & Rinnooy Kan [152]
*	$P2 \mid chains \mid \sum C_i$	Du et al. [86]
*	$P2 \mid r_i \mid \sum C_i$	Single-machine problem
	$P2 \parallel \sum w_i C_i$	Bruno et al. [58]
*	$P \parallel \sum w_i C_i$	Lenstra [150]
*	$P2 \mid p_i = 1; chains \mid \sum w_i C_i$	Timkovsky [201]
*	$P2 \mid p_i = 1; chains \mid \sum U_i$	Single-machine problem
*	$P2 \mid p_i = 1; chains \mid \sum T_i$	Single-machine problem

Table 5.3: $\mathcal{NP}$-hard parallel machine problems without preemption.

$P \mid pmtn \mid C_{\max}$	McNaughton [165]
	5.1.1 $O(n)$
$P \mid outtree; pmtn; r_i \mid C_{max}$	Lawler [139]
	$O(n^2)$
$P \mid tree; pmtn \mid C_{max}$	Gonzalez & Johnson [103]
	$O(n \log m)$
$Q \mid pmtn; r_i \mid C_{max}$	Labetoulle et al. [133]
	$O(n \log n + mn)$
$Q \mid chains; pmtn \mid C_{max}$	Gonzalez & Sahni [105]
	5.1.2 $O(n + m \log n)$
$P \mid intree; pmtn \mid L_{max}$	Lawler [139]
	$O(n^2)$
$Q2 \mid prec; pmtn; r_j \mid L_{max}$	Lawler [139]
	$O(n^2)$
$Q2 \mid prec; pmtn; r_i \mid L_{max}$	Lawler [139]
	$O(n^6)$
$P \mid pmtn \mid L_{\max}$	Baptiste [17]
	$O(n \log n)$
$Q \mid pmtn \mid L_{max}$	Labetoulle et al. [133]
	$O(n \log n + mn)$
$Q \mid pmtn, r_i; d_i \mid -$	Federgruen & Gronevelt [89]
	5.1.2 $O(mn^3)$
$R \mid pmtn; r_i \mid L_{max}$	Lawler & Labetoulle [142]
	5.1.3 lin. progr.
$P \mid p_i = p; outtree; pmtn \mid \sum C_i$	Brucker et al. [38]
	$O(n^2)$
$P \mid p_i = 1; outtree; pmtn; r_i \mid \sum C_i$	Brucker et al. [38]
	$O(n^2)$
$P2 \mid p_i = p; prec; ; pmtn \mid \sum C_i$	Coffman et al. [68]
$P2 \mid p_i = p; outtree; pmtn; r_i \mid \sum C_i$	Lushchakova [163]
$P2 \mid p_i = p; pmtn; r_i \mid \sum C_i$	Herrbach & Leung [111]
	$O(n \log n)$
$P \mid p_i = p; pmtn; r_i \mid \sum C_i$	Brucker & Kravchenko [52]
	lin. progr.
$Q \mid pmtn \mid \sum C_i$	Labetoulle et al. [133]
	5.1.2 $O(n \log n + mn)$
$P \mid p_i = p; pmtn \mid \sum w_i C_i$	McNaughton [165]
	5.1.1 $O(n \log n)$
$Q \mid p_i = p; pmtn \mid \sum U_i$	Baptiste et al. [21]
$Qm \mid pmtn \mid \sum U_i$	Lawler [138], Lawler & Martel [146]
	$O(n^{3(m-1)})$
$Pm \mid p_i = p; pmtn \mid \sum w_i U_i$	Baptiste [18], Baptiste [17]
	$O(n^{3m+4})$
$P \mid p_i = 1; pmtn; r_i \mid \sum w_i U_i$	Brucker et al. [37]
	$O(mn^3)$
$P \mid p_i = p; pmtn \mid \sum T_i$	Baptiste et al. [21]
	$O(n^3)$
$P \mid p_i = 1; pmtn; r_i \mid \sum w_i T_i$	Baptiste [19]
	$O(mn^3)$

Table 5.4: Polynomially solvable preemptive parallel machine problems.

$Pm \mid pmtn \mid \sum w_i C_i$ McNaughton [165], Lawler et al. [145]

$Qm \mid pmtn \mid \sum w_i U_i$ Lawler [138] , Lawler & Martel [146]

Table 5.5: Pseudopolynomially solvable preemptive parallel machine problems.

*	$P \mid intree; pmtn; r_i \mid C_{max}$	Lenstra [150]
*	$P \mid p_i = 1; prec; pmtn \mid C_{max}$	Ullman [204]
*	$R2 \mid chains; pmtn \mid C_{max}$	Lenstra [150]
*	$P \mid outtree; pmtn \mid L_{max}$	Lenstra [150]
	$P2 \mid pmtn; r_i \mid \sum C_i$	Du et al. [85]
*	$P2 \mid chains; pmtn \mid \sum C_i$	Du et al. [86]
*	$P \mid pmtn; r_i \mid \sum C_i$	Brucker & Kravchenko [51]
*	$R \mid pmtn \mid \sum C_i$	Sitters [187]
*	$P2 \mid p_i = 1; chains; pmtn \mid \sum w_i C_i$	Du et al. [86]
	$P2 \mid pmtn \mid \sum w_i C_i$	Bruno et al. [58]
*	$P \mid p_i = p; pmtn; r_i \mid \sum w_i C_i$	Leung & Young [158]
*	$P \mid pmtn \mid \sum w_i C_i$	Lenstra [150]
*	$P2 \mid pmtn; r_i \mid \sum w_i C_i$	Labetoulle et al. [133]
	$P \mid pmtn \mid \sum U_i$	Lawler [140]
	$P2 \mid pmtn; r_i \mid \sum U_i$	Du et al. [84]
*	$P2 \mid p_i = 1; chains; pmtn \mid \sum U_i$	Baptiste et al. [21]
*	$R \mid pmtn; r_i \mid \sum U_i$	Du & Leung [82]
*	$R \mid pmtn \mid \sum U_i$	Sitters [187]
	$P \mid p_i = p; pmtn \mid \sum w_i U_i$	Brucker & Kravchenko [50]
	$P2 \mid pmtn \mid \sum w_i U_i$	Single-machine problem

Table 5.6: $\mathcal{NP}$-hard preemptive parallel machine problems.

Chapter 6

Shop Scheduling Problems

In this chapter we will discuss **shop scheduling problems**, such as open shop problems, flow shop problems, job shop problems, and mixed shop problems, which are widely used for modeling industrial production processes. All of these problems are special cases of the general shop problem.

The **general shop problem** may be defined as follows. We have n jobs $i = 1, \ldots, n$ and m machines $M_1, \ldots, M_m$. Each job i consists of a set of operations O_{ij} ($j = 1, \ldots, n_i$) with processing times p_{ij}. Each operation O_{ij} must be processed on a machine $\mu_{ij} \in \{M_1, \ldots, M_m\}$. There may be precedence relations between the operations of all jobs. Each job can only be processed only by one machine at a time and each machine can only process one job at a time. The objective is to find a feasible schedule that minimizes some objective function of the finishing times C_i of the jobs $i = 1, \ldots, n$. The objective functions are assumed to be regular.

In Section 6.1 we will introduce disjunctive graphs, which are a useful tool for representing feasible schedules for shop problems. In subsequent sections we will discuss open shop problems (Section 6.2), flow shop problems (Section 6.3), job shop problems (Section 6.4), and mixed shop problems (Section 6.5). In Section 6.6 complexity results for shop scheduling problems are presented. Unless otherwise stated, preemption is not allowed.

6.1   The Disjunctive Graph Model

Disjunctive graphs can be used to represent certain feasible schedules
for general shop problems. If the objective function is regular, the set
of feasible schedules represented in this way always contains an optimal
solution for the problem. Thus, the disjunctive graph model may be used
to construct optimal schedules.

For a given instance of the general shop problem, the **disjunctive graph**
$G = (V, C, D)$ is defined as follows.

V is the set of nodes representing the operations of all jobs. In addition, there are two special nodes, a source $0 \in V$, and a sink $* \in V$.
A weight is associated with each node. The weights of 0 and $*$ are
zero, while the weights of the other nodes are the processing times
of the corresponding operations.

C is the set of directed **conjunctive** arcs. These arcs reflect the
precedence relations between the operations. Additionally, there
are conjunctive arcs between the source and all operations without
a predecessor, and between all operations without a successor and
the sink.

D is the set of undirected **disjunctive** arcs. Such an arc exists for
each pair of operations belonging to the same job which are not connected by a chain of conjunctive arcs and for each pair of operations
to be processed on the same machine which are not connected by
a chain of conjunctive arcs.

Figure 6.1 shows a disjunctive graph for a general shop problem with
4 jobs and 4 machines. Each node has a label indicating the machine
on which the corresponding operation has to be processed. The basic
scheduling decision is to define an ordering between the operations connected by disjunctive arcs. This can be done by turning the **undirected**
disjunctive arcs into **directed** ones. A **selection** S is a set of directed
disjunctive arcs. Disjunctive arcs which have been directed are called
fixed. A selection is a **complete selection** if

- each disjunctive arc has been fixed, and

- the resulting graph $G(S) = (V, C \cup S)$ is acyclic.

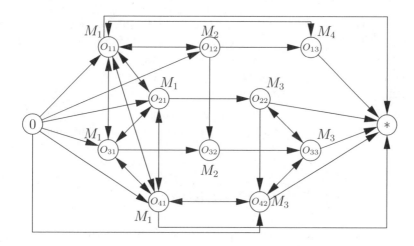

Figure 6.1: Disjunctive graph for a general shop problem with 4 jobs and 4 machines.

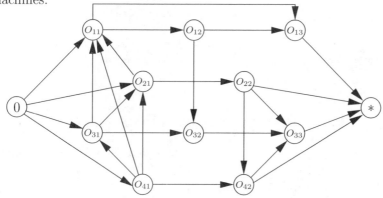

Figure 6.2: Complete selection for the example presented in Figure 6.1.

Figure 6.2 shows a complete selection for the example presented in Figure 6.1. Given a complete selection S, we may construct a corresponding nonpreemptive (semi-active) schedule $x = (x_i)$ defined by the starting times of all operations i. For each path p from vertex i to vertex j in $G(S)$, define the length of p to be the sum of all labels of nodes in p, j excluded. For each operation i, let $l(i)$ be the length of a longest path from 0 to the vertex representing i. If we define $x_i = l(i)$ for all operations i, then we get the feasible schedule x associated with S.

On the other hand, an arbitrary feasible schedule x defines an order of operations for each job and each machine. This induces a complete selection S and, given a regular objective function, the corresponding schedule x' is not worse than x. Thus, a complete selection always exists which represents an optimal schedule.

If the objective function is to minimize makespan, then the length $l(*)$ of a longest $0-*-$path is the $C_{\max}$-value which corresponds with a complete selection.

6.2   Open Shop Problems

An **open shop problem** is a special case of the general shop in which

- each job i consists of m operations O_{ij} $(j = 1, \ldots, m)$ where O_{ij} must be processed on machine M_j, and

- there are no precedence relations between the operations.

Thus, the problem is to find **job orders** (orders of operations belonging to the same job) and **machine orders** (orders of operations to be processed on the same machine).

6.2.1   Arbitrary Processing Times

If the processing times p_{ij} are arbitrary and preemption is not allowed, then $O2 \parallel C_{\max}$ (or symmetrically $O \mid n = 2 \mid C_{\max}$) seems to be the only problem which is polynomially solvable.

An $O(n)$-algorithm for problem $O2 \parallel C_{\max}$ can be described as follows.

Let A and B be the two machines and denote by a_i and b_i the processing times of job i $(i = 1, \ldots, n)$ on machines A and B, respectively. Furthermore, define

$$I = \{i \mid a_i \leq b_i; \; i = 1, \ldots, n\} \quad \text{and}$$
$$J = \{i \mid b_i < a_i; \; i = 1, \ldots, n\}.$$

We consider two cases.

Case 1:
$$a_r = \max\{\max\{a_i \mid i \in I\}, \max\{b_i \mid i \in J\}\}$$

An optimal schedule is constructed by scheduling

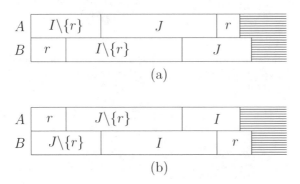

Figure 6.3: Optimal schedules for $O2 \parallel C_{\max}$.

- first all jobs in $I\backslash\{r\}$ in an arbitrary order on machine A, then all jobs in J in an arbitrary order, and, finally, job r,

- first job r on machine B, then all jobs in $I\backslash\{r\}$ in the same order as jobs in $I\backslash\{r\}$ are scheduled on A, and, finally, all jobs in J in the same order as on machine A, and

- first job r on machine B and then on machine A, while all other jobs are first scheduled on machine A (see Figure 6.3(a)).

Case 2:
$$b_r = \max\{\max\{a_i \mid i \in I\}, \max\{b_i \mid i \in J\}\}$$

We have to interchange the machines and sets I and J before applying the same rule (see Figure 6.3(b)).

The complexity of this procedure is $O(n)$.

To prove the correctness of this procedure we consider only Case 1 (Case 2 is similar).

Let $G(S)$ be the network induced by the solution S. Then it is sufficient to show that one of the following paths is a longest path in $G(S)$:

(i) $0 \to a_i \ (i \in I\backslash\{r\}) \longrightarrow a_i \ (i \in J) \longrightarrow a_r \to *$

(ii) $0 \to b_r \longrightarrow b_i \ (i \in I\backslash\{r\}) \longrightarrow b_i(i \in J) \to *$

(iii) $0 \to b_r \longrightarrow a_r \to *$

Here a_i $(I\backslash\{r\}), a_i$ $(i \in J)$, etc. stand for corresponding subpaths.

Because the length of each of these three paths is a lower bound for the open shop problem, the solution must be optimal.

To simplify the notation we assume that the jobs are enumerated according to the sequence on machine A. Thus, $I\backslash\{r\} = \{1, \ldots, |I| - 1\}$, $J = \{|I|, \ldots, n - 1\}$, and $r = n$.

The only paths other than (i), (ii), and (iii) that exist in $G(S)$ are paths of the form

$$0 \to a_1 \to \ldots \to a_i \to b_i \to \ldots \to b_{n-1} \to * \quad (i = 1, \ldots, n - 1).$$

We show that none of these paths is longer than the longest of (i), (ii), (iii).

If $i \in I$, then

$$\sum_{j=1}^{i} a_j + \sum_{j=i}^{n-1} b_j \le \sum_{j=1}^{i-1} b_j + a_i + \sum_{j=i}^{n-1} b_j \le \sum_{j=1}^{n} b_j$$

because $a_i \le \max\{a_j \mid j \in I\} = a_n \le b_n$.

If $i \in J$, then

$$\sum_{j=1}^{i} a_j + \sum_{j=i}^{n-1} b_j \le \sum_{j=1}^{i} a_j + b_i + \sum_{j=i+1}^{n-1} a_j \le \sum_{j=1}^{n} a_j$$

because $b_i \le \max\{b_j \mid j \in J\} \le \max\{\max\{a_i \mid i \in I\}, \max\{b_j \mid j \in J\}\} = a_n$. □

In Section 2.4 we showed that problem $O \mid pmtn \mid C_{\max}$ can be solved in $O(n^{5/2}m)$ time. Similar results can be obtained for the minimization of maximum lateness if preemption is allowed. Lawler, Lenstra & Rinnooy Kan [144] give an $O(n)$ time algorithm for $O2 \mid pmtn \mid L_{\max}$ and, by symmetry, for $O2 \mid pmtn, r_i \mid C_{\max}$. For $O \mid r_i; pmtn \mid L_{\max}$ Cho & Sahni [66] show that a trial value of $L_{\max}$ can be tested for feasibility by linear programming; binary search is then applied to minimize $L_{\max}$ in polynomial time.

The following problems are $\mathcal{NP}$-hard: $O \mid pmtn \mid \sum C_i$, $O2 \mid pmtn; d_i \mid \sum C_i$ (Liu & Bulfin [160]), and $O2 \mid pmtn \mid \sum C_i$ (Du & Leung [83]).

6.2.2   Unit Processing Times

To solve an open shop problem P with unit processing times we proceed as follows.

We transform P into a problem $\overline{P}$ by replacing

- the machines by m identical parallel machines, and

- each job i by a chain of m unit time jobs O_{ik} $(k = 1, \ldots, m)$,

and solve problem $\overline{P}$.

A schedule for problem $\overline{P}$ may be represented by a binary matrix $A = (a_{it})$ where $a_{it} = 1$ iff O_{ik} is scheduled in time period t for some k ($k = 1, \ldots, m$). Such a schedule can be transformed into a feasible schedule of the original open shop problem by assigning machines to the unit time operations in such a way that

- all m unit time operations belonging to the same chain are assigned to different machines, and

- all unit time operations scheduled at the same time are assigned to different machines.

This machine assignment problem is equivalent to coloring the arcs of the bipartite graph G defined by A with exactly m colors. According to the results in Section 2.6, this is always possible because m is the maximum degree of G. Note that G has nm edges. Furthermore, we assume that $m \leq n$. Then the machine assignment can be done in $O(n^2 m)$ time using the edge coloring algorithm of Section 2.6. If we use the more sophisticated algorithm of Gabow & Kariv [95], we get a time bound of $O(nm \log^2(nm))$ because the number of columns in A are bounded by $O(nm)$.

An optimal solution of $\overline{P}$ yields an optimal solution of the original problem P. This follows from the fact that $\overline{P}$ is a relaxation of P and that a solution of $\overline{P}$ also defines a solution for P.

Problem $\overline{P}$ is equivalent to the problem $\hat{P}$ of scheduling identical jobs with processing time m on m identical machines where preemption and restart is only allowed at integer times.

We have considered the case $m \leq n$. If $n < m$, then it is always possible to construct a schedule in which job i finishes at time $r_i + m$. Such a

1	2	3	
	1	2	3
3		1	2
2	3		1

$n = 3,\ m = 4$

Figure 6.4: Optimal schedule for an instance of $O \mid p_{ij} = 1 \mid \gamma$ with $n < m$.

1	2	3	4	5	6	7
7	1	2	3	4	5	6
6	7	1	2	3	4	5
5	6	7	1	2	3	4

$m = 4,\ n = 7$

Figure 6.5: Optimal schedule for an instance of $O \mid p_{ij} = 1 \mid C_{\max}$.

schedule must be optimal if the objective function is regular. Figure 6.4 shows such a schedule for the case in which all release times r_i are zero.

Table 6.1 in Section 6.6 shows open shop problems P that can be solved polynomially due to the fact that the corresponding parallel machine problem $\hat{P}$ with processing times m and integer preemption can be solved polynomially. The complexity of problem P is given by the maximum of the complexity for $\hat{P}$ and $O(nm \log^2(nm))$. Most of the parallel machine problems have been discussed in the previous chapter. Other results will be derived in this section. However, we will first discuss some open shop problems with unit processing times for which an optimal solution can be constructed directly, i.e. without applying the assignment procedure. As before, we assume $m \leq n$.

$O \mid p_{ij} = 1 \mid C_{\max}$

The results derived in 5.1.1 show that problem $P \mid p_i = m; pmtn \mid C_{\max}$ with n jobs has a solution with an optimal $C_{\max}$-value equal to n. Thus, n is a lower bound for the solution value. It is also not difficult to construct a schedule for the corresponding problem $O \mid p_{ij} = 1 \mid C_{\max}$ with a makespan equal to n. Figure 6.5 shows an example for such a schedule which is an optimal solution for the open shop problem.

Block 1			Block 2			Block 3			Block 4	
1	2	3	4	5	6	7	8	9	10	11
3	1	2	6	4	5	9	7	8	10	11
2	3	1	5	6	4	8	9	7	11	10

Figure 6.6: Optimal schedule for an instance of $O \mid p_{ij} = 1 \mid \sum w_i C_i$.

$O \mid p_{ij} = 1 \mid \sum w_i C_i$

We first investigate how to solve the corresponding problem $P \mid p_i = m; pmtn \mid \sum w_i C_i$. In Section 5.1.1, we saw that preemptions are not advantageous when solving $P \mid pmtn \mid \sum w_i C_i$, i.e. an instance of $P \parallel \sum w_i C_i$ has the same optimal objective value as the corresponding instance of $P \mid pmtn \mid \sum w_i C_i$.

Thus, it is sufficient to solve $P \mid p_i = m \mid \sum w_i C_i$. This is accomplished by scheduling the jobs in order of nonincreasing w_i-values (see 5.1.1). If we assume that $n = lm + r$ with $r < m$, we get l blocks of jobs, each consisting of exactly m jobs, and a block $l+1$ consisting of the remaining r jobs. All jobs of block k $(k = 1, \ldots, l+1)$ are scheduled in the time interval $[(k-1)m, km]$. To construct a schedule for the corresponding $O \mid p_{ij} = 1 \mid \sum w_i C_i$-problem, we schedule each of the first l blocks as shown in Figure 6.5 and the last block as shown in Figure 6.4. Figure 6.6 shows the total schedule for the case $m = 3$ and $n = 11$.

Problem $O \mid p_{ij} = 1; d_i \mid$ - is to determine whether a feasible schedule exists for the open shop problem with unit processing times in which no jobs finish later than their deadlines.

In the next sections we will present algorithms for this problem and other problems involving due dates. We will assume that the jobs are enumerated in such a way that

$$d_1 \leq d_2 \leq \ldots \leq d_n. \tag{6.1}$$

$O \mid p_{ij} = 1; d_i \mid -$

If $d_1 < m$, then $C_1 > d_1$ in any schedule for $O \mid p_{ij} = 1; d_i \mid -$. Thus, we may assume that $m \leq d_i$ for all $i = 1, \ldots, n$.

Algorithm $O \mid p_{ij} = 1; d_i \mid -$ solves problem $O \mid p_{ij} = 1; d_i \mid -$ for

m machines. Later we will show that this algorithm has an $O(nm)$-implementation.

The idea of Algorithm $O \mid p_{ij} = 1; d_i \mid -$ is to assign the m unit operations of each job to the time slots $[t-1, t]$ for $t = 1, \ldots, T := \max\{d_i \mid i = 1, \ldots, n\}$. Job i is first assigned to time slots $d_i - m + 1, \ldots, d_i$. If some time slot $t > 1$ contains $m + 1$ operations, then an operation from the smallest time slot $t > 1$ with this property is moved one unit to the left and the process is repeated if necessary. Thus, only the first time slot may accumulate more than m operations and this happens if and only if the decision problem $O \mid p_{ij} = 1; d_i \mid -$ has a negative answer. We denote by $h(t)$ the number of operations accumulated in time slot $[t-1, t]$.

Algorithm O $\mid$ p$_{ij}$ = 1; d$_i$ $\mid$ −
1. $T := \max\{d_i \mid i = 1, \ldots, n\}$;
2. FOR $t := 1$ TO T DO $h(t) := 0$;
3. FOR $i := 1$ TO n DO
            BEGIN
4.   FOR $j := d_i$ DOWN TO $d_i - m + 1$ DO $h(j) := h(j) + 1$;
5.   WHILE there exists a $t > 1$ with $h(t) = m + 1$ DO
                  BEGIN
6.   Find a minimal $t_0 > 1$ with $h(t_0) = m + 1$;
7. $h(t_0 - 1) := h(t_0 - 1) + 1$;
8. $h(t_0) := m$
                  END
            END
9. IF $h(1) \leq m$ THEN there exists a schedule without late jobs

We call the vector h calculated by the algorithm the **frequency vector**. The frequency vector does not depend on the numeration of jobs.

It remains to show that Algorithm $O \mid p_{ij} = 1; d_i \mid -$ is correct.

Lemma 6.1 For a set of jobs with deadlines $d_1, \ldots, d_n$ problem $O \mid p_{ij} = 1; d_i \mid -$ has a feasible solution if and only if $h(1) \leq m$ holds.

Proof: If $h(1) > m$, the capacity of machines is not sufficient to perform all operations in time.

Algorithm $O \mid p_{ij} = 1; d_i \mid -$ initially assigns all operations of the same job to pairwise different time slots. If there is a $t > 1$ with $h(t) = m + 1$

and $h(t-1) \leq m$, then there must exist at least one job which is assigned to time t but not to time $t-1$. Thus, after shifting one operation the vector h still corresponds to an assignment of each job to m different time slots. If $h(1) \leq m$, then vector h satisfies $h(t) \leq m$ for all $t = 1, \ldots, T$, i.e. it corresponds to a feasible schedule for the corresponding problem on parallel machines. Using the coloring algorithm in Section 2.6, we can construct a feasible solution for $O \mid p_{ij} = 1; d_i \mid -$.   □

Remark 6.2 If there exists a schedule without late jobs, such a schedule can be constructed using Algorithm $O \mid p_{ij} = 1; d_i \mid -$ by replacing Step 4 by

4'. FOR $j := d_i$ DOWN TO $d_i - m + 1$ DO
        BEGIN $h(j) := h(j) + 1$; Schedule job i in $[j - 1, j]$ END

and adding

8a. Move a job not scheduled in time slot $t_0 - 1$ but in time slot t_0
    to time slot $t_0 - 1$

after Step 8.

Next we will show that $O \mid p_{ij} = 1; d_i \mid -$ can be solved in $O(nm)$ steps.

First, we consider the following question. Let U be a set of jobs with the property that a schedule exists for U without late jobs. Furthermore, let i be a job not belonging to U with $d_j \leq d_i$ for all $j \in U$. Is it possible to schedule all jobs in $V := U \cup \{i\}$ such that no job in V is late?

Before answering this question, we introduce some further notations. The h-vectors corresponding to U and V are denoted by h^U and h^V, respectively. Furthermore, let $x(d_i)$ be the number of time periods t with $d_i - m + 1 \leq t \leq d_i$ and $h^U(t) < m$. Finally, we state that a set of jobs can be scheduled **early** if a schedule exists for this set with no late jobs.

Theorem 6.3 Let U be a set of jobs which can be scheduled early and let i be a job not belonging to U with $d_j \leq d_i$ for all $j \in U$. Then the set of jobs $V = U \cup \{i\}$ can be scheduled early if and only if

$$x(d_i) + \sum_{t=1}^{d_i - m} (m - h^U(t)) \geq m. \qquad (6.2)$$

For the proof of this theorem we need

Lemma 6.4 Consider jobs $1, 2, \ldots, i$ with $d_1 \leq d_2 \leq \ldots \leq d_i$ and let $U := \{1, \ldots, i-1\}$, $V := U \cup \{i\}$. Then for all $j = d_i - m + 1, \ldots, d_i$ with $h^U(j) < m$ we have $h^V(j) = h^U(j) + 1$.

Proof: We get vectors h^U and h^V after $i-1$ and i iterations of Algorithm $O \mid p_{ij} = 1; d_i \mid -$. During the algorithm, components of the h-vector with $h(j) \leq m$ never decrease.

Thus, if $d_i - m + 1 \leq j \leq d_i$ and $h^U(j) < m$, then $h^V(j) \geq h^U(j) + 1$. To prove that $h^V(j) \geq h^U(j) + 2$ is not possible for $d_i - m + 1 \leq j \leq d_i$, we consider the schedule which can be constructed by Algorithm $O \mid p_{ij} = 1; d_i \mid -$ (see Remark 6.2).

If $h^V(j) \geq h^U(j) + 2$, then during the i-th iteration an operation of job i is added to time slot j and at least one operation of some other job, say k, is moved from time slot $j+1$ to time slot j. This is only possible if no operation of job k is scheduled before time slot j (no operation is moved from j to $j-1$ as long as $h(j) < m$). Thus, job k is scheduled in time slot j and time slots $\nu > j+1$ which implies $j < d_k - m + 1 \leq d_i - m + 1$, i.e. a contradiction. $\square$

Proof of Theorem 6.3: Condition (6.2) is equivalent to

$$(d_i - m)m \geq \sum_{i=1}^{d_i - m} h^U(t) + m - x(d_i). \tag{6.3}$$

Due to Lemma 6.4 we have

$$\sum_{j=d_i-m+1}^{d_i} h^V(j) = \sum_{j=d_i-m+1}^{d_i} h^U(j) + x(d_i).$$

Subtracting this equation from

$$\sum_{j=1}^{d_i} h^V(j) = \sum_{j=1}^{d_i} h^U(j) + m$$

we get

$$\sum_{t=1}^{d_i - m} h^V(t) = m - x(d_i) + \sum_{t=1}^{d_i - m} h^U(t).$$

Thus, (6.2) or (6.3) is equivalent to

$$Tm \geq \sum_{t=1}^{T} h^V(t) \tag{6.4}$$

with $T := d_i - m$.

It remains to show that if (6.4) holds for $T = d_i - m$, then (6.4) also holds for $T = 1, \ldots, d_i - m - 1$. By Lemma 6.1 $h^V(1) \leq m$ implies that all jobs in V can be scheduled early. If, on the other hand, $h^V(1) \leq m$, then (6.4) holds because $h^V(t) \leq m$ for all $t \geq 2$ by construction of h^V.

We prove that (6.4) holds for all $T = 1, \ldots, d_i - m$ by induction on T.

Assume that (6.4) holds for some T with $1 < T \leq d_i - m$. We consider two cases depending on the value $h^V(T)$.

Case 1: $h^V(T) = m$

Because (6.4) holds for T we have

$$(T - 1)m \geq \sum_{t=1}^{T} h^V(t) - m = \sum_{t=1}^{T-1} h^V(t),$$

i.e. (6.4) holds for $T - 1$.

Case 2: $h^V(T) < m$

In the V-schedule all operations of job i must have been assigned to $[T - 1, d_i]$ because $T \leq d_i - m$ and there is an idle machine during $[T - 1, T]$. By the same reasoning, all operations in the U-schedule assigned to $[T - 1, d_i]$ are also assigned to $[T - 1, d_i]$ by the V-schedule.

Thus, we have

$$(T - 1)m \geq \sum_{t=1}^{T-1} h^U(t) = \sum_{t=1}^{T-1} h^V(t),$$

i.e. (6.4) holds for $T - 1$. Note that the last inequality holds, since a feasible schedule exists for the jobs of U. $\square$

Let k be the cardinality of the set U. Then we have

$$\sum_{j=1}^{d_i - m} (m - h^U(j)) = m(d_i - m) - \sum_{j=1}^{d_i - m} h^U(j)$$

$$= m(d_i - m) - (km - \sum_{j=d_i - m + 1}^{d_i} h^U(j))$$

and (6.2) becomes

$$m(d_i - m) - (km - \sum_{j=1}^{m} h^U(d_i - m + j)) + x(d_i) \geq m. \qquad (6.5)$$

We conclude that we only need to know the values $h^U(d_i - m + 1)$, $\ldots, h^U(d_i)$ and the cardinality k of the set U to check whether (6.5) holds, i.e. whether $V = U \cup \{i\}$ can be scheduled early. Furthermore, (6.5) can be checked in $O(m)$ time.

To solve problem $O \mid p_{ij} = 1; d_i \mid -$ for jobs $i = 1, \ldots, n$ with $d_1 \leq d_2 \leq \ldots \leq d_n$ for each $i = 1, \ldots, n$ we check whether the job set $U_i = \{1, \ldots, i\}$ can be scheduled early if U_{i-1} can be scheduled early. This is done in $O(m)$ time by checking (6.5). Furthermore, due to Lemma 6.4, the values $h^{U_i}(d_i - m + 1), \ldots, h^{U_i}(d_i)$ can be updated in $O(m)$ time. Therefore, Algorithm $O \mid p_{ij} = 1; d_i \mid -$ can be implemented such that the running time is $O(nm)$ if the jobs are ordered according to nondecreasing due dates.

The $O(nm)$-algorithm for solving $O \mid p_{ij} = 1; d_i \mid -$ may be used to calculate the optimal objective value of $O \mid p_{ij} = 1 \mid \sum U_i$ in $O(mn \log n)$ time. This will be discussed in the next section.

$O \mid p_{ij} = 1 \mid \sum U_i$

We will first solve the parallel machine problem corresponding to $O \mid p_{ij} = 1 \mid \sum U_i$. An optimal schedule of this problem consists of a schedule for the set E of early jobs followed by the set $L := \{1, \ldots, n\} \backslash E$ of tardy jobs scheduled arbitrarily.

Again we assume that (6.1) holds. An easy exchange argument shows that a maximal set E^* of early jobs has the form $E^* = \{k^*, k^*+1, \ldots, n\}$. We can calculate k^* by binary search using the $O(nm)$-algorithm which solves $O \mid p_{ij} = 1 \mid d_i \mid -$ as a subroutine. This provides an $O(mn \log n)$-algorithm for solving the parallel machine problem.

To construct a schedule in which all jobs in E^* are early, we may apply an $O(nm \log^2(nm))$-algorithm to be discussed later in this section, which solves problem $O \mid p_{ij} = 1 \mid \sum T_i$.

Finally, we would like to mention that Tautenhahn [195] has developed an $O(nm + n \log n)$-algorithm for solving problem $O \mid p_{ij} = 1; r_i \mid \sum U_i$.

$O \mid p_{ij} = 1 \mid \sum w_i U_i$

To solve this problem we have to find a set U^* of jobs which can be scheduled early such that $\sum_{i \notin U^*} w_i$, i.e. the sum of the weights of jobs not scheduled in U^* is minimized. We solve this problem by dynamic programming using the results developed in connection with problem $O \mid p_{ij} = 1; d_i \mid -$.

Again, assume that $d_1 \leq d_2 \leq \ldots \leq d_n$. For each job i we have to decide whether it should be scheduled early or late. Assume that we have already made this decision for jobs $1, 2, \ldots, i - 1$, i.e. we have a subset $U \subseteq \{1, \ldots, i - 1\}$ of jobs which can be scheduled early. Let h^U be the frequency vector for U. To decide whether $U \cup \{i\}$ can be scheduled early we have to check condition (6.5):

$$m(d_i - m) - (km - \sum_{j=1}^{m} h^U(d_i - m + j)) + x(d_i) \geq m$$

where k is the cardinality of U and $x(d_i)$ denotes the number of time periods $d_i - m + 1 \leq t \leq d_i$ with $h^U(t) < m$. $U \cup \{i\}$ can be scheduled early iff (6.5) holds. To check this, we only need m components $h^U(t), t = d_i - m + 1, \ldots, d_i$. Therefore, we introduce the variables

$$k_j := \begin{cases} h^U(d_i - m + j) & \text{if } j \in \{1, \ldots, m\} \\ 0 & \text{otherwise.} \end{cases}$$

Furthermore, it is convenient to define additional variables.

$$l_j := \begin{cases} 1 & \text{if } j \in \{1, \ldots, m\} \text{ and } k_j < m \\ 0 & \text{otherwise.} \end{cases}$$

Note that $x(d_i) = \sum_{j=1}^{m} l_j$. Therefore, (6.5) implies

$$m(d_i - m) - (km - \sum_{j=1}^{m} k_j) + \sum_{j=1}^{m} l_j \geq m$$

or

$$m(d_i - m - k) + \sum_{j=1}^{m} (k_j + l_j) \geq m. \tag{6.6}$$

For the dynamic programming approach, we define $f_i(k, k_1, \ldots, k_m)$ to be the minimum cost of scheduling jobs $i, i + 1, \ldots, n$ given that a set U of k jobs in $\{1, \ldots, i-1\}$ is scheduled early, and $k_j = h^U(d_i - m + j)(j =$

$1, \ldots, m$). Moreover, let $p := d_{i+1} - d_i$. Then we have the following recurrence relations:

$$f_i(k, k_1, \ldots, k_m) = \begin{cases} f_{i+1}(k, k_{1+p}, k_{2+p}, \ldots, k_{m+p}) + w_i \qquad (6.7) \\ \qquad \text{if } m(d_i - m - k) + \sum_{j=1}^{m}(k_j + l_j) < m \\ \\ \min\{f_{i+1}(k, k_{1+p}, k_{2+p}, \ldots, k_{m+p}) + w_i, \\ \qquad f_{i+1}(k + 1, k_{1+p} + l_{1+p}, k_{2+p} + l_{2+p}, \ldots \qquad (6.8) \\ \qquad \ldots, k_{m+p} + l_{m+p})\} \text{ otherwise.} \end{cases}$$

The boundary conditions are

$$f_{n+1}(k, k_1, \ldots, k_m) = 0 \qquad (k, k_1, \ldots, k_m = 0, 1, \ldots, m).$$

(6.7) describes the case in which job i cannot be scheduled early due to inequality (6.5). Thus, the objective value increases by w_i. The frequency vector does not change but the indices of the variables k_j have to be increased by p because, when considering job $i + 1$, the new variables must reflect the frequency vector at positions $t = d_{i+1} - m + 1, \ldots, d_{i+1}$.

In the second case (see (6.8)), job i may be scheduled early or late. If job i is scheduled early, then there is no increase in the objective function, but the frequency vector changes. This is reflected by increasing each variable k_j by $l_j (j = 1, \ldots, m)$. Moreover, analogously to the first case, the indices of the variables k_j have to be increased by p. If job i is scheduled late, we get the same formula as in the first case (namely formula (6.7)).

Note that the values $f_i(k, k_1, \ldots, k_m)$ can only be calculated if all values $f_{i+1}(k, k_1, \ldots, k_m)$ are already known. Therefore, the recurrence relations are first evaluated for $i = n$, then for $i = n - 1$, etc. The cost of the optimal schedule is $f_1(0, 0, \ldots, 0)$.

To calculate the time complexity of this dynamic program, note that the range of i and k is $0, \ldots, n$ and the range of k_j is $0, \ldots, m$ for each $j = 1, \ldots, m$. Each $f_i(k, k_1, \ldots, k_m)$-value may be calculated in $O(m)$ time. Thus, the complexity of the algorithm is $O(n^2 m^{m+1})$, which is $O(n^2)$ for a fixed number of machines. The final calculation of a feasible schedule for the early jobs can be done in $O(mn \log^2(mn))$ time using an algorithm to be derived in the next section for solving problem $O \mid p_{ij} = 1 \mid \sum T_i$.

$O \mid p_{ij} = 1 \mid \sum T_i$

Again, we consider the corresponding parallel machine problem. This means that we have to schedule n jobs, each consisting of m unit time operations, in such a way that $\sum_{i=1}^{n} \max\{0, C_i - d_i\}$ is minimized, where C_i is the finishing time of the last operation of job $i (i = 1, \ldots, n)$. Recall that the operations have to be scheduled in such a way that no two operations of the same job are processed in the same time slot and that at the most m jobs are scheduled in each time slot.

As before, we assume that $d_1 \leq d_2 \leq \ldots \leq d_n$. Then the following lemma holds.

Lemma 6.5 An optimal schedule always exists with $C_1 \leq C_2 \leq \ldots \leq C_n$.

Proof: By a simple exchange argument. $\square$

Next we consider only optimal schedules with $C_1 \leq C_2 \leq \ldots \leq C_n$. Then we have:

Theorem 6.6 An optimal schedule always exists with $C_i \leq m + i - 1$ for $i = 1, \ldots, n$.

Proof: Consider an optimal schedule B with $C_i \leq m + i - 1$ for $i = 1, \ldots, k - 1$ and $C_k > m + k - 1$ where k is maximal.

k is at least two, because if we have an optimal schedule with $C_1 > m$ and job 1 is scheduled in period t but not in period $t - 1$, then there exists a (possibly empty) operation scheduled in period $t - 1$ and not scheduled in period t. We exchange this operation with the operation of job 1 scheduled in period t. The C_i-values do not increase because C_1 is the smallest C_i-value. If we continue this process, we get an optimal schedule with $C_1 = m$.

Now let $C_k = m + k + t$, $t \geq 0$. Let W be the set of all operations of jobs $i = 1, 2, \ldots, k - 1$, let X be the set of all operations scheduled after time $k + m + t$ in schedule B, and let Y be the set of operations of jobs $i = k + 1, \ldots, n$ which were scheduled by time $k + m + t$ in schedule B. These sets are mutually exclusive and, with job k, are collectively exhaustive.

We construct a new schedule B' by first scheduling all operations in $W \cup X$ as in schedule B. Because $C_i \leq m + i - 1$ for $i = 1, \ldots, k - 1$ and no operations in X are scheduled before time $k + m + t$, there are m different idle periods between time 1 and time $k + m - 1$ in which we schedule job k. Thus $C_k \leq m + k - 1$. We then assign machines to the operations scheduled before time $k + m + t$ such that there are $k + m + t - k = m + t$ empty time cells between time 1 and time $k + m + t$ on each machine. Because $|Y| \leq (k + m + t)m - km = (m + t)m$, it is also possible to schedule the operations belonging to Y before $m + k + t$, and to transform this schedule into a schedule of the open shop problem which again is optimal, because the jobs j with operations of Y had a finishing time $C_j \geq C_k = m + k + t$. However, this contradicts the maximality of k. $\qquad\square$

The idea of the algorithm is to schedule the jobs in order of nondecreasing due dates. To schedule the current job i, we first calculate a time limit T_i. The processing periods of i are m time periods $1 \leq t_1 < t_2 < \ldots < t_m \leq T_i$ with the smallest frequency values $h(t)$. Details are given by the following algorithm.

Algorithm $O \mid p_{ij} = 1 \mid \sum T_i$
1. FOR $t := 1$ TO $m + n - 1$ DO $h(t) := 0$;
2. FOR $i := 1$ TO n DO
   BEGIN
3.   IF $d_i < m + i - 1$ THEN
       BEGIN
4.   Calculate the number z of time slots $t = 1, \ldots, d_i$ with $h(t) < m$;
5.   IF $z \geq m$ THEN $T_i := d_i$
6.   ELSE $T_i := d_i + m - z$
       END
7.   ELSE $T_i := m + i - 1$;
8.   Calculate time periods $1 \leq t_1 < t_2 < \ldots < t_m \leq T_i$ with the m smallest $h(t)$-values;
9.   FOR $j := 1$ TO m DO
       BEGIN
10.   Schedule job i in period $[t_j - 1, t_j]$;
11. $h(t_j) := h(t_j) + 1$
       END
   END

The algorithm can be implemented in such a way that its running time is $O(nm)$. To get an algorithm with this complexity, we schedule the jobs such that after each step i the following invariance property holds: $l_1 \geq l_2 \geq \ldots \geq l_m$ exists with $l_1 \leq T_i$ such that on machine M_j ($j = 1, \ldots, m$) all time slots $1, \ldots, l_j$ are occupied.

Clearly, the invariance property is initially satisfied with $l_1 = l_2 = \ldots = l_m = 0$. Assume that the invariance property holds after step $i - 1$. Then we have $T_{i-1} \leq T_i$ and schedule job i by filling time slots in the following order

$$l_1 + 1, \ldots, T_i \text{ on } M_1,$$
$$l_2 + 1, \ldots, l_1 \text{ on } M_2,$$
$$\vdots$$
$$l_m + 1, \ldots, l_{m-1} \text{ on } M_m.$$

We still have to prove the correctness of the algorithm.

Theorem 6.7 Algorithm $O \mid p_{ij} = 1 \mid \sum T_i$ calculates an optimal schedule for the parallel machine problem corresponding with problem $O \mid p_{ij} = 1 \mid \sum T_i$.

Proof: We use interchange arguments to prove this theorem. According to Lemma 6.5 and Theorem 6.6, an optimal schedule exists with $C_1 \leq C_2 \leq \ldots \leq C_n$ and

$$C_i \leq m + i - 1 \text{ for } i = 1, \ldots, n. \tag{6.9}$$

Let B be an optimal schedule satisfying (6.9) with the property that jobs $1, \ldots, k - 1$ are scheduled in the same time slots as in the schedule A constructed by Algorithm $O \mid p_{ij} = 1 \mid \sum T_i$. Furthermore, assume that B is chosen such that k is maximal.

Assume that $C_k > T_k$. Since job k is scheduled before T_k in A, a time slot $t \leq T_k$ exists in which job k is not processed in B. Thus, in B this time slot is either empty or it is occupied by a job $r > k$. If this time slot is empty, we move the operation of k scheduled in time slot C_k to this time slot. If job r is scheduled at time t but not at time C_k, then we switch the operations of jobs k and r. If job r is scheduled at times t and C_k, then either there is an empty slot at $C_r + 1$ or there must be a job, say v, which is scheduled at time $C_r + 1$ but not scheduled at time C_k. This must be possible since r and k are scheduled at time C_k but not at time $C_r + 1$.

If there is an empty slot at $C_r + 1$, move job r from time t to $C_r + 1$ and job k from time C_k to t. If there is no empty slot at $C_r + 1$, we can move r from t to $C_r + 1$, k from C_k to t, and v from $C_r + 1$ to C_k. Since C_k must improve by at least one unit and C_r increases by at the most one unit the new schedule is as good as the old one.

If we continue this process, we get an optimal schedule B' with $C_k \leq T_k$ in which jobs $1, \ldots, k - 1$ are scheduled as in A.

Now let h be the frequency vector for the partial schedule for jobs $1, \ldots, k - 1$. Assume that $h(t') < h(t)$ and job k is scheduled in time slot t but not in time slot t' in B'. If in B' a machine is idle at time t', we can move job k from time slot t to time slot t'. Otherwise a job $r > k$ is scheduled in time slot t' but not in time slot t. We can move r to t and k to t' without increasing $\sum T_i$ because $C_k \leq C_r$. Continuing in this way, we reach an optimal schedule in which jobs $1, \ldots, k$ are scheduled as in A. This is a contradiction to the maximality of k.   □

Again, the coloring algorithm of Gabow & Kariv [GK82] can be used to provide an optimal solution for the open shop problem. This shows that problem $O \mid p_{ij} = 1 \mid \sum U_i$ can be solved in $O(nm \log^2(nm))$ time.

6.3   Flow Shop Problems

The **flow shop problem** is a general shop problem in which

- each job i consists of m operations O_{ij} with processing times p_{ij} $(j = 1, \ldots, m)$ where O_{ij} must be processed on machine M_j, and

- there are precedence constraints of the form $O_{ij} \to O_{i,j+1}$ $(i = 1, \ldots, m - 1)$ for each $i = 1, \ldots, n$, i.e. each job is first processed on machine 1, then on machine 2, then on machine 3, etc.

Thus, the problem is to find a job order π_j for each machine j. We will restrict our discussion to flow shop problems with $C_{\max}$-objective function. All other problems turn out to be $\mathcal{NP}$-hard if we admit arbitrary processing times.

6.3.1   Minimizing Makespan

Problem $F2 \parallel C_{\max}$ is the only flow shop problem with $C_{\max}$-criterion which is polynomially solvable if the processing times are arbitrary. A corresponding algorithm has been developed by Johnson [120].

To find an optimal solution for problem $F2 \parallel C_{max}$ we may restrict our attention to schedules in which the job sequence on both machines is the same. This is an immediate consequence of the following lemma.

Lemma 6.8 For problem $Fm \parallel C_{max}$ an optimal schedule exists with the following properties:

(i) The job sequence on the first two machines is the same.

(ii) The job sequence on the last two machines is the same.

Proof: The proof of (i) is similar to the proof of Theorem 3.5. The proof of (ii) is symmetric to the proof of (i).   □

A flow shop is called a **permutation flow shop** if solutions are restricted to job sequences $\pi_1, \ldots, \pi_m$ with $\pi_1 = \pi_2 = \ldots = \pi_m$. Lemma 6.8 shows that for two or three machines the optimal solution of the flow shop problem is not better than that of the corresponding permutation flow shop. This is not the case if there are more than three machines.

Next we will present Johnson's algorithm for solving the two-machine flow shop problem. We have to find a permutation

$$L : L(1), \ldots, L(n)$$

of all jobs such that if all jobs are scheduled in this order on both machines, then the makespan is minimized.

An optimal order is constructed by calculating a left list $T : L(1), \ldots, L(t)$ and a right list $R : L(t+1), \ldots, L(n)$, and then concatenating them to obtain $L = T \circ R := L(1), \ldots, L(n)$. The lists T and R are constructed step by step.

At each step we consider an operation $O_{i^*j^*}$ with the smallest $p_{i^*j^*}$-value. If $j^* = 1$, then we put job i^* at the end of list T, i.e. we replace T by $T \circ i^*$. Otherwise we put i^* at the beginning of list R, i.e. we replace R by $i^* \circ R$. Job i^* and processing times p_{i^*1} and p_{i^*2} are then deleted from consideration.

Algorithm F2 $\parallel$ C$_{max}$
1. $X := \{1, \ldots, n\}; T := \phi; R := \phi;$
2. While $X \neq \phi$ DO

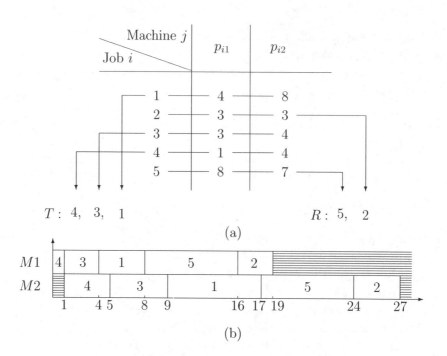

Figure 6.7: Application of Algorithm $F2 \parallel C_{\max}$

        BEGIN
3.   Find i^*, j^* with $p_{i^* j^*} = \min\{p_{ij} \mid i \in X; j = 1, 2\}$;
4.   If $j^* = 1$ THEN $T := T \circ i^*$ ELSE $R := i^* \circ R$;
5. $X := X \backslash \{i^*\}$
        END;
6. $L := T \circ R$

The example in Figure 6.7 shows how Algorithm $F2 \parallel C_{\max}$ works. The schedule constructed in Figure 6.7(a) is shown in Figure 6.7(b). To prove that Algorithm $F2 \parallel C_{\max}$ is correct we need the following two lemmas.

Lemma 6.9 Let $L := L(1), \ldots, L(n)$ be a list constructed by Algorithm $F2 \parallel C_{\max}$. Then

$$\min\{p_{i1}, p_{j2}\} < \min\{p_{j1}, p_{i2}\}$$

implies that job i appears before job j in L.

Proof: If $p_{i1} < \min\{p_{j1}, p_{i2}\}$, then $p_{i1} < p_{i2}$ implies that job i belongs

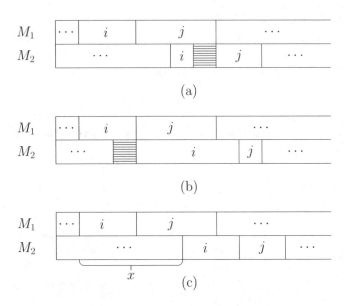

Figure 6.8: Three possible cases if j is scheduled immediately after i.

to T. If j is added to R, we have finished. Otherwise j appears after i in T because $p_{i1} < p_{j_1}$. If $p_{j2} < \min\{p_{j1}, p_{i2}\}$, we argue in a similar way. $\square$

Lemma 6.10 Consider a schedule in which job j is scheduled immediately after job i. Then

$$\min\{p_{j1}, p_{i2}\} \leq \min\{p_{i1}, p_{j2}\} \tag{6.10}$$

implies that i and j can be swapped without increasing the $C_{\max}$-value.

Proof: If j is scheduled immediately after i, then we have three possible cases which are shown in Figure 6.8. Denote by w_{ij} the length of the time period from the start of job i to the finishing time of job j in this situation. We have

$$w_{ij} = \max\{p_{i1} + p_{j1} + p_{j2}, p_{i1} + p_{i2} + p_{j2}, x + p_{i2} + p_{j2}\}$$
$$= \max\{p_{i1} + p_{j2} + \max\{p_{j1}, p_{i2}\}, x + p_{i2} + p_{j2}\}$$

Similarly, we have

$$w_{ji} = \max\{p_{j1} + p_{i2} + \max\{p_{i1}, p_{j2}\}, x + p_{i2} + p_{j2}\}$$

if i is scheduled immediately after j.

Now (6.10) implies

$$\max\{-p_{i1}, -p_{j2}\} \leq \max\{-p_{j1}, -p_{i2}\}.$$

Adding $p_{i1} + p_{i2} + p_{j1} + p_{j2}$ to both sides of this inequality, we get

$$p_{j1} + p_{i2} + \max\{p_{i1}, p_{j2}\} \leq p_{i1} + p_{j2} + \max\{p_{j1}, p_{i2}\},$$

which implies $w_{ji} \leq w_{ij}$.

Thus, swapping i and j will not increase the $C_{\max}$-value.   □

Now it is not difficult to prove the correctness of Algorithm $F2 \parallel C_{\max}$.

Theorem 6.11 The sequence $L : L(1), \ldots, L(n)$ constructed by Algorithm $F2 \parallel C_{\max}$ is optimal.

Proof: Let $\mathcal{L}$ be the set of all optimal sequences and assume that $L \notin \mathcal{L}$. Then we consider a sequence $R \in \mathcal{L}$ with

$$L(\nu) = R(\nu) \text{ for } \nu = 1, \ldots, s-1 \text{ and } i := L(s) \neq R(s) =: j$$

where s is maximal. Then job i is a (not necessarily immediate) successor of j in R. Let k be a job scheduled between job j and job i or $k = j$ in R. In L, job k is scheduled after job i. Thus, by Lemma 6.9 we must have

$$\min\{p_{k1}, p_{i2}\} \geq \min\{p_{i1}, p_{k2}\} \qquad (6.11)$$

(otherwise job i would follow job k in L).

(6.11) holds for each such job k. Applying Lemma (6.10) to R, we may swap each immediate predecessor k of job i with i without increasing the objective value. We finally get a sequence $\overline{R} \in \mathcal{L}$ with $\overline{R}(\nu) = L(\nu)$ for $\nu = 1, \ldots, s$ which contradicts the maximality of s.   □

6.4   Job Shop Problems

The **job shop problem** is a special case of the general shop problem which generalizes the flow shop problem. We are given n jobs $i = 1, \ldots, n$ and m machines $M_1, \ldots, M_m$. Job i consists of a sequence of n_i operations

$$O_{i1}, O_{i2}, \ldots, O_{in_i}$$

which must be processed in this order, i.e. we have precedence constraints of the form $O_{ij} \to O_{i,j+1}$ $(j = 1, \ldots, n_i - 1)$. There is a machine $\mu_{ij} \in \{M_1, \ldots, M_m\}$ and a processing time p_{ij} associated with each operation O_{ij}. O_{ij} must be processed for p_{ij} time units on machine μ_{ij}. The problem is to find a feasible schedule which minimizes some objective function depending on the finishing times C_i of the last operations O_{i,n_i} of the jobs. If not stated differently we assume that $\mu_{ij} \neq \mu_{i,j+1}$ for $j = 1, \ldots, n_i - 1$.

In Sections 6.4.1 and 6.4.2 we will discuss job shop problems which are polynomially solvable. In Section 6.4.3, a branch-and-bound method for the general problem $J \parallel C_{\max}$ will be developed. This method solves the famous 10x10 problem given in Muth & Thompson [174] in less than 15 minutes. Section 6.4.4 is devoted to heuristics based on iterative improvement.

6.4.1 Problems with Two Machines

There are only a few special job shop problems which can be solved polynomially or pseudopolynomially.

$J2 \mid n_i \leq 2 \mid C_{\max}$

This two-machine job shop problem with at the most two operations per job can be solved by a reduction to the two-machine flow shop problem. To describe this reduction, it is convenient to divide the set of jobs into the following subsets:

I_1 jobs which are processed only on machine 1

I_2 jobs which are processed only on machine 2

$I_{1,2}$ jobs which are processed first on machine 1 and then on machine 2

$I_{2,1}$ jobs which are processed first on machine 2 and then on machine 1

Note that jobs in I_1 and I_2 consist of only one operation.

To construct an optimal solution for problem $J2 \mid n_i \leq 2 \mid C_{\max}$ we have to apply the following steps.

1. Calculate an optimal sequence $R_{1,2}$ for the flow shop problem with job set $I_{1,2}$.

2. Calculate an optimal sequence $R_{2,1}$ for the flow shop problem with job set $I_{2,1}$.

3. On machine 1 first schedule $I_{1,2}$ according to $R_{1,2}$, then all jobs in I_1 in an arbitrary order, and, finally, $I_{2,1}$ according to $R_{2,1}$.

4. On machine 2 first schedule $I_{2,1}$ according to $R_{2,1}$, then all jobs in I_2 in an arbitrary order, and, finally, $I_{1,2}$ according to $R_{1,2}$.

We may assume that the schedule constructed in this way is active. Then at least one machine processes the jobs without idle time. More specifically, if

$$\sum_{i \in I_{2,1}} p_{i2} \leq \sum_{i \in I_{1,2}} p_{i1} + \sum_{i \in I_1} p_{i1}$$

then there is no idle time on machine 1. Otherwise there is no idle time on machine 2.

To prove that the schedule is optimal we assume w.l.o.g. that there is no idle time on machine 1. If there is also no idle time on machine 2 or if

$$\max_{i=1}^{n} C_i = \sum_{i \in I_{1,2} \cup I_1 \cup I_{2,1}} p_{i1},$$

then we have finished. Otherwise the solution value is equal to that of the problem restricted to $I_{1,2}$, which is also optimal.

A related problem is

$J2 \mid p_{ij} = 1 \mid L_{\max}$

Given are n jobs $i = 1, \ldots, n$ and two machines denoted by A and B. Job i has n_i unit time operations O_{ij}, $j = 1, \ldots, n_i$. If operation O_{ij} is processed on machine A (B), then operation $O_{i,j+1}$ must be processed on machine B (A) $(j = 1, \ldots, n_i - 1)$. Thus, job i may be characterized by the number n_i of operations and the machine on which the first operation must be processed. Let $r = \sum_{i=1}^{n} n_i$ be the total number of operations.

Again, assume that zero time is the earliest time an operation can be started. Furthermore, let $t_{\max}$ be an upper bound for the latest starting time of any operation. For example, we may choose $t_{\max} = r$. Then a schedule may be defined by two arrays $A(t)$ and $B(t)$ $(t = 0, \ldots, t_{\max})$ where $A(t) = O_{ij}$ if operation O_{ij} is to be processed on machine A at time t and $A(t) = \phi$ if machine A is idle during the time period from t to $t+1$. We call ϕ an empty operation. For each operation O_{ij} to be processed on machine A, there exists a time t with $A(t) = O_{ij}$. $B(t)$ is defined similarly. A schedule is feasible if and only if $A(t) = O_{ij}$ $(B(t) = O_{ij})$ with $1 < j \leq n_i$ implies that $O_{i,j-1} = B(s)$ $(O_{i,j-1} = A(s))$ for some $s < t$, and the first operation of each job is scheduled on the right machine. A permutation of all operations is called a list. Given a list L, a feasible schedule can be constructed in the following way. Schedule the operations in the order given by L, where each operation is scheduled as early as possible. Such a schedule is called a list schedule corresponding to L.

The finishing time C_i of job i in a feasible schedule $y = (A(t), B(t))$ is given by

$$C_i := \max\{t + 1 \mid A(t) \text{ or } B(t) \text{ is an operation of job } i\}.$$

Given a due date $d_i \geq 0$ associated with each job i, the problem we consider in this section is to find a feasible schedule such that the maximum lateness

$$\max\{C_i - d_i \mid i = 1, \ldots, n\}$$

is minimized.

The following algorithm solves this problem.

Algorithm 1 J2 | $p_{ij} = 1$ | L_{max}

1. Associate with each operation O_{ij} the label $l(O_{ij}) = d_i - n_i + j$;

2. Construct a list L of all operations ordered according to nondecreasing $l(O_{ij})$-values;

3. Find a list schedule corresponding to L.

This algorithm can be implemented in $O(r \log r)$ time. However, we will use hash techniques (compare Section 4.2, $1 \mid prec; p_j = 1 \mid L_{max}$) to derive an $O(r)$-implementation of this algorithm.

As in Section 4.2, we may assume that $d_i \geq 0$ for $i = 1, \ldots, n$ and $d_i = 0$ for at least one job i. Otherwise, replace d_i by $d_i' = d_i - d$ where $d = \min\{d_i \mid i = 1, \ldots, n\}$.

Because $C_i \geq 1$ for all $i = 1, \ldots, n$ and $d_i = 0$ for at least one i, we have $L_i = C_i - d_i \geq 1$ for at least one i. Furthermore, we may assume that $C_i \leq r$. Thus, jobs with $d_i > r - 1$, i.e. with $L_i = C_i - d_i < 1$ may be ignored. They do not contribute to the objective function $\max L_i$ because $L_i \geq 1$ for some i. We may schedule these jobs after all others in an arbitrary order. For the operations O_{ij} of the remaining jobs we have

$$-r + 1 \leq l(O_{ij}) = d_i - n_i + j \leq r - 1.$$

We put each of these operations in a corresponding bucket $L(k)$ where $k = l(O_{ij}) = d_i - n_i + j$ $(-r + 1 \leq k \leq r - 1)$. In a second step, we schedule the operations according to increasing bucket numbers k where operations from the same bucket may be scheduled in an arbitrary order.

Details are given by the following algorithm. In this algorithm $T1$ and $T2$ denote the first period $t \geq 0$ where machines A and B, respectively, are idle. LAST (i) denotes the finishing time of the last scheduled operation of job i. Z denotes the set of jobs i with $d_i \geq r$.

Algorithm 2 J2 | $p_{ij} = 1$ | L_{max}
1. FOR $k := -r + 1$ TO $r - 1$ DO $L(k) := \phi$; $Z := \phi$;
2. FOR $i := 1$ TO n DO
3.   IF $d_i < r$ THEN
4.   FOR $j := 1$ TO n_i DO add O_{ij} to $L(d_i - n_i + j)$
      ELSE
5.   add job i to Z;
6. FOR $i := 1$ TO n DO LAST $(i) := 0$;
7. $T1 := 0$; $T2 := 0$;
8. FOR $k := -r + 1$ TO $r - 1$ DO
9.   WHILE $L(k) \neq \phi$ DO
      BEGIN
10.   Choose a task O_{ij} from $L(k)$;
11. $L(k) := L(k) \backslash \{O_{ij}\}$;
12.   Schedule O_{ij}
     END
13. WHILE $Z \neq \phi$ DO
     BEGIN
14.   Choose job i from Z;
15. $Z := Z \backslash \{i\}$;
16.   FOR $j := 1$ TO n_i Schedule O_{ij}
     END

The module Schedule O_{ij} schedules operation O_{ij}. It may be formulated as follows.

Scheduled O$_{ij}$
1. IF $\mu_{ij} = A$ THEN DO
2.   IF $T1 <$ LAST (i) THEN
       BEGIN
3. $t :=$ LAST (i);
4. $A(t) := O_{ij}$
       END
     ELSE
       BEGIN
5. $t := T1$;
6. $A(t) := O_{ij}$;
7.   WHILE $A(T_1) \neq \phi$ DO $T1 := T1 + 1$
       END
   ELSE $\{\mu_{ij} = B\}$
8.   IF $T2 <$ LAST (i) THEN
       BEGIN
9. $t :=$ LAST (i);
10. $B(t) := O_{ij}$
       END
     ELSE
       BEGIN
11. $t := T2$;
12. $B(t) := O_{ij}$;
13.   WHILE $B(T_2) \neq \phi$ DO $T2 := T2 + 1$
       END;
14.   LAST $(i) := t + 1$

Clearly, the number of steps of Algorithm 2 $J2 \mid p_{ij} = 1 \mid L_{\max}$ is bounded by $O(r)$.

To prove that Algorithm 2 $J2 \mid p_{ij} = 1 \mid L_{\max}$ is correct we first have to show that a feasible schedule is constructed. This is true if and only if, before setting $A(t) := O_{ij}$ and $B(t) := O_{ij}$ in Steps 4 and 10 of the module Schedule O_{ij}, we have $A(t) = \phi$ and $B(t) = \phi$, respectively. Otherwise two different operations would be scheduled at the same time on the same machine.

To show feasibility we first prove

Lemma 6.12 Let $Y = (A(t), B(t))$ be a list schedule with $B(t) = \phi$ $(A(t) = \phi)$. Then for each $s > t$ with $B(s) = O_{ij}$ $(A(s) = O_{ij})$ we have $A(s - 1) = O_{i,j-1}$ $(B(s - 1) = O_{i,j-1})$.

Proof: We show by induction on s that $B(s) = O_{ij}$, $s > t$ implies $A(s - 1) = O_{i,j-1}$. This is certainly true for $s = t + 1$ because if $B(t + 1) = O_{ij}$ and $A(t)$ does not belong to job i, then $B(t) = \phi$ implies that operation O_{ij} must be scheduled earlier in the list schedule.

Now, assume that Lemma 6.12 holds for all v with $t < v < s$ and that $B(s) = O_{ij}$. Choose a maximal l with $t \leq l < s$ and $B(l) = \phi$. By the induction assumption, $A(v - 1)$ and $B(v)$ belong to the same job for $v = l + 1, \ldots, s - 1$. Suppose that $A(s - 1)$ does not belong to job i. Then for each $v \in \{l, l + 1, \ldots, s - 1\}$ operation $A(v)$ does not belong to job i for $v = l, \ldots, s - 1$. Thus O_{ij} can be processed at time l, which contradicts the fact that Y is a list schedule.   □

Theorem 6.13 Let O_{ij} be the operation scheduled in Step 4 (Step 10) of the module Schedule O_{ij} and assume that $t = \text{LAST } (i) > T1(T2)$. Then $A(t) = \phi$ $(B(t) = \phi)$.

Proof: Assume that $A(t) \neq \phi$ $(B(t) \neq \phi)$. Because $A(T1) = \phi$ $(B(T2) = \phi)$, the previous Lemma implies that $A(t)$ and $B(t-1)$ $(B(t)$ and $A(t-1))$ are operations of the same job k. Because $\text{LAST } (i) = t$, we must have $k \neq i$. This is not possible because $\text{LAST } (i) = t$ and $\mu_{ij} = A(\mu_{ij} = B)$ imply that $B(t - 1) = O_{i,j-1}$ $(A(t - 1) = O_{i,j-1})$.   □

Finally, we show that the list schedule constructed by the algorithm is optimal.

Lemma 6.14 If a schedule exists in which no job is late, then the schedule $Y = (A(t), B(t))$ constructed by Algorithm 2 $J2 \mid p_{ij} = 1 \mid L_{\max}$ has this property.

Proof: We will show that if there is a late job in the schedule constructed by Algorithm 2 $J2 \mid p_{ij} = 1 \mid L_{\max}$, then there is a late job in each schedule.

If there is a late job in $Y = (A(t), B(t))$, then there exists an operation $A(t)$ or $B(t)$ with $l(A(t)) < t + 1$ or $l(B(t)) < t + 1$. For example, this inequality is true for the last operation in a late job. Choose a minimal t with this property and assume that $l(A(t)) < t + 1$.

Then we will prove that

$$l(A(v)) \leq l(A(t)) \quad \text{for } v = 1, \ldots, t-1$$
$$l(A(0)) \leq l(A(t)) \quad \text{if } A(0) \neq \phi. \tag{6.12}$$

Thus, in each schedule at least one late job must exist because $A(0) \neq \phi$ implies $l(A(v)) < t+1$ for $v = 0, \ldots, t$ and we must schedule $t+1$ operations in the time interval $[0, t]$, which is impossible. If, on the other hand, $A(0) = \phi$, then all jobs start on machine B and t operations must be processed in the time interval $[1, t]$, which again is not possible.

To prove (6.12), note that (6.12) is true if $A(t)$ is the first operation of a job, for if

$$l(A(t)) < l(A(v)) \quad \text{for some } v = 0 \ldots, t-1,$$

then the algorithm must schedule $A(t)$ before $A(v)$.

Now let

$$A(t) = O_{i,j} \quad \text{for some } i \text{ and } j > 1.$$

Then we have

$$O_{i,j-1} = B(s) \quad \text{with } s < t-1$$

because $s = t-1$ implies $l(B(s)) = l(A(t)) - 1 < t = s+1$, which contradicts the minimality of t. It follows that

$$l(A(v)) \leq l(A(t)) \quad \text{for } v = s+1, \ldots, t-1$$

because otherwise $A(t)$ must be scheduled earlier. Also

$$l(A(s)) \leq l(A(s+1))$$

because otherwise $A(s+1)$ should be scheduled at time s since $A(s+1)$ and $B(s)$ are operations of different jobs. If $s = 0$, we have already proved (6.12). Otherwise let $A(s) = O_{i',j'}$. If $A(s)$ is the first operation of a job, we have finished. Otherwise, if

$$O_{i',j'-1} = B(r) \quad \text{with } r < s-1,$$

we again have

$$l(A(v)) \leq l(A(s)) \quad \text{for } v = r, \ldots, s-1.$$

If, however, $O_{i',j'-1} = B(s-1)$, then we let $r \leq s-1$ be the smallest integer with the property that $B(v)$ and $A(v+1)$ are successive operations of the same job for $v = r, \ldots, s-1$. $A(s+1)$ does not belong to job i and we again have $l(A(v)) \leq l(A(s+1))$ for $v = r, \ldots, s$. If $r = 0$, we have finished. If $r > 0$, we continue in the same way. □

Theorem 6.15 A schedule constructed by Algorithm 2 $J2 \mid p_{ij} = 1 \mid L_{\max}$ is optimal.

Proof: Let l be the maximum lateness of an optimal schedule. Then

$$\max_{i=1}^{n} L(i) = \max_{i=1}^{n} \{C_i - d_i\} \leq l,$$

which is equivalent to

$$\max_{i=1}^{n} \{C_i - (d_i + l)\} \leq 0.$$

Due to Lemma 6.14, Algorithm 2 $J2 \mid p_{ij} = 1 \mid L_{\max}$ applied to the problem with due dates $d_i + l$ yields an optimal schedule for the original problem. Furthermore, this schedule is the same as the schedule we get by applying Algorithm 2 $J2 \mid p_{ij} = 1 \mid L_{\max}$ to the due dates d_i. □

Note that the algorithm, although fast, is not polynomial if we encode the problem by the numbers n_i and, for each job i, the machine number on which the first operation of job i has to be processed. It is only a pseudopolynomial algorithm. Timkovsky [199] and Kubiak et al. [130] presented algorithms which are polynomial even for this encoding for the special case with $C_{\max}$ objective function. The following more general result has been derived by Timkovsky [199]: $J2 \mid p_{ij} = 1 \mid L_{\max}$ (and symmetrically $J2 \mid p_{ij} = 1; r_i \mid C_{\max}$) can be solved in $O(n^2)$ time. That $J2 \mid p_{ij} = 1 \mid \sum C_i$ can be solved in $O(n \log n)$ time has been shown by Kubiak & Timkovsky [131]. An $O(n^6)$-algorithm for $J2 \mid p_{ij} = 1 \sum U_i$ is due to Kravchenko [126]. The problems $J2 \mid p_{ij} = 1; r_i \mid \sum C_i$, $J2 \mid p_{ij} = 1 \mid \sum w_i C_i$, and $J2 \mid p_{ij} = 1 \mid \sum T_i$ are $\mathcal{NP}$-hard.

6.4.2 Problems with Two Jobs. A Geometric Approach

Job shop problems with two jobs can be solved polynomially even with objective functions $f(C_1, C_2)$ which are regular, i.e. monotone nondecreasing functions of the finishing times C_1 and C_2 of both jobs. These

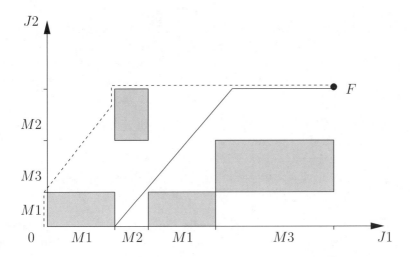

Figure 6.9: Graphical representation of a solution for a job shop problem with 2 jobs.

problems can be reduced to shortest path problems in appropriate networks. First, we will derive this reduction for problem $J \mid n = 2 \mid C_{\max}$. Later we will show how to modify the corresponding algorithm to solve the general problem $J \mid n = 2 \mid f$ with regular f.

$J \mid n = 2 \mid C_{\max}$

Problem $J \mid n = 2 \mid C_{\max}$ may be formulated as a shortest path problem in the plane with rectangular objects as obstacles (Akers & Friedman [8]). Figure 6.9 shows a shortest path problem with obstacles which corresponds to a job shop problem with two jobs with $n_1 = 4$ and $n_2 = 3$. The processing times of the operations of job 1 (job 2) are represented by intervals on the x-axis (y-axis) which are arranged in the order in which the corresponding operations are to be processed. Furthermore, the intervals are labeled by the machines on which the corresponding operations must be processed. A feasible schedule corresponds to a path from 0 to F. This path has the following properties:

(i) the path consists of segments which are either parallel to one of the axes (an operation of only one job is processed) or diagonal (operations of both jobs are processed in parallel);

(ii) the path has to avoid the interior of any rectangular obstacle of the form $I_1 \times I_2$, where I_1 and I_2 are intervals on the x-axis and y-axis which correspond to the same machine. This follows from the fact that two operations cannot be processed simultaneously on the same machine and that preemption is not allowed;

(iii) the length of the path, which corresponds to the schedule length, is equal to:

$$\text{length of horizontal parts} + \text{length of vertical parts} + (\text{length of diagonal parts})/\sqrt{2}.$$

In general, we have consecutive intervals $I_\nu^x(I_\nu^y)$ of length $p_{1\nu}(p_{2\nu})$ where $\nu = 1, \ldots, n_1(n_2)$. Furthermore, the rectangles $I_i^x \times I_j^y$ are forbidden regions if and only if $\mu_{1i} = \mu_{2j}$. Finally, define

$$a = \sum_{\nu=1}^{n_1} p_{1\nu} \text{ and } b = \sum_{\nu=1}^{n_2} p_{2\nu}.$$

We have to find a shortest path from $O = (o, o)$ to $F = (a, b)$ which has only horizontal, vertical, and diagonal segments and which does not pass through the interior of any of the forbidden regions. We denote this problem by Q. Next we will show that the problem can be reduced to an unrestricted shortest path problem in an appropriate network N. Furthermore, the unrestricted path problem will be solved in time which is linear in the number of obstacles.

The network $N = (V, A, d)$ is constructed as follows. The set of vertices V consists of O, F, and the set of north-west corners (NW-corners) and south-east corners (SE-corners) of all obstacles. O is considered as a degenerate obstacle in which both the NW-corner and the SE-corner coincide. Each vertex $i \in V \setminus \{F\}$ coincides with at the most two arcs going out of i. To construct these arcs, we go from i diagonally in a NE direction until we hit either the boundary of the rectangle defined by O and F or the boundary of an obstacle. In the first case, F is the only successor of i and arc (i, F) consists of the path which goes from i diagonally to the boundary and continues along the boundary to F (see Figure 6.10(b)). If we hit an obstacle D, then there are two arcs (i, j) and (i, k) where j and k are the NW-corner and SE-corner of D, respectively. The corresponding polygons are shown in Figure 6.10(a). The length $d(i, j)$ of an arc (i, j) is equal to the length of the vertical or

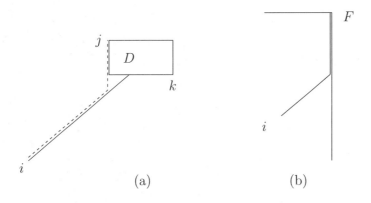

Figure 6.10: Successors of vertex i.

horizontal piece plus the length of the projection of the diagonal piece on the x-axis (or equivalently, y-axis).

It is easy to see that an $O - F$-path (i.e. a path from O to F) in $N = (V, A, d)$ corresponds to a feasible schedule, and its length is equal to the corresponding C_{max}-value. The next theorem shows that an optimal schedule corresponds with a shortest $O - F$-path in N.

Theorem 6.16 A shortest path from O to F in $N = (V, A, d)$ corresponds to an optimal solution of the shortest path problem with obstacles (i.e. with an optimal solution of the corresponding job-shop scheduling problem).

Proof: It is clear from the preceding discussion that an $O - F$-path in N corresponds to a path p from O to F which avoids obstacles. p consists of arcs, as shown in Figure 6.10. We have to prove that an optimal solution of Q exists consisting of a sequence of arcs.

Consider an optimal solution p^* with a longest starting sequence of arcs. If p^* is equal to this sequence, we have finished. Otherwise assume that the last arc in this sequence ends at vertex i. Consider the situation shown in Figure 6.11. Let D be the obstacle we hit at some point s if we go diagonally from i in the NE-direction. Denote by l the line through the SE-corner k of D which is parallel to the x-axis and by l' the line through the NW-corner j of D which is parallel to the y-axis. Furthermore, denote the SW-corner of D by u. Assume without loss of generality that s is on l. Path p^* crosses line l at some point t. If $t = u$

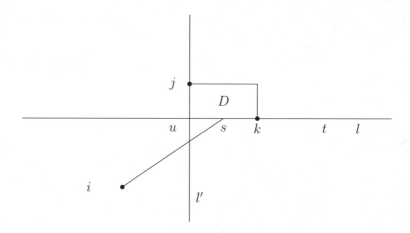

Figure 6.11: Proof of Theorem 6.16.

and p^* continues to k or if t is between u and k or $t = k$, then we may replace the part of p^* going from i to k by arc i, s, k without increasing the length of p^*. If t is to the right of k, then we may replace the part of p^* between i and t by i, s, k, t without increasing the length of p^*. In both cases we get an optimal path with a longer beginning sequence of arcs which contradicts the maximality assumption. Finally, if t is to the left of u, then p^* crosses l' at some point t' above u and a similar argument (but now using t' and l') leads to a contradiction.   □

To find a shortest path from O to F in the network $N = (V, A, d)$, we first order the forbidden regions according to the lexicographic order of their NW-corners (i.e. $D_i < D_j$ if for the corresponding NW-corners (x_i, y_i) and (x_j, y_j) we have $y_i < y_j$ or $y_i = y_j, x_i < x_j$).

Assume that we have r forbidden regions and that they are indexed such that

$$D_1 < D_2 < \ldots < D_r.$$

Then the following algorithm calculates the length d^* of a shortest path from O to F.

Algorithm J | n = 2 | C$_{\max}$
1. FOR ALL vertices $i \in V$ DO $d(i) := \infty$;
2. FOR ALL successors j of O DO $d(j) := d(O, j)$;
3. FOR $i := 1$ TO r DO

```
         BEGIN
4.       FOR ALL successors j of the NW-corner k of D_i
5.       DO d(j) := min{d(j), d(k) + d(k, j)};
6.       FOR ALL successors j of the SE-corner k of D_i
7.       DO d(j) := min{d(j), d(k) + d(k, j)}
         END
```
8. $d^* := d(F)$

Algorithm $J \mid n = 2 \mid C_{\max}$ may be easily modified to find the shortest path as well as the corresponding optimal schedule. Its complexity is $O(r)$.

Next we will show that the network N can be constructed in $O(r \log r)$ steps. Thus, the total time to solve the job shop problem is $O(r \log r)$. Note that r may be as large as $O(n_1 \cdot n_2)$. This is the case if we only have two machines. If each job is only processed once on a machine, then $r = \min\{n_1, n_2\}$.

To construct the network $N = (V, A, d)$ we apply a line sweep with the SW-NE-line $y - x = c$. We move this line parallel to itself from northwest to south-east. The sweep line intersects the obstacles creating an ordered set of intervals. Let S be the corresponding set of obstacles, together with the order induced by the intervals on the sweep line. We keep track of changes in S during the sweep. There are two possible events where changes occur.

(i) If the sweep line hits an NW-corner i of an obstacle D_l, then we have to insert D_l into the ordered set S. If there is a next element D_h in S, which has an NW-corner j and a SE-corner k, then the arcs (i, j) and (i, k) must be inserted into A and we have to calculate $d(i, j)$ and $d(i, k)$. Otherwise we have to insert (i, F) into A and calculate $d(i, F)$.

(ii) The sweep line hits a SE-corner i of an obstacle D_l. If there is a next element D_h in S with an NW-corner j and a SE-corner k, then we insert (i, j) and (i, k) into A and calculate $d(i, j)$ and $d(i, k)$. Otherwise we have to insert (i, F) into A and calculate $d(i, F)$. Finally, D_l must be deleted from S.

The arcs $(i, j), (i, k)$ and the distances $d(i, j), d(i, k)$ can be calculated in constant time. Furthermore, if we use a balanced tree, e.g. 2-3 tree (see

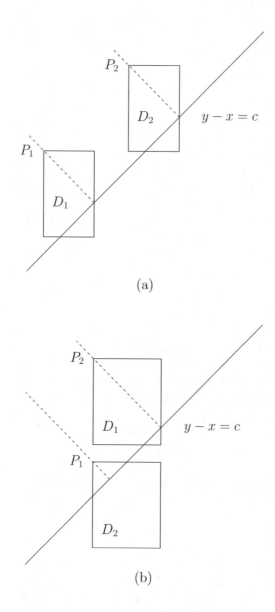

(a)

(b)

Figure 6.12: Ordering of intervals induced by obstacles on the sweep line. Case $x_1 \leq x_2$.

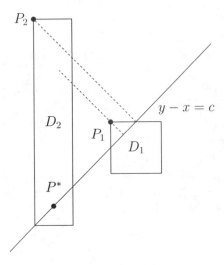

Figure 6.13: Ordering of intervals induced by obstacles on the sweep line. Case $x_2 < x_1$.

Aho, Hopcroft, Ullman [4]), then the insert and delete operations can be done in $O(\log r)$ time. Thus, N can be constructed in $O(r \log r)$ time. When implementing this algorithm the following result is very useful.

Theorem 6.17 If we order the obstacles in S according to the $(x + y)$-values of their NW-corners, this ordering is identical to the ordering induced by the intervals on the corresponding sweep line.

Proof: Consider two different obstacles D_1 and D_2 intersecting the sweep line $y - x = c$ in I_1 and I_2. Furthermore, let $P_1 = (x_1, y_1)$ and $P_2 = (x_2, y_2)$ be the NW-corners of D_1 and D_2. Assume without loss of generality that $y_1 \leq y_2$. If $x_1 \leq x_2$, then we have the situation shown in Figure 6.12. I_1 is south-west of I_2 as well as $x_1 + y_1 < x_2 + y_2$ ($x_1 + y_1 = x_2 + y_2$ is not possible because D_1 and D_2 are disjoint).

The claim also holds if $x_2 < x_1$. To see this assume that $x_2 + y_2 \geq x_1 + y_1$ and that I_2 is to the south-west of I_1. Then we have $y_2 > y_1$. Furthermore, there is a point $P^* = (x^0, y^0) \in I_2$ with $y^0 < y_1$ (see Figure 6.13). However, this is a contradiction to the fact that different intervals on the y-axis are not contained within each other.   □

J | n = 2 | f

Now we will discuss how to modify Algorithm $J \mid n = 2 \mid C_{\max}$ if we replace $C_{\max}$ by a regular objective function $f(C_1, C_2)$. In this case the optimal objective value depends on all points where paths from O to F hit the boundary of the rectangle R, defined by O and F. If P is such a point and P lies on the northern boundary of R, then the best solution among all those represented by a path going through P has the value $f(d(P) + d(P, F), d(P))$ where $d(P)$ is the length of the shortest path from O to P and $d(P, F)$ is the length of the horizontal segment between P and F. Similarly, if P lies on the eastern boundary of R, we get the best solution value $f(d(P), d(P) + d(P, F))$.

These ideas lead to the following algorithm derived from Algorithm $J \mid n = 2 \mid C_{\max}$ in which the current best objective value d^* is updated each time we hit the boundary.

Algorithm J | n = 2 | f
1. FOR ALL vertices $i \in V$ DO $d(i) := \infty$;
2. $d^* = \infty$;
3. FOR ALL successors j of O DO
4.   IF $j = F$ THEN update (d^*, O)
      ELSE $d(j) := d(O, j)$;
5. FOR $i := 1$ TO r DO
      BEGIN
6.   FOR ALL successors j of the NW-corner k of D_i DO
           IF $j = F$ THEN update (d^*, k)
           ELSE $d(j) := \min\{d(j), d(k) + d(k, j)\}$;
7.   FOR ALL successors j of the SE-corner k of D_i DO
           IF $j = F$ THEN update (d^*, k)
           ELSE $d(j) := \min\{d(j), d(k) + d(k, j)\}$
      END

Update (d^*, k) updates the current best objective value as described previously:

Update (d*, k)
1. Calculate the distance $l(k)$ between k and the point P where the half-line starting in k and going in the NE-direction hits the borderline;

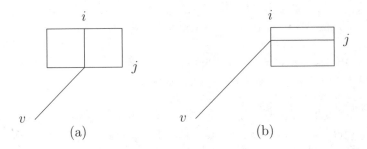

Figure 6.14: Successors of vertex v if preemption is allowed.

2. IF P lies on the northern borderline THEN
$$d^* := \min\{d^*, f(d(k) + d(k, F), d(k) + l(k))\}$$
ELSE $\{P$ lies on the eastern borderline$\}$
$$d^* := \min\{d^*, f(d(k) + l(k), d(k) + d(k, F))\}$$

If the function $f(C_1, C_2)$ can be evaluated in constant time, this algorithm has the same complexity as the previous one.

Preemptive job shop problems with two jobs can be solved similarly.

$J \mid n = 2; \text{pmtn} \mid f$

If preemption is allowed in the previous problem, then we may go horizontally or vertically through obstacles. For this reason, the network $N = (V, A, d)$ must be defined differently.

The vertex set is defined recursively by

(i) O is a vertex.

(ii) If v is a vertex and the half-line starting from v and going in a NE-direction hits an obstacle, then v has the two successors i and j shown in Figure 6.14(a) or (b).

(iii) If v is a vertex and the half-line starting from v and going in a NE-direction hits the borderline given by the rectangle defined by O and F, then F is the only successor of v.

We denote the modified network by $\overline{N}$.

Arcs (i, j) and arc lengths $d(i, j)$ are defined as before. If in Algorithm $J \mid n = 2 \mid f$ the "NW-corner" and "SE-corner" are replaced by "north boundary point" and "east boundary point", respectively, this modified algorithm applied to $\overline{N}$ solves problem $J \mid n = 2; pmtn \mid f$. The running time of this modified algorithm is bounded by $O(n_{\max}^3)$ where $n_{\max} = \max\{n_1, n_2\}$. This can be seen as follows.

Consider for each SE-corner or NW-corner v, which can be reached from O, the unique path starting from v which avoids the boundaries of the obstacles it hits. If such a path hits the SW-corner t of an obstacle (or a boundary point t' of the rectangle R, defined by O and F), this path terminates in t (or in F). There are at most $O(n_1, n_2)$ of these paths and each has at the most $n_1 + n_2$ arcs. Furthermore, the set of all these paths covers all arcs going through the interior of obstacles. Thus, the total number of arcs which go through the interior of obstacles is bounded by $O(n_{\max}^3)$. Because the number of arcs not going through the interior of obstacles is bounded by $O(n_1 n_2)$ and the total computation time of the shortest path algorithm is proportional to the number of all arcs, we have an $O(n_{\max}^3)$-algorithm.

Finally, we remark that all of the geometric methods also work if we drop the assumption that $\mu_{ij} \neq \mu_{i,j+1}$ for all i and $j = 1, \ldots, n_i - 1$.

6.4.3   Job Shop Problems with Two Machines

In the previous section we showed that job shop problems with two jobs are polynomially solvable. Sotskov & Shakhlevich [190] showed that the problems $J3 \mid n = 3 \mid C_{\max}$ and $J3 \mid n = 3 \mid \sum C_i$ are $\mathcal{NP}$-hard. Also $J2 \parallel C_{max}$ is $\mathcal{NP}$-hard (Lenstra & Rinnooy Kan [153]). Thus, the complexity of the job shop problem with two machines and a fixed number k of jobs remains open. In this section we will show that problem $J2 \mid n = k \mid C_{\max}$ is polynomially solvable even if machine repetition is allowed, i.e. if $\mu_{ij} = \mu_{i,j+1}$ is possible for jobs i.

We first show that $J2 \mid n = k \mid C_{\max}$ can be reduced to a shortest path problem in an acyclic network with $O(r^k)$ vertices where $r = \max\limits_{i=1}^{n} n_i$. Then we show that this network can be constructed in $O(r^{2k})$ steps, providing an overall complexity of $O(r^{2k})$. Finally, we present a simple $O(r^4)$-algorithm for problem $J2 \mid n = 3 \mid C_{\max}$ with no machine repetition.

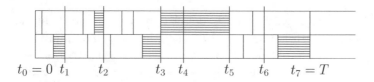

$$t_0 = 0 \; t_1 \qquad t_2 \qquad\quad t_3 \; t_4 \qquad t_5 \qquad t_6 \qquad t_7 = T$$

Figure 6.15: Decomposition of a $J2 \mid n = k \mid C_{\max}-$ schedule into blocks.

A shortest path formulation

In this section we will give a shortest path formulation for the two-machine job shop problem with k jobs and makespan objective. The corresponding network is acyclic and has at the most $O(r^k)$ vertices where $r = \overset{k}{\underset{i=1}{\max}} \, n_i$. Thus, the job shop problem can be solved in $O(r^{2k})$ steps if the network is given. The two machines are denoted by A and B. We consider only active schedules, i.e. schedules in which no operation can be started earlier without violating feasibility. Each schedule can be transformed into an active one without increasing the $C_{\max}$-value.

Given an active schedule S, we have a unique sequence

$$t_0 = 0 < t_1 < t_2 < \ldots < t_q$$

of all times at which either two operations begin processing jointly on both machines or one operation begins processing on one machine while an idle period is starting on the other machine (see Figure 6.15). We define $t_{q+1} = T$ where T is the $C_{\max}$-value of the schedule.

Furthermore, we call the set D_ν of operations scheduled in the interval $[t_\nu, t_{\nu+1}]$ $(\nu = 0, \ldots, q)$ a **block**. For a block D, let $D^A(D^B)$ be the set of operations of D processed on machine $A(B)$ and denote the sum of processing times of all operations in $D^A(D^B)$ by $l_D^A(l_D^B)$. A block D associated with the interval $[t_i, t_{i+1}]$ has the property that

- all jobs in $D^A(D^B)$ are scheduled in $[t_i, t_i + l_D^A]$ ($[t_i, t_i + l_D^B]$),

- $t_{i+1} = t_i + \max\{l_D^A, l_D^B\}$, and

- one machine is idle in $[\min\{l_D^A, l_D^B\}, t_{i+1}]$.

$l_D := \max\{l_D^A, l_D^B\} = t_{i+1} - t_i$ is called the **length** of block D.

It follows that a schedule is defined by a sequence of blocks and the schedule length is the sum of the lengths of all blocks in that sequence. To formulate problem $J2 \mid n = k \mid C_{\max}$ as a shortest path problem in some network $N = (V, A, l)$, we characterize blocks in a different way. For each job i, let $j_\nu(i)$ be the index of the last operation $O_{i,j_\nu(i)}$ which is processed before t_ν and define $\mathbf{j}_\nu := (j_\nu(i))_{i=1}^k$. Then D_ν is defined by $\mathbf{j}_\nu$ and $\mathbf{j}_{\nu+1}$. Generally, blocks can be described by pairs $(\mathbf{j}, \mathbf{h})$ of index tuples $\mathbf{j} = (j(i))$, $\mathbf{h} = (h(i))$ with $0 \le j(i) \le h(i) \le n_i$ for $i = 1, \ldots, k$. However, not all pairs of index tuples $(\mathbf{j}, \mathbf{h})$ define blocks.

The network $N = (V, A, l)$ is defined by

- the set V of all index tuples $\mathbf{j} = (j(i))$ with $0 \le j(i) \le n_i$ for $i = 1, \ldots, k$. The vertex $\mathbf{s} = \mathbf{j}$ with $j(i) = 0$ for all $i = 1, \ldots, k$ is called the **initial vertex**. The vertex $\mathbf{t} = \mathbf{j}$, with $j(i) = n_i$ for $i = 1, \ldots, k$, is called the **terminal vertex**,

- $(\mathbf{u}, \mathbf{v}) \in A$ if and only if $\mathbf{u} < \mathbf{v}$ and the set of operations
$$\{O_{i,j(i)} \mid i = 1, \ldots, k; u(i) < j(i) \le v(i)\}$$
defines a block, and

- for each $(\mathbf{u}, \mathbf{v}) \in A$, its length $l(\mathbf{u}, \mathbf{v})$ is the length of the block corresponding to $(\mathbf{u}, \mathbf{v})$.

In N, each $\mathbf{s} - \mathbf{t}$-path p corresponds to a feasible schedule and the length of p is equal to the makespan of this schedule. We obtain this schedule by scheduling the blocks corresponding to the arcs in p consecutively as shown in Figure 6.15. Furthermore, there is an $\mathbf{s} - \mathbf{t}$-path corresponding to an optimal schedule. Thus, to solve the job shop problem we have to find a shortest $\mathbf{s} - \mathbf{t}$-path in N.

It remains to show that the network can be constructed in polynomial time. This is the case if, for each vertex $\mathbf{u} \in V$, all successors of $\mathbf{u}$ can be calculated in polynomial time. In the next section we will derive an algorithm which does this in $O(r^k)$ time for each vertex. Thus, the total time needed to construct the network is $O(r^{2k})$.

Constructing the network N

In this section we will present an $O(r^k)$ algorithm which, for a given vertex $\mathbf{u}$, finds all arcs $(\mathbf{u}, \mathbf{v})$ which define a block. W.l.o.g. let $\mathbf{u} = \mathbf{s}$ where $\mathbf{s}$ is the starting vertex defined in the previous section.

A block may be decomposed as shown in Figure 6.16.

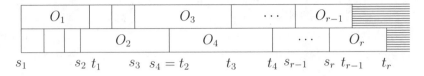

Figure 6.16: Structure of a block.

This decomposition is defined by operations $O_i (i = 1, \ldots, r)$ with starting times s_i and finishing times t_i satisfying the following properties:

- $s_1 \leq s_2$, $t_{r-1} \leq t_r$ and $s_i < t_{i-1} \leq s_{i+1}$ for $i = 2, 3, \ldots, r-1$. Thus, O_i and O_{i+1} are processed on different machines and O_i overlaps with O_{i-1} and O_{i+1}.

- The time between $t = 0$ and the starting time s_2 of O_2 as well as the time between the finishing time t_i of O_i and the starting time s_{i+2} of O_{i+2} ($i = 1, \ldots, r-2$) is completely filled with other operations.

We call the partial schedule consisting of operation O_i and all operations scheduled between O_{i-2} and O_i a **bar** (see Figure 6.17). Let B_i be the set of operations in this bar. O_i is called the **main operation** of B_i.

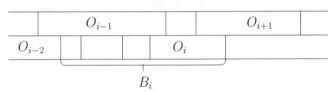

Figure 6.17: Definition of a bar.

Next we will construct a graph $\tilde{G} = (\tilde{V}, \tilde{A})$ with $\mathbf{s} \in \tilde{V}$ such that the blocks correspond with paths in $\tilde{G}$ starting in $\mathbf{s}$. The arcs in this graph represent bars. More specifically, $\tilde{G} = (\tilde{V}, \tilde{A})$ is defined by

- the set $\tilde{V} = V' \cup \{\mathbf{s}\}$, where V' is the set of all pairs $(\mathbf{j}, h)$ of index-tupels $\mathbf{j} = (j(i))$ combined with an additional index h representing the job of the main operation $O_{h,j(h)}$ such that

$$t_j^A - p_{h,j(h)} < t_j^B \leq t_j^A \ (t_j^B - p_{h,j(h)} < t_j^A \leq t_j^B) \tag{6.13}$$

if $O_{h,j(h)}$ is processed on machine $A(B)$. Here $t_j^A(t_j^B)$ is the sum of the processing times of all operations O_{ij} ($i = 1, \ldots, k$; $j = 1, \ldots, j(i)$) which are processed on machine $A(B)$. If $t_j^A - p_{h,j(h)} = 0$ ($t_j^B - p_{h,j(h)} = 0$), the strict inequality in condition (6.13) is replaced by "$\leq$",

- $(\tilde{u}, \tilde{v})$ with $\tilde{u} = (\mathbf{u}, h), \tilde{v} = (\mathbf{v}, l) \in V'$ is an arc if and only if $(\tilde{u}, \tilde{v})$ defines a bar, and

- $(\mathbf{s}, \tilde{v})$ with $\tilde{v} = (\mathbf{v}, l) \in V'$ is an arc if and only if

$$v(j) = \begin{cases} 1 \text{ if } j = l \\ 0 \text{ otherwise} \end{cases}$$

for some job index l.

To construct all blocks, we have to find all paths in $\tilde{G}$ starting from s. Because $\tilde{G}$ is acyclic and has at the most $O(r^k)$ vertices, this can be done in $O(r^{2k})$ time. However, the complexity can be reduced by adding a single operation in each step of the search process. There are at the most k operations which can be added. Thus, the total complexity is $O(kr^k) = O(r^k)$ because k is fixed.

Problem J2 | n = 3 | $C_{\max}$ with no machine repetition

In this section we will show that a simple $O(r^4)$-algorithm for problem $J2 \mid n = 3 \mid C_{\max}$ with no machine repetition can be easily derived using the concepts introduced previously.

As before, we denote the two machines by A and B. Furthermore, assume that the three jobs denoted by 1,2,3 have operations O_{ij} where $i = 1, 2, 3$ and $j = 1, \ldots, n_i$. p_{ij} is the processing time of operations O_{ij}, which must be processed on machine μ_{ij}. We assume that

$$\mu_{ij} \neq \mu_{i,j+1} \text{ for } i = 1, 2, 3 \text{ and } j = 1, \ldots, n_i - 1.$$

We use the algorithm presented in the previous section to solve this problem. However, due to the fact that machine repetition is not allowed, blocks containing at least two operations have a special structure which may be characterized by the following two properties (see Figure 6.18):

Figure 6.18: Block structure for $J2 \mid n = 3 \mid C_{\max}$.

(a) With the exception of a first and a last operation, each operation in the block overlaps exactly two other operations.

(b) The job indices are repeated periodically, i.e. the operations ordered according to increasing starting times yield a sequence

$$O_{ir},\ O_{js},\ O_{kt}, O_{i,r+1},\ O_{j,s+1},\ O_{k,t+1},\ O_{i,r+2},\ \ldots$$

These properties follow from the fact that if two operations O and P of jobs i and j with finishing times t_1 and t_2, respectively, overlap and $t_1 < t_2$, then the first operation Q of job k scheduled at time t_1 or later in the same block must be processed starting at time t_1. Furthermore, the block ends at time t_2 if the processing time of Q is not larger than $t_2 - t_1$.

However, it is also possible that a block consists of exactly one operation.

For a block B there are at the most three one-element blocks which may be a successor of B. In a successor block of B containing more than one operation, two operations begin at the same time. Given these two operations, there is a unique maximal block satisfying conditions (a) and (b) and this maximal block can be constructed in $O(r)$ time. Each initial part of this maximal block may be a successor of B. Due to the fact that there are only these two possibilities to start a successor block of B, it follows that block B has at the most $O(r)$ successors and these successors can be constructed in $O(r)$ time.

This implies that the network has at the most $O(r^4)$ arcs and can be constructed in $O(r^4)$ time. Thus, we have an $O(r^4)$-algorithm to solve $J2 \mid n = 3 \mid C_{\max}$.

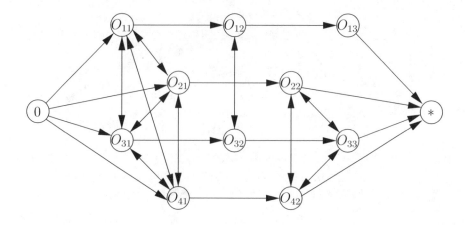

Figure 6.19: Disjunctive graph for a job shop problem with 4 jobs and 4 machines.

6.4.4 A Branch-and-Bound Algorithm

Carlier & Pinson [63] first solved the 10x10-job shop problem of Muth & Thompson [174]. Their solution is based on a branch-and-bound method combined with the concept of immediate selection. Other effective branch-and-bound methods have been developed by Applegate & Cook [10] and Brucker, Jurisch, and Sievers [43].

In this section we present a branch-and-bound method based on concepts from Brucker, Jurisch, and Sievers [43] and Brucker, Jurisch, and Krämer [41].

Branch-and-Bound Algorithm

The most effective branch-and-bound methods are based on the disjunctive graph model. We introduced this model in connection with the general shop problem in Section 6.1. In a job shop problem, all operations of the same job are connected by a chain of conjunctive arcs and we have disjunctive arcs between the operations to be processed on the same machine. Figure 6.19 shows the disjunctive graph for a job shop problem with four jobs to be processed on four machines.

The basic scheduling decision is to order the operations on each machine, i.e. to fix precedence relations between these operations.

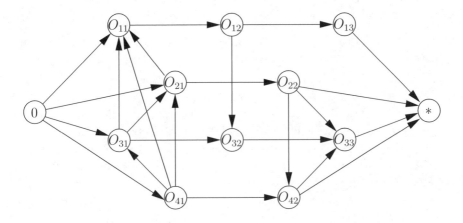

Figure 6.20: Complete selection for the example presented in Figure 6.19.

In the disjunctive graph model this is done by turning undirected (disjunctive) arcs into directed ones. A set of these "fixed" disjunctions is called a selection. Obviously, a selection S defines a feasible schedule if and only if

- every disjunctive arc has been fixed, and

- the resulting graph $G(S) = (V, C \cup S)$ is acyclic.

In this case we call the set S a complete selection. See Figure 6.20 for a selection that defines a feasible schedule.

For a given schedule (i.e. a complete selection S), the maximal completion time of all jobs $C_{max}(S)$ is equal to the length of the longest weighted path from the source 0 to the sink $*$ in the acyclic graph $G(S) = (V, C \cup S)$. This path is usually called a **critical path**.

Next, a short description of a branch-and-bound algorithm for the job shop scheduling problem will be given. The algorithm will be represented by a search tree. Initially, the tree contains only one node, the root. No disjunctions are fixed in this node, i.e. it represents all feasible solutions to the problem. The successors of the root are calculated by fixing disjunctions. The corresponding disjunctive graph represents all solutions to the problem respecting these disjunctions. After this, each successor is handled recursively in the same way. The examination of a search tree node stops if it represents only one solution (i.e. the set S of fixed disjunctive arcs is a complete selection), or it can be shown that the node does not contain an optimal solution.

More precisely: A search tree node r corresponds to a graph $G(F_r) = (V, C \cup F_r)$. F_r denotes the set of fixed disjunctive arcs in node r. The node represents all solutions $Y(r)$ respecting the partial order given by F_r. Branching is done by dividing $Y(r)$ into disjoint subsets $Y(s_1), ..., Y(s_q)$. Each $Y(s_i)$ is the solution set of a problem with a graph $G(F_{s_i}) = (V, C \cup F_{s_i})$ where $F_r \subset F_{s_i}$, which means that $G(F_{s_i})$ is derived from $G(F_r)$ by fixing additional disjunctions. This branching creates immediate successors $s_1, ..., s_q$ of node r in the branching tree which are treated recursively. For each node r, a value $LB(r)$, bounding from below the objective values of all solutions in $Y(r)$, is calculated. We set $LB(r) = \infty$ if the corresponding graph $G(F_r)$ has a cycle. Furthermore, we have an upper bound UB for the solution value of the original problem. UB is updated whenever a new feasible solution is found which improves UB.

The following recursive procedure describes a branch-and-bound scheme based on depth-first search. Initially, we set $UB = \infty$ and $F_r = \emptyset$.

PROCEDURE Branch-and-Bound (r)
1. Calculate a solution $S \in Y(r)$ using heuristics;
2. IF $C_{max}(S) < UB$ THEN $UB := C_{max}(S)$;
3. WHILE there is a successor s of r which has not yet been examined DO
4. IF $LB(s) < UB$ THEN Branch-and-Bound (s)

To specify the branch-and-bound procedure in more detail we have to

  (a) introduce a branching scheme, and

  (b) discuss methods for calculating bounds.

The next sections are devoted to these issues.

A branching scheme

The branching scheme presented here is based on an approach used by Grabowski et al. [107] in connection with single-machine scheduling with release dates and due dates. It is based on a feasible schedule which corresponds with the graph $G(S) = (V, C \cup S)$. Let P be a critical path in $G(S)$. Let $L(S)$ be the length of this critical path. A sequence $u_1, ..., u_k$ of successive nodes in P is called a **block** if the following two properties are satisfied:

(a) The sequence contains at least two nodes.

(b) The sequence represents a maximal number of operations to be processed on the same machine.

We denote the j'th block on the critical path by B_j. See Figure 6.21 for blocks and conjunctive arcs on a critical path.

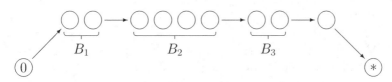

Figure 6.21: Blocks on a critical path.

The following theorem is the basis of this section.

Theorem 6.18 Let S be a complete selection corresponding to some solution of the job shop scheduling problem. If another complete selection S' exists such that $L(S') < L(S)$, then at least one operation of some block B of $G(S)$ has to be processed in S' before the first or after the last operation of B.

Proof: Let $P = (0, u_1^1, u_2^1, ..., u_{m_1}^1, ..., u_1^k, u_2^k, ..., u_{m_k}^k, *)$ be a critical path in $G(S) = (V, C \cup S)$. $u_1^j, ..., u_{m_j}^j$ $(j = 1, ..., k)$ denotes a maximal subsequence of operations to be processed on the same machine (i.e. a block if $m_j > 1$). Assume that there is a complete selection S' with $L(S') < L(S)$ and in S' no operation of any block of S is processed before the first or after the last operation of its block.

Thus $G(S')$ contains a path

$$(0, u_1^1, v_2^1, ..., v_{m_1-1}^1, u_{m_1}^1, ..., u_1^k, v_2^k, ..., v_{m_k-1}^k, u_{m_k}^k, *)$$

where, for $j = 1, ..., k$, the sequence $v_2^j, ..., v_{m_j-1}^j$ is a permutation of $u_2^j, ..., u_{m_j-1}^j$.

The length of the critical path in $G(S')$ is not less than the length of this path. We have:

$$L(S') \geq \sum_{j=1}^{k} \left(p_{u_1^j} + \sum_{i=2}^{m_j-1} p_{v_i^j} + p_{u_{m_j}^j} \right)$$

$$= \sum_{j=1}^{k} \left(p_{u_1^j} + \sum_{i=2}^{m_j-1} p_{u_i^j} + p_{u_{m_j}^j} \right)$$

$$= L(S)$$

which is a contradiction.   □

The following fact is an immediate consequence of the previous theorem: If there are two complete selections S, S' with $L(S') < L(S)$, then at least one of the two conditions (i) or (ii) holds.

(i) At least one operation of one block B in $G(S)$, different from the first operation in B, has to be processed **before** all other operations of B in the schedule defined by $G(S')$.

(ii) At least one operation of one block B in $G(S)$, different from the last operation in B, has to be processed **after** all other operations of B in the schedule defined by $G(S')$.

Now consider a node r of the search tree and a solution $y \in Y_r$. Usually y is calculated using some heuristic. Let S be the complete selection corresponding to y. A critical path in $G(S)$ defines blocks $B_1, ..., B_k$. For block $B_j : u_1^j, ..., u_{m_j}^j$, the jobs in

$$E_j^B := B_j \setminus \{u_1^j\} \text{ and } E_j^A := B_j \setminus \{u_{m_j}^j\}$$

are called **before-candidates** and **after-candidates**.

At least one of the candidates must be moved in order to improve S. Furthermore, we define the arc-sets

$$F_j := \{u_1^j \longrightarrow \ell \mid \ell = u_2^j, ..., u_{m_j}^j\}$$
$$L_j := \{\ell \longrightarrow u_{m_j}^j \mid \ell = u_1^j, ..., u_{m_j-1}^j\}$$

for $j = 1, ..., k$ and consider a permutation

$$R_1, R_2, ..., R_{2k} \tag{6.14}$$

of all F_j and L_j.

Next we will describe a branching $Y(s_1), ..., Y(s_q)$ of Y_r which depends on this permutation (6.14). We describe the sets $Y(s_\nu)$ by specifying the arc sets to be joined with the arc-set F_r of Y_r. They are constructed in the following way:

- For each before-candidate $\ell \in E_j^B$ $(j = 1, ..., k)$ find the index $m = \alpha(\ell)$ with $R_m = F_j$ and define

$$S_\ell^B := R_1 \cup R_2 \cup \cdots \cup R_{m-1} \cup \{\ell \to i \mid i \in B_j \setminus \{\ell\}\}.$$

- For each after-candidate $\ell \in E_j^A$ $(j = 1, ..., k)$ find the index $m = \alpha(\ell)$ with $R_m = L_j$ and define

$$S_\ell^A := R_1 \cup R_2 \cup \cdots \cup R_{m-1} \cup \{i \to \ell \mid i \in B_j \setminus \{\ell\}\}.$$

- Take $R := R_1 \cup R_2 \cup \cdots \cup R_{2k}$.

This construction is illustrated in the following example.

Example 6.1

Consider a critical path with two blocks of the form.

If we take the permutation

$$R_1 = F_2, \quad R_2 = L_1, \quad R_3 = L_2, \quad R_4 = F_1$$

we get the arc sets shown in Figure 6.22.

Note that S_5^A and S_4^B contain cycles. Cycles may also be created in connection with the arcs in F_r which have been fixed previously. If cycles are created, the corresponding sets $Y(s_\nu)$ of feasible solutions are empty.

□

It is advantageous to check the "direct" cycles during the calculation of the before– and after– candidates in a search tree node r. This means

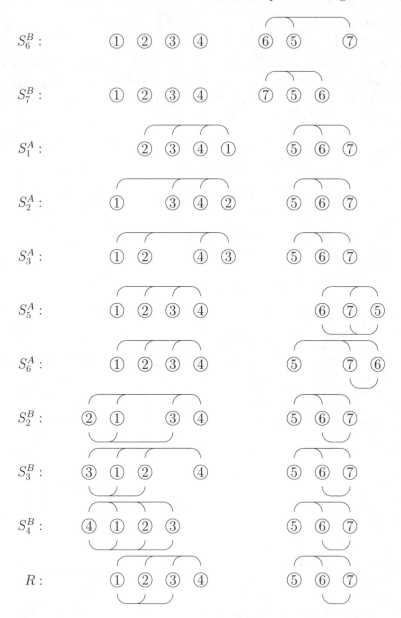

Figure 6.22: Branching for Example 6.1.

that for the block $B_\ell : u_1^\ell, ..., u_{m_\ell}^\ell$ if a disjunctive arc $i \rightarrow j$ $(i, j \in B_\ell)$ is already fixed in the actual search tree node, then operation j (operation i) is not inserted into the set $E_\ell^B (E_\ell^A)$. The cycles in the preceding example can be eliminated by this method. A complete cycle-check is done during the computation of heads and tails which will be introduced in the next section.

The resulting solution sets created by this branching rule are pairwise disjoint. This can be seen as follows. If we have two sets S_ℓ^B and $S_{\ell'}^B$ with $\ell, \ell' \in E_j^B$, then $(\ell, \ell') \in S_\ell^B$ and $(\ell', \ell) \in S_{\ell'}^B$. Thus, the corresponding sets $Y(s_\nu)$ have an empty intersection. The same reasoning applies if we have sets S_ℓ^A and $S_{\ell'}^A$ with $\ell, \ell' \in E_j^A$. Note that these two cases are characterized by the fact that $\alpha(\ell) = \alpha(\ell')$. If, on the other hand, we have two sets S_ℓ^ν and $S_{\ell'}^{\nu'}$ with $\alpha(\ell) < \alpha(\ell')$, then if ℓ is a before-candidate (after-candidate) in the block B_j, we have $\ell \longrightarrow u_1^j$ $(u_{m_j}^j \longrightarrow \ell)$ in S_ℓ^ν but $u_1^j \longrightarrow \ell$ $(\ell \longrightarrow u_{m_j}^j)$ in $S_{\ell'}^{\nu'}$.

By Theorem 6.18, solutions associated with R do not improve the solution S. Thus, the corresponding successor node of r will not be considered.

We have not yet specified how to choose the permutation $R_1, ..., R_{2k}$ of the sets F_j and L_j $(j = 1, ..., k)$. The objective is to fix a large number of disjunctive arcs as early as possible. Hence we arrange the sets F_j and L_j $(j = 1, ..., k)$ according to nonincreasing cardinalities of the corresponding blocks. Additionally, we always take the set L_j as a direct successor of the set F_j. More precisely, we choose

$$R_{2i-1} := F_{\pi(i)}, \quad R_{2i} := L_{\pi(i)} \quad (i = 1, ..., k)$$

where π is a permutation of $1, ..., k$ such that $|B_{\pi(i)}| \geq |B_{\pi(j)}|$ if $i < j$.

Now it is possible to formulate a branch-and-bound procedure based on the branching rule introduced in this section.

PROCEDURE Branch-and-Bound (r)
1. Calculate a solution $S \in Y(r)$ using heuristics;
2. IF $C_{max}(S) < UB$ THEN $UB := C_{max}(S)$;
3. Calculate a critical path P;
4. Calculate the blocks of P;
5. Calculate the sets E_j^B and E_j^A;
6. WHILE an operation $i \in E_j^\nu$ exists with $j = 1, ..., k$ and
   $\nu = A, B$ DO
          BEGIN

7.   Delete i from E_j^{ν};
8.   Fix disjunctions for the corresponding successor s;
9.   Calculate a lower bound $LB(s)$ for node s;
10.   IF $LB(s) < UB$ THEN Branch-and-Bound (s)
          END

Note that the handling of a node s terminates if

- the lower bound $LB(s)$ is greater than or equal to the best solution value (this is the case if the corresponding disjunctive graph has cycles, i.e. $LB(s) = \infty$) or

- the critical path of the heuristic solution calculated for S does not contain any blocks or

- the sets E_j^B and E_j^A are empty for all blocks B_j.

We did not specify in which order the operations $i \in E_j^{\nu}$ are chosen, i.e. the order of the successors of a search tree node r. The following rule seems to be promising. Sort the candidates according to nondecreasing heads of before-candidates and tails of after-candidates and deal with the successors of a search tree node in this order. Heads and tails are explained below.

Heads and tails

With each operation i we may associate a head and a tail. Heads and tails are important for lower bound calculations. They are also used in heuristics.

A **head** r_i of operation i is a lower bound for an earliest possible starting time of i.

A **tail** q_i of operation i is a lower bound for the time period between the finishing time of operation i and the optimal makespan.

Calculations of heads and tails are based on all conjunctive arcs and the fixed disjunctive arcs. Thus, they depend on the specific search tree node r.

A simple way to get heads r_i for operation i would be to calculate the length of the longest weighted path from 0 to i in the disjunctive graph $G = (V, C \cup F_r)$. Similarly, for each i the tail q_i could be calculated as the length of the longest weighted path from i to $*$ in $G = (V, C \cup F_r)$.

A more sophisticated method for calculating heads is as follows.
If $P(i)$ is the set of disjunctive predecessors of operation i in a search
tree node, the value

$$\max_{J \subseteq P(i)} \left\{ \min_{j \in J} r_j + \sum_{j \in J} p_j \right\}$$

defines a lower bound for the earliest possible starting time of operation
i. Using the head of the conjunctive predecessor $h(i)$ of i, we get the
lower bound $r_{h(i)} + p_{h(i)}$. Using these formulas, we may define the head
r_i of an operation i recursively:

$$r_0 := 0;$$

$$r_i := \max \left\{ r_{h(i)} + p_{h(i)}; \; \max_{J \subseteq P(i)} \left\{ \min_{j \in J} r_j + \sum_{j \in J} p_j \right\} \right\}$$

The same ideas lead to a formula for the tails q_i of all operations:

$$q_* := 0;$$

$$q_i := \max \left\{ p_{k(i)} + q_{k(i)}; \; \max_{J \subseteq S(i)} \left\{ \sum_{j \in J} p_j + \min_{j \in J} q_j \right\} \right\}$$

Here $k(i)$ is the conjunctive successor of i, and $S(i)$ denotes the set of
disjunctive successors of i.

The calculation of heads can be combined with a cycle-check. We call
an operation a labeled operation if its head is calculated. Furthermore,
we keep a set D of all operations which can be labeled next, i.e. all
unlabeled operations with the property that all their predecessors are
labeled. Initially, $D = \{0\}$. If we label an operation $i \in D$, then i is
eliminated from D and all successors of i are checked for possible insertion
into D. The procedure continues until D is empty. The disjunctive graph
$G = (V, C \cup F)$ contains a cycle if and only if no head has been assigned
to the dummy operation $*$ by this procedure. It is not difficult to prove
this property which is a consequence of the special structure of G.

In the following sections we will see how to use heads and tails in different
parts of the branch-and-bound algorithm.

Immediate Selection

One of the objectives of the introduced branching scheme was to add large numbers of fixed disjunctions to the set F_r when going from node r to its successors. A fast increase of the sets of fixed disjunctions is essential for the quality of a branch-and-bound algorithm because

- more successors s of r contain cycles in the disjunctive graph and need not be inspected ,

- generally, the value of the lower bound increases because more fixed disjunctive arcs have to be respected, and

- if we have the additional information that j succeeds i in a solution which improves a current upper bound, then a heuristic will not look for schedules where j is processed before i. Therefore, such a heuristic generally calculates better solutions.

In this section we will present a method due to Carlier and Pinson [63] which fixes additional disjunctive arcs between jobs belonging to a set of operations to be processed on the same machine. The method, called immediate selection, is independent of the branching process. It uses an upper bound UB for the optimal makespan and simple lower bounds. From now on we assume that I is the set of all operations to be processed on a given machine. Furthermore, let n be the number of elements in I. Let $J \subset I$ and $c \in I \backslash J$. If condition

$$\min_{j \in J \cup \{c\}} r_j + \sum_{j \in J \cup \{c\}} p_j + \min_{j \in J} q_j \geq UB \tag{6.15}$$

holds, then all operations $j \in J$ must be processed before operation c if we want to improve the current upper bound UB. This follows from the fact that the left-hand side of (6.15) is a lower bound for all schedules in which c does not succeed all jobs in J. Due to integrality, (6.15) is equivalent to

$$\min_{j \in J \cup \{c\}} r_j + \sum_{j \in J \cup \{c\}} p_j + \min_{j \in J} q_j > UB - 1$$

or

$$\min_{j \in J \cup \{c\}} r_j + \sum_{j \in J \cup \{c\}} p_j > \max_{j \in J} d_j \tag{6.16}$$

where $d_j := UB - q_j - 1$.

(J, c) is called a **primal pair** if (6.15) or, equivalently, (6.16) holds. The corresponding arcs $j \to c$ with $j \in J$ are called **primal arcs**. Similarly, (c, J) is called a **dual pair** and arcs $c \to j$ are called **dual arcs** if

$$\min_{j \in J} r_j + \sum_{j \in J \cup \{c\}} p_j > \max_{j \in J \cup \{c\}} d_j \qquad (6.17)$$

holds. In this case all operations $j \in J$ must be processed after operation c if we want to improve the current solution value UB.

If J is a one-element set, then (6.15) may be replaced by the weaker condition

$$r_c + p_c + p_j + q_j \geq UB \qquad (6.18)$$

which is equivalent to

$$p_c + p_j > d_j - r_c. \qquad (6.19)$$

If these conditions hold, then we can fix the disjunction $j \to c$. The corresponding arc is called a **direct arc**.

In (6.16), (6.17), and (6.19) the d_j-values may be interpreted as deadlines. Next we will present an algorithm for fixing all primal and dual arcs in $O(n^2)$ time. This algorithm is based on a method for improving heads and due dates.

Improving Heads and Deadlines

In this section we consider the problem of finding a feasible schedule for a set I of n operations with processing times p_k, heads r_k, and deadlines d_k to be scheduled on one machine.

We assume that the corresponding problem with preemption has a feasible solution. Such a solution can be found by calculating **Jackson's Preemptive Schedule** (JPS) (Carlier [62]). JPS is calculated from left to right by applying the following rule: At each time t, which is given by a head or a completion time of an operation, schedule an unfinished operation i with $r_i \leq t$ and $d_i = \min\{d_j | r_j \leq t; j$ is not finished$\}$. Figure 6.23(a) shows an example for JPS. Note that the starting and restarting times of the operations are always integer if r_k, p_k are integer. There is a dual version of JPS which calculates a schedule from right to left applying the following dual rule: At each time t, which is given by a deadline or a starting time of an operation, schedule backwards a not completely scheduled operation i with $d_i \geq t$ and $r_i = \max\{r_j | d_j \geq t; j$ is not completely scheduled$\}$. We call such a schedule **Backwards Jackson's Preemptive Schedule** (BJPS). It is not difficult to see that JPS is feasible if and only if BJPS is feasible.

Now the objective is to improve the head r_c of an operation $c \in I$ in the original problem without preemption. The idea is to compute a lower bound s_c for the completion time of operation c under the assumption that release dates and deadlines are respected but preemptions at integer times are allowed. We call this time s_c the **earliest possible completion time** of operation c. Clearly, s_c is also a lower bound for the finishing time of operation c with respect to nonpreemptive schedules and r_c may be improved to

$$r'_c = s_c - p_c \tag{6.20}$$

if $r_c < r'_c$. Next we present methods for calculating s_c. We assume that

$$d_n \leq d_{n-1} \leq \ldots \leq d_1 = d \text{ and } r = \min_{j \in I} r_j.$$

s_c may be calculated by

Algorithm Improving Heads

1. Calculate JPS up to r_c;

2. Calculate BJPS without c in $[r_c, d]$ using the remaining processing times p_k^+;

3. Schedule operation c from left to right using the earliest idle periods in $[r_c, d]$. Let s_c be the completion time of operation c;

4. IF $s_c - p_c > r_c$ THEN $r_c := s_c - p_c$

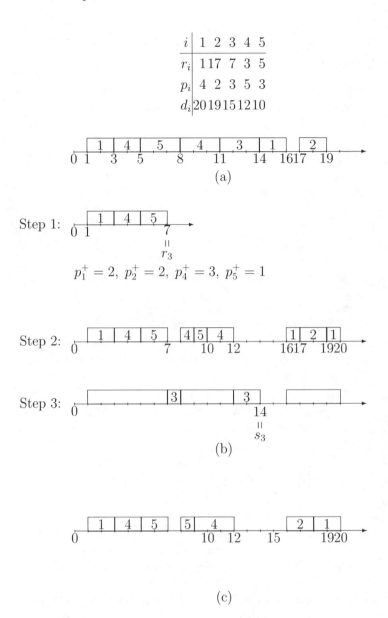

Figure 6.23: Calculation of earliest completion times r_c.

Figure 6.23(b) shows the results of the three steps of this algorithm applied to $c = 3$.

Theorem 6.19   (i) The schedule S calculated by Algorithm Improving Heads is feasible.

   (ii) Algorithm Improving Heads provides a lower bound for the completion time of operation c under the assumption that preemption at integer times is allowed.

Proof:

   (i) We only need to consider the interval $[r_c, d]$.
       By assumption JPS is feasible. Thus, we have a feasible preemptive schedule in $[r_c, d]$ for the processing times p_k^+ and BJPS provides such a feasible schedule even if c is included. Let f denote the completion time of operation c in this BJPS. Then $s_c \leq f \leq d_c$ and thus operation c also respects its release time and deadlines in S.

   (ii) We use simple exchange arguments.
        Assume that a feasible schedule exists in which the finishing time f_1 of c is smaller than s_c. Among all such schedules consider one S_1 coinciding with S as long as possible, i.e. S and S_1 coincide on $[r, t]$ with t maximal. Due to the fact that we have to consider only schedules with preemptions on integer times, such a t exists and is integer. Suppose $t < r_c$. If no operation in S is scheduled in $[t, t+1]$, then no operation can be scheduled in $[t, t+1]$ in S_1, contradicting maximality of t. Now assume that in S operation j is scheduled in $[t, t+1]$ and in S_1 operation $k \neq j$ is scheduled in $[t, t+1]$. Then a time unit $[t', t'+1], t' > t$ exists in which j is scheduled in S_1. Since $d_j \leq d_k$, operations j and k may be exchanged in S_1. f_1 does not change because $t < r_c$ implies $k \neq c$ and $j \neq c$. This again contradicts the maximality of t. Similarly, we have a contradiction if in S_1 no operation is scheduled in $[t, t+1]$. Hence S_1 and S coincide at least in $[r, r_c]$. With the same argument it can be shown that a schedule S_2 exists coinciding with S at least on $[r, r_c] \cup [s_c, d]$ in which the finishing time f_2 of c is smaller than s_c. Now the total remaining processing time of all operations to be scheduled in $[r_c, s_c]$ is exactly $s_c - r_c$ because S has this property. Only operation c may be scheduled in $[s_c - 1, s_c]$. So it must be scheduled in $[s_c - 1, s_c]$ which contradicts the fact that $f_2 < s_c$.

$\square$

The calculation of the earliest possible completion time s_c for a given operation $c \in I$ can be simplified due to the following ideas.

To apply Step 3 of Algorithm Improving Heads we only need to know the idle periods which are generated by BJPS in Step 2 of the algorithm. These idle periods can also be calculated using the following modified Step 2.

2. Starting from time d, schedule backwards in an order of nonincreasing deadlines the operations $j \in I\backslash\{c\}$ with processing times p_j^+ without preemption.

It is easy to see that this algorithm generates the same idle periods as BJPS. Figure 6.23(c) shows the resulting schedule after applying the modified Step 2.

The deadlines can be improved (decreased) in a similar way. The corresponding procedures are symmetric to those derived for the release times.

Fixing all Primal and Dual Arcs

The following simple procedure fixes all direct arcs associated with the set I of n jobs in $O(n^2)$ time.

Procedure Select
1. FOR ALL $c, j \in I, c \neq j$ DO
2.   IF $p_c + p_j > d_j - r_c$ THEN
3.   fix direct arc $j \rightarrow c$;

Next we will prove that Procedure Select calculates all primal and dual pairs associated with I if we replace the r_j-values and d_j-values by the modified r_j-values and d_j-values, respectively (see previous section).

Let r_i' and d_i' denote the release date and deadlines of operation i that are improved by the procedure given in the last section (note that $r_i' \geq r_i$ and $d_i' \leq d_i$ for $i = 1, \ldots, n$).

We get the following

Theorem 6.20 Let I be a set of operations to be processed on one machine with release dates r_i, deadlines d_i, modified release dates r_i', and modified deadlines d_i' for $i = 1, \ldots, n$.

(a) For each primal pair (J, c) with $J \subset I, c \in I \backslash J$ we have

$$r'_c + p_c + p_j > d_j \geq d'_j$$

for all $j \in J$.

(b) For each dual pair (c, J) with $J \subset I, c \in I \backslash J$ we have

$$r'_j + p_j + p_c \geq r_j + p_j + p_c > d'_c$$

for all $j \in J$.

(a) means that we can calculate all disjunctive arcs associated with primal arcs using Procedure Select with modified release dates r'_i $(i = 1, \ldots, n)$. The corresponding result for dual pairs is given by (b).

Proof: We will only prove (a). (b) can be proved similarly. Let (J, c) be a primal pair, i.e.

$$\min_{j \in J \cup \{c\}} r_j + \sum_{j \in J \cup \{c\}} p_j > \max_{j \in J} d_j.$$

This implies that in all feasible preemptive schedules parts of c have to be processed after $\max_{j \in J} d_j$.

In the last section we calculated a feasible preemptive schedule in which operation c finished as early as possible. We thereby obtained an earliest possible finishing time s_c for operation c and the modified release date $r'_c = s_c - p_c$. By the arguments given above, we have $s_c > d_j$ for all $j \in J$ and

$$\begin{aligned} d_j - r'_c &= d_j - (s_c - p_c) \\ &= (d_j - s_c) + p_c \\ &< p_c \\ &< p_c + p_j. \end{aligned}$$

$\square$

Combining the results of this section and the last section we get an $O(n^2)$-procedure for fixing all primal arcs and dual arcs for a set I of n jobs to be processed on the same machine. The time bound can be reduced to $O(\max\{n \log n, d\})$ (see Brucker et al. [41]) where d denotes the number of arcs to be fixed by the algorithm.

Application of Immediate Selection

The calculation of all disjunctive arcs by immediate selection is undertaken before the computation of a heuristic solution. One may proceed as follows:

(1) Calculation of all primal arcs for all machines.

(2) Calculation of new heads and deadlines.

(3) Calculation of all dual arcs for all machines.

(4) Calculation of new heads and deadlines.

In (1) and (3) we improve heads and deadlines, respectively, and apply Procedure Select. The computation of new heads and deadlines in steps (2) and (4) is undertaken because the additional arcs influence the heads and deadlines of all operations. Steps (1) to (4) are repeated as long as new disjunctive arcs are fixed.

Calculation of Lower Bounds

Let r be a search tree node with a set F_r of fixed disjunctive arcs. Based on the arcs in F_r, a head r_i and a tail q_i is given for each operation i. A lower bound $LB(s)$ is calculated for each successor s of r. If this value exceeds or is equal to the actual upper bound UB, then an inspection of s is not necessary.

Different methods for calculating lower bounds have been tested. The best strategy was to compute different lower bounds at different places of the algorithm:

(1) Lower bound calculation during the computation of the sets E_ℓ^B and E_ℓ^A : If operation i should be moved before block B, all disjunctive arcs $\{i \rightarrow j : j \in B \setminus \{i\}\}$ are fixed. Thus the value

$$r_i + p_i + \max \left\{ \max_{j \in B \setminus \{i\}} (p_j + q_j); \sum_{j \in B \setminus \{i\}} p_j + \min_{j \in B \setminus \{i\}} q_j \right\}$$

is a simple lower bound for the search tree node s. Similarly, the value

$$
\max \left\{ \max_{j \in B \setminus \{i\}} (r_j + p_j); \min_{j \in B \setminus \{i\}} r_j + \sum_{j \in B \setminus \{i\}} p_j \right\} + p_i + q_i
$$

is a lower bound for the node s if i should be moved after block B.

(2) Lower bound calculation during the computation of heads and tails: If the value $r_i + p_i + q_i$ of an operation i exceeds the actual upper bound, the node need not be inspected. Also the head r_* of the sink and the tail q_0 of the source of the disjunctive graph are used as lower bounds for all solutions in the search tree node s.

(3) Lower bound calculation after the computation of heads and tails: The Jackson Preemptive Schedule is calculated for each machine. The maximal makespan of these schedules gives a lower bound for the search tree node s.

Note that the value of the lower bound $LB(s)$ may increase if additional disjunctions are fixed. Thus, it is advantageous to check $LB(s)$ each time additional disjunctive arcs are fixed.

The calculation of all these lower bounds is advantageous because every time a lower bound exceeds or is equal to an upper bound, a time-consuming part of the algorithm (e.g. the computation of heads and tails or the fixation of disjunctions) is no longer necessary.

Calculation of heuristic solutions

The branching scheme we used was based on a heuristic solution of the problem.

In connection with the 10×10-problem, a priority dispatching rule based heuristic gave the best result (see Jurisch & Sievers [43]). The heuristic successively calculates the operation to be scheduled next. This is done in the following way:

- Calculate the set C of all operations which can be scheduled next, i.e. C is the set of operations c with the property that all predecessors of c are already scheduled. Initially, C contains the source 0 of the disjunctive graph.

- Let $u \in C$ be the operation with minimal value $r_u + p_u$, i.e. $r_u + p_u = \min_{c \in C}\{r_c + p_c\}$. Let M_k be the machine which has to process operation u. We define the set $\bar{C}$ by

$$\bar{C} := \{s \in C \mid r_s < r_u + p_u; s \text{ has to be processed on } M_k\}.$$

- For each operation $c \in \bar{C}$ we calculate a lower bound for the makespan of the schedule if we schedule c next. We choose the operation $\bar{c} \in \bar{C}$ with minimal lower bound to be scheduled next.

- The set C is updated by inspecting all successors s of $\bar{c}$. If all predecessors of s have already been scheduled, we set $C = C \cup \{s\}$.

  After this, $\bar{c}$ is deleted from C and we start again.

Different methods to calculate lower bounds for the operations $c \in \bar{C}$ have been tested. The bound which gave the best results was calculated as follows.

Let T be the set of operations on machine M_k that are not yet scheduled (note that $\bar{C}$ is a subset of T). Take as a lower bound the solution value of Jackson's Preemptive Schedule for the set T assuming that c has to be scheduled first.

6.4.5 Applying Tabu-Search to the Job Shop Problem

In this section we will describe how the Algorithm Tabu-Search presented in Section 3.4.1 can be implemented for the job shop problem. Firstly, several neighborhoods will be discussed. These neighborhoods can also be used in connection with other local search methods. Then, following Dell'Amico & Trubian [75], we will describe the organization of the tabu-list and the aspiration criterion to be used. For a more detailed discussion of the application of simulated annealing and tabu-search to the job shop scheduling problem we refer to Van Laarhoven et al. [206] and Dell'Amico & Trubian [75].

All processing times p_{ij} considered in this section are assumed to be positive.

Neighborhood Structures

The quality of local search heuristics strongly depends on the neighborhood used. In this section we will define neighborhoods that yield good results for simulated annealing and tabu-search methods. Again we use disjunctive graphs $G = (V, C, D)$ for representing job shop scheduling problems. Thus, solutions can be represented by complete selections. A complete selection S induces the acyclic graph $G(S) = (V, C \cup S)$.

The following Lemma motivates the first neighborhood N_1.

Lemma 6.21 Let S be a complete selection and let p be a longest path in $G(S)$. Let (v, w) be an arc of p such that v and w are processed on the same machine. Then S' derived from S by reversing (v, w) is again a complete selection.

Proof: We have to show that $G(S')$ is acyclic. If $G(S')$ is cyclic, then (w, v) must be belong to a cycle c because $G(S)$ has no cycles. (v, w) does not belong to c. Thus, c contains at least three vertices. Furthermore, v and w are the only vertices which belong to both c and p. If we now replace the arc (v, w) in p by the subpath of c going from v to w, we have in $G(S)$ a path which is longer than p. This contradicts the fact that p is a longest path in $G(S)$.   □

For a complete selection S we now denote by $\mathbf{N_1(S)}$ the set of all complete selections derived from S by reversing an arc (v, w) on a critical path in $G(S)$, where v and w are to be processed on the same machine. Thus, the moves corresponding to N_1 are reversals of certain critical arcs.

A neighborhood N is called **opt-connected** if, from each solution S, some optimal solution can be reached by a finite sequence of moves, i.e. there exists a sequence of complete selections $S_0, S_1, \ldots, S_k$ with $S_0 = S$, S_k is optimal, and $S_{i+1} \in N(S_i)$ for $i = 0, 1, \ldots, k - 1$.

Connectivity is a desired property for local search methods, such as simulated annealing and tabu-search. In connection with simulated annealing and tabu-search, connected neighborhoods generally provide better results.

Theorem 6.22 N_1 is opt-connected.

Proof: We have to show that we can get from an arbitrary complete selection S to an optimal selection by a finite sequence of moves. This is accomplished by the following procedure which is guided by an arbitrary but given optimal selection S_{opt}.

1. $i = 0;\ S_i := S$;
2. WHILE S_i is not optimal DO
        BEGIN
3.   Find $(v, w) \in S_i$ on a critical path in $G(S_i)$ such that
          (v, w) does not belong to S_{opt};
4. $S_{i+1} := (S_i \backslash \{(v, w)\}) \cup \{(w, v)\}$;
5. $i := i + 1$
        END

In Step 3 of this procedure we can always find an arc (v, w) on a critical path with respect to S_i which does not belong to S_{opt}. Otherwise all arcs on a critical path in $G(S_i)$ belong to S_{opt} which implies $C_{\max}(S_i) \leq C_{\max}(S_{opt})$ and S_i must be optimal, too. Thus the procedure must reach S_{opt} after a finite number of steps unless some $S_i \neq S_{opt}$ is optimal. □

A disadvantage of N_1 is that for all (v, w) on a critical path where v and w belong to the same block and neither v is the first operation in the block nor w is the last operation in the block, the move which corresponds to (v, w) does not improve the $C_{\max}$-value. Thus, generally several moves are necessary to improve the objective value. To decrease this number of moves, N_1 can be extended in the following way.

Let (v, w) be on a critical path with respect to S, where v and w are to be processed on the same machine, and denote by $PM(v)$ $(SM(w))$ the immediate disjunctive predecessor (successor) of $v(w)$, if it exists. Instead of the reversal of (v, w), we consider as moves all possible permutations of $\{PM(v), v, w\}$ and $\{v, w, SM(w)\}$ in which arc (v, w) is inverted. Denote this neighborhood by $\mathbf{N_2}$. Then we clearly have $N_1(S) \subseteq N_2(S)$ for all complete selections S. Thus, N_2 is also opt-connected.

Another alternative would be to consider the neighborhood $\mathbf{N_3}$ defined by all moves shifting an operation of some block at the beginning or the end of the block. Such moves are not defined if the resulting selections are not complete, i.e. contain cycles. Unfortunately, it is an open question whether N_3 is opt-connected.

N_3 can be extended to a neighborhood $\mathbf{N_4}$ which is opt-connected by defining neighbors S' of S in the following way.

Let p be a critical path in $G(S)$. Then S' is derived from S by moving one operation of a block B of p, which is different from the first (last) operation j in B, before (after) all other operations in B if the resulting selection is feasible. Otherwise j is moved to the position inside block B closest to the first (last) position of B such that the resulting schedule is feasible. Note that $N_3(S) \subseteq N_4(S)$ for all complete selections S.

Theorem 6.23 N_4 is opt-connected.

Proof: Let S_{opt} be an optimal solution and, for an arbitrary complete selection S, denote by $n(S)$ the number of disjunctive arcs fixed in different directions in S and S_{opt}.

If S is not optimal, then according to Theorem 6.18 a block B exists in a critical path of S such that at least one operation j in B is processed before or after all other operations of B in S_{opt}. Assume w.l.o.g. that j has to be processed before all other operations of B. Then we move j to the position closest to the beginning of B such that the resulting schedule S' is feasible. This is one of the moves in N_4. Note that due to Lemma 6.21 it is always possible to move j to the position of its immediate predecessor in B. Furthermore, $n(S') < n(S)$. $\qquad\square$

Organization of the Tabu-List

The main components of a tabu-search algorithm are memory structures, in order to have a trace of the evolution of the search, and strategies for using the memory information in the best possible way.

The fundamental memory structure is a so-called tabu list, which stores attributes characterizing solutions that should not be considered again for a certain length of time. Usually a first-in-first-out (FIFO) strategy is applied to the list. Old attributes are deleted as new attributes are inserted.

In connection with the job shop scheduling problem and the neighborhoods N_1 to N_4, disjunctive arcs (i, j) reversed by recent moves will be used as attributes. A solution S is defined to be tabu if an arc belonging to the attribute set is contained in S.

As a supporting data structure we may use a square matrix $A = (a_{ij})$ with a dimension equal to the maximum number of operations. a_{ij} contains the count of the iteration in which arc (i, j) was last reversed. We forbid the swapping of arc (i, j) if the previous a_{ij}-value a_{ij}^{old} plus the length l of the tabu list is greater than the count a_{ij}^{new} of the current iteration, i.e.

$l > a_{ij}^{new} - a_{ij}^{old}$. Thus, a solution is not considered again after less than l iterations.

Dell'Amico & Trubian [75] suggest using a variable length l for the tabu list, defined according to the following rules:

- if the current objective function value is less than the best value found before, then set $l = 1$.

- if we are in an improving phase of the search (i.e. the value of the objective function of the current solution is less than the value at the previous iteration) and the length of the list is greater than a threshold *MIN*, then decrease the list length by one unit.

- if we are not in an improving phase of the search (i.e. the value of the objective function of the current solution is greater than or equal to the value at the previous iteration) and the length of the list is less than a given *MAX*, then increase the length by one unit.

Such a tabu list is called **dynamic**.

Finally, we note that A is usually sparse and can be stored in a compact way if its dimension is large.

Aspiration Criterion

An aspiration criterion is introduced as a condition for cancelling the effect of tabu status on a move. A basic condition for allowing a forbidden move from solution S to solution S' is:

An estimation $estim(S, S')$ for the solution value S' which depends on S is less than the value of the best solution found before the current iteration.

One may define $estim(S, S')$ as follows. Let $B(S, S')$ be the set of all operations j such that (i, j) or (j, i) is reversed by the move from S to S'. Furthermore, for each operation i, let $r_i(r_i')$ be the length of the longest path from 0 to i in $G(S)$ $(G(S'))$ and let $q_i(q_i')$ be the length of the longest path from i to $\star$ in $G(S)$ $(G(S'))$. Then we set

$$estim(S, S') = \max\{r_j' + p_j + q_j' \mid j \in B(S, S')\}. \qquad (6.21)$$

The values r_j' and q_j' can be calculated using the r_j- and q_j-values. The r_j- and q_j-values are found by longest path calculations in $G(S)$ (see Dell'Amico & Trubian [75]).

The idea behind such an aspiration criterion is that we are interested in moving to a solution S' which improves the best previous solution even if the corresponding move is tabu. To check whether S' is an improving solution we have to calculate the value $C_{\max}(S')$. Since this may be too time-consuming, an alternative is to replace $C_{\max}(S')$ by an estimate $estim(S, S')$ for $C_{\max}(S')$. $Estim(S, S')$ defined by (6.21) is a lower bound for $C_{\max}(S')$ which can be easily calculated.

A more recent and improved tabu-search implementation is described in Nowicki & Smutnicki [177]. Dorndorf & Pesch [77] apply genetic algorithms to the job shop problem. Genetic algorithms are generalizations of local search methods. A detailed computational study of local search methods for shop scheduling problems can be found in Aarts et al. [1].

6.5   Mixed Shop Problems

In this section we consider mixed shop problems, denoted by the symbol X. The mixed shop is a combination of the job shop problem and the open shop problem. Thus, we have open shop jobs and job shop jobs. As before, the number of operations of job i is denoted by n_i. n_J and n_O are bounds on the number of job shop and open shop jobs, respectively.

6.5.1   Problems with Two Machines

Due to the complexity of job shop scheduling problems, only problems with two machines, in which the number of jobs is fixed or each job shop job has at the most two operations, can be expected to be polynomially solvable. Strusevich [192] has shown that both problems $X2 \mid n_i \leq 2 \mid C_{\max}$ and $X2 \mid pmtn; n_i \leq 2 \mid C_{\max}$ can be solved in $O(n \log n)$ steps. His approach consists of a complicated case analysis. He considers thirteen cases which depend on the operations and their processing times. For each case he describes an optimal schedule. For details we refer to Strusevich [192]. Shaklevich et al. [184] present an $O(r^3 + n)$-algorithm for problem $X2 \mid n_J = 2; pmtn \mid C_{\max}$ and show that $X2 \mid n_J = k; n_O = l \mid C_{\max}$ can be solved in $O(r^{3n_J} 2^{n_O})$ time by using techniques similar to those presented in Section 6.4.3.

6.5.2 Problems with Two Jobs

Shakhlevich & Sotskov [183] have shown that the problems $X \mid n = 2 \mid C_{\max}$ and $X \mid n = 2 \mid \sum C_i$ are $\mathcal{NP}$-hard. They also suggested an $O(r)$-algorithm for the preemptive problem consisting of one open shop job and one job shop job with an arbitrary regular objective function $f(C_1, C_2)$. As before, r is the maximum number of operations of both jobs. This algorithm will be presented in this section.

Assume that we have two jobs, J_1 and J_2. Let J_1 be a job shop job with operations O_{1j} $(j = 1, \ldots, n_1)$. O_{1j} has the processing time p_{1j} and is to be processed on machine $\mu_j \in \{M_1, \ldots, M_m\}$. Job J_2 is an open shop job with operations O_{2j} $(j = 1, \ldots, n_2 = m)$, where O_{2j} has the processing time p_{2j} and must be processed on M_j. The order in which the operations O_{2j} are processed is arbitrary.

Let $t_i = \sum_{j=1}^{n_i} p_{ij}$ be the total processing time of J_i $(i = 1, 2)$. We consider the two cases $t_2 \leq t_1$ and $t_1 < t_2$.

Case: $t_2 \leq t_1$

We assume that an index l $(1 \leq l < n_1)$ exists with $\sum_{j=1}^{l} p_{1j} = t_2$. Otherwise we split an operation of J_1 into two operations.

For each $k = 1, \ldots, m$ we define

$$s_k = p_{2k} + \sum_{\substack{\mu_j = M_k \\ j \leq l}} p_{1j}$$

and set $s = s_{k^*} := \max_{k=1}^{n} s_k$.

We consider two subcases.

Subcase: $s \leq t_2$

We will construct a schedule with $C_1 = t_1$ and $C_2 = t_2$ which is optimal. It is sufficient to show that for the truncated problem obtained by replacing J_1 by $O_{11}, \ldots, O_{1l}$ a schedule S exists which finishes at time t_2. If, additionally, the remaining operations $O_{1,l+1}, \ldots, O_{1,n_1}$ are processed

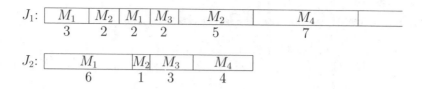

Figure 6.24: Two jobs.

from time t_2 without interruption, then we get a schedule with $C_1 = t_1$ and $C_2 = t_2$.

To construct S we first solve the two-job open shop problem with processing times

$$\bar{p}_{1k} = \sum_{\substack{\mu_j = M_k \\ j \leq l}} p_{1j} \text{ and } \bar{p}_{2k} = p_{2k} \text{ for } k = 1, \ldots, m.$$

Because for open shops there is a complete symmetry between jobs and machines, this can be done by using the algorithm described in Section 6.2.1. Because $\bar{p}_{1k} + \bar{p}_{2k} \leq t_2$, all operations can be scheduled in $[0, t_2]$. To illustrate this step we consider the following example.

Example 6.2

Consider two jobs represented by Figure 6.24.

We have $t_2 = 14 < t_1 = 21$.

We truncate this problem by eliminating the last operation of J_1. The corresponding two-job open shop problem is defined by the following $\bar{p}_{ij}$-values

i	1	2	3	4
a_i	5	7	2	0
b_i	6	1	3	4

Applying the algorithm given in Section 6.2.1, we get $I = \{1, 3, 4\}$, $J = \{2\}$, $5 = a_1 = \max\{\max\{5, 2, 0\}, 1\}$ and the schedule shown in Figure 6.25.   □

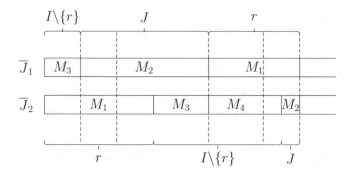

Figure 6.25: Application of the algorithm form Section 6.2.1.

The final step is to cut the schedule along the operations of J_1 into slices and to reschedule these slices in such a way that we get a preemptive schedule for the truncated original problem in $[0, t_2]$. Adding the operations of J_1 scheduled after t_2, we get an optimal solution for $X \mid n = 2; pmtn \mid f$ (see Figure 6.26).

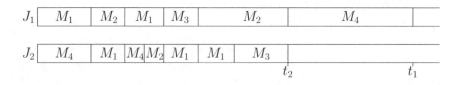

Figure 6.26: Optimal schedule for an instance of $X \mid n = 2; pmtn \mid f$.

The open shop problem can be solved in $O(m)$ time. Furthermore, the number of "slices" we have to rearrange in the last step of the algorithm is at the most n_1. Thus, the computational time is bounded by $O(\max\{m, n_1\})$. Note that we have at the most n_1 preemptions of J_2-operations.

Subcase: $s = s_{k^*} > t_2$

No schedule exists with $C_i = t_i$ for $i = 1, 2$ because if $C_2 = t_2$, then at least one operation O_{1j} with $\mu_j = M_{k^*}$ and $j \leq l$ must finish later than time t_2. This implies that J_1 may finish later than t_1 (see Figure 6.27(c)).

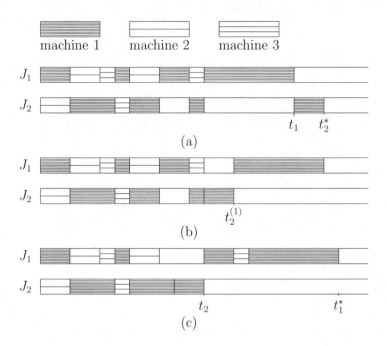

Figure 6.27: An example for Subcase $s > t_2$ of Case $t_2 \leq t_1$.

To avoid excessive formalism, we will use the example in Figure 6.27 to explain how to proceed in this case. In the example, $k^* = 1$. We first consider the two extreme cases in which

(1) $C_1 = t_1$ and C_2 is minimized (see Figure 6.27(a)) or

(2) $C_2 = t_2$ and C_1 is minimized (see Figure 6.27(c)).

Denote the minimal C_2-value in Case (1) by t_2^* and the minimal C_1-value in Case (2) by t_1^* .
For each $t_2 \leq t \leq t_2^*$ define

$$f(t) = \min\{f(s,t) \mid t_1 \leq s \leq t_1^*\}.$$

Then $f(t^*) = \min\{f(t) \mid t_2 \leq t \leq t_2^*\}$ is the optimal solution of the problem. To calculate t^* we need to consider at the most n_1 different t-values which can be calculated in $O(n_1)$ time. This can be explained as follows using Figure 6.27.

We start with the optimal schedule for $t = t_2^*$ shown in Figure 6.27(a). The only way to decrease t is to increase s from t_1 to t_2^*. To minimize $f(s,t)$ for fixed $s = t_2^*$ in Figure 6.27(a) we move the last processing period of J_1 on machine 1 $t_2^* - t_1$ time units to the right and shift the last processing period of J_2 on machine 1 as far as possible to the left. The resulting new schedule is shown in Figure 6.27(b). Let $t_2^{(1)}$ be the new finishing time of J_2. Then

$$f(t_2^{(1)}) = \min\{f(t) \mid t_2^{(1)} \le t < t_2^*\}.$$

To decrease $t = t_2^{(1)}$ we need to move the last M_1-processing period of J_1 to the right in such a way that it finishes at time $t_2^{(1)}$. Also shifting the last M_1-block of J_2 to the left yields the schedule of Figure 6.27(c) in which the new finishing time of J_2 is equal to t_2. Thus, a further decrease of the finishing time of J_2 is not possible and we have $f(t^*) = \min\{f(t_2^*), f(t_2^{(1)}), f(t_2)\}$.

It is not difficult to write a procedure which solves the general problem in $O(n_1)$ time if the objective function $f(s,t)$ can be evaluated in constant time for given (s,t).

Next we consider the

Case: $t_1 < t_2$

We define

$$s_k = \sum_{\mu_j = M_k} p_{1j} + p_{2k} \qquad \text{for } k = 1, \ldots, m.$$

If $s = \max s_k \le t_1$, then, as in the previous case, a schedule exists with $C_i = t_i$ for $i = 1, 2$ which is optimal.

Therefore, we assume that $s_k > t_1$ for some k. If $s_k \le t_2$, then again a schedule exists with $C_i = t_i$ for $i = 1, 2$ (see Figure 6.28).

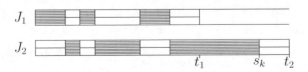

Figure 6.28: Schedule with $C_i = t_i$ for $i = 1, 2$

Finally, let $s_k > t_2$. In this case we proceed as in the previous second subcase. For an example, see Figure 6.29.

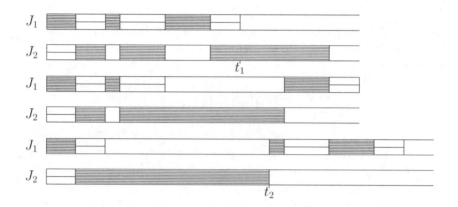

Figure 6.29: Schedule for Subcase $s_k > t_2$ of Case $t_1 < t_2$.

6.6 Complexity of Shop Scheduling Problems

In this section we will give a survey on complexity results for shop scheduling problems.

Complexity results for open shop problems are summarized in Tables 6.1 to 6.3. We have to add $O(nm \log^2 nm)$, the complexity for the coloring procedure, to get the complexities of the open shop problems P in Table 6.1.

Table 6.4 shows that problem $F2 \parallel C_{\max}$ is the only nontrivial flow shop problem without preemptions which is polynomially solvable if the processing times are arbitrary. Similar results hold for preemptive flow shop scheduling problems. Flow shop problems with m stages and unit processing times are closely related to corresponding problems with m identical parallel machines and unit processing times.

Tables 6.6 to 6.8 present complexity results for job shop scheduling problems. f is an arbitrary regular objective function.

Note that $r = \max\{n_i, \ldots, n_n\}$ is the maximum number of operations of the jobs.

Tables 6.9 and 6.10 present complexity results for mixed shop problems. Again f is an arbitrary regular function and $r = \max\{n_1, \ldots, n_k\}$. We assume that $f(C_1, C_2)$ can be evaluated in constant time.

Problem P	Problem $\hat{P}$	Complexity of $\hat{P}$
$O \mid p_{ij} = 1; r_i \mid C_{\max}$	$P \mid r_i; pmtn \mid C_{\max}$	Horn [115] $O(n^2)$ Gonzales & Johnson [103] $O(nm)$
$O \mid p_{ij} = 1; tree \mid C_{\max}$	$P \mid tree; pmtn \mid C_{\max}$	Muntz & Coffman [173] $O(n^2)$ Gonzales & Johnson [103] $O(n \log m)$
$O2 \mid p_{ij} = 1; prec \mid C_{\max}$	$P2 \mid prec; pmtn \mid C_{\max}$	Muntz & Coffman [172] Gonzales & Johnson [103] (nr)
$O \mid p_{ij} = 1; r_i; d_i \mid -$	$P \mid r_i; d_i; pmtn \mid -$	Horn [115] (n^3)
$O \mid p_{ij} = 1 \mid L_{\max}$	$P \mid pmtn \mid L_{\max}$	Horn [115] (n^2) Gonzales & Johnson [103] $O(nm)$
$O \mid p_{ij} = 1; r_i \mid L_{\max}$	$P \mid r_i; pmtn \mid L_{\max}$	Labetoulle et al. [133] $O(n^3 \min\{n^2, \log n + \log \max_j p_j\})$
$O \mid p_{ij} = 1; intree \mid L_{\max}$	$P \mid intree; p_i = m; pmtn \mid L_{\max}$	Garey & Johnson [96] $O(nm \log nm)$ Monma [169] $O(nm)$
$2 \mid p_{ij} = 1; prec \mid L_{\max}$	$P2 \mid prec; pmtn \mid L_{\max}$	Lawler [139] $O(n^2)$
$O2 \mid p_{ij} = 1; r_i; prec \mid L_{\max}$	$P2 \mid; r_i; prec; pmtn \mid L_{\max}$	Lawler [139] $O(n^6)$ Garey & Johnson [96] $O(n^3 m^3)$
$O \mid p_{ij} = 1 \mid \sum w_i C_i$	$P \mid p_i = m; pmtn \mid \sum w_i C_i$	Mc Naughton [165] $(n \log n)$
$O \mid p_{ij} = 1 \mid \sum T_i$	$P \mid p_i = m; pmtn \mid \sum T_i$	Liu & Bulfin [161] $O(nm + n \log n)$
$O \mid p_{ij} = 1 \mid \sum U_i$	$P \mid p_i = m; pmtn \mid \sum U_i$	Liu & Bulfin [161] $O(nm + n \log n)$

Table 6.1: Complexities of transformed problems $\hat{P}$.

$O \mid p_{ij} = 1; tree \mid C_{\max}$	Bräsel et al. [31]	$O(nm)$
$O2 \parallel C_{\max}$	6.2.1 Gonzalez & Sahni [104]	$O(n)$
$O \mid p_{ij} = 1; intree \mid L_{\max}$	6.2.2 Brucker et al. [40],	$O(mn \log^2 mn)$
$O \mid p_{ij} = 1; r_i \mid L_{\max}$	Brucker et al. [40]	Networkflow-problem
$O \mid r_i; pmtn \mid L_{\max}$	Cho & Sahni [66]	lin. progr.
$O2 \mid p_{ij} = 1; prec; r_i \mid L_{\max}$	Brucker et al. [40]	
	Lawler [139]	$O(n^6)$
$O \mid p_{ij} = 1; chains; r_i \mid L_{\max}$	Baptiste et al. [21]	$O(n^9)$
$O \mid p_{ij} = 1; outtree \mid \sum C_i$	Bräsel et al. [32]	$O(nm)$
$O \mid p_{ij} = 1; outtree; r_i \mid C_{\max}$	Lushchakova [163]	
$O2 \mid p_{ij} = 1; prec \mid \sum C_i$	Coffman et al. [68]	$O(n)$
$Om \mid p_{ij} = 1; r_i \mid \sum C_i$	Tautenhahn & Wöginger [196]	$O(n^2 m^{6m})$
$O \mid p_{ij} = 1; r_i \mid \sum C_i$	Brucker& Kravchenko [51]	lin. progr.
$O \mid p_{ij} = 1 \mid \sum w_i C_i$	6.2.2 Brucker et al. [40]	
	Tanaev et al. [194]	$O(mn + n \log n)$
$O \mid p_{ij} = 1 \mid \sum U_i$	6.2.2 Liu & Bulfin [161]	$O(n^2 m)$
$Om \mid p_{ij} = 1; r_i \mid \sum w_i U_i$	Baptiste [15]	$O(n^{4m^2 - m + 10})$
$O \mid p_{ij} = 1 \mid \sum T_i$	6.2.2 Liu & Bulfin [161]	$O(nm \log^2(mn))$

Table 6.2: Polynomially solvable open shop problems.

$O3 \parallel C_{\max}$	Gonzalez & Sahni [104]
$O \mid n = 3 \mid C_{\max}$	Gonzalez & Sahni [104]
$*O \parallel C_{\max}$	Lenstra [150]
$*O \mid p_{ij} = 1; outtree; r_i \mid C_{\max}$	Timkovsky [202]
$*O \mid p_{ij} = 1; prec \mid C_{\max}$	Timkovsky [202]
$*O2 \mid chains \mid C_{\max}$	Tanaev et al. [194]
$*O2 \mid chains; pmtn \mid C_{\max}$	Lenstra [150]
$*O2 \mid r_i \mid C_{\max}$	Lawler et al. [143],[144]
$*O \mid p_{ij} = 1; outtree \mid L_{\max}$	Timkovsky [202]
$*O2 \parallel L_{\max}$	Lawler et al. [143],[144]
$*O2 \parallel \sum C_i$	Achugbue & Chin [2]
$O2 \mid pmtn \mid \sum C_i$	Du & Leung [83]
$*O3 \mid pmtn \mid \sum C_i$	Liu & Bulfin [160]
$*O2 \mid r_i; pmtn \mid \sum C_i$	Sriskandarajah & Wagneur [191]
$*O2 \mid chains; pmtn \mid \sum C_i$	Lenstra [150]
$*Om \mid p_{ij} = 1; chains \mid \sum w_i C_i$ for each $m \geq 2$	Timkovsky [202]
$*O2 \mid pmtn \mid \sum w_i C_i$	Lenstra [150]
$*O2 \mid pmtn \mid \sum U_i$	Lawler et al. [143],[144]
$*O \mid p_{ij} = 1; r_i \mid \sum U_i$	Kravchenko [127]
$*Om \mid p_{ij} = 1; chains \mid \sum U_i$ for each $m \geq 2$	Timkovsky [202]
$*Om \mid p_{ij} = 1; chains \mid \sum T_i$ for each $m \geq 2$	Timkovsky [202]

Table 6.3: $\mathcal{NP}$-hard open shop problems.

$F2 \mid p_{ij} = 1; prec; r_i \mid \sum C_i$	Baptiste & Timkowsky [23]	
$Fm \mid p_{ij} = 1; intree \mid \sum C_i$	Averbakh etal.[11]	
$F \mid p_{ij} = 1; outtree; r_i \mid C_{\max}$	Bruno et al. [60]	$O(n^2)$
$F \mid p_{ij} = 1; tree \mid C_{\max}$	Bruno et al.[60]	$O(n)$
$F2 \parallel C_{\max}$	Johnson [120]	$O(n \log n)$
	6.2.1	
$F2 \mid pmtn \mid C_{\max}$	Gonzales & Sahni [105]	$O(n \log n)$
$F \mid p_{ij} = 1; intree \mid L_{\max}$	Bruno et al. [60]	$O(n^2)$
$F2 \mid p_{ij} = 1; prec; r_i \mid L_{\max}$	Bruno et al. [60]	$O(n^3 \log n)$
$F \mid p_{ij} = 1; outtree; r_i \mid \sum C_i$	Brucker & Knust [44]	$O(n \log n)$
$F2 \mid p_{ij} = 1; prec \mid \sum C_i$	Brucker & Knust [44]	$O(n^{\log 7})$
$F \mid p_{ij} = 1; r_i \mid \sum w_i U_i$	Single machine problem	$O(n^3)$
$F \mid p_{ij} = 1; r_i \mid \sum w_i T_i$	Single machine problem	$O(n^3)$

Table 6.4: Polynomially solvable flow shop problems.

$* \; F \mid p_{ij} = 1; intree; r_i \mid C_{\max}$ Brucker & Knust [44]

$* \; F \mid p_{ij} = 1; prec \mid C_{\max}$ Leung et al. [156]

$* \; F2 \mid chains \mid C_{\max}$ Lenstra et al. [155]

$* \; F2 \mid chains; pmtn \mid C_{\max}$ Lenstra [150]

$* \; F2 \mid r_i \mid C_{\max}$ Lenstra et al. [155]

$* \; F2 \mid r_i; pmtn \mid C_{\max}$ Gonzales & Sahni [105]

$* \; F3 \parallel C_{\max}$ Garey et al. [100]

$* \; F3 \mid pmtn \mid C_{\max}$ Gonzales & Sahni [105]

$* \; F \mid p_{ij} = 1; outtree \mid L_{\max}$ Brucker & Knust [44]

$* \; F2 \parallel L_{\max}$ Lenstra et al. [155]

$* \; F2 \mid pmtn \mid L_{\max}$ Gonzales & Sahni [105]

$* \; F2 \parallel \sum C_i$ Garey et al. [100]

$* \; F2 \mid pmtn \mid \sum C_i$ Du & Leung [83]

$* \; Fm \mid p_{ij} = 1; chains \mid \sum w_i C_i$ Tanaev et al. [194]

$* \; Fm \mid p_{ij} = 1; chains \mid \sum U_i$ Brucker & Knust [44]
for each $m \geq 2$

$* \; Fm \mid p_{ij} = 1; chains \mid \sum T_i$ Brucker & Knust [44]
for each $m \geq 2$

Table 6.5: $\mathcal{NP}$-hard flow shop problems.

$J2 \mid n_i \leq 2 \mid C_{\max}$	Jackson [119] 6.4.1	$O(n \log n)$
$J2 \mid p_{ij} = 1 \mid C_{\max}$	Timkovsky [198]	$O(n \log(nr))$
$J2 \mid p_{ij} = 1; r_i \mid C_{\max}$	Timkovsky [200]	$O(n^2)$
$J2 \mid n = k \mid C_{\max}$	Brucker [34]]	$O(r^{2k})$
$J2 \mid p_{ij} = 1 \mid L_{\max}$	Timkovsky [199]	$O(n^2)$
$J \mid prec; p_{ij} = 1; r_i; n = k \mid f_{\max}$	Brucker & Krämer [49]	$O(k^2 2^k m r^{k+1})$
$J2 \mid p_{ij} = 1 \mid \sum C_i$	Kubiak & Timkovsky [131]	$O(n \log n)$
$J2 \mid p_{ij} = 1 \mid \sum U_i$	Kravchenko [126]	$O(n^6)$
$J2 \mid n = k \mid f$	Brucker et al. [54]	$O(r^{1.5(k^2+k)})$
$J \mid prec; r_i; n = 2 \mid f$	Sotskov [189], Brucker [33] 6.4.2	$O(r^2 \log r)$
$J \mid prec; r_i; n = 2; pmtn \mid f$	Sotskov [189] 6.4.2	$O(r^3)$
$J \mid prec; p_{ij} = 1; r_i; n = k \mid \sum f_i$	Brucker & Krämer [46]	$O(k^2 2^k m r^{k+1})$

Table 6.6: Polynomially solvable job shop problems.

$J \mid prec; r_i; n = k \mid \sum w_i U_i$	Middendorf & Timkovsky [167]
$J2 \mid p_{ij} = 1 \mid \sum w_i U_i$	Kravchenko [127]
$J \mid prec; r_i; n = k \mid \sum w_i T_i$	Middendorf & Timkovsky [167]
$J \mid prec; r_i; n = k; pmtn \mid \sum w_i U_i$	Middendorf & Timkovsky [167]
$J \mid prec; r_i; n = k; pmtn \mid \sum w_i T_i$	Middendorf & Timkovsky [167]

Table 6.7: Pseudopolynomially solvable job shop problems.

$*J2 \mid p_{ij} \in \{1,2\} \mid C_{\max}$ Lenstra & Rinnooy Kan [153]

$*J2 \mid chains; p_{ij} = 1 \mid C_{\max}$ Timkovsky [198]

$*J2 \mid pmtn \mid C_{\max}$ Lenstra & Rinnooy Kan [153]

$J2 \mid n = 3; pmtn \mid C_{\max}$ Brucker et al. [55]

$*J3 \mid p_{ij} = 1 \mid C_{\max}$ Lenstra & Rinnooy Kan [153]

$J3 \mid n = 3 \mid C_{\max}$ Sotskov & Shakhlevich [190]

$*J2 \parallel \sum C_i$ Garey et al. [100]

$*J2 \mid chains; p_{ij} = 1 \mid \sum C_i$ Timkovsky [199]

$J2 \mid p_{ij} = 1; r_i \mid \sum C_i$ Timkovsky [199]

$*J2 \mid pmtn \mid \sum C_i$ Lenstra [150]

$J2 \mid n = 3; pmtn \mid \sum C_i$ Brucker et al. [55]

$J3 \mid n = 3 \mid \sum C_i$ Sotskov & Shakhlevich [190]

$*J3 \mid p_{ij} = 1 \mid \sum C_i$ Lenstra [150]

$J2 \mid p_{ij} = 1 \mid \sum w_i C_i$ Timkovsky [199]

$*J2 \mid p_{ij} = 1; r_i \mid \sum w_i C_i$ Timkovsky [199]

$J2 \mid p_{ij} = 1; r_i \mid \sum U_i$ Timkovsky [202]

$J2 \mid p_{ij} = 1 \mid \sum w_i U_i$ Kravchenko [126]

$J2 \mid p_{ij} = 1 \mid \sum T_i$ Timkovsky [199]

$*J2 \mid p_{ij} = 1 \mid \sum w_i T_i$ Timkovsky [199]

Table 6.8: $\mathcal{NP}$-hard job shop problems.

$X2 \mid n_i \leq 2 \mid C_{\max}$ Strusevich [192]
$O(n \log n)$

$X2 \mid n_i \leq 2; pmtn \mid C_{\max}$ Strusevich [192]
$O(n \log n)$

$X2 \mid n_J = 2; pmtn \mid C_{\max}$ Shakhlevich et al. [184]
$O(r^3 + n)$

$X2 \mid n_J = k; n_O = l \mid C_{\max}$ Shakhlevich et al. [184]
$O(r^{3n_J} 2^{n_O})$

$Xm \mid n_J \leq 2; n_O = l \mid C_{\max}$ Shakhlevich et al. [184]
$O((r^2 \log r)^{n_O m + 1} (n_O m)!)$

$X \mid n_J = 1; pmtn \mid C_{\max}$ Shakhlevich et al. [184]
$O(nm(\min\{nm, m^2\} + m \log n) + r)$

$X2 \mid n_J = 1; n_O = 1; pmtn \mid f$ 6.5.2 Shakhlevich& Sotskov [183]
$O(r)$

Table 6.9: Polynomially solvable mixed shop problems.

$*X2 \mid n_O = 0; p_{ij} \in \{1, 2\} \mid C_{\max}$ Lenstra & Rinnooy Kan [153]

$*X \mid n_J = 1; n_O = 1 \mid C_{\max}$ Shakhlevich & Sotskov [183]

$*X2 \mid n_J = 1 \mid C_{\max}$ Shakhlevich et al. [184]

$X2 \mid n_J = 3; n_O = 0; pmtn \mid C_{\max}$ Brucker et al. [54]

$X3 \mid n_J = 3; n_O = 0 \mid C_{\max}$ Shakhlevich & Sotskov [183]

$X3 \mid n_J = 2; n_O = 1; pmtn \mid C_{\max}$ Shakhlevich et al. [184]

$*X \mid n_J = 1; n_O = 1 \mid \sum C_i$ Shakhlevich & Sotskov [183]

Table 6.10: $\mathcal{NP}$-hard mixed shop problems.

Chapter 7

Due-Date Scheduling

New production technologies like "just-in-time" production lead to special scheduling problems involving due dates d_i. Contrary to classical scheduling problems where the objective function simply involves lateness $L_i = C_i - d_i$ or tardiness $T_i = \max\{0, C_i - d_i\}$ penalties, earliness $E_i = \max\{0, d_i - C_i\}$ is now also of importance. Objective functions such as $\sum w_i \mid L_i \mid$ and $\sum w_i L_i^2$ are typical of "just-in-time" situations. Note that $L_i = T_i + E_i$ and $L_i^2 = T_i^2 + E_i^2$. From the practical and theoretical point of view, situations in which all due dates are equal are of importance. This due date d may be a given parameter of the problem or it may be a variable, i.e. we are interested in an optimal due date d_{opt} with respect to the objective function. To indicate these special situations we add d or d_{opt} to the job characteristics of the problem. If the due date is a variable, then we may add due-date assignment costs $w_d \cdot d$ to the objective function.

Another objective function considered in the literature in connection with single-machine problems is $\sum w_i \mid L_{\sigma(i)} \mid$, where $\sigma : \sigma(1), \ldots, \sigma(n)$ denotes the sequence in which the jobs are processed on the machine. In this case the weights w_i do not correspond with the jobs but with the positions in which the jobs are scheduled.

In this chapter we will present polynomial and pseudo-polynomial algorithms for such due-date scheduling problems. In general, we will restrict ourselves to the one-machine case. Furthermore, we assume that there are no precedence constraints between jobs and that preemption is not allowed.

In the next sections we show that the d_{opt}-version of the problem with objective function $\sum w_i \mid L_{\sigma(i)} \mid$ can be solved efficiently.

7.1   Problem $1 \mid d_{opt} \mid \sum w_i |L_{\sigma(i)}| + w_0 \cdot d$

Given non-negative weights w_i $(i = 0, \ldots, n)$, we have to schedule jobs
with processing times p_i $(i = 1, \ldots, n)$ on one machine and find a common
due date d_{opt} such that

$$\sum_{i=1}^{n} w_i \mid C_{\sigma(i)} - d_{opt} \mid +w_0 d_{opt} \tag{7.1}$$

is minimized. $\sigma(i)$ denotes the job scheduled in position i on the machine.
Thus, the weights are position weights rather than weights associated
with the jobs.

Next we will derive properties of an optimal schedule for this problem.

Lemma 7.1 An optimal schedule exists in which the machine is not idle
between the processing of jobs.

Proof: Assume that we have an optimal schedule where the machine is
idle between the processing of jobs i and j as shown in Figure 7.1.

Figure 7.1: Idle period between jobs i and j.

Thus, we have $t < s$ for the completion time t of i and the starting time
s of j. If $d_{opt} < t$, we move job j and the jobs scheduled after j' by an
amount of $\triangle = s - t$ units to the left without increasing the objective
value. If $d_{opt} > s$, we may move job i and the jobs scheduled before i by
the same amount of units to the right without increasing the objective
value. If $t \leq d_{opt} \leq s$, we may move i with its predecessors to the right
and j with its successors to the left such that i finishes at time d_{opt} and
j starts at time d_{opt} without increasing the objective value. After at
the most $n - 1$ such steps we get an optimal schedule without idle time
between the jobs. $\square$

We may assume that the first job starts at time 0 in an optimal schedule. If this is not the case, i.e. if the first job starts at time $t \neq 0$, replace d_{opt} and the starting times x_i of all jobs $i = 1, \ldots, n$ by $d_{opt} - t$ and $x_i - t$ without changing the objective value.

It is convenient to introduce a dummy job 0 with processing time $p_0 = 0$ and weight w_0 which is always scheduled at time 0, i.e. we define $\sigma(0) = 0$. Then the objective function is

$$\sum_{i=0}^{n} w_i \mid C_{\sigma(i)} - d_{opt} \mid . \tag{7.2}$$

We conclude that an optimal schedule is given by a sequence $\sigma(0)$, $\sigma(1), \ldots, \sigma(n)$ with $\sigma(0) = 0$.

Theorem 7.2 Let k be a median for the sequence $w_0, w_1, \ldots, w_n$, i.e.

$$\sum_{j=0}^{k-1} w_j \leq \sum_{j=k}^{n} w_j \text{ and } \sum_{j=0}^{k} w_j \geq \sum_{j=k+1}^{n} w_j. \tag{7.3}$$

Then $d_{opt} = \sum_{i=0}^{k} p_{\sigma(i)}$ for some optimal sequence σ.

Proof: We first show that in an optimal solution d_{opt} is the finishing time of some job.

Consider a solution σ, d with $C_{\sigma(i)} < d < C_{\sigma(i+1)}$ and let Z be the corresponding objective value. Define $x := d - C_{\sigma(i)}$ and $y := C_{\sigma(i+1)} - d$. Let Z' and Z'' be the objective value for $d = C_{\sigma(i)}$ and $d = C_{\sigma(i+1)}$. Then

$$Z' = Z + x \sum_{j=i+1}^{n} w_j - x \sum_{j=0}^{i} w_j = Z + x \left(\sum_{j=i+1}^{n} w_j - \sum_{j=0}^{i} w_j \right) \tag{7.4}$$

and

$$Z'' = Z - y \sum_{j=i+1}^{n} w_j + y \sum_{j=0}^{i} w_j = Z - y \left(\sum_{j=i+1}^{n} w_j - \sum_{j=0}^{i} w_j \right) \tag{7.5}$$

(see Figure 7.2).

Thus, we have $Z' \leq Z$ if $\sum_{j=i+1}^{n} w_j - \sum_{j=0}^{i} w_j \leq 0$ and $Z'' < Z$ otherwise.

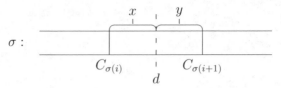

Figure 7.2: A solution with $C_{\sigma(i)} < d < C_{\sigma(i+1)}$.

$$
\begin{array}{cc}
\overset{x}{\overbrace{\hphantom{C_{\sigma(k-1)} \quad d_{opt} = C_{\sigma(k)}}}} & \overset{y}{\overbrace{\hphantom{d_{opt} = C_{\sigma(k)} \quad C_{\sigma(k+1)}}}} \\
C_{\sigma(k-1)} \quad d_{opt} = C_{\sigma(k)} & d_{opt} = C_{\sigma(k)} \quad C_{\sigma(k+1)} \\
\text{(a)} & \text{(b)}
\end{array}
$$

Figure 7.3: A solution with $d_{opt} = C_{\sigma(k)}$.

This implies that an optimal solution exists in which d_{opt} is equal to the completion time of some job $\sigma(k)$.

To prove that k satisfies (7.3), assume that $d_{opt} = C_{\sigma(k)}$, where σ is an optimal sequence. Let Z be the optimal solution value. Applying (7.4) and (7.5) to the situation shown in Figures 7.3(a) and 7.3(b), respectively, we conclude that

$$
\sum_{j=0}^{k} w_j - \sum_{j=k+1}^{n} w_j \geq 0 \text{ and } \sum_{j=k}^{n} w_j - \sum_{j=0}^{k-1} w_j \geq 0.
$$

$\square$

A job sequence $\sigma : \sigma(1), \ldots, \sigma(n)$ is called **V-shaped with respect to the p_i-values** if no three indices $i < j < k$ exist with $p_{\sigma(i)} < p_{\sigma(j)} > p_{\sigma(k)}$. It is not difficult to see that a sequence is V-shaped if and only if

$$
p_{\sigma(1)} \geq p_{\sigma(2)} \geq \cdots \geq p_{\sigma(k)} \text{ and } p_{\sigma(k)} \leq p_{\sigma(k+1)} \leq \cdots \leq p_{\sigma(n)} \qquad (7.6)
$$

for some $1 \leq k \leq n$.

If $k = 1$, then σ is a SPT-sequence. If $k = n$, then σ is a LPT-sequence.

Theorem 7.3 An optimal sequence exists which is V-shaped with respect to the p_i-values.

Proof: Let $\sigma : \sigma(1), \ldots, \sigma(n)$ and $d_{opt} = C_{\sigma(k)}$ be an optimal solution such that (7.3) is satisfied. For the corresponding objective value we have

$$\sum_{j=0}^{k} w_j(C_{\sigma(k)} - C_{\sigma(j)}) + \sum_{j=k+1}^{n} w_j(C_{\sigma(j)} - C_{\sigma(k)}) = \sum_{j=0}^{k} w_j \sum_{\nu=j+1}^{k} p_{\sigma(\nu)}$$

$$+ \sum_{j=k+1}^{n} w_j \sum_{\nu=k+1}^{j} p_{\sigma(\nu)} = \sum_{\nu=1}^{k} p_{\sigma(\nu)}(\sum_{j=0}^{\nu-1} w_j) + \sum_{\nu=k+1}^{n} p_{\sigma(\nu)}(\sum_{j=\nu}^{n} w_j).$$

$$= \sum_{j=1}^{n} p_{\sigma(j)} \lambda_j$$

with

$$\lambda_j = \begin{cases} \sum_{\nu=0}^{j-1} w_\nu & \text{for } j = 1, \ldots, k \\ \sum_{\nu=j}^{n} w_\nu & \text{for } j = k+1, \ldots, n. \end{cases} \tag{7.7}$$

Because $\lambda_1 \leq \lambda_2 \leq \ldots \leq \lambda_k$ and $\lambda_{k+1} \geq \lambda_{k+2} \geq \ldots \geq \lambda_n$, the objective value does not increase if we reorder σ in such a way that in the sum $\sum_{j=1}^{n} p_{\sigma(j)} \lambda_j$ the smallest p_i-values are assigned to the largest λ_j-values. This yields a sequence which is V-shaped with respect to the p_i-values.   □

To solve problem $1 \mid d_{opt} \mid \sum w_i \mid L_{\sigma(i)} \mid + w_0 d$, we first calculate k according to (7.3) and the corresponding λ_j-values. Using the λ_j-values, an optimal sequence σ is constructed and $d_{opt} = \sum_{j=1}^{k} p_{\sigma(j)}$ is calculated.

σ is constructed by matching the smallest p_i-values with the largest λ_j. More specifically, we compare λ_k and λ_{k+1}. If $\lambda_k \geq \lambda_{k+1}$, then a job with the smallest processing time is scheduled in position k and λ_k is replaced by λ_{k-1}. Otherwise such a job is scheduled in position $k+1$, and λ_{k+1} is replaced by λ_{k+2}, etc.

The computational complexity of this algorithm is $O(n \log n)$.

7.2   Problem $1|d_{opt}|w_E \sum E_i + w_T \sum T_i + w_0 d$

In "just-in-time" production models we have to consider a penalty not only if a job is late but also if a job is early with respect to a given due date d. A simple objective function modeling such a situation is $w_E \sum E_i + w_T \sum T_i + w_0 d$, where $E_i = \max\{0, -L_i\} = \max\{0, d_i - C_i\}$, $T_i = \max\{0, L_i\} = \max\{0, C_i - d_i\}$, and $w_E, w_T > 0$. Problem $1 \mid d_{opt} \mid$

$w_E \sum E_i + w_T \sum T_i + w_0 d$ can be solved using techniques described in the last section.

This is due to the fact that each solution of problem $1 \mid d_{opt} \mid w_E \sum E_i + w_T \sum T_i + w_0 d$ is a solution of problem $1 \mid d_{opt} \mid \sum w_i \mid L_{\sigma(i)} \mid + w_0 d$ with special weights (namely w_0 for the dummy job, w_E for each of the first jobs which is early, and w_T for each of the last jobs which is late).

Again, if we have an optimal solution, there is no idle time between two jobs and d_{opt} is equal to the finishing time of some job. If $d_{opt} = \sum_{\nu=1}^{k} p_{\sigma(\nu)}$, then the following inequalities hold

$$w_0 + (k-1)w_E \le (n-k+1)w_T \tag{7.8}$$

$$w_0 + k w_E \ge (n-k)w_T \tag{7.9}$$

(compare (7.3) and the proof of Theorem 7.2).

Inequalities (7.8) and (7.9) are equivalent to

$$\frac{n w_T - w_0}{w_E + w_T} \le k \le \frac{n w_T - w_0}{w_E + w_T} + 1. \tag{7.10}$$

We have to find an integer k satisfying (7.10). If $\frac{n w_T - w_0}{w_E + w_T}$ is not integer, then

$$k := \left\lceil \frac{n w_T - w_0}{w_E + w_T} \right\rceil \tag{7.11}$$

is the only k satisfying (7.10). Otherwise we have two solutions k and $k+1$ where k is given by (7.11). In this case, each d with $\sum_{\nu=1}^{k} p_{\sigma(\nu)} \le d \le \sum_{\nu=1}^{k+1} p_{\sigma(\nu)}$ provides the same objective value. This can be seen as follows.

Let $Z(\sigma, d)$ be the objective value for the sequence $\sigma : \sigma(1), \ldots, \sigma(n)$ and the due-date d. Then for $d^* = C_{\sigma(k)} := \sum_{j=1}^{k} p_{\sigma(\nu)}$ we have

$$Z(\sigma, d^*) = w_E \sum_{j=1}^{k} \mid C_{\sigma(j)} - d^* \mid + w_T \sum_{j=k+1}^{n} \mid C_{\sigma(j)} - d^* \mid + w_0 d^*.$$

Replacing d^* by $d^* + \triangle$ with $0 \le \triangle \le p_{\sigma(k+1)}$ yields

$$
\begin{aligned}
Z(\sigma, d^* + \triangle) &= Z(\sigma, d^*) + w_E k \triangle - w_T(n - k) \triangle + w_0 \triangle \\
&= Z(\sigma, d^*) + \triangle(k(w_E + w_T) + w_0 - n w_T) \\
&= Z(\sigma, d^*) + \triangle \cdot \left(\frac{n w_T - w_0}{w_E + w_T} (w_E + w_T) + w_0 - n w_T \right) \\
&= Z(\sigma, d^*).
\end{aligned}
$$

Therefore, regardless of whether k is integer or not, we may choose k as defined by (7.11). However, for large w_0 this value may be negative. In this case, we have to replace k by

$$
k := \max \left\{ 0, \left\lceil \frac{n w_T - w_0}{w_E + w_T} \right\rceil \right\}. \tag{7.12}
$$

Given k, for the corresponding λ_j-values we have

$$
\lambda_j = \begin{cases} w_E(j - 1) + w_0 & \text{for } 1 \le j \le k \\ w_T(n - j + 1) & \text{for } k + 1 \le j \le n \end{cases} \tag{7.13}
$$

(see (7.7)).

Using (7.12) and (7.13), an optimal solution for problem $1 \mid d_{opt} \mid w_E \sum E_i + w_T \sum T_i + w_0 d$ can be found using the algorithm described at the end of Section 7.2. The corresponding algorithm was first formulated by Panwalkar et al. [179].

If we set $w_E = w_T = 1$ and $w_0 = 0$, we get problem $1 \mid d_{opt} \mid \sum \mid L_i \mid$. Our algorithm also solves this problem if we set

$$
k := \left\lceil \frac{n}{2} \right\rceil
$$

and

$$
\lambda_j = \begin{cases} j - 1 & \text{for } 1 \le j \le k \\ n - j + 1 & \text{for } k + 1 \le j \le n \end{cases}
$$

(see Kanet [123]).

Finally, we mention that problem $P2 \mid d_{opt} \mid \sum \mid L_i \mid$ is $\mathcal{NP}$-hard.

7.3 Problem $1 \mid d \mid \sum w_i \mid L_{\sigma(i)} \mid$

If in problem $1 \mid d_{opt} \mid \sum \mid L_{\sigma(i)} \mid$ we replace d_{opt} by d, i.e. if the due date is given and a job cannot start before time $t = 0$, then the problem becomes $\mathcal{NP}$-hard (Kahlbacher [122]).

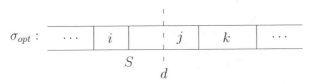

Figure 7.4: A schedule with $C_i < d < C_j$.

In this section we will derive a pseudo-polynomial algorithm for the problem $1 \mid d \mid \sum w_i \mid L_{\sigma(i)} \mid$ with positive w_i-values and given due date d. Such an algorithm is based on the fact that an optimal schedule exists with the following properties:

- the machine is not idle between jobs, and

- the schedule is V-shaped with respect to the p_i-values.

The first property follows as in Section 7.1. It implies that an optimal schedule is characterized by a sequence σ of all jobs and the starting time of the first job. Next we will prove the second property.

Theorem 7.4 For problem $1 \mid d \mid \sum w_i \mid L_{\sigma(i)} \mid$ an optimal schedule exists which is V-shaped with respect to the p_i-values.

Proof: All jobs which finish not later than the given due date d can be ordered according to nonincreasing processing times in an optimal schedule. This follows from a simple interchange argument. Similarly, all jobs starting not earlier than d can be ordered according to nondecreasing processing times.

Thus, if in an optimal schedule the finishing time of a job is equal to its due date d we have finished. Otherwise we have to show that job j overlapping with d, its immediate predecessor i, and its immediate successor k builds a V-shaped subsequence.

Assume that this is not the case, i.e. that we have $C_i < d < C_j$ and $p_i < p_j > p_k$. Let $S := C_i$ and denote by σ_{opt} the optimal sequence (see Figure 7.4).

Let $\sigma_{ji}(\sigma_{kj})$ be the sequence derived from σ_{opt} by swapping i and j (j and k). Furthermore, denote by $Z(\sigma)$ the objective value associated with σ. If job i is on position p in σ_{opt}, then we have

$$Z(\sigma_{ji}) - Z(\sigma_{opt}) = w_p(\mid S - p_i + p_j - d \mid - \mid S - d \mid) \quad \geq 0$$
$$Z(\sigma_{kj}) - Z(\sigma_{opt}) = w_{p+1}(\mid S + p_k - d \mid - \mid S + p_j - d \mid) \geq 0$$

because σ_{opt} is optimal. This implies

$$\mid S - p_i + p_j - d \mid \geq d - S \qquad (7.14)$$
$$\mid S + p_k - d \mid \; \geq S + p_j - d \qquad (7.15)$$

because $S < d < S + p_j$.

We must have $S - p_i + p_j - d \geq 0$ because otherwise (7.14) is equivalent to $-S + p_i - p_j + d \geq d - S$, i.e. $p_i \geq p_j$, which is a contradiction. Similarly, due to (7.15), we must have $S + p_k - d \leq 0$. Thus, (7.14) and (7.15) can be written in the form

$$S - p_i + p_j - d \geq d - S \qquad (7.16)$$
$$-S - p_k + d \; \geq S + p_j - d. \qquad (7.17)$$

Adding inequalities (7.16) and (7.17) gives $p_i + p_k \leq 0$, which implies $p_i = p_k = 0$. Thus we can swap i with j or i with k without increasing the objective value. If we continue this process, we get a V-shaped sequence. □

Let d^* be the optimal due date for the corresponding problem $1 \mid d_{opt} \mid \sum w_i \mid L_{\sigma(i)} \mid$. We may assume that the optimal schedule of this problem starts at time $t = 0$. Let σ^* be the optimal sequence of the jobs. If $d \geq d^*$, then the starting time $d - d^*$ and σ^* define an optimal schedule for our problem $1 \mid d \mid \sum w_i \mid L_{\sigma(i)} \mid$. If $d < d^*$, then we can show that an optimal schedule starts at time $t = 0$. However, finding an optimal sequence is $\mathcal{NP}$-hard. We solve this problem by dynamic programming.

We assume that the jobs are indexed according to nondecreasing processing time, i.e. that

$$p_1 \leq p_2 \leq \ldots \leq p_n$$

holds. Since an optimal solution exists which is V-shaped, we may assume that in an optimal solution jobs $1, \ldots, k (1 \leq k \leq n)$ are scheduled as a contiguous block.

Let $S(k, i, e)$ be an optimal schedule for jobs $1, \ldots, k$ with positional weights $w_i, w_{i+1}, \ldots, w_{i+k-1}$ and due date e starting at time 0. Let $\sigma(k, i, e)$ be the corresponding sequence and let $Z(k, i, e)$ be the corresponding objective value.

We will now derive a recursion for the $Z(k, i, e)$-values and corresponding sequences $\sigma(k, i, e)$, where $1 \leq k \leq n$, $1 \leq i \leq n - k + 1$, and $0 \leq e \leq d$.

Clearly, we have

$$Z(1, i, e) = w_i \mid p_1 - e \mid$$
$$\sigma(1, i, e) = 1$$

for all $1 \leq i \leq n$, $0 \leq e \leq d$.

We get an optimal sequence for the jobs $1, \ldots, k$ by adding k to the beginning or the end of an optimal sequence for jobs $1, \ldots, k-1$. Therefore, we have to consider two cases.

Case 1: k is scheduled at the beginning.

The costs for scheduling k are $w_i \mid p_k - e \mid$. The costs for the remaining jobs $1, \ldots, k-1$ scheduled in $[p_k, \sum_{j=1}^{k} p_j]$ with due date e are the same as the costs for scheduling them in $[0, \sum_{j=1}^{k-1} p_j]$ with due date $e - p_k$. If the corresponding positional weights are $w_{i+1}, \ldots, w_{i+k-1}$, then these costs are given by $Z(k-1, i+1, e-p_k)$. Thus, the costs for scheduling $1, \ldots, k$ are given by

$$Z_1(k, i, e) = w_i \mid p_k - e \mid + Z(k-1, i+1, e-p_k).$$

Case 2: k is scheduled at the end.

The scheduling costs for k are $w_{i+k-1} \mid \sum_{j=1}^{k} p_j - e \mid$. The remaining cost are for scheduling $1, \ldots, k-1$ in $[0, \sum_{j=1}^{k-1} p_j]$ with due date e and weights $w_i, \ldots, w_{i+k-2}$. They are given by $Z(k-1, i, e)$. Thus, the total costs are

$$Z_2(k, i, e) = w_{i+k-1} \mid \sum_{j=1}^{k} p_j - e \mid + Z(k-1, i, e).$$

Combining both cases, we get

$$Z(k, i, e) = \min\{Z_1(k, i, e), Z_2(k, i, e)\}$$
$$= \min\{w_i \mid p_k - e \mid + Z(k-1, i+1, e-p_k),$$
$$w_{i+k-1} \mid \sum_{j=1}^{k} p_j - e \mid + Z(k-1, i, e)\}$$

and

$$\sigma(k, i, e) = \begin{cases} k \circ \sigma(k-1, i+1, e-p_k) & \text{if } Z_1(k, i, e) \leq Z_2(k, i, e) \\ \sigma(k-1, i, e) \circ k & \text{otherwise.} \end{cases}$$

We have to calculate $Z(k, i, e)$ for $k = 1, \ldots, n$, $i = 1, \ldots, n - k + 1$, and $e = 0, \ldots, d$.

$\sigma(n, 1, d)$ is an optimal sequence and $Z(n, 1, d)$ is its solution value.

To evaluate $Z(k, i, e)$ we need the value $Z(k - 1, i + 1, e - p_k)$, which may have a negative argument $e - p_k$. However, for negative e we have $\sigma(k, i, e) : 1, 2, \ldots, k$. Thus, in this case

$$Z(k, i, e) = \sum_{\nu=1}^{k} w_{i+\nu-1} \sum_{j=1}^{\nu} p_j - e \sum_{\nu=1}^{k} w_{i+\nu-1}. \tag{7.18}$$

The values

$$G(k, i) := \sum_{\nu=1}^{k} w_{i+\nu-1} \sum_{j=1}^{\nu} p_j$$

and

$$W(k, i) := \sum_{\nu=1}^{k} w_{i+\nu-1}$$

for all $k = 1, \ldots, n$; $i = 1, \ldots, n - k + 1$ can be calculated during a preprocessing step in $0(n^2)$ time. Using these values, (7.18) becomes

$$Z(k, i, e) = G(k, i) - eW(k, i).$$

Summarizing these results, we get the following algorithm.

Algorithm $1 \mid d \mid \sum \mathbf{w_i} \mid \mathbf{L_{\sigma(i)}} \mid$
1. Choose the job indices such that $p_1 \leq p_2 \leq \ldots \leq p_n$;
2. Calculate an optimal due date d^* and an optimal sequence σ^* for the problem $1 \mid d_{opt} \mid \sum w_j \mid L_{\sigma(j)} \mid$;
3. IF $d \geq d^*$ THEN
4.   BEGIN $s := d - d^*$; $\sigma := \sigma^*$ END
    ELSE
        BEGIN
5. $s := 0$;
6.   IF $d \leq 0$ THEN $\sigma :=$ SPT-sequence
      ELSE
          BEGIN
7.   FOR $k := 1$ TO n DO
8.   FOR $i := 1$ TO $n - k + 1$ DO
9.   Calculate $G(k, i)$ and $W(k, i)$;

```
10.        FOR i := 1 TO n DO
11.          FOR e := -p₂ TO d DO
12.            BEGIN Z(1,i,e) := wᵢ | p₁ - e |; σ(1,i,e) := 1 END;
13.          FOR k := 2 TO n DO
14.            FOR i := 1 TO n - k + 1 DO
15.              FOR e := -p_{k+1} TO d DO
                   BEGIN
16.                  IF e < 0 THEN Z(k,i,e) := G(k,i) - eW(k,i)
                     ELSE
                     BEGIN
17.                    Z₁(k,i,e) := Z(k-1,i+1,e-p_k)
                       +wᵢ | p_k - e |;
18.                    Z₂(k,i,e) := Z(k-1,i,e) + w_{i+k-1}
                       | Σ_{j=1}^{k} p_j - e |;
19.                    IF Z₁(k,i,e) ≤ Z₂(k,i,e) THEN
                       BEGIN
20.                      Z(k,i,e) := Z₁(k,i,e);
21.                      σ(k,i,e) := k ∘ σ(k-1,i+1,e-p_k)
                         END
                     ELSE
                     BEGIN
22.                    Z(k,i,e) := Z₂(k,i,e);
23.                    σ(k,i,e) := σ(k-1,i,e) ∘ k
                       END
                     END
                   END;
24.          σ := σ(n,1,d)
             END
          END
```

The computational complexity of this algorithm is $O(n^2 d)$.

We developed this algorithm for the case that jobs can be scheduled only in $[0, +\infty[$. If we allow jobs to be scheduled in $] -\infty, +\infty[$, then the solution is much easier. We solve $1 \mid d_{opt} \mid \sum w_i \mid L_{\sigma(i)} \mid$ by calculating an optimal due date d^* for an optimal schedule starting at $s = 0$ and an optimal sequence σ^*. Then we schedule the jobs according to this sequence starting at time $d - d^*$.

7.4 Problem $1 \mid d \mid \mathbf{w_E} \sum \mathbf{E_i} + \mathbf{w_T} \sum \mathbf{T_i}$

For this problem an optimal schedule also exists with no idle time between jobs which is V-shaped with respect to the p_i-values. The proof for this is nearly identical to the corresponding proof in the previous section.

To construct an optimal schedule we may proceed as in the previous section. However, due to the special objective function, the dynamic programming can be made more efficient. Instead of considering states defined by the three variables i, k, e, we only need the two variables k and e. More specifically, we again assume $p_1 \leq p_2 \leq \ldots \leq p_n$ and for each $k = 1, \ldots, n$ and each due date e, we define $\sigma(k, e)$ to be an optimal sequence for jobs $1, \ldots, k$ and due date $e \leq d$. Let $Z(k, e)$ be the objective value of a corresponding optimal schedule starting at time $s = 0$.

We have

$$\sigma(1, e) = 1$$

$$Z(1, e) = \begin{cases} w_E(e - p_1) & \text{if } p_1 \leq e \leq d \\ w_T(p_1 - e) & \text{if } e < p_1 \end{cases}$$

as initial conditions.

Furthermore, if k is scheduled before an optimal sequence for the jobs $1, \ldots, k-1$, then we have

$$Z_1(k, e) = w_E(e - p_k)^+ + w_T(p_k - e)^+ + Z(k - 1, e - p_k)$$

(for arbitrary numbers x we define $x^+ = \max\{0, x\}$).

If k is scheduled after an optimal sequence for the jobs $1, \ldots, k-1$, then we have

$$Z_2(k, e) = w_E(e - \sum_{j=1}^{k} p_j)^+ + w_T(\sum_{j=1}^{k} p_j - e)^+ + Z(k - 1, e).$$

Thus we get

$$Z(k, e) = \min\{Z_1(k, e), Z_2(k, e)\}$$

and

$$\sigma(k, e) = \begin{cases} k \circ \sigma(k - 1, e - p_k) & \text{if } Z_1(k, e) \leq Z_2(k, e) \\ \sigma(k - 1, e) \circ k & \text{otherwise.} \end{cases}$$

These recursions hold for $k = 2, \ldots, n$ and $0 \le e \le d$. If $e < 0$, then the SPT-sequence is optimal and we have

$$Z(k, e) = w_T \left(\sum_{\nu=1}^{k} \sum_{j=1}^{\nu} p_j - ke \right).$$

If all values

$$G(k) := \sum_{\nu=1}^{k} \sum_{j=1}^{\nu} p_j \quad k = 1, 2, \ldots, n$$

are calculated during a preprocessing step, then each value

$$Z(k, e) = w_T (G(k) - k \cdot e)$$

can be calculated in constant time. The preprocessing can be done in $O(n)$ time.

It is not difficult to formulate the algorithm along the lines of the previous section.

Algorithm 1 | d | $\mathbf{w_E} \sum \mathbf{E_i} + \mathbf{w_T} \sum \mathbf{T_i}$

1. Choose the job indices such that $p_1 \le p_2 \le \ldots \le p_n$;
2. Calculate an optimal due date d^* and an optimal sequence σ^* for the corresponding problem $1 \mid d_{opt} \mid w_E \sum E_i + w_T \sum T_i$;
3. IF $d \ge d^*$ THEN
4.   BEGIN $s := d - d^*$; $\sigma := \sigma^*$ END
    ELSE
       BEGIN
5. $s := 0$;
6.   IF $d \le 0$ THEN $\sigma := $ SPT-sequence
    ELSE
       BEGIN
7.   FOR $k = 1$ TO n DO calculate $G(k)$;
8.   FOR $e := -p_2$ TO d DO
       BEGIN
9. $\sigma(1, e) = 1$;
10.   IF $e < p_1$ THEN $Z(1, e) := w_T(p_1 - e)$
       ELSE $Z(1, e) := w_E(e - p_1)$;
       END;
11.   FOR $k := 2$ TO n DO
12.   FOR $e := -p_{k+1}$ TO d DO

           BEGIN

13.   IF $e < 0$ THEN $Z(k, e) := w_T(G(k) - ke)$

           ELSE

           BEGIN

14. $Z_1(k, e) := w_E(e - p_k)^+ + w_T(p_k - e)^+$

                $+Z(k - 1, e - p_k);$

15. $Z_2(k, e) := w_E(e - \sum_{j=1}^{k} p_j)^+ + w_T(\sum_{j=1}^{k} p_j - e)^+$

                $+Z(k - 1, e);$

16.   IF $Z_1(k, e) \leq Z_2(k, e)$ THEN

           BEGIN

17. $Z(k, e) := Z_1(k, e);$

18. $\sigma(k, e) := k \circ \sigma(k - 1, e - p_k)$

           END

           ELSE

           BEGIN

19. $Z(k, e) := Z_2(k, e);$

20. $\sigma(k, e) := \sigma(k - 1, e) \circ k$

           END

           END

         END;

21. $\sigma := \sigma(n, d)$

         END

       END

The complexity of this algorithm is $O(n \log n + nd)$.

7.5   Problem $1 \mid d \mid |L_i|_{\max}$ and $1 \mid d_{opt} \mid |L_i|_{\max}$

We now consider the objective function $\max\limits_{i=1}^{n} \mid C_i - d \mid$ (Kahlbacher [122]). As before, for variable and fixed d there exists an optimal schedule without idle time between jobs.

We first consider problem $1 \mid d \mid L_i \mid_{\max}$. If $\sigma(1)$ is the first job and this job starts at time s, then the objective value can be written in the form

$$\mid L_i \mid_{\max} = \max\limits_{i=1}^{n} \mid C_i - d \mid = \max\{\mid s + p_{\sigma(1)} - d \mid, \mid s + \sum_{i=1}^{n} p_i - d \mid\} \quad (7.19)$$

The next theorem shows that $\sigma(1)$ can always be chosen to be the longest job.

Theorem 7.5 An optimal sequence exists in which a longest job is scheduled at the first position.

Proof: Let $p_l = \max\limits_{i=1}^{n} p_i$. Then due to (7.19) it is sufficient to show that

$$\max\{|\, s + p_l - d\,|,\ |\, s + \sum_{i=1}^{n} p_i - d\,|\}$$

$$\leq \max\{|\, s + p_i - d\,|,\ |\, s + \sum_{i=1}^{n} p_i - d\,|\} \quad (7.20)$$

holds for all $i = 1, \ldots, n$. We consider the following two cases.

Case 1: $s + p_l > d$

Then

$$\max\{|\, s + p_l - d\,|,\ |\, s + \sum_{i=1}^{n} p_i - d\,|\} = s + \sum_{i=1}^{n} p_i - d$$

$$\leq \max\{|\, s + p_i - d\,|,\ |\, s + \sum_{i=1}^{n} p_i - d\,|\}$$

for all $i = 1, \ldots, n$.

Case 2: $s + p_l \leq d$

Then $|s + p_l - d| = d - s - p_l \leq d - s - p_i = |s + p_i - d|$, which implies (7.20) for all $i = 1, \ldots, n$. □

Due to this theorem, the objective function can be written as follows

$$f(s) = \max\{|\, s + p_l - d\,|,\ |\, s + \sum_{j=1}^{n} p_j - d\,|\} \text{ with } p_l = \max\limits_{j=1}^{n} p_j. \quad (7.21)$$

f is minimized if we choose $s^* = d - \frac{1}{2}(\sum_{j=1}^{n} p_j + p_l)$ (see Figure 7.5). If s^* is negative, we have to replace s^* by 0. We have

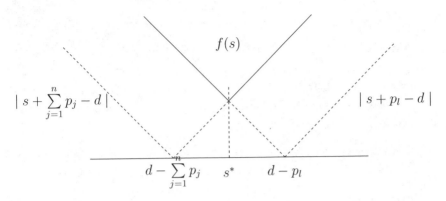

Figure 7.5: Function f.

Theorem 7.6 Any schedule which starts with a job l with a largest processing time at time

$$t := \max\{0, d - \frac{1}{2}(\sum_{j=1}^{n} p_j + p_l)\}$$

and processes the other jobs without idle time after l in an arbitrary sequence is optimal for problem $1 \mid d \mid\mid L_i \mid_{\max}$. □

Note that such an optimal schedule can be found in $O(n)$ time.

To solve problem $1 \mid d_{opt} \mid\mid L_i \mid_{\max}$, we have to find a value d^* which minimizes (7.21). We may assume that $s = 0$. In other words, we get a solution for problem $1 \mid d_{opt} \mid\mid L_i \mid_{\max}$ if we set $d = 0$ and $s = -d$ in (7.21). This leads to

Theorem 7.7 An optimal solution for problem $1 \mid d_{opt} \mid\mid L_i \mid_{\max}$ is obtained by scheduling a longest job l as the first job starting at time $s = 0$ and setting

$$d_{opt} = \frac{1}{2}(\sum_{j=1}^{n} p_j + p_l).$$

□

7.6 Problem 1 | d_{opt} | $\sum w_i |L_i|$

In this problem we assume that all w_j-values are positive integers. Hall & Posner [109] have shown that problem $1 \mid d_{opt} \mid \sum w_i \mid L_i \mid$ is $\mathcal{NP}$-hard.

We will develop two pseudo-polynomial algorithms for this problem. One has complexity $O(n \sum_{i=1}^{n} p_i)$, the other has complexity $O(n \sum_{i=1}^{n} w_i)$. The following theorems are the basis for these algorithms. Again, it is sufficient to consider only schedules without idle time between jobs in which the first job starts at time 0. We have to find an optimal sequence σ^* and an optimal due date d^*.

Theorem 7.8 Given a sequence $\sigma(1), \ldots, \sigma(n)$, a corresponding optimal due date is given by the finishing time $C_{\sigma(r)}$ of a job $\sigma(r)$. Moreover,

$$\sum_{j=1}^{r-1} w_{\sigma(j)} \le \sum_{j=r}^{n} w_{\sigma(j)} \text{ and } \sum_{j=1}^{r} w_{\sigma(j)} \ge \sum_{j=r+1}^{n} w_{\sigma(j)}.$$

Proof: Similar to the proof of Theorem 7.2.   □

The next theorem states that an optimal sequence exists which is V-shaped with respect to the ratios p_i/w_i.

Theorem 7.9 An optimal sequence exists in which the early jobs are sequenced according to nonincreasing (p_i/w_i)-values and the late jobs are sequenced according to nondecreasing (p_i/w_i)-values.

Proof: By a simple exchange argument (see also Smith's ratio rule in Section 4.3.1).   □

Again, we use dynamic programming approaches to solve problem $1 \mid d_{opt} \mid \sum w_i \mid L_i \mid$. We assume that the jobs are numerated such that

$$p_1/w_1 \le p_2/w_2 \le \ldots \le p_n/w_n.$$

In the first approach, we define for each $k = 1, \ldots, n$ and integer p with $0 \le p \le \sum_{i=1}^{k} p_i$ the optimal value $Z(k, p)$ for scheduling jobs $1, \ldots, k$ under the condition that the total processing time of all early jobs, i.e. the due date, equals p.

For $k = 1$ we set

$$Z(1, p) = \begin{cases} 0 & \text{if } p \in \{0, p_1, \ldots, p_n\} \\ \infty & \text{otherwise .} \end{cases}$$

Now assume that $Z(k - 1, p)$ is known for each p. We get an optimal sequence for jobs $1, \ldots, k$ by adding job k either at the beginning or at the end of the optimal sequence for the jobs $1, \ldots, k-1$. In the first case we have

$$Z_1(k, p) = Z(k - 1, p - p_k) + w_k(p - p_k).$$

In the second case we get

$$Z_2(k, p) = Z(k - 1, p) + w_k\left(\sum_{i=1}^{k} p_i - p\right).$$

Combining both cases yields the recursion

$$\begin{aligned}
Z(k, p) &= \min\{Z_1(k, p), Z_2(k, p)\} \\
&= \min\{Z(k - 1, p - p_k) + w_k(p - p_k), \\
&\quad Z(k - 1, p) + w_k\left(\sum_{i=1}^{k} p_i - p\right)\}
\end{aligned}$$

which holds for $k = 2, \ldots, n$ and $0 \leq p \leq \sum_{i=1}^{k} p_i$.

Note that $Z(k, p)$ is finite only if $p = \sum_{i \in E} p_i$ for some set E of (early) jobs.

The optimal solution value is given by

$$Z^* = \min\{Z(n, p) \mid p = 0, \ldots, \sum_{i=1}^{n} p_i\}.$$

Clearly, the computational time needed to calculate Z^* is $O(n \sum_{i=1}^{n} p_i)$.

The second approach is based on the fact that, given an optimal sequence σ and an optimal due date $d = \sum_{i=1}^{r} p_{\sigma(i)}$, the objective value can be written as follows

$$p_{\sigma(2)} w_{\sigma(1)} + p_{\sigma(3)}\left(w_{\sigma(1)} + w_{\sigma(2)}\right) + \ldots + p_{\sigma(r)} \sum_{i=1}^{r-1} w_{\sigma(i)} +$$

$$p_{\sigma(r+1)} \sum_{i=r+1}^{n} w_{\sigma(i)} + \ldots + p_{\sigma(n)} w_{\sigma(n)}.$$

For each $k = n, n - 1, \ldots, 1$ and integer $0 \leq w \leq \sum_{i=k}^{n} w_i$, let $Z(k, w)$ be the optimal objective value for scheduling jobs $k, k + 1, \ldots, n$ under the condition that the total weight of all early jobs equals w.

For $k = n$ we set

$$Z(n, w) = \begin{cases} 0 & \text{if } w \in \{0, w_1, \ldots, w_n\} \\ \infty & \text{otherwise.} \end{cases}$$

We get an optimal sequence for jobs $k \ldots, n$ from an optimal sequence for jobs $k + 1, \ldots, n$ by considering k as either the last early job or as the first late job. In the first case we have

$$Z_1(k, w) = Z(k + 1, w - w_k) + p_k(w - w_k).$$

In the second case we get

$$Z_2(k, w) = Z(k + 1, w) + p_k(\sum_{i=k}^{n} w_i - w).$$

Combining both yields

$$Z(k, w) = \min\{Z_1(k, w), Z_2(k, w)\}.$$

The optimal solution value is given by

$$Z^* = \min\{Z(1, w) \mid w = 0, \ldots, \sum_{i=1}^{n} w_i\}$$

and can be calculated in $O(n \sum_{i=1}^{n} w_i)$ time.

Notice the close relationship and high symmetry between both approaches.

7.7 Problem $1 \mid d \mid \sum w_i |L_i|$

Contrary to problem $1 \mid d_{opt} \mid \sum w_i \mid L_i \mid$, for problem $1 \mid d \mid \sum w_i \mid L_i \mid$ there need not exist an optimal solution which is V-shaped with respect to the (p_i/w_i)-values, as the following example shows.

Example 7.1: Consider a problem with 3 jobs where $p_1 = 4, p_2 = 5, p_3 = 2, w_1 = 5, w_2 = 7, w_3 = 3$, and $d = 7.5$. Then $p_1/w_1 > p_2/w_2 > p_3/w_3$, but $\sigma^* : 2, 1, 3$ is the only optimal solution. $\Box$

However, we have the following result.

Theorem 7.10 An optimal sequence exists in which all jobs finishing not later than time d are scheduled according to nonincreasing (p_i/w_i)-values and all jobs starting not earlier than time d are scheduled according to nondecreasing (p_i/w_i)-values.

Proof: By an exchange argument (see Smith's rule in Section 4.3.1). □

Thus, one job at the most starts before and finishes after d which, together with its predecessors and successor, violates the V-shape property. We call this job a d-job.

We solve the problem again by dynamic programming, assuming that

$$p_1/w_1 \geq p_2/w_2 \geq \ldots \geq p_n/w_n.$$

We consider two cases.

Case 1: An optimal solution exists in which d is the finishing time or the starting time of a job.

Then the corresponding optimal sequence is V-shaped. In this case we denote, by $F(k,t)$ for each integer $0 \leq t \leq d$ and $k = 1, \ldots, n$ the optimal solution value for the problem of scheduling jobs $n - k + 1, \ldots, n$ in the interval

$$[d - t, d - t + \sum_{i=n-k+1}^{n} p_i],$$

i.e. starting at time $d - t$.

We define

$$F(k,t) = \begin{cases} 0 & \text{if } t = 0, k = 0 \\ \infty & \text{otherwise.} \end{cases}$$

The recursion is

$$\begin{aligned} F(k,t) = \min\{ & F(k-1, t - p_{n-k+1}) + w_{n-k+1}(t - p_{n-k+1}), \\ & F(k-1, t) + w_{n-k+1} \mid \sum_{i=n-k+1}^{n} p_i - t \mid \} \end{aligned} \tag{7.22}$$

for $k = 1, 2, \ldots, n$ and $0 \leq t \leq d$.

In (7.22) the minimum is taken from the optimal solution value if job $n - k + 1$ is scheduled first, and the optimal solution value if $n - k + 1$ is scheduled at the end.

The optimal solution value for scheduling all jobs is given by

$$F^* = \min_{t=0}^{d} F(n, t).$$

It can be calculated in $O(nd)$ time.

If in an optimal solution the first job starts later than time $t = 0$, then we must have Case 1. To prove this, consider the optimal due date d^* for problem $1 \mid d_{opt} \mid \sum w_i \mid L_i \mid$. If $d^* = d$, we have finished (see Theorem 7.8). Otherwise we may improve the objective value by moving the starting time of the first job, which is a contradiction.

Case 2: The first job in an optimal schedule starts at time 0.

Under the assumption that job h is the d-job for $k = 1, \ldots, n$ and $0 \le t \le d$, let $G(h, k, t)$ be the optimal solution value for scheduling the jobs in $\{1, \ldots, k\} \backslash \{h\}$ in the intervals

$$[0, t] \quad \text{and} \quad [t + \sum_{\substack{i=k \\ i \neq h}}^{n} p_i + p_h, \sum_{i=1}^{n} p_i].$$

We define

$$G(h, k, t) = \begin{cases} 0 & \text{if } t = 0, k = 0 \\ \infty & \text{otherwise.} \end{cases}$$

To derive a recursion formula for $G(h, k, t)$, we consider two cases.

(a) Job k is scheduled as the last job in $[0, t]$. Then the $G(h, k, t)$-value is

$$G_1(h, k, t) = G(h, k - 1, t - p_k) + w_k(d - t).$$

(b) Job k is scheduled as the first job in $[t + \sum_{\substack{i=k+1 \\ i \neq h}}^{n} p_i + p_h, \sum_{i=1}^{n} p_i]$. Then the $G(h, k, t)$-value is

$$G_2(h, k, t) = G(h, k - 1, t) + w_k \mid t + \sum_{\substack{i=k \\ i \neq h}}^{n} np_i + p_h - d \mid.$$

Note that if $t < p_k$, then only case (b) can occur and if $\sum_{i=1}^{n} p_i - t - \sum_{\substack{i=k \\ i \neq h}}^{n} p_i -$ $p_h < p_k$, then only case (a) can occur. Finally, we have $G(h, h, t) =$

$G(h, h-1, t)$. Summarizing, we get

$$
G(h, k, t) = \begin{cases}
G(h, k-1, t) & \text{if } k = h \\
G_1(h, k, t) & \text{if } \sum\limits_{i=1}^{n} p_i - t - \sum\limits_{\substack{i=k \\ i \neq h}}^{n} p_i - p_h < p_k \\
G_2(h, k, t) & \text{if } t < p_k \\
\min\{G_1(h, k, t), G_2(h, k, t)\} & \text{otherwise}
\end{cases}
$$

for $h = 1, \ldots, n, k = 1, \ldots, n, 0 \le t \le d$.
Finally,

$$
G^*(h) = \min\{G(h, n, t) + w_h(t + p_h - d) \mid d - p_h \le t \le d\}
$$

is the optimal solution value under the constraint that h is a d-job and

$$
G^* = \min_{h=1}^{n} G^*(h)
$$

is the optimal value in Case 2.

G^* can be calculated in $0(n^2 d)$ time.

If we combine Case 1 and Case 2, we get the overall optimal solution value

$$
H^* = \min\{F^*, G^*\}
$$

in $O(n^2 d)$ time.

Chapter 8

Batching Problems

Batching means that sets of jobs which are processed on the same machine must be grouped into batches. A batch is a set of jobs which must be processed jointly. The finishing time of all jobs in a batch is defined to be equal to the finishing time of the last job in the batch. There is a setup time s for each batch, which is assumed to be the same for all batches. A batching problem is to group the jobs on each machine into batches and to schedule these batches. Depending on the calculation of the length of a batch, two types of batching problems have been considered. For s-batching (p-batching) problems the length is the sum (maximum) of the processing times of the jobs in the batch. Batching problems have been identified by adding the symbol "s-batch" or "p-batch" to the β-field of our classification scheme.

In the next two sections we discuss single machine s-batching and p-batching problems. Section 8.3 presents some complexity results for such batching problems.

8.1 Single Machine s-Batching Problems

In Section 2.7 we discussed single machine s-batching problems with objective function $\sum w_i C_i$. We have shown that, given a sequence of n jobs, an optimal partitioning of this sequence into s-batches can be found by solving a special shortest path problem in $O(n)$ time. Furthermore, we showed that for the problems $1 \mid s-batch \mid \sum C_i$ and $1 \mid p_i = p; s-batch \mid \sum w_i C_i$ optimal sequences can be found by ordering the jobs according to nondecreasing processing times and nonincreasing weights, respectively. Similarly, the problem $1 \mid prec; p_i = p; s - batch \mid \sum C_i$ can be solved: Find a sequence which is compatible with the precedence constraints and calculate an optimal partitioning for this sequence. The first step can be done in $O(n^2)$ time by sorting the jobs topologically.

Next we will present two dynamic programming algorithms for the problem $1 \mid s - batch \mid \sum w_i U_i$ which lead to polynomial algorithms for the special cases in which $p_i = p$ or $w_i = 1$ for all jobs i.

$1 \mid s - \text{batch} \mid \sum w_i U_i$

Before presenting the two dynamic programming algorithms, we derive some properties of an optimal schedule for problem $1 \mid s - batch \mid \sum w_i U_i$. The first property is that we can put all late jobs into one batch scheduled after all other "early" batches. In the following, we assume that the jobs are enumerated such that

$$d_1 \leq d_2 \leq \ldots \leq d_n \tag{8.1}$$

holds and that for at least one i we have $s + p_i \leq d_i$. Then we have

Lemma 8.1 For $1 \mid s - batch \mid \sum w_i U_i$ there exists an optimal schedule S with the property: if i belongs to batch B_l, job j belongs to batch B_t, both are early, and B_l is scheduled before B_t, then $i < j$.

Proof: Consider an optimal schedule for which the property of Lemma 8.1 does not hold, i.e. we have batch B_l scheduled before batch B_t with $i \in B_l$, $j \in B_t$, and $i > j$. Then $d_j \leq d_i$. Furthermore, because $j \in B_t$ and all jobs in B_t are early, the finishing time of batch B_t is not greater than d_j. Thus, if we move job i from B_l to B_t, we get a schedule in which the early batches remain early. Continuing this exchange process we get an optimal schedule with the desired properties. $\qquad \square$

For the first dynamic programming algorithm we assume that all weights w_i are integer. We define $C_j(w, d)$ to be the minimal completion time of the last early job in a schedule S for jobs $1, \ldots, j$, which has the following properties:

- the $\sum w_i U_i$-value of S is w, and

- the earliest due date in the last early batch of S is equal to d.

To derive a recursion for the $C_j(w, d)$ -values we consider the following cases.

Case 1: In a schedule defining $C_j(w, d)$, job j is late. Then

$$C_j(w, d) = C_{j-1}(w - w_j, d).$$ (8.2)

Case 2: In a schedule defining $C_j(w, d)$, job j is scheduled early jointly with at least one other job in the last early batch. In this case we have $C_{j-1}(w, d) + p_j \leq d$ and

$$C_j(w, d) = C_{j-1}(w, d) + p_j.$$ (8.3)

Case 3: In a schedule defining $C_j(w, d)$, job j is the only job scheduled in the last early batch. Then we must have $d = d_j$ and

$$C_j(w, d) = \min_{\nu=1}^{j-1} C_{j-1}(w, d_\nu) + s + p_j.$$ (8.4)

Combining (8.2), (8.3), and (8.4) yields the recursion

$$C_j(w, d) = \min \begin{cases} C_{j-1}(w - w_j, d) \\ C_{j-1}(w, d) + p_j & \text{if } C_{j-1}(w, d) + p_j \leq d \\ & \text{and } C_{j-1}(w, d) > 0 \\ K & \text{if } d = d_j \end{cases}$$ (8.5)

where

$$K = \min\{C_{j-1}(w, d_\nu) + s + p_j \mid C_{j-1}(w, d_\nu) + s + p_j \leq d; \ \nu = 1, \ldots, j-1\}.$$

As initial conditions, we first set

$$C_j(w, d) = \infty \text{ for all } j = 1, \ldots, n, \ w \in \{-w_{\max}, -w_{\max} + 1, \ldots, \sum_{j=1}^{n} w_j\}$$

and $d \in \{d_1, \ldots, d_n\}$, where $w_{\max} = \max_{j=1}^{n} w_j$, and then we set

$$C_0(0, d) = 0 \text{ for all } d \in \{d_1, \ldots, d_n\}.$$

To solve problem $1 \mid s - batch \mid \sum w_j U_j$ for $j = 1, 2, \ldots, n$ we calculate $C_j(w, d)$ for all $w \in \{0, 1, \ldots, \sum_{j=1}^{n} w_j\}$ and $d \in \{d_1, \ldots, d_n\}$ using the recursion (8.5). Finally,

$$w^* = \min\{w \mid C_n(w, d) < \infty, \, 0 \le w \le \sum_{j=1}^{n} w_j, d \in \{d_1, \ldots, d_n\}\}$$

is the optimal value.

Clearly, for each j, all values $C_j(w, d)$ can be calculated by (8.5) in $O(n \sum_{j=1}^{n} w_j)$ time. Thus, the problem can be solved in $O(n^2 \sum_{j=1}^{n} w_j)$ time. If we set $w_j = 1$ for $j = 1, \ldots, n$, we have an $O(n^3)$ algorithm which solves problem $1 \mid s - batch \mid \sum U_j$.

For the second dynamic programming approach, which is due to Hochbaum & Landy [112], the roles of the weights and the processing times are interchanged. Thus, we assume that all processing times are integer. Furthermore, instead of forward dynamic programming backward dynamic programming is applied.

We define $F_j(t, d)$ to be the minimum cost of scheduling jobs $j, j + 1, \ldots, n$, starting at time t, given that d is the earliest due date of a job in the last early batch of a partial schedule for jobs $1, \ldots, j - 1$. Again, we have three cases.

Case 1: Job j is scheduled late. Then

$$F_j(t, d) = F_{j+1}(t, d) + w_j. \tag{8.6}$$

Case 2: Job j is part of the last early batch of the partial schedule for jobs $1, \ldots, j - 1$. This is only possible if $t + p_j \le d$ and in this case we have

$$F_j(t, d) = F_{j+1}(t + p_j, d). \tag{8.7}$$

Case 3: Job j starts a new early batch. This is only possible if $t + s + p_j \le d_j$ and in this case we have

$$F_j(t, d) = F_{j+1}(t + s + p_j, d_j). \tag{8.8}$$

Combining (8.6), (8.7), and (8.8), we get

$$F_j(t, d) = \min \begin{cases} F_{j+1}(t, d) + w_j & \\ F_{j+1}(t + p_j, d) & \text{if } t + p_j \le d \\ F_{j+1}(t + s + p_j, d_j) & \text{if } t + s + p_j \le d_j. \end{cases} \tag{8.9}$$

To solve problem $1 \mid s - batch \mid \sum w_j U_j$, we calculate for $j = n, n - 1, \ldots, 1$ the $F_j(t, d)$-values for all $0 \leq t \leq \sum_{j=1}^{n} p_j + ns$ and $d \in \{d_1, \ldots, d_j\}$ using recursion (8.9) and the initial conditions

$$F_{n+1}(t, d) = 0 \text{ for all } 0 \leq t \leq \sum_{j=1}^{n} p_j + ns \text{ and } d \in \{d_1, \ldots, d_n\}.$$

This can be done in $O(n^2(\sum_{j=1}^{n} p_j + ns))$ time.

The optimal solution value is given by

$$\min_{j=1}^{n}\{F_{j+1}(s + p_j, d_j) + \sum_{\nu=1}^{j-1} w_\nu\}$$

which can be calculated in $O(n)$ time given the $F_j(t, d)$-values. Thus, we have an algorithm with overall complexity $O(n^2(\sum_{j=1}^{n} p_j + ns))$.

If $p_i = p$ for all $i = 1, \ldots, n$, then the relevant t-values have the form

$$as + bp \text{ with } a, b \in \{1, \ldots, n\},$$

i.e. we have to consider at the most $O(n^2)$ t-values, which leads to an $O(n^4)$ algorithm for problem $1 \mid p_i = p; s - batch \mid \sum w_i U_i$.

8.2 Single Machine p-Batching Problems

In this section we will discuss single machine p-batching problems, i.e. batching problems where the batch length is the maximum of the processing times of the jobs in a batch. The machine is called a batching machine. It can handle up to b job simultaneously. We analyze two variants: the unbounded model, where $b \geq n$ (Section 8.2.1); and the bounded model, where $b < n$ (Section 8.2.2). In connection with p-batching problems it is easy to deal with batch set-up times s. We have to add s to each processing time and to solve the corresponding problem without set up. Therefore, in this section we assume that $s = 0$. To describe the bounded case we add $b < n$ to the β-field of the $\alpha|\beta|\gamma$-notation.

8.2.1   The Unbounded Model

In this section we assume that $b \geq n$ and hence that the batching machine can process any number of jobs at the same time. The problem $1 \mid p - batch \mid C_{\max}$ of minimizing the makespan is solved easily by putting all jobs into one batch.

For the remainder of this section we assume that the jobs are indexed according to the shortest processing time (SPT) rule so that $p_1 \leq p_2 \leq \ldots \leq p_n$. The algorithms for the unbounded model are based on the following observation.

Lemma 8.2 For minimizing any regular objective function, there exists an optimal schedule $B_1, B_2, \ldots, B_r$ where $B_\nu = \{i_\nu, i_\nu + 1, \ldots, i_{\nu+1} - 1\}$ and $1 = i_1 < i_2 < \ldots < i_r < i_{r+1} = n + 1$.

Proof: Consider an optimal schedule $\sigma : B_1, B_2, \ldots, B_r$ with $k \in B_l$, $j \in B_q$, $l < q$ and $p_k > p_j$. If we move job j from batch B_q to batch B_l, the length of both batches will not increase. Since the objective function is regular the new schedule is also optimal. A finite number of repetitions of this procedure yields an optimal schedule of the required form.   □

We call a schedule described in Lemma 8.2 an **SPT-batch schedule**.

Next we present a forward dynamic programming algorithm which solves the problem of minimizing an arbitrary regular objective function $\sum_{i=1}^{n} f_i(C_i)$.

$1 \mid p - batch \mid \sum f_i$

Let $F_j(t)$ be the minimum objective value for SPT-batch schedules containing jobs $1, 2, \ldots, j$ subject to the condition that the last batch is completed at time t. Due to Lemma 8.2 there exists a schedule corresponding to $F_j(t)$ in which the last batch has the form $\{i+1, \ldots, j\}$ with $i < j$. Thus, we have the following recursion

$$F_j(t) = \min_{0 \leq i \leq j-1} \{F_i(t - p_j) + \sum_{k=i+1}^{j} f_k(t)\} \qquad (8.10)$$

with

$$F_0(t) = \begin{cases} 0 & \text{if } t = 0 \\ \infty & \text{otherwise.} \end{cases}$$

To solve the problem we evaluate (8.10) for $j = 1, \ldots, n$ and $t = p_j, \ldots,$ $\sum_{k=1}^{j} p_k$. The optimal solution value is equal to $\min\{F_n(t) \mid p_n \leq t \leq P\}$ where $P = \sum_{k=1}^{n} p_k$.

To implement the algorithm efficiently, the partial sums $\sum_{k=1}^{j} f_k(t)$ are evaluated and stored for $j = 1, \ldots, n$ and $t = p_j, \ldots, \sum_{k=1}^{j} p_k$ in a pre-processing step in $O(nP)$ time. Then each application of the recursion equation (8.10) requires $O(n)$ time. Thus, the dynamic programming algorithm requires $O(n^2 P)$ time and $O(nP)$ space.

$1 \mid p - batch \mid \sum U_i$

To solve this problem in polynomial time we use the objective value as the state variable and the makespan as the value of a state. Furthermore, we build the schedule by adding single jobs instead of complete batches and fix the last job to be scheduled in the current batch.

More specifically, we define a schedule for jobs $1, 2, \ldots, j$ to be in state (j, u, k) where $u \leq j \leq k$ if it contains exactly u tardy jobs. Additionally, the last batch, if completed, contains the additional jobs $j+1, \ldots, k$ which are contained in the same batch, and this batch has processing time p_k. Let $F_j(u, k)$ be the minimum makespan for SPT-batch schedules in state (j, u, k). A schedule in state (j, u, k) with value $F_j(u, k)$ is created by taking one of the following decisions in a previous state:

- add job j so that it does not start the last batch.

  In this case $j - 1$ and j belong to the last batch with processing time p_k. This processing time contributes to the makespan of the previous state, which is $F_{j-1}(u, k)$ or $F_{j-1}(u - 1, k)$ depending on whether j is on time or tardy. If $F_{j-1}(u, k) \leq d_j$, then we consider $(j - 1, u, k)$ as a previous state in which j is scheduled on time and $F_j(u, k) = F_{j-1}(u, k)$. If $F_{j-1}(u - 1, k) > d_j$, then j must be tardy. Thus, $(j - 1, u - 1, k)$ is considered as a previous state and $F_j(u, k) = F_{j-1}(u - 1, k)$.

- add job j so that it starts the last batch.

The previous batch ends with job $j - 1$ and the processing time of the new batch is p_k. After adding the contribution from the previous state, the makespan becomes $F_{j-1}(u, j-1) + p_k$ or $F_{j-1}(u-1, j-1) + p_k$, depending on whether j is on time or tardy. If $F_{j-1}(u, j-1) + p_k \leq d_j$, then we consider $(j-1, u, j-1)$ as a previous state (the last batch ends with $j-1$ with j scheduled to be on time. If $F_{j-1}(u-1, j-1) + p_k > d_j$, then we consider $(j-1, u-1, j-1)$ as a previous state with j scheduled to be tardy.

Summarizing, we have the recursion for $j = 1, \ldots, n$, $u = 0, \ldots, j$, and $k = j, \ldots, n$:

$$
F_j(u, k) = \min \begin{cases}
F_{j-1}(u, k), & \text{if } F_{j-1}(u, k) \leq d_j \\
F_{j-1}(u-1, k), & \text{if } F_{j-1}(u-1, k) > d_j \\
F_{j-1}(u, j-1) + p_k, & \text{if } F_{j-1}(u, j-1) + p_k \leq d_j \\
F_{j-1}(u-1, j-1) + p_k, & \text{if } F_{j-1}(u-1, j-1) + p_k > d_j \\
\infty, & \text{otherwise.}
\end{cases}
$$

The initialization is

$$
F_0(u, k) = \begin{cases}
0, & \text{if } u = 0 \text{ and } k = 0 \\
\infty, & \text{otherwise.}
\end{cases}
$$

The minimum number of tardy jobs is then equal to the smallest value u for which $F_n(u, n) < \infty$. The algorithm requires $O(n^3)$ time and $O(n^3)$ space.

$1 \mid p - \text{batch} \mid \sum w_i C_i$

To solve this problem we apply backward dynamic programming. Let F_j be the minimum total weighted completion time for SPT-batch schedules containing the last $n-j+1$ jobs $j, j+1, \ldots, n$. Processing of the first batch in the schedule starts at zero time. Furthermore, whenever a new batch is added to the beginning of this schedule, there is a corresponding delay to the processing of all batches. Suppose that a batch $\{j, \ldots, k-1\}$, which has processing time p_{k-1}, is inserted at the start of a schedule for jobs $k, \ldots, n$. The total weighted completion time of jobs $k, \ldots, n$ increases by $p_{k-1} \sum_{\nu=k}^{n} w_\nu$, while the total weighted completion time for jobs $j, \ldots, k-1$

is $p_{k-1} \sum_{\nu=j}^{k-1} w_\nu$. Thus, the overall increase in total weighted completion time is $p_{k-1} \sum_{\nu=j}^{n} w_\nu$.

The dynamic programming recursion can now be formulated as follows. The initialization is

$$F_{n+1} = 0$$

and for $j = n, n-1, \ldots, 1$ we have

$$F_j = \min_{j < k \leq n+1} \{F_k + p_{k-1} \sum_{\nu=j}^{n} w_\nu\}.$$

The optimal solution value is equal to F_1.

F_j can be interpreted as the length of a shortest path from j to $n+1$ in a network with vertices $1, \ldots, n+1$, arcs (j, k) with $j < k$ and arc lengths

$$c_{jk} = p_{k-1} \sum_{\nu=j}^{n} w_\nu.$$

The arc lengths c_{jk} satisfy the product property

$$c_{jl} - c_{jk} = (p_{l-1} - p_{k-1}) \sum_{\nu=j}^{n} w_\nu = h(k,l)f(j), \quad j < k < l$$

with $h(k, l) \geq 0$ and $f(j)$ nonincreasing. Thus, all values $F_j (j = n, n-1, \ldots, 1)$ can be calculated in $O(n)$ time (see Section 2.7) if the jobs are enumerated according to nondecreasing p_i-values. Therefore, the problem can be solved in time $O(n \log n)$.

$1 \mid p - batch \mid L_{max}$

Again, we apply backward dynamic programming. Let F_j be the minimum value for the maximum lateness for SPT-batch schedules containing jobs $j, \ldots, n$, where processing starts at zero time. If batch $\{j, \ldots, k-1\}$, which has processing time p_{k-1}, is inserted at the start of a schedule for jobs $k, \ldots, n$, then the maximum lateness of jobs $k, \ldots, n$ increases by p_{k-1}, while the maximum lateness for jobs $j, \ldots, k$ is $\max_{j \leq \nu \leq k-1} (p_{k-1} - d_\nu)$.

We are now ready to give the dynamic programming recursion. The initialization is

$$F_{n+1} = -\infty,$$

and the recursion for $j = n, n-1, \ldots, 1$ is

$$F_j = \min_{j < k \leq n+1} \max\{F_k + p_{k-1}, \max_{j \leq \nu \leq k-1}\{p_{k-1} - d_\nu\}\}.$$

The optimal solution is then equal to F_1. Clearly, the algorithm requires $O(n^2)$ time and $O(n)$ space.

Next we will show that this algorithm for the $L_{\max}$-problem can be used as a subroutine for solving the $f_{\max}$-problem.

$1 \mid p-\mathbf{batch} \mid \mathbf{f}_{\max}$

Let $f_{\max} = \max_{i=1}^{n} f_i(C_i)$, where each f_i is a nondecreasing function of the finishing time of job i. We assume that the optimal solution value of the problem is an integer whose logarithm is polynomially bounded in the size of the input. Then $1 \mid p-batch \mid f_{\max}$ can be solved polynomially if, for any integer k, there is a polynomial algorithm which solves the decision problem $P(k)$: Does there exist a solution with $f_{\max} \leq k$?

Such an algorithm for solving $P(k)$ can be obtained as follows. A schedule satisfies the condition $f_{\max} \leq k$ if and only if $f_j(C_j) \leq k$ for all $j = 1, \ldots, n$. The condition $f_j(C_j) \leq k$ induces a deadline d_j on the completion time of job j which can be determined in $O(\log P)$ time by binary search over the $P+1$ possible completion times where $P := \sum_{\nu=1}^{n} p_\nu$.

Once the deadlines have been determined, we can use the algorithm for minimizing $L_{\max}$ to find out if there is a solution with $f_j(C_j) \leq k$ by checking the condition $L_{\max} \leq 0$. Hence, the question "is $f_{\max} \leq k$?" can be answered in $O(n^2 + n \log P)$ time.

This is almost as far as we can get with polynomial algorithms because the problems $1 \mid p-batch \mid \sum w_i U_i$ and $1 \mid p-batch \mid \sum w_i T_i$ have been shown to be NP-hard.

8.2.2   The Bounded Model

It is easy to show that $1 \mid p-batch; b < n \mid C_{\max}$ can be solved in $O(n \log n)$ time: We assume that n is a multiple of b. If this is not the case, we add dummy jobs with zero processing times. Now the batches are constructed as follow. Assign the b jobs with smallest processing times to the first batch B_1, then b jobs with the next smallest processing times to B_2, and so on, until all jobs are assigned. An easy exchange argument shows that this must be optimal.

On the other hand, problems of type $1 \mid p-batch; b = 1 \mid f$ are equivalent to the corresponding single machine problems. Thus, NP-hardness results for single machine problems are also valid for p-batching problems with bounded batch size. Furthermore, $1 \mid p - batch; b = 2 \mid L_{\max}$ is strongly NP-hard.

8.3 Complexity Results for Single Machine Batching Problems

Tables 8.1 and 8.2 present complexity results for single machine s-batching problems. Several problems are $\mathcal{NP}$-hard because the corresponding single machine problem without batching (i.e. with $s = 0$) are $\mathcal{NP}$-hard.

Tables 8.3 and 8.4 contain complexity results for single machine p-batching problems. Note that we have shown that $1 \mid p-batch \mid \sum f_i$ can be solved in time $O(n^2 P)$. Serial batching problems and bounded parallel batching problems with constant processing times, release dates, and the objective function $\sum w_i C_i$, $\sum w_i U_i$, $\sum T_i$ can be solved polynomially using a dynamic programming approach related to the one discussed in Section 4.6.

Complexity results for some bounded parallel batching problems with constant processing times are derived from the fact that these problems are equivalent to corresponding problems with identical parallel machines.

$1 \mid prec; s - batch \mid L_{\max}$	Ng et al. [176]	$O(n^2)$
$1 \mid prec; p_i = p; s - batch \mid \sum C_i$ 8.1	Albers & Brucker [9]	$O(n^2)$
$1 \mid s - batch \mid \sum C_i$	2.7 Coffman et al. [71]	$O(n \log n)$
$1 \mid p_i = p; s - batch \mid \sum w_i C_i$	2.7 Albers & Brucker [9]	$O(n \log n)$
$1 \mid p_i = p; s - batch; r_i \mid \sum w_i C_i$	Baptiste [16]	$O(n^{14})$
$1 \mid s - batch \mid \sum U_i$	8.1 Brucker & Kovalyov [46]	$O(n^3)$
$1 \mid p_i = p; s - batch \mid \sum w_i U_i$	8.1 Hochbaum & Landy [112]	$O(n^4)$
$1 \mid p_i = p; s - batch; r_i \mid \sum w_i U_i$	Baptiste [16]	$O(n^{14})$
$1 \mid p_i = p; s - batch; r_i \mid \sum T_i$	Baptiste [16]	$O(n^{14})$

Table 8.1: Polynomially solvable serial batching problems.

$*1 \mid r_i; s-batch \mid L_{\max}$	Lenstra et al. [151]
$1 \mid chains; s-batch \mid \sum C_i$	Albers & Brucker [9]
$*1 \mid prec; s-batch \mid \sum C_i$	Lawler [137]
$*1 \mid r_i; s-batch \mid \sum C_i$	Lenstra et al. [151]
$*1 \mid s-batch \mid \sum w_i C_i$	Albers & Brucker [9]
$*1 \mid chains; p_i = 1; s-batch \mid \sum w_i C_i$	Albers & Brucker [9]
$*1 \mid chains; p_i = 1; s-batch \mid \sum U_i$	Lenstra & Rinnooy Kan [154]
$1 \mid s-batch \mid \sum w_i U_i$	Karp [124]
$1 \mid s-batch \mid \sum T_i$	Du & Leung [81]
$*1 \mid chains; p_i = 1; s-batch \mid \sum T_i$	Leung & Young [158]

Table 8.2: $\mathcal{NP}$-hard serial batching problems.

$1 \mid p - batch \mid C_{\max}$	8.2.1	Brucker et al. [36]
		$O(n)$
$1 \mid outtree; p_i = p; p - batch; r_i; b < n \mid C_{max}$		Brucker et al. [35]
		$O(n)$ '
$1 \mid p - batch; b < n \mid C_{max}$	8.2.1	Brucker et al. [36]
		$O(n \log n)$
$1 \mid tree; p_i = p; p - batch; b < n \mid C_{max}$		Hu [116]
		$O(n)$
$1 \mid p - batch \mid L_{\max}$	8.2.1	Brucker et al. [36]
		$O(n \log n)$
$1 \mid chains; p_i = 1; p - batch; r_i; b < n \mid L_{max}$		Parallel machine problem
$1 \mid intree; p_i = p; p - batch; b < n \mid L_{max}$		Brucker et al. [35]
		$O(n)$
$1 \mid outtree; p_i = 1; p - batch; r_i; b < n \mid \sum C_i$		Brucker et al. [38]
		$O(n^2)$
$1 \mid tree; p_i = p; p - batch; b < n \mid \sum C_i$		Parallel machine problem
$1 \mid p - batch \mid \sum w_i C_i$	8.2.1	Brucker et al. [36]
		$O(n \log n)$
$1 \mid p_i = p; p - batch; r_i; b < n \mid \sum w_i C_i$		Baptiste [16]
		$O(n^8)$
$1 \mid p - batch \mid \sum U_i$	8.2.1	Brucker et al. [36]
		$O(n^3)$
$1 \mid p_i = p; p - batch; r_i; b < n \mid \sum w_i U_i$		Baptiste [16]
		$O(n^8)$
$1 \mid prec; p_i = p; p - batch \mid \sum w_i U_i$		Earliest Start Schedule
		$O(n^2)$
$1 \mid p_i = p; p - batch; r_i; b < n \mid \sum T_i$		Baptiste [16]
		$O(n^8)$
$1 \mid p_i = 1; p - batch; r_i; b < n \mid \sum w_i T_i$		Network flow problem
$1 \mid p_i = p; p - batch; b < n \mid \sum w_i T_i$		Network flow problem
$1 \mid p_i = p; p - batch; r_i; \mid \sum w_i U_i$		Baptiste et al. [21]
		$O(n^{11})$
$1 \mid prec; p_i = p; p - batch \mid \sum w_i T_i$		Earliest Start Schedule
		$O(n^2)$

Table 8.3: Polynomially solvable parallel batching problems.

$*1 \mid intree; p_i = 1; p - batch; r_i; b < n \mid C_{max}$ Brucker et al. [35]

$*1 \mid p - batch; r_i; b < n \mid C_{max}$ Brucker et al. [36]

$*1 \mid prec; p_i = 1; p - batch; b < n \mid C_{max}$ Ullman [203]

$*1 \mid outtree; p_i = 1; p - batch; b < n \mid L_{max}$ Brucker et al. [35]

$*1 \mid p - batch; b = 2 \mid L_{max}$ Brucker et al. [36]

$*1 \mid intree; p_i = 1; p - batch; r_i; b < n \mid \sum C_i$ Lenstra [150]

$*1 \mid p - batch; r_i; b < n \mid \sum C_i$ Lenstra et al. [151]

$*1 \mid prec; p_i = 1; p - batch; b < n \mid \sum C_i$ Lenstra & Rinnooy

                                                                  Kan [152]

$*1 \mid chains; p_i = 1; p - batch; b < n \mid \sum w_i C_i$ Timkovsky [202]

$*1 \mid chains; p_i = 1; p - batch; b < n \mid \sum U_i$ Lenstra & Rinnooy

                                                                  Kan [154]

$1 \mid p - batch \mid \sum w_i U_i$ Brucker et al. [36]

$*1 \mid chains; p_i = 1; p - batch; b < n \mid \sum T_i$ Leung & Young [157]

$1 \mid p - batch \mid \sum w_i T_i$ Brucker et al. [36]

Table 8.4: $\mathcal{NP}$-hard parallel batching problems.

Chapter 9

Changeover Times and Transportation Times

In this chapter we consider scheduling problems in which the set I of all jobs or all operations (in connection with shop problems) is partitioned into disjoint sets $I_1, \ldots, I_r$ called groups, i.e. $I = I_1 \cup I_2 \cup \ldots \cup I_r$ and $I_f \cap I_g = \phi$ for $f, g \in \{1, \ldots, r\}$, $f \neq g$. Let N_j be the number of jobs in I_j. Furthermore, we have the additional restrictions that for any two jobs (operations) i, j with $i \in I_f$ and $j \in I_g$ to be processed on the same machine M_k, job (operation) j cannot be started until s_{fgk} time units after the finishing time of job (operation) i, or job (operation) i cannot be started until s_{gfk} time units after the finishing time of job (operation) j. In a typical application, the groups correspond to different types of jobs (operations) and s_{fgk} may be interpreted as a machine dependent changeover time. During the changeover period, the machine cannot process another job. We assume that $s_{fgk} = 0$ for all $f, g \in \{1, \ldots, r\}$, $k \in \{1, \ldots, m\}$ with $f = g$, and that the triangle inequality holds:

$$s_{fgk} + s_{ghk} \geq s_{fhk} \text{ for all } f, g, h \in \{1, \ldots, r\}, k \in \{1, \ldots, m\}. \quad (9.1)$$

Both assumptions are realistic in practice.

If we consider single machine problems or if the changeover times are machine independent, we replace s_{fgk} by s_{fg}. If the changeover times do not depend on both groups I_f and I_g, but only on the group I_g to which the job to be processed next belongs, then we replace s_{fg} by s_g. In the latter case, the changeover times are called **sequence independent**, contrary to the general case in which they are called **sequence dependent**. If

$s_{fg} = s$ for all $f, g = 1, \ldots, r$, then we have **constant** changeover times. To indicate problems with changeover times, we add $\beta_7 \in \{s_{fgk}, s_{fg}, s_g, s\}$ to the β-part of our general classification scheme.

In Section 9.1, single machine problems with changeover times will be discussed. Section 9.2 describes some results on parallel machine problems with changeover times, while in the last section, shop problems with changeover and/or transportation times are introduced.

9.1 Single Machine Problems

While problems $1 \mid s_{fg} \mid C_{\max}$ and $1 \mid s_g \mid L_{\max}$ are $\mathcal{NP}$-hard (Bruno & Downey [59]), problem $1 \mid s_g \mid C_{\max}$ can be solved polynomially by scheduling the jobs group by group in any order.

Next we will present dynamic programming procedures for the problems $1 \mid s_{fg} \mid L_{\max}$, $1 \mid s_{fg} \mid \sum w_i C_i$, and $1 \mid s_{fg} \mid \sum w_i U_i$, which are due to Monma & Potts [170]. The following theorem is the basis for these procedures.

Theorem 9.1   (a) For problem $1 \mid s_{fg} \mid \sum w_i U_i$, there exists an optimal schedule where the early jobs within each group are ordered according to nondecreasing due dates.

(b) For problem $1 \mid s_{fg} \mid \sum w_i C_i$, there exists an optimal schedule where the jobs within each group are ordered according to nondecreasing p_i/w_i-values.

(c) For problem $1 \mid s_{fg} \mid L_{\max}$, there exists an optimal schedule where the jobs within each group are ordered according to nondecreasing due dates.

Proof: Consider a schedule of the form D, j, E, i, F, where jobs i and j are from the same group and D, E, F represent arbitrary blocks, i.e. partial sequences of jobs. Due to the triangle inequality (9.1), the total changeover times will not increase if D, j, E, i, F is replaced by D, E, i, j, F or D, i, j, E, F. We have to show that if $d_i < d_j$ for early jobs i, j, or $p_i/w_i < p_j/w_j$, or $d_i < d_j$, then $\sum w_i U_i$, or $\sum w_i C_i$, or the $L_{\max}$-value will not increase when moving from the sequence D, j, E, i, F to one of the two sequences D, E, i, j, F or D, i, j, E, F.

(a) If we have the objective function $\sum w_i U_i$, then the fact that i is early in D, j, E, i, F implies that i, j are early in D, E, i, j, F because $d_i < d_j$.

(b) Consider the objective function $\sum w_i C_i$ and let $p_i/w_i < p_j/w_j$.

It is convenient to replace changeover times by set-up jobs with processing time equal to the changeover time and zero weight. Furthermore, we assume that all set ups after j and before i in D, j, E, i, F are included in the partial sequence E. Define

$$p(E) = \sum_{i \in E} p_i \text{ and } w(E) = \sum_{i \in E} w_i.$$

Then an easy calculation shows that job j and block E can be swapped without increasing the objective value if $p_j/w_j > p(E)/w(E)$. Similarly, i and E can be swapped if $p(E)/w(E) > p_i/w_i$. In the first case we first swap j and E and then j and i without increasing the objective value. This provides the sequence D, E, i, j, F. If $p_j/w_j \leq p(E)/w(E)$, then $p_i/w_i < p(E)/w(E)$ and we get D, i, j, E, F after two swaps.

(c) Consider the objective function $L_{\max}$ and let $d_i < d_j$. Again, changeover times are replaced by set-up jobs with the changeover time as the processing time and a very large due date. To see the effect of swapping a job j scheduled before a block $E = i_r, i_{r-1}, \ldots, i_1$, we replace E by a job with processing time $p_{i_r, i_{r-1}, \ldots, i_1} = p(E)$ and a due date $d_{i_r, i_{r-1}, \ldots, i_1}$, where $d_{i_r, i_{r-1}, \ldots, i_1}$ is calculated by the recursion

$$d_{i_{\vartheta+1}, \ldots, i_1} = \min\{d_{i_\vartheta, \ldots, i_1}, d_{i_{\vartheta+1}} + \sum_{k=1}^{\vartheta} p_{i_k}\} \text{ for } \vartheta = 1, 2, \ldots, r-1.$$

This follows by induction using the fact that, for two jobs i and j with finishing times C_j and $C_i = C_j - p_j$, we have

$$\max\{C_j - d_j, C_j - p_j - d_i\} = C_j - \min\{d_j, d_i + p_j\}.$$

Now we can proceed as in Part (b). If $d_j > d_E := d_{i_r, i_{r-1}, \ldots, i_1}$, then we can first swap j and E and then j and i without increasing the objective value. Otherwise, we have $d_i < d_j \leq d_E$ and we can first swap i and E and then j and i. $\qquad \square$

For the following dynamic programming algorithms, we assume that the jobs in each group are ordered according to Theorem 9.1. We first derive an algorithm for problem $1 \mid s_{fg} \mid \sum w_i C_i$.

We define $C(n_1, n_2, \ldots, n_r, t, h)$ to be the minimum cost of a partial schedule containing the first n_j jobs of group I_j ($j = 1, \ldots, r$), where the last job scheduled comes from group I_h and is completed at time t. We have

$$0 \le n_j \le N_j \text{ for } j = 1, \ldots, r$$

and

$$0 \le t \le T := \sum_{i \in I} p_i + \sum_{j=1}^{r} N_j \max\{s_{fj} \mid 1 \le f \le r\}.$$

The recursion is

$$
\begin{aligned}
&C(n_1, n_2, \ldots, n_r, t, h) \\
&= \min\{C(n_1', n_2', \ldots, n_r', t', f) + w_{n_h}^h t \mid 1 \le f \le r\}
\end{aligned}
\tag{9.2}
$$

where $n_j' = n_j$ for $j \ne h$, $n_h' = n_h - 1$, $t' = t - p_{n_h}^h - s_{fh}$, and $w_{n_h}^h$ and $p_{n_h}^h$ are the weight and processing time of the n_h-th job in group I_h.

Initially, we set $C(0, 0, \ldots, 0, 0, 0) = 0$ and all other C-values to infinity.

The optimal schedule cost is found by selecting the smallest value of the form $C(N_1, \ldots, N_r, t, h)$ for some schedule completion time $0 \le t \le T$ and some group I_h to which the final job belongs.

Because the number of states is bounded by $O(rn^r T)$ and (9.2) can be calculated in $O(r)$ steps, we have an $O(r^2 n^r T)$-algorithm.

Alternatively, we can replace the state variable t by variables t_{fh} ($f, h = 1, \ldots, r$) representing the number of set ups from group f to group h. Note that t is readily computed from the state variables using

$$t = \sum_{f,h=1}^{r} t_{fh} s_{fh} + \sum_{h=1}^{r} \sum_{\nu=1}^{n_h} p_\nu^h.$$

The complexity of this version is $O(r^2 n^{r+s})$, where s is the number of different values for changeover times. Note that $s \le r^2$ in general and $s \le r$ in the case of sequence-independent changeover times. If the number of groups is fixed, we have a polynomial algorithm.

Similarly, we solve problem $1 \mid s_{fg} \mid L_{\max}$. In this case (9.2) is replaced by

$$C(n_1, n_2, \ldots, n_r, t, h)$$
$$= \min\{\max\{C(n_1', n_2', \ldots, n_r', t', f), t - d_{n_k}^h\} \mid 1 \le f \le r\}. \tag{9.3}$$

The problem with the weighted number of late jobs is solved differently. By Theorem 9.1(a), we only know an order for early jobs; those jobs that are late must also be determined by the algorithm. The late jobs may be appended in any order to the schedule of on-time jobs.

We define $C(n_1, n_2, \ldots, n_r, t, h)$ to be the minimum weighted number of late jobs for the partial schedule containing the first n_j jobs of group I_j $(j = 1, \ldots, r)$, where the last on-time job comes from group I_h and is completed at time t. We have

$$0 \le n_j \le N_j \text{ for } j = 1, \ldots, r$$

and

$$0 \le t \le T := \min\{\max_{i \in I} d_i, \sum_{i \in I} p_i + \sum_{j=1}^{r} N_j \max\{s_{fj} \mid 1 \le f \le r\}\}.$$

The recursion is

$$C(n_1, n_2, \ldots, n_r, t, h) = \begin{cases} \min\{\min_{1 \le f \le r} C(n_1', n_2', \ldots, n_r', t', f), \\ \qquad C(n_1', n_2', \ldots, n_r', t, h) + w_{n_h}^h\} & \text{if } t \le d_{n_h}^h \\ C(n_1', n_2', \ldots, n_r', t, h) + w_{n_h}^h & \text{if } t > d_{n_h}^h \end{cases} \tag{9.4}$$

where $n_j' = n_j$ if $j \ne h$, $n_h' = n_h - 1$, $t' = t - p_{n_h}^h - s_{fh}$.
The initial values are

$$C(n_1, n_2, \ldots, n_r, 0, 0) = \sum_{j=1}^{r} \sum_{\nu=1}^{n_j} w_\nu^j$$

for $0 \le n_j \le N_j$, where $j = 1, \ldots, r$. All other initial values are set to infinity.

The minimum weighted number of late jobs is found by selecting the smallest value of the form $C(N_1, N_2, \ldots, N_r, t, h)$ for some completion time of on-time jobs, where $0 \leq t \leq T$, and for some group I_h containing the final on-time job.

The complexity is $O(r^2 n^r T)$. Again, it may be desirable to eliminate the state variable t from the recursion. To achieve this, we switch the state variable t with the objective function value as follows.

Define $C(n_1, n_2, \ldots, n_r, w, h)$ to be the minimum completion time of on-time jobs for a partial schedule containing the first n_j jobs of each group I_j, where the weighted number of late jobs is equal to w, and the last on-time job comes from group I_h. The initial values are $C(n_1, n_2, \ldots, n_r, w, 0) = 0$, where $w = \sum_{j=1}^{r} \sum_{\nu=1}^{n_j} w_\nu^j$ for $0 \leq n_j \leq N_j$ $(j = 1, \ldots, r)$, and all other values are set to infinity.

The recursion is

$$C(n_1, n_2, \ldots, n_r, w, h) = \min\{ \min_{1 \leq f \leq r} \{C(n_1', n_2', \ldots, n_r', w, f) + p_{fh}' \mid$$
$$C(n_1', n_2', \ldots, n_r', w, f) + p_{fh}' \leq d_{n_h}^h \}, C(n_1', n_2', \ldots, n_r', w', h)\}$$

where $n_j' = n_j$ if $j \neq h$, $n_h' = n_h - 1$, $p_{fh}' = p_{n_h}^h + s_{fh}$ and $w' = w - w_{n_h}^h$. As in (9.4), the first term in the minimization chooses the n_h-th job in group I_h to be scheduled on time, if possible, and chooses the previous on-time job from group I_f; the second term selects the n_h-th job of group I_h to be late.

The minimum weighted number of late jobs is found by selecting the smallest w for which $\min_{0 \leq h \leq r} C(N_1, N_2, \ldots, N_r, w, h)$ is finite.

The complexity is $O(r^2 n^r W)$, where $W = \sum_{i \in I} w_i$. It reduces to $O(r^2 n^{r+1})$ for the total number of late jobs problem.

9.2 Problems with Parallel Machines

In this section we consider changeover times in connection with parallel, identical (uniform, unrelated) machines. For unrelated machines, we have machine dependent changeover times s_{fgk}. In the case of uniform machines, the changeover time depends on the speed r_k of machine k, more specifically $s_{fgk} = s_{fg}/r_k$.

We saw in the last section that even in the one machine case, problems with sequence dependent changeover times are $\mathcal{NP}$-hard in all but trivial cases. Therefore, we restrict ourselves to parallel machine problems with sequence independent changeover times $s_{gk}, s_{gk} = s_g/r_k$, or s_g for unrelated, uniform, or identical machines. As before, there are r job groups $I_1, \ldots, I_r$, where N_j is the number of jobs in group I_j.

The two problems $P2 \mid p_j = 1; s_g = 1 \mid C_{\max}$ and $Q \mid p_j = 1; s_g = 1; N_j = h \mid C_{\max}$ are $\mathcal{NP}$-hard (Brucker et al. [47]). Thus, we can only expect polynomial algorithms in special situations.

One such problem is $P \mid p_j = p; s_g = p; N_j = h \mid C_{\max}$, i.e. a problem with identical parallel machines where all groups have equal sizes and all processing and changeover times are equal to p.

Let $P(y)$ be the problem of finding a schedule for $P \mid p_j = p; s_g = p; N_j = h \mid C_{\max}$ with $C_{\max} \leq y$ if such a schedule exists. $P(y)$ can be solved by applying Mc Naughton's Wrapping Around Rule: Schedule the groups one after the other in the interval $[0, y]$ by filling this interval for each machine, one machine after the other. Continue to schedule a group on the next machine if the group cannot be completed on the current machine.

Theorem 9.2 Problem $P(y)$ has a solution if and only if all jobs can be scheduled by applying the Wrapping Around Rule.

Proof: Consider a feasible schedule. Assume that all groups scheduled completely on $M1$ are scheduled at the beginning of the interval $[0, y]$. Let i be the first group not completely scheduled on $M1$ and assume that the i-jobs, i.e. the jobs belonging to group i, are scheduled immediately after the last complete group on $M1$. Let c be the completion time of the last i-job.

There exists a machine, say M_2, on which other i-jobs are scheduled. Assume that on M_2 all i-jobs are scheduled at the beginning of $[0, y]$ and that the last i-job on M_2 finishes at time a. Then we consider three cases.

Case 1: $y - c < 2p$

If $y - c < p$, no further job can be scheduled on $M1$. If $y - c \geq p$, then we move one i-job from $M2$ to $M1$.

Case 2: $y - c \geq 2p$ and $a \leq y - c$

We exchange the jobs (including set-up jobs) scheduled on $M1$ in the interval $[c, c + a]$ with the i-jobs and the set-up job scheduled on M_2 in $[0, a]$ as shown in Figures 9.1(a) and 9.1(b).

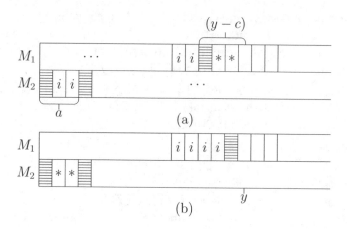

(a)

(b)

Figure 9.1: Extending group of i-job on M_1: Case 2.

Case 3: $y - c \geq 2p$ and $a > y - c$

We have the situation as shown in Figure 9.2(a) and transform this schedule into the one in Figure 9.2(b).

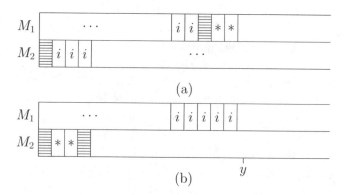

(a)

(b)

Figure 9.2: Extending group of i-job on M_1: Case 3.

The whole process is repeated until after a finite number of steps we get a schedule with the desired properties.

Due to the fact that all job groups have equal sizes and all machines are identical, the wrapping around rule creates a feasible schedule. □

The computation time of the Wrapping Around Algorithm is bounded by $O(m)$. To find an optimal $C_{\max}$-value C^*, we exploit the following facts:

- $L := \lceil \frac{r(h+1)}{m} \rceil p$ is a lower bound for C^*, and

- $L + p$ is an upper bound for C^* (the Wrapping Around schedule for $y = L + p$ is always feasible because the extra p-value allows for an additional set up on each machine).

Thus, we only need to solve the two problems $P(L)$ and $P(L + p)$. This provides us with $O(m)$-algorithm.

Mc Naughton's Wrapping Around Rule solves the problem even if the changeover time is a multiple of the processing time p, i.e. if $p_j = p$ and $s_g = lp$ where l is an arbitrary positive integer. The interchange arguments in the proof of Theorem 9.2 are almost the same.

If we replace the identical machines by uniform machines, then the exchange arguments of Theorem 9.2 are still valid. However, Mc Naughton's Wrapping Around Rule does not solve the corresponding problem $Q \mid p_j = p; s_g = lp; N_j = h; d_j = y \mid -$. The reason for this is that the Wrapping Around Rule depends on the order of the uniform machines. To solve the problem we may apply the Wrapping Around Rule to each of the $m!$ possible orders which yields an $O(mm!)$-algorithm. This algorithm is polynomial if m is fixed.

Finally, note that the $O(m)$-algorithm which solves $P(y)$ by applying the Wrapping Around Rule is not a polynomial one. Next, an $O(\log m)$-algorithm will be presented which solves problem $P(y)$. This algorithm can be described as follows.

Let $s = lp$. In the interval $[0, Y]$ with $Y = (hp+s) \lfloor y/(hp+s) \rfloor$ we schedule as many groups as possible without splitting them into subgroups. If all groups can be scheduled, we have finished. Otherwise each of the remaining groups is divided into subgroups including $U := \lfloor (y-Y-s)/p \rfloor$ jobs, except possibly the last subgroups including $Q < U$ jobs. We schedule the subgroups with U jobs without splitting them on the m available machines. If all of these subgroups are scheduled and $Q = 0$, we have finished. If the number r of these subgroups is greater than m or $r = m$ and $Q > 0$, no feasible schedule exists. Otherwise, we set $m' = m - r$, $y' = y - Y, p' = p, h' = Q$ and apply the same procedure recursively to the problem specified by m', y', p', h'.

Note that we may assume that $r > \lfloor \frac{m}{2} \rfloor$, because otherwise all batches with Q jobs can be scheduled in $[Y, y]$ on the remaining $m' = m - r > \lfloor \frac{m}{2} \rfloor$ machines and we have finished. Thus, the number of recursive calls is at the most $O(\log m)$. In each recursive step the corresponding schedule can be calculated in constant time.

Using the interchange techniques described in the proof of Theorem 9.2, it can be shown that an optimal schedule exists with the described structure. This leads to

Theorem 9.3 Problem $P \mid p_j = p; s_g = lp; N_j = h \mid C_{\max}$ can be solved in time $O(\log m)$.

9.3 General Shop Problems

In connection with general shop problems, we may have changeover times and transportation times. For changeover times, we have a partition of the set $I = \{1, \ldots, t\}$ of operations of all jobs into disjoint sets $I_1, \ldots, I_r$. Again, we call these sets groups. If, on a specific machine M_k, an operation i from group I_h is processed immediately after an operation j from group I_l, a changeover time t_{lhk} occurs between i and j. In the disjunctive graph model we can take care of the changeover time from operation j to operation i by labeling the fixed disjunctive arc (j, i) with t_{lhk}. Furthermore, the length of a path in the corresponding network is now equal to the sum of all vertex labels and arc labels on the path. Using these concepts, it is possible to generalize the branch-and-bound method presented in Section 6.4.3 to this more general situation (see Brucker & Thiele [57]).

If in the general shop model we replace "sets of operations to be processed on the same machine" by "sets of operations belonging to the same job" and introduce a changeover time t_{lhi} if an operation of job i belonging to group I_l is processed immediately before an operation of job i belonging to group I_h, then we get a model which is mathematically equivalent to the previous one. If group I_k is the set of operations to be processed on machine M_k, then t_{lhi} may be interpreted as the time to transport job i from machine M_l to machine M_h. Due to the equivalence of both models, an algorithm which solves the general shop problem with changeover times solves the general shop problem with transportation times. It should be noted that in the transportation model we assume that there is sufficient transportation capacity to handle all jobs to be transported simultaneously.

We can go a step further by considering problems with both changeover times and transportation times.

Chapter 10

Multi-Purpose Machines

In a multi-purpose machine (MPM) model there is a set of machines $\mu_i(\mu_{ij}) \subseteq \{M_1, \ldots, M_m\}$ associated with a job J_i (operation O_{ij}). $J_i(O_{ij})$ has to be processed by one machine in the set $\mu_i(\mu_{ij})$. Thus, scheduling problems with multi-purpose machines combine assignment and scheduling problems: we have to schedule each job J_i (operation O_{ij}) on exactly one machine from the set $\mu_i(\mu_{ij})$.

If we have single operation jobs and the multi-purpose machines have identical (uniform) speeds, we denote the corresponding situation by $PMPM$ $(QMPM)$. Note that $P(Q)$ is the special case of $PMPM$ $(QMPM)$ in which all machine sets μ_i contain all m machines. Furthermore, $PMPM$ is a special case of $QMPM$. We also may introduce $RMPM$ to denote MPM problems with unrelated machines which generalize $QMPM$ problems. However in combination with regular objective functions $RMPM$ is equivalent to R because we may set $p_{ij} = \infty$ if $M_j \notin \mu_i$.

Shop problems with MPM are defined similarly. In a general shop with MPM, denoted by $GMPM$, there is a machine set μ_{ij} associated with each operation. The MPM job shop problem, denoted by $JMPM$, is the corresponding special case of $GMPM$. For MPM flow shop problems and MPM open shops, denoted by $FMPM$ and $OMPM$, respectively, we need special definitions. For the MPM flow shop problem, each job J_i has exactly r operations O_{ij} $(j = 1, \ldots, r)$ and there is the same machine set μ_j associated with the j-th operation of each job. r is called the **number of stages** of the problem. Furthermore, all machine sets are assumed to be different, i.e. $\mu_j \neq \mu_k$ for $j \neq k$. As in the classical case for $j = 2, \ldots, r$, O_{ij} cannot start before $O_{i,j-1}$ is completed.

MPM open shop problems are defined like MPM flow shop problems. However, there are no precedence constraints between the operations of an MPM open shop. In connection with $FMPM$ problems and $OMPM$ problems, r is called the number of stages. Shop problems are MPM shop problems with one-element machine sets μ_{ij}.

To describe and classify MPM problems, we combine $PMPM$, $QMPM$, $GMPM$, $JMPM$, etc. with the other symbols used for the classification of scheduling problems.

In Section 10.1, MPM problems with identical and uniform machines will be discussed. Section 10.2 is devoted to MPM shop problems.

10.1   MPM Problems with Identical and Uniform Machines

Problem $RMPM\| \sum C_i$ is equivalent to problem $R\| \sum C_i$. This problem can be formulated as a weighted matching problem in a bipartite graph and can be solved in $O(n^3)$ time.

All other problems with arbitrary processing times and parallel multi-purpose machines are $\mathcal{NP}$-hard because $P2\|C_{\max}$ and $P2\| \sum w_i C_i$ are $\mathcal{NP}$-hard (Garey and Johnson [99] and Bruno et al. [58]).

Now let us consider problems with unit processing times.

Problems QMPM | $p_i = 1$ | $\sum w_i U_i (\sum w_i T_i)$

Again, we reduce the problems to minimum cost bipartite matching problems. Consider first problem $QMPM \mid p_i = 1 \mid \sum w_i U_i$. The corresponding bipartite graph is $(V_1 \cup V_2, A)$, where

- V_1 is the set of jobs,

- V_2 is the set of all pairs (j, t), where j represents M_j and t represents unit-time period $[(t-1)/s_j, t/s_j]$ $(j = 1, \ldots, m; t = 1, \ldots, n)$,

- for each $t = 1, \ldots, n$ an arc from i to (j, t) exists if $M_j \in \mu_i$, and

- the cost associated with the arc from i to (j, t) is given by w_i if $t/s_j > d_j$ and 0 otherwise.

Problem $QMPM \mid p_i = 1 \mid \sum w_i T_i$ can be solved in the same way if we replace the cost associated with the arc from i to (j,t) by

$$w_i \cdot \max\{0, t/s_j - d_i\}.$$

Problems PMPM $\mid$ $p_i = 1; r_i \mid \sum w_i U_i (\sum w_i T_i)$

These problems are also formulated as minimum cost matching problems in bipartite graphs which are nearly identical with those defined above. The main difference is that the time slots $t = 1, \ldots, n$ have to be replaced by different time slots $t_1, t_2, \ldots, t_n$, which are the earliest possible time slots for scheduling n unit-time jobs with release times $r_1, \ldots, r_n$ on one machine. Furthermore, we have to set $s_j = 1$ for $j = 1, \ldots, m$.

Problems PMPM 2 $\mid$ $p_i = 1;$ chains $\mid$ $C_{\max}$

Surprisingly, problem $PMPM\,2 \mid p_i = 1; chains \mid C_{\max}$ is $\mathcal{NP}$-hard. This follows from an $\mathcal{NP}$-hardness proof for problem $PMPT\,2 \mid p_i = 1; chains \mid C_{\max}$ given by Hoogeveen et al. [113].

Now let us consider

QMPM- and PMPM Problems with Preemption

Problem PMPM $\mid$ pmtn $\mid \sum C_i$

We will show that every schedule with a finite number of preemptions can be transformed into a nonpreemptive one without increasing the objective value. Thus, the problem can be solved in $O(n^3)$ time by applying the algorithm for $R \| \sum C_i$.

Theorem 10.1 Any schedule for problem $PMPM \mid pmtn \mid \sum C_i$ can be transformed into a nonpreemptive one without increasing the objective value.

Proof: Consider an arbitrary schedule S for an instance of problem $PMPM \mid pmtn \mid \sum C_i$ with a finite number of preemptions. Since the claim clearly holds for single machine problems, it suffices to transform this schedule into a preemptive one where every job is processed by only one machine.

Figure 10.1: Parts of job j_0 are scheduled on M_k and M_l.

Let $t_1 < t_2 < \ldots < t_r$ denote a sequence which contains all starting, preemption, restarting, and completion times of jobs in S.

If each job is processed by only one machine, we have finished. Otherwise, consider a maximal value i such that there exists a job j that is processed in $[t_{i-1}, t_i]$ on machine M_ν and also processed later than t_i on a machine other than M_ν.

Let J be the set of jobs of this type, i.e. $J = \{j \mid j$ is processed in $[t_{i-1}, t_i]$ and later than t_i on different machines$\}$.

Let M denote the set of machines used by the jobs of J in $[t_{i-1}, t_i]$ and let M' denote the set of machines used by the jobs of J later than t_i.

If $M \subseteq M'$, then $M = M'$ and we reassign the jobs in $[t_{i-1}, t_i]$ such that each job uses the same machine as it uses later. Thus, the maximal value i with the above property is reduced by at least one.

Otherwise if $M \not\subseteq M'$, a machine $M_k \in M \backslash M'$ exists. Let j_0 denote the job that is processed on M_k in $[t_{i-1}, t_i]$. Let M_l denote the machine on which the later parts of job j_0 are scheduled. This situation is depicted in Figure 10.1.

Let $L_k = t_i - t_{i-1}$ and let L_l be the sum of the lengths of all parts of job j_0 processed later than t_i. Let F_k denote the number of jobs finished on machine M_k later than t_i and let F_l denote the number of jobs finished on machine M_l later than C_{j_0}.

If $F_l < F_k$, we may schedule the part of job j_0 scheduled on M_k on M_l during the time interval $[C_{j_0}, C_{j_0} + L_k]$, shift the jobs scheduled on M_l later than C_{j_0} by L_k units to the right, and shift the jobs scheduled on M_k later than t_i by L_k units to the left. The resulting schedule is feasible because after the shifts no job processed in $[t_{i-1}, t_i]$ on machine M_k is processed on any other machine in the same time period because $M_k \notin M'$. Furthermore, the objective value does not increase because $(F_l + 1)L_k - F_k L_k \leq 0$.

Conversely, if $F_l \geq F_k$, we may schedule the parts of job j_0 scheduled later than t_i on M_l in $[t_i, t_i + L_l]$ on M_k, shift the jobs scheduled on M_k later than t_i by L_l units to the right, and shift the remaining jobs scheduled on M_l later than t_i as far to the left as possible. Due to the maximality of i, the resulting schedule is feasible. The objective value does not increase because $F_k L_l - F_l L_l \leq 0$.

Thus, we have reduced the set J by one element. This process can be repeated until the set J is empty. Hence the maximal value i with the above property is again reduced by at least one. □

$P2 \mid pmtn \mid \sum w_i C_i$ is $\mathcal{NP}$-hard since for problem $P \mid pmtn \mid \sum w_i C_i$ preemptive schedules do not yield a smaller optimal objective value than nonpreemptive schedules (see Theorem 5.6) and $P2 \parallel \sum w_i C_i$ is $\mathcal{NP}$-hard (Bruno et al. [58]).

QMPM and PMPM Problems with Preemption and Release Dates

Problem $R \mid pmtn; r_i \mid L_{\max}$ can be formulated as a linear program (see Section 5.1.3). This implies that $QMPM \mid pmtn; r_i \mid L_{max}$ is polynomially solvable. However, this is as far as we can get because $PMPM2 \mid pmtn; r_i \mid \sum C_i$ and $PMPM2 \mid pmtn; r_i \mid \sum U_i$ are $\mathcal{NP}$-hard. These $\mathcal{NP}$-hardness results are a consequence of the fact that the corresponding parallel machine problems are $\mathcal{NP}$-hard (Du et al. [85], Du et al. [84]).

In this section we will derive an ε-approximation algorithm for problem $PMPM \mid pmtn; r_i \mid L_{\max}$ which is based on network flow concepts.

For a given threshold value L, we consider the decision problem of whether a feasible solution exists with $L_{\max} \leq L$. Because $L_{\max} \leq L$ is equivalent to

$$C_i \leq d_i^L := d_i + L \text{ for } i = 1, \ldots, n$$

this problem is equivalent to the time window problem: Given release times r_i and deadlines d_i for each job, does there exist a feasible schedule with

$$C_i \leq d_i \text{ for } i = 1, \ldots, n?$$

To solve the time window problem, we generalize the network flow approach described in Section 5.1.1.

Let $t_1, t_2, \ldots, t_{p+1}$ be a sequence of the release times r_i and the due dates

d_i such that $t_j < t_{j+1}$ for $j = 1, \ldots, p$. The sequence $t_1, t_2, \ldots, t_{p+1}$ defines time intervals $I_j = [t_j, t_{j+1}]$ of length $T_j = t_{j+1} - t_j$ $(j = 1, \ldots, p)$. Using these time intervals, we define the following network $N = (V, A)$.

The set V consists of

- a source s,

- job-nodes J_i $(i = 1, \ldots, n)$,

- job-interval-nodes $J_i I_j$ $(i = 1, \ldots, n; j = 1, \ldots, p)$,

- interval-machine-nodes $I_j M_k$ $(j = 1, \ldots, p; k = 1, \ldots, m)$, and

- a sink t.

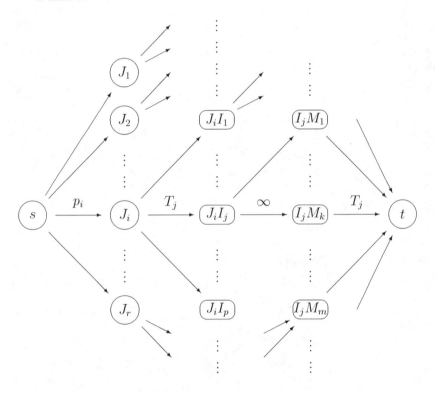

Figure 10.2: Network for problem $PMTM \mid pmtn; r_i; d_i \mid -$.

A denotes the set of arcs with restricted capacities. A contains

- arcs (s, J_i) with capacity p_i $(i = 1, \ldots, n)$,

- arcs $(J_i, J_i I_j)$ with capacity T_j if J_i can be processed in time interval I_j, i.e. $r_i \leq t_j$ and $d_i \geq t_{j+1}$ $(i = 1, \ldots, n; j = 1, \ldots, p)$,

- arcs $(J_i I_j, I_j M_k)$ with infinite capacity if $M_k \in \mu_i$ $(i = 1, \ldots, n; j = 1, \ldots, p; k = 1, \ldots, m)$, and

- arcs $(I_j M_k, t)$ with capacity T_j $(j = 1, \ldots, p; k = 1, \ldots, m)$.

Figure 10.2 shows a part of the resulting network.

We have the following

Theorem 10.2 For a given instance of $PMPM|pmtn; r_i; d_i|-$, there exists a feasible schedule if and only if there exists a flow from s to t in the corresponding network $N = (V, A)$ with flow value $\sum_{i=1}^{r} p_i$.

Proof: First assume that there exists a feasible flow $x = (x(i, j) : (i, j) \in A)$ with flow value $P := \sum_{i=1}^{r} p_i$. For all job-nodes J_i $(i = 1, \ldots, n)$ we have $x(s, J_i) = p_i$ because $P = \sum_{i=1}^{r} p_i$. A feasible schedule of $PMPM|pmtn; r_i; d_i|-$ can be defined as follows.

(i) If $x(J_i, J_i I_j) = l$, then we schedule l time units of J_i in time interval I_j. This is possible because $x(J_i, J_i I_j) \leq T_j$.

(ii) If $x(J_i I_j, I_j M_k) = l$, then we schedule l time units of J_i in time interval I_j on machine M_k. Because $x(I_j M_k, t) \leq T_j$, machine M_k is busy for at the most T_j time units during time interval I_j.

We obtain a classical open shop problem $O|pmtn|C_{max}$ in each time interval I_j by defining

$$p_{ik} := x(J_i I_j, I_j M_k) \quad (i = 1, \ldots, n; k = 1, \ldots, m).$$

Because of (i) we have

$$A_i := \sum_{k=1}^{m} p_{ik} \leq T_j \quad (i = 1, \ldots, n; j = 1, \ldots, p).$$

Moreover, because of (ii) we have

$$B_k := \sum_{i=1}^{r} p_{ik} \leq T_j \quad (k = 1, \ldots, m; j = 1, \ldots, p).$$

As shown in Section 2.4, the optimal solution value of the open shop problem is given by $\max\{\max_{i=1}^{n} A_i, \max_{k=1}^{m} B_k\} \leq T_j$. Therefore, we can schedule $x(J_i I_j, I_j M_k)$ time units of job J_i on machine M_k in time interval I_j without violating any capacity constraints. By combining the schedules obtained in all time intervals, we get a feasible schedule for $PMPM|pmtn; r_i; d_i|-$.

Now let there be a feasible schedule for a given instance of $PMPM$ $|pmtn; r_i; d_i|-$. Using (i) and (ii), it is easy to define a feasible flow $x = (x(i,j) : (i,j) \in A)$ with flow value $P = \sum_{i=1}^{r} p_i$ based on this schedule. $\square$

To find a solution with an objective value that differs from the optimal objective value by at the most ε time units, we do binary search on the set of values $L_{low} + i\varepsilon (i = 1, \ldots, \lceil \frac{L_{up} - L_{low}}{\varepsilon} \rceil)$, where $L_{low}(L_{up})$ is a lower (upper) bound for the optimal $L_{\max}$-value.

10.2   *MPM* Problems with Shop Characteristics

In this section we study job shop, flow shop, and open shop problems with multi-purpose machines. In Section 10.2.1, problems with arbitrary processing times are discussed. Section 10.2.2 is devoted to problems with unit-processing times.

10.2.1   Arbitrary Processing Times

Job shop, flow shop, and open shop problems without preemption are investigated first. Then preemptive open shop scheduling problems are analyzed.

MPM Job Shop Problems

First we consider job shop problems with a fixed number of jobs to be processed on multi-purpose machines. Contrary to the classical job shop problem, the MPM job shop problem with two machines and three jobs is already $\mathcal{NP}$-hard. On the other hand, the geometrical approach described in Section 6.4.2 can be extended to problem $JMPM \mid n = 2 \mid C_{\max}$. This can be seen as follows.

Assume that we have two jobs J_1 and J_2, and that μ assigns a machine $\mu(O_{ij})$ to each of the operations O_{ij} of both jobs. For a fixed assignment μ, the problem may be formulated as a shortest path problem in the plane with rectangular objects as obstacles. The obstacles are of the form $I_{1i} \times I_{2j}$ with $\mu(O_{1i}) = \mu(O_{2j})$, where $I_{1i}(I_{2j})$ are consecutive intervals of length $p_{1i}(p_{2j})$ on the x-axis (y-axis). The path goes either diagonally or parallel to the axes and has to avoid the interior of the obstacles (see Figure 6.9).

As shown in Section 6.4.2, this shortest path problem can be reduced to the problem of finding a shortest path from an origin to some destination in a network $N(\mu) = (V(\mu), A(\mu), l(\mu))$, where

(i) $V(\mu) = \{O, F\} \cup \{$ north-west corners of obstacles$\}$
$\cup \{$ south-east corners of obstacles$\}$.

(ii) Each vertex i has at the most two immediate successors which are calculated as follows. Assume R is the obstacle we hit first if we go diagonally starting in i. Then the north-west corner and south-east corner of R are immediate successors of i. If we do not hit any obstacle, then F is the immediate successor of i.

(iii) O is the origin and F is the destination.

(vi) The length $l_{ij}(\mu) = l_{ij}$ of arc (i, j) is defined by $l_{ij} = \max\{p_{ij}^x, p_{ij}^y\}$, where p_{ij}^x and p_{ij}^y are the lengths of the two projections of the line segment connecting i and j.

$N(\mu)$ can be constructed in $O(r^2 \log r)$ time, where $r = \max\{n_1, n_2\}$.

Let $\mathcal{A}$ be the set of all possible assignments μ. Then we define the network $N = (V, A, l)$ by setting

$$V = \bigcup_{\mu \in \mathcal{A}} V(\mu), \quad A = \bigcup_{\mu \in \mathcal{A}} A(\mu).$$

l_{ij} is defined as before.

Theorem 10.3 A shortest path from O to F in N corresponds to an optimal solution of the MPM job shop problem.

Proof: If μ^* is an optimal assignment, then an optimal solution of the problem corresponds with some path from O to F in $N(\mu^*)$. Furthermore, if we have an arbitrary path p from O to F in N, then an assignment μ can be defined such that p is a path in $N(\mu)$. To see this, let (i, j) be an arc in p and assume that i is a north-west corner of an obstacle and j is a south-east corner of an obstacle with respect to some assignment μ'. This situation is shown in Figure 10.3.

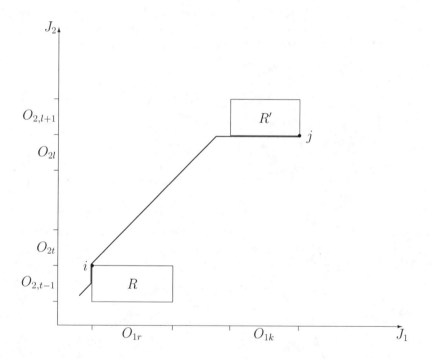

Figure 10.3: Arc (i, j) in p.

Then we set $\mu(O_{1\nu}) = \mu'(O_{1\nu})$ for $\nu = r, r+1, ..., k$ and $\mu(O_{2\nu}) = \mu'(O_{2\nu})$ for $\nu = t, t+1, ..., l$. All other cases are treated similarly. The assignment μ is well defined and has the desired property.   □

The set V consists of all north-west and south-east corners of potential obstacles. A **potential obstacle** is a rectangle $I_{1i} \times I_{2j}$ with $\mu_{1i} \cap \mu_{2j} \neq \emptyset$. O and F are regarded as degenerate potential obstacles where the north-west and south-east corner coincide. There are at the most $n_1 \cdot n_2$ potential obstacles which can be found in time $s_1 \cdot s_2$, where

$$s_i = \sum_{\nu=1}^{n_i} |\mu_{i\nu}| \quad (i = 1, 2).$$

To construct A we have to find the set $S(i)$ of all immediate successors for each vertex i. Assume that i is the north-west corner of some potential obstacle R. Then we have to find the **first unavoidable obstacle R'** **with respect to i**, i.e. a potential obstacle R' with the property that

- an assignment μ exists such that R' is hit first by the diagonal line l starting in i, and

- the length of the line segment $\breve{s}$ between i and the point at which l hits R' is as long as possible.

Let $R = I_{1r} \times I_{2,t-1}$ and $R' = I_{1k} \times I_{2,l+1}$. Then $S(i)$ consists of all north-west and south-east corners of potential obstacles $I_{1i} \times I_{2j}$ that correspond to the overlapping intervals I_{1i} and I_{2j} having the additional property that $\mu_{1i} \cap \mu_{2j} \neq \emptyset$ (see Figure 10.4.).

Figure 10.4: First unavoidable obstacle R' with respect to i.

Thus it is easy to find all immediate successors of i if the first unavoidable obstacle is known.

If i is a south-east corner of some potential obstacle R, then R' and $S(i)$ are defined similarly.

Notice that each vertex i has at the most $O(r)$ successors. Therefore, the network N has at the most $O(r^3)$ arcs.

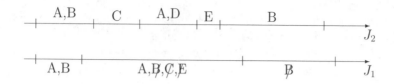

Figure 10.5: Forward scan.

We now describe a procedure for finding the first unavoidable obstacle if we start at some vertex i. Assume without loss of generality that i is the north-west corner of $I_{1r} \times I_{2,t-1}$ (see Figure 10.3). Then we scan the intervals I_{ij} shown in Figure 10.4 in order of nondecreasing finishing times of the corresponding operations O_{ij}. During this scan the following operations are applied to the intervals I_{ij}.

- If $i = 1$ ($i = 2$) and μ_{ij} contains only one machine M, then M is deleted from all sets μ_{2k} (μ_{1k}) with the property that I_{2k} (I_{1k}) overlaps I_{ij}.

- If $\mu_{ij} = \emptyset$, then I_{ij}, together with the first interval I_{lk} with $I_{ij} \cap I_{lk} \neq \emptyset$ and $|\mu_{lk}| = 1$, defines the first unavoidable obstacle.

Figure 10.5 shows an example of this **forward scan**.

Applying the forward scan, we proceed from a vertex i of an obstacle R to the next unavoidable obstacle R'. The new sets μ_{ij} after the scan are called **modified sets**. A (partial) assignment which enables us to get from i to R' diagonally may be constructed by a **backward scan** using the modified sets μ'_{ij}.

Starting with I_{2l} or $I_{1,k-1}$ (see Figure 10.3), we scan the intervals I_{ij} of Figure 10.4 in nonincreasing order of the finishing times of the corresponding operations O_{ij}. During the scan the following operations are applied to the intervals I_{ij}.

- If $i = 1$ ($i = 2$) and μ'_{ij} contains only one machine M, then M is deleted from all sets μ_{2k} (μ_{1k}) with the property that I_{2k} (I_{1k}) overlaps I_{ij}. Furthermore, we set $\mu(O_{ij}) := M$.

- If μ'_{ij} contains more than one machine, we arbitrarily choose one machine $M \in \mu'_{ij}$ and set $\mu(O_{ij}) := M$.

If we apply the backward scan to the modified sets in Figure 10.5, we get the assignment shown by the encircled machines in Figure 10.6.

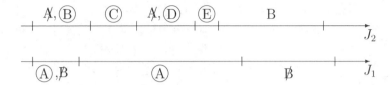

Figure 10.6: Backward scan applied to modified sets in Figure 10.5.

Note that we may get stuck if we try to construct an assignment by a forward scan through the modified sets. This is demonstrated in Figure 10.7 .

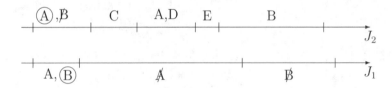

Figure 10.7: A forward scan through modified sets may fail to find a feasible assignment.

To prove that the backward scan always works, we have to show that the deletion of additional machines during the scan never results in an empty set.

Assume that during the backward scan we reach a situation in which we have two overlapping intervals I_{1i} and I_{2j} with $\mu'_{1i} = \mu'_{2j} = \{M\}$. Furthermore, assume that I_{1i} is scanned before I_{2j}. In this case, I_{2j} was scanned before I_{1i} during the forward scan and so M must have been deleted from the set μ'_{1i}, which is a contradiction.

The algorithm can now be summarized as follows.

1. Construct the network $N = (V, A, l)$;

2. Calculate a shortest path p from O to F in N;

3. Calculate an assignment corresponding to p by backward scanning through p.

Steps 1 and 2 can be combined. Starting from O, we may construct only that part of the network which is relevant while simultaneously doing the shortest path calculation. This is possible since N is acyclic. If we do not count the work for doing operations on the sets μ_{ij}, the complexity of the algorithm is $O(r^3)$.

A further generalization leads to an $O(\max\{n_1, n_2\}^5)$-algorithm for $JMPM \mid n = 2; prec; r_i \mid L_{\max}$ (Jurisch [121]). Multi-purpose machine problems with 3 jobs are $\mathcal{NP}$-hard even if the number of machines is restricted to 2 (Brucker et al. [42]).

MPM Flow Shop and Open Shop Problems

Proceeding as for problem $JMPM2|n = 3|C_{max}$, $FMPM|n = 3|C_{max}$ and $OMPM|n = 3|C_{max}$ can be shown to be $\mathcal{NP}$-hard. If we fix the number of machines, even the simplest problems $FMPM2|stages = 1|C_{max}$ and $OMPM2|stages = 1|C_{max}$ are also $\mathcal{NP}$-hard since they generalize problem $P2||C_{max}$. Here stage $= 1$ indicates that we have only one stage.

Next we consider open shop problems where preemption is allowed. We will show that the decision version of $OMPM|pmtn|C_{max}$ for a threshold value T is solvable in $O((m + \sum_{i=1}^{n} n_i)^3 + (\min\{m, n\})^4)$ time. This yields an ϵ-approximation algorithm for problem $OMPM|pmtn|C_{max}$. Furthermore, an ϵ-approximation algorithm is presented for problem $OMPM|pmtn, r_i|L_{max}$.

OMPM|pmtn|C$_{\max}$

Let there be a given threshold value T. We denote the corresponding decision problem by $OMPM|pmtn; C_i \leq T|-$. To answer the question of whether there exists a feasible schedule for an instance of $OMPM|pmtn; C_i \leq T|-$ with makespan less than or equal to T, we consider the following network $N_T = (V, A)$.

V, the set of vertices, consists of different types of nodes:

- a source s,

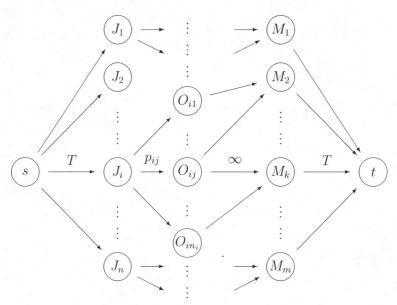

Figure 10.8: Network for problem $OMPM \mid pmtn; C_i \leq T \mid -$.

- job-nodes J_i $(i = 1, \ldots, n)$,

- operation-nodes O_{ij} $(i = 1, \ldots, n; j = 1, \ldots, n_i)$,

- machine-nodes M_j $(j = 1, \ldots, m)$, and

- a sink t.

A denotes the set of arcs with restricted capacities. A contains

- arcs (s, J_i) with capacity T $(i = 1, \ldots, n)$,

- arcs (J_i, O_{ij}) with capacity p_{ij} $(i = 1, \ldots, n; j = 1, \ldots, n_i)$,

- arcs (O_{ij}, M_k) with capacity ∞ $(i = 1, \ldots, n; j = 1, \ldots, n_i; M_k \in \mathcal{M}_{ij})$, and

- arcs (M_k, t) with capacity T $(k = 1, \ldots, m)$.

Figure 10.8 shows a part of the resulting network.

We will show that there exists a solution of a given instance of $OMPM$ $|pmtn|C_{max}$ with makespan less than or equal to T if and only if there exists a feasible flow from s to t in the corresponding network N_T with flow value $\sum_{i=1}^{n} \sum_{j=1}^{n_i} p_{ij}$.

First assume that for a given instance of $OMPM|pmtn|C_{max}$ there exists a feasible schedule y with makespan less than or equal to T. We obtain a feasible flow x from s to t in N_T with value $P = \sum_{i=1}^{n} \sum_{j=1}^{n_i} p_{ij}$ as follows:

- $x(s, J_i) = \sum_{j=1}^{n_i} p_{ij} \quad (i = 1, \ldots, n)$.

- $x(J_i, O_{ij}) = p_{ij} \quad (i = 1, \ldots, n; j = 1, \ldots, n_i)$.

- Define $x(O_{ij}, M_k)$ to be the time during which operation O_{ij} is processed on M_k in schedule y $\quad (i = 1, \ldots, n; j = 1, \ldots, n_i; k = 1, \ldots, m)$.

- Define $x(M_k, t)$ to be the length of all parts of operations which are processed on M_k in y $\quad (k = 1, \ldots, m)$.

Because no machine has to work for more than T time units ($C_{max} \leq T$), the flow x is a feasible flow from s to t in N_T with flow value P.

Now assume that there is a feasible flow x from s to t in N_T with flow value P. We obtain a classical open-shop problem by defining

$$p_{ik} = \sum_{j=1}^{n_i} x(O_{ij}, M_k) \quad (i = 1, \ldots, n; k = 1, \ldots, m).$$

As shown in Section 2.4, this problem has a solution with makespan less than or equal to T. This solution defines a feasible schedule for the given instance of $O\,MPM|pmtn|C_{max}$.

The max-flow problem in N_T can be solved with time complexity $O((n + m + \sum_{i=1}^{n} n_i)^3)$ (e.g. Malhotra, Kumar, Maheshwari [164]). The calculation of a feasible schedule by solving the classical open-shop problem needs $O((\min\{n, m\})^4)$ (Gonzalez [102]). Thus, we obtain an overall complexity of $O((m + \sum_{i=1}^{n} n_i)^3 + (\min\{m, n\})^4)$ to decide if a feasible schedule exists and to calculate such a schedule.

Of course, the solution of $OMPM|pmtn; d_i = T|-$ can be used for an ϵ-approximation algorithm for $OMPM|pmtn|C_{max}$. To find a solution for $OMPM|pmtn|C_{max}$ which differs from the optimal objective value by at the most ϵ time units, we do binary search on the set of values

$$C_{low} + i\epsilon \ (i = 1, \ldots, \lceil \frac{C_{up} - C_{low}}{\epsilon} \rceil),$$

where $C_{low}(C_{up})$ is a lower (upper) bound for the optimal C_{max}-value.

OMPM|pmtn; r_i|L$_{max}$

Now we will present an ϵ-approximation algorithm for $OMPM|pmtn; r_i|L_{max}$.

For a given threshold value T we consider the decision problem of whether there exists a feasible solution with $L_{max} \leq T$. This problem is equivalent to the time window problem: Given release dates r_i and due dates d_i for each job, does there exist a feasible schedule with $C_i \leq d_i$ for $i = 1, \ldots, n$? The time window problem is denoted by $OMPM|pmtn; r_i; d_i|-$. It can be solved by linear programming.

Let $t_1, \ldots, t_{p+1}$ be a sequence of release dates and due dates such that $t_l < t_{l+1}$ for $l = 1, \ldots, p$. The sequence $t_1, \ldots, t_{p+1}$ defines time intervals $I_l = [t_l, t_{l+1}]$ of length $T_l = t_{l+1} - t_l$ for $l = 1, \ldots, p$.

We use a linear program with variables

$$x_{ijkl} \ (i = 1, \ldots, n; \ \text{(job indices)}$$
$$j = 1, \ldots, n_i; \text{(operation indices)}$$
$$k = 1, \ldots, m; \text{(machine indices)}$$
$$l = 1, \ldots, p \ \text{(time-interval indices))}.$$

The 4-tuple (i, j, k, l) is called **feasible** if and only if O_{ij} can be processed on M_k in time interval I_l, i.e. if

- $M_k \in \mathcal{M}_{ij}$, and

- $r_i \leq t_l$ and $d_i \geq t_{l+1}$.

We consider the following linear program

$$\text{max} \quad - \quad \text{s.t.}$$

$$\text{(I)} \quad \sum_{\substack{k,l \\ (i,j,k,l) \\ feasible}} x_{ijkl} = p_{ij} \, (i = 1, \ldots, n; j = 1, \ldots, n_i)$$

$$\text{(II)} \quad \sum_{\substack{j,k \\ (i,j,k,l) \\ feasible}} x_{ijkl} \leq T_l \ (i = 1, \ldots, n; l = 1, \ldots, p)$$

$$\text{(III)} \quad \sum_{\substack{i,j \\ (i,j,k,l) \\ feasible}} x_{ijkl} \leq T_l \ (k = 1, \ldots, m; l = 1, \ldots, p)$$

$$x_{ijkl} \geq 0 \ ((i, j, k, l) \text{ feasible}).$$

We will show that for a given instance of $OMPM|pmtn; r_i; d_i|-$ there exists a feasible schedule if and only if there exists a feasible solution of the corresponding linear program.

First we will show that a feasible solution of the linear program defines a feasible solution of $OMPM|pmtn; r_i; d_i|-$.

If $x_{ijkl} = t$, then t time units of operation O_{ij} are processed on M_k in time interval I_l. By fulfilling equations (I), all operations are processed for p_{ij} time units. Because of inequalities (II), the sum of the processing times of all operations of one job in one time interval is not greater than the length of the interval. Due to inequalities (III), the sum of the processing times of all operations on one machine in one time interval is not greater than the length of the interval. Thus, due to the results in Section 2.4, each operation O_{ij} can be processed on machine M_k in time interval I_l for x_{ijkl} time units without violating any capacity constraints. By combining the resulting schedules of all time intervals, we get a feasible solution of $OMPM|pmtn; r_i; d_i|-$.

Using these ideas, it is easy to define a feasible solution $x = (x_{ijkl})$ of the linear program based on a given feasible schedule for $OMPM|pmtn; r_i; d_i|-$.

Again, for $OMPM|pmtn; r_i|L_{max}$ we obtain a solution which differs from the optimal objective value by at the most ϵ time units if we do binary search on the set of values $L_{low} + i\epsilon \ (i = 1, \ldots, \lceil \frac{L_{up} - L_{low}}{\epsilon} \rceil)$.

10.2.2 Unit Processing Times

In this section we show that some *MPM* shop problems with unit processing times can be formulated as shortest path problems in suitable networks.

MPM Job Shop Problems

We generalize an approach of Meyer [166] for problem $J\,MPM\mid p_{ij} = 1; n = k|C_{max}$.

J MPM $\mid \mathbf{p_{ij}} = 1; \mathbf{r_i}; \mathbf{prec}; \mathbf{n} = \mathbf{k}\mid \max \mathbf{f_i}\,(\sum \mathbf{f_i})$

Here f_i denotes a monotonic nondecreasing function of the completion time of job i.

To solve this problem, we first determine time slots $t_1, \ldots, t_l$ $(l = \sum_{i=1}^{k} n_i)$ which are sufficient to schedule all jobs in some active schedule for the problem. To calculate such time slots we may assume $r_i < r_j$ whenever i precedes j, and schedule jobs with processing time n_i $(i = 1, \ldots, k)$ on one machine in order of nondecreasing release dates r_i. $t_1, \ldots, t_l$ are defined by all the time slots occupied by this schedule.

Now the original problem will be formulated as the problem of finding a shortest path from some initial vertex to some terminal vertex in the following network $N = (V, A, l)$. In this network each path from the initial vertex to the terminal vertex corresponds to a feasible schedule.

- The set V of vertices consists of $(k + 1)$-tupels $(t_j, i_1, \ldots, i_k)$ for $j = 1, \ldots, l$ and $0 \le i_\nu \le n_\nu (\nu = 1, \ldots, k)$. Such a vertex represents a partial schedule for the interval $[0, t_j]$, where i_ν indicates the last operation of job ν which is already scheduled. We also have an initial vertex $(t_1 - 1, 0, \ldots, 0)$ and a terminal vertex $(t_l + 1, n_1, \ldots, n_k)$.

- We have arcs between vertices $(t_j, i_1, \ldots, i_k)$ and $(t_{j+1}, i'_1, \ldots, i'_k)$ representing the operations scheduled in time slot t_{j+1}. Thus, we have an arc between two vertices if a k-tupel $(x_1, \ldots, x_k) \in \{0, 1\}^k$ exists with $i'_\nu = i_\nu + x_\nu, \nu = 1, \ldots, k$ such that:

    - the operations of $S = \{O_{\nu, i_\nu + 1} | x_\nu = 1\}$ can be processed in parallel, i.e. a feasible assignment of the operations of S to the machines exists. This can be checked by constructing a bipartite graph in $O(km)$ time and finding a maximal matching in $O(m^{2.5})$ time (Even & Kariv [88]),

- the release dates are respected, i.e. $O_{\nu,i_\nu+1} \in S$ implies $r_\nu < t_{j+1}$, and

- the precedences are respected, i.e. if job μ precedes job ν and $x_\nu = 1$, the value of i_μ must equal n_μ.

- The arcs are weighted with the maximum (sum) of all $f_\nu(t_{j+1})$-values of jobs finishing exactly at time t_{j+1}, i.e. jobs ν with $x_\nu = 1$ and $i_\nu + x_\nu = n_\nu$. If no job finishes at time t_{j+1}, the arc weight is set to $-\infty(0)$.

Each feasible schedule corresponds to a path from the initial vertex to the terminal vertex and vice versa. The corresponding objective value is given by the length of the path, which is the maximum (sum) of all arc values. Thus, we only need to find a shortest path which takes $O((km + m^{2.5})2^k \sum\limits_{i=1}^{k} n_i \prod\limits_{i=1}^{k} n_i)$ time since we have $O(\sum\limits_{i=1}^{k} n_i \prod\limits_{i=1}^{k} n_i)$ vertices and $O(2^k)$ arcs incident at each vertex. Thus we obtain $O(2^k \sum\limits_{i=1}^{k} n_i \prod\limits_{i=1}^{k} n_i)$ arcs. Since the inspection of an arc takes $O(km + m^{2.5})$ time, we get the given complexity.

MPM Flow Shop Problems

First we consider the flow shop problem

FMPM | $p_{ij} = 1$; stages = r | $\sum w_i C_i$

We may assume $w_1 \geq w_2 \geq \ldots \geq w_n$. Then there always exists an optimal schedule in which job i finishes not later than job j if $i < j$.

We define a network as follows.

The set V of vertices consists of $(2r + 2)$-tupels $(i, i_0, \ldots, i_r, j_1, \ldots, j_r)$ for $i = 1, \ldots, nr, i_k = 0, \ldots, n$ $(k = 0, \ldots, r)$, and $j_k = 0, \ldots, m$ $(k = 1, \ldots, r)$. Additionally, we assume $\sum\limits_{n=0}^{r} i_k = n$ and $j_k \leq i_k$ for all $k = 1, \ldots, r$.

A vertex represents a partial schedule for the interval $[0, i]$. Here i_k indicates the number of jobs which are finished up to stage k. The entry j_k denotes the number of jobs of this partial schedule which are processed in stage k in $[i - 1, i]$. We consider only vertices such that j_1 operations of stage 1, j_2 operations of stage 2, $\ldots$, and j_r operations of stage r can be processed in parallel, i.e. a feasible assignment of the $\sum_{k=1}^{r} j_k$ operations to the m machines exists. This can be checked in $O(mr + m^{2.5})$ time by constructing a bipartite graph and finding a maximal matching (Even & Kariv [88]).

Note that i_r equals the number of jobs which are completely finished. Additionally, we have an initial vertex $(0, n, 0, \ldots, 0)$. The vertex $(nr + 1, 0, \ldots, 0, i_r, 0, \ldots, 0)$ with $i_r = n$ is defined as the terminal vertex.

The set A of arcs consists of two different types of arcs. Arcs of the first type are between vertices $(i, i_0, \ldots, i_r, j_1, \ldots, j_r)$ and $(i, i'_0, \ldots, i'_r, j'_1, \ldots, j'_r)$ belonging to the same time i. They represent the processing of a job in stage k in interval $[i - 1, i]$. Hence we have an arc if $i'_k = i_k + 1, i'_{k-1} = i_{k-1} - 1, j'_k = j_k + 1$ and $i'_\nu = i_\nu, j'_\nu = j_\nu$ otherwise. This arc is weighted with 0 if $k < r$. If $k = r$, a job is finished and this arc is weighted with iw_{i_r+1}. Arcs of the second type are between vertices $(i, i_0, \ldots, i_r, j_1, \ldots, j_r)$ and $(i + 1, i_0, \ldots, i_r, 0, \ldots, 0)$. In this situation no operation is scheduled. Hence these arcs are weighted with 0.

Now each schedule in which the jobs are finished in order of nonincreasing weights corresponds to a path from the initial vertex to the terminal vertex. The objective value is given by the length of the path. Conversely, from each such path a schedule with objective value equal to the length of the path can be constructed. Note that we may always construct a permutation flow-shop schedule, i.e. a schedule in which the job order for each stage is the same.

The network has $O(nrn^r m^r)$ vertices since i_r is uniquely determined by $i_0, \ldots, i_{r-1}$. Hence the network has $O(r^2 m^r n^{r+1})$ arcs. Calculating a maximal matching for each vertex takes $O(rm + m^{2.5})$ time. Inspecting an arc takes $O(r)$ time since a vertex has $O(r)$ entries, implying that $O(r)$ binary symbols are needed to encode a vertex. Thus, it takes $O((r^2 + rm + m^{2.5})r \cdot m^r \cdot n^{r+1})$ time to construct the network and to calculate a shortest path, i.e. an optimal schedule.

By modifying this approach as described in Section 11.3, $FMPM \mid p_{ij} = 1; stages = r \mid \sum T_i(\sum w_i U_i)$ and $FMPM \mid p_{ij} = 1; stages = r; r_i \mid$

$\sum C_i(C_{\max})$ can be solved in $O(r(r^2 + rm + m^{2.5})m^r n^{r+1})$ time.

Recall that a fixed number of machines induces a bounded number of stages of a flow shop problem. Thus, the problems $FMPM\ m \mid p_{ij} = 1 \mid f$ for $f \in \{\sum w_i C_i, \sum T_i, \sum w_i U_i\}$ and $FMPM\ m \mid p_{ij} = 1; r_i \mid f$ for $f \in \{C_{\max}, \sum C_i\}$ are also solvable in polynomial time.

MPM Open Shop Problems

In an open shop problem, the tasks of a job might be processed in an arbitrary order. By prespecifying for each possible order the number of jobs which have to be processed according to this order, we obtain a scheduling problem which can be solved by generalizations of the approaches for flow shop problems presented in the last section.

In such a problem each job is processed according to one of the $C = r!$ possible (stage) orders $\pi_1, \ldots, \pi_C$. Thus each schedule defines a C-tupel $(n_1, \ldots, n_C)$, where n_i denotes the number of jobs which are processed according to π_i. Hence we have to calculate all different tupels $(n_1, \ldots, n_C)$ with $0 \le n_i \le n$ for all $i = 1, \ldots, C$ and $\sum_{i=1}^{C} n_i = n$, and solve for each such tupel the corresponding optimization problem. Then the best schedule of all these subproblems gives the optimal schedule of the open-shop problem.

Based on these ideas, but using more complicated networks (see Section 11.3), problems $OMPM \mid p_{ij} = 1; stages = r \mid f$ for $f \in \{\sum w_i C_i, \sum T_i, \sum w_i U_i\}$ and $OMPM \mid p_{ij} = 1; stages = r; r_i \mid f$ for $f \in \{C_i, C_{\max}\}$ can be solved polynomially. These networks have $O(r \cdot m^r \cdot n^{r!r+1})$ vertices and $O(r!r)$ arcs incident at each vertex. The consideration of arcs and the feasibility check takes $O(m^{2.5} + mr!r)$ time per arc. Hence these problems can be solved in $O(r^2 \cdot r!(mr!r + m^{2.5})m^r \cdot n^{r!r+1})$ time. Similar to the flow shop situation, we conclude that problem $OMPM\ m \mid p_{ij} = 1 \mid f$ for $f \in \{\sum u_i C_i, \sum T_i, \sum w_i U_i\}$ and $OMPM\ m \mid p_{ij} = 1; r_i \mid f$ for $f \in \{C_{\max}, \sum C_i\}$ are also solvable in polynomial time.

10.3 Complexity Results

Table 10.1 summarizes the polynomially solvable problems discussed in Section 10.1. The corresponding results for Section 10.2 can be found in Table 10.2 in which we denote $\max\{n_1, n_2\}$ by $n_{\max}$. The following problems are binary $\mathcal{NP}$-hard: $PMPM2 \mid chains; p_i = 1 \mid C_{\max}$, $FMPM \mid n = 3 \mid C_{\max}$ (Brucker et al. [42]), and $JMPM2 \mid n = 3 \mid C_{\max}$ (Meyer [166]). Furthermore, since parallel machine problems and shop scheduling problems are special cases of their MPM-counterparts, the MPM-problems corresponding to the problems in Tables 5.3, 5.6, 6.3, 6.5, 6.8 are $\mathcal{NP}$-hard as well.

$R \mid pmtn; r_i \mid L_{\max}$	5.1.3	Brucker et al. [42]
		lin. prog.
$R \parallel \sum C_i$	5.1.3	Bruno et al. [58]
		$O(mn^3)$
$PMPM \mid pmtn \mid \sum C_i$	10.1	Brucker et al. [42]
		$O(n^3)$
$RMPM \mid pmtn \mid \sum C_i$	5.1.3	Brucker et al. [42]
		lin. prog.
$PMPM \mid p_i = 1; r_i \mid \sum w_i U_i$	10.1	Brucker et al. [42]
		$O(n^2 m(n + \log m))$
$QMPM \mid p_i = 1 \mid \sum w_i U_i$	10.1	Brucker et al. [42]
		$O(n^2 m(n + \log m))$
$PMPM \mid p_i = 1; r_i \mid \sum w_i T_i$	10.1	Brucker et al. [42]
		$O(n^2 m(n + \log m))$
$QMPM \mid p_i = 1 \mid \sum w_i T_i$	10.1	Brucker et al. [42]
		$O(n^2 m(n + \log m))$

Table 10.1: Polynomially solvable MPM-problems with identical and uniform machines.

$FMPMm \mid r_i; p_{ij} = 1; stages = r \mid C_{max}$ Brucker et al. [42]
$O(r(r^2 + rm + m^{2.5})m^r n^{r+1})$

$FMPMm \mid r_i; p_{ij} = 1; stages = r \mid \sum C_i$ Brucker et al. [42]
$O(r(r^2 + rm + m^{2.5})m^r n^{r+1})$

$FMPMm \mid p_{ij} = 1; stages = r \mid \sum w_i C_i$ Brucker et al. [42]
$O(r(r^2 + rm + m^{2.5})m^r n^{r+1})$

$FMPMm \mid p_{ij} = 1; stages = r \mid \sum w_i U_i$ Brucker et al. [42]
$O(r(r^2 + rm + m^{2.5})m^r n^{r+1})$

$FMPMm \mid p_{ij} = 1; stages = r \mid \sum T_i$ Brucker et al. [42]
$O(r(r^2 + rm + m^{2.5})m^r n^{r+1})$

$JMPM \mid m = 2 \mid C_{max}$ Brucker & Schlie [56]
$O(n_{max}^3)$

$JMPM \mid prec; r_i; n = 2 \mid L_{max}$ Jurisch [121]
$O(n_{max}^5)$

$JMPM \mid prec; r_i; p_{ij} = 1; n = k \mid \sum w_i U_i$ Brucker et al. [42]
$O((km + m^{2.5})2^k \sum_{i=1}^{k} n_i \prod_{i=1}^{k} n_i)$

$JMPM \mid prec; r_i; p_{ij} = 1; n = k \mid \sum w_i T_i$ Brucker et al. [42]
$O((km + m^{2.5})2^k \sum_{i=1}^{k} n_i \prod_{i=1}^{k} n_i)$

$OMPMm \mid r_i; p_{ij} = 1; stages = r \mid C_{max}$ Brucker et al. [42]
$O(r^2 r!(mr!r + m^{2.5})m^r n^{r!r+1})$

$OMPMm \mid r_i; p_{ij} = 1; stages = r \mid \sum C_i$ Brucker et al. [42]
$O(r^2 r!(mr!r + m^{2.5})m^r n^{r!r+1})$

$OMPMm \mid p_{ij} = 1; stages = r \mid \sum w_i C_i$ Brucker et al. [42]
$O(r^2 r!(mr!r + m^{2.5})m^r n^{r!r+1})$

$OMPMm \mid p_{ij} = 1; stages = r \mid \sum w_i U_i$ Brucker et al. [42]
$O(r^2 r!(mr!r + m^{2.5})m^r n^{r!r+1})$

$OMPMm \mid p_{ij} = 1; stages = r \mid \sum T_i$ Brucker et al. [42]
$O(r^2 r!(mr!r + m^{2.5})m^r n^{r!r+1})$

Table 10.2: Polynomially solvable shop problems with multipurpose machines.

Chapter 11

Multiprocessor Tasks

Contrary to the scheduling problems discussed thus far in which each job (or task) is processed by at the most one machine (processor) at a time, in a system with **multiprocessor tasks** (MPT) tasks require one or more processors at a time.

More specifically, we have m different processors $M_1, \ldots, M_m$ and n tasks $i = 1, \ldots, n$. Each task i requires during a processing period p_i all processors belonging to a subset $\mu_i \subseteq \{M_1, \ldots, M_m\}$. Tasks requiring the same processor cannot be processed simultaneously. Such tasks are called **incompatible**. Otherwise they are called **compatible**.

The **general shop problem with multiprocessor tasks** is defined similarly. Each job i consists of n_i multiprocessor tasks $O_{i1}, \ldots, O_{i,n_i}$ with processing times p_{ij} and processor sets $\mu_{ij} \subseteq \{M_1, \ldots, M_m\}$. During the processing period p_{ij}, O_{ij} requires each processor in the set μ_{ij}. The **multiprocessor task job shop problem** is a special case of the general shop problem with MPT in which each job consists of a chain of tasks. The **flow shop problem with** MPT is a special case of the job shop problem with MPT in which $n_i = r$ for $i = 1, \ldots, n$. Furthermore, we assume that $\mu_{ij} = \mu_j \subseteq \{M_1, \ldots, M_m\}$ for stages $j = 1, \ldots, r$ and $\mu_j \neq \mu_l$ for $j \neq l$.

Open shop problems with MPT are defined as flow shop problems with MPT but without precedence constraints between tasks. However, no pair of tasks of the same job can be processed simultaneously.

To describe different types of multiprocessor task scheduling problems, we modify the α-field of the $\alpha|\beta|\gamma$-notation introduced in Chapter 1. We set $\alpha = MPT$ if we have a task system with an arbitrary number of processors. Shop problems with multiprocessor tasks are denoted by $GMPT, JMPT, FMPT, OMPT$. If the number of processors is fixed, we add the symbol m after the symbol MPT.

11.1   Multiprocessor Task Systems

In this section we consider the problem of scheduling a set of multiprocessor tasks. $MPT2 \parallel C_{\max}$ is the simplest problem of this type. Due to the fact that there are only two processors, we have only three types of tasks: bi-processor tasks and two types of single-processor tasks. Clearly, we get an optimal schedule by first scheduling each single-processor task on its processor without causing idle time.

This, however, is as far as we can get with polynomial algorithms for multiprocessor task systems with arbitrary processing times. Hoogeveen et al. [113] have shown that the following problems are $\mathcal{NP}$-hard: $MPT3 \parallel C_{max}$, $MPT2 \parallel \sum C_i$, $MPT2 \mid r_i \mid C_{max}$.

The situation is different if we consider task systems with unit processing times. Blazewicz & Ecker [26] have shown that $MPTm \mid p_i = 1 \mid C_{\max}$ can be solved in time which is linear in the number of jobs. The more general problem $MPTm \mid p_i = 1; r_i \mid C_{\max}$, as well as $MPTm \mid p_i = 1; r_i \mid \sum C_i$, had open complexity status (Hoogeveen et al. [113]).

We will show that these and other related open problems can be solved polynomially by reductions to shortest (or longest) path problems. We show this reduction for problem $MPTm \mid p_i = 1 \mid \sum w_i C_i$. Reductions for the problems mentioned above and for the additional problems $PMPTm \mid p_i = 1 \mid \sum T_i$ and $MPTm \mid p_i = 1 \mid \sum w_i U_i$ are very similar and will be explained later.

MPTm | p$_i$ = 1 | $\sum$ w$_i$C$_i$

We have n multiprocessor tasks $i = 1, \ldots, n$ with unit processing times. Associated with task i is a set μ_i of processors which are all needed to process task i. The set μ_i defines the **type** of task i. Let $R \le 2^m - 1$ be the number of different types in the system and denote by $I_j (j = 1, \ldots, R)$ the set of all tasks of type j. Let n_j be the number of tasks in I_j. By exchange arguments one can show that there exists an optimal schedule S such that the following property holds for each $j = 1, \ldots, R$ (see Section

4.3): The tasks in I_j are processed in order of nonincreasing weights w_i. For each I_j, let

$$j_1, j_2, \ldots, j_{n_j}$$

be an ordered sequence of all tasks from I_j. For technical reasons we add a dummy task j_0 at the beginning of the sequence. Next we show that problem $MPTm \mid p_i = 1 \mid \sum w_i C_i$ can be formulated as a shortest path problem in some network $N = (V, A, l)$. This network is defined by:

- The set V of vertices consisting of $(R+1)$-tuples $(t; i_1, \ldots, i_R)$ where $0 \le t \le n$ and $0 \le i_j \le n_j$. $(t; i_1, \ldots, i_R)$ represents a partial schedule consisting of all tasks j_ν with $1 \le j \le R$ and $1 \le \nu \le i_j$ scheduled in the time interval $[0, t]$. $(0; 0, \ldots, 0)$ is the initial vertex and $(n; n_1, \ldots, n_R)$ is the terminal vertex.

- The immediate successors of vertex $u = (t; i_1, \ldots, i_R)$ are given by all $v = (t + 1; i_1 + x_1, \ldots, i_R + x_R)$ where $x_1, \ldots, x_R$ satisfy the following conditions:

  - $x_\nu \in \{0, 1\}$ for $\nu = 1, \ldots, R$
  - during one time period, exactly one task from each set I_ν with $x_\nu = 1$ can be scheduled, i.e. for each pair (ν, α) with $\nu \ne \alpha$ and $x_\nu = x_\alpha = 1$, tasks from I_ν and I_α are compatible.

- The cost $l(u, v)$ associated with arc (u, v) is given by

$$\sum_{i \in S} w_i(t + 1) \tag{11.1}$$

  where $S = \{j_{i_\nu + 1} \mid x_\nu = 1; 1 \le \nu \le R\}$.

Clearly, a feasible schedule corresponds to a path in N from $(0; 0, \ldots, 0)$ to $(n; n_1, \ldots, n_R)$ and vice versa. The shortest such path provides an optimal solution of the problem.

In a preprocessing step, all feasible $(x_1, \ldots, x_R)$-tupels are calculated. The number of vertices is bounded by $n \prod_{j=1}^{R} n_j \le n^{R+1}$ and each vertex has at the most 2^R successors. Thus, the network has at the most $2^R n^{R+1}$ arcs, which means that a shortest path can be calculated in $O(R 2^R n^{R+1})$ time where $R \le 2^m - 1$. The factor R takes care of the calculation of arc weights.

MPTm | $p_i = 1$ | $\sum T_i$

To solve this problem we have to order the tasks in each set I_j according to nondecreasing due dates. Furthermore, the cost (11.1) is replaced by

$$\sum_{i \in S} \max\{0, t + 1 - d_i\}.$$

MPTm | $p_i = 1; r_i$ | $C_{\max}$ and MPTm | $p_i = 1; r_i$ | $\sum C_i$

To solve these problems the tasks are ordered according to nondecreasing release times r_i in each set I_j (see Sections 4.2 and 4.3). Furthermore, we may restrict the schedule to a set of at the most n time periods $[t-1, t]$. Let T be the set of corresponding t-values (see Section 4.1.2). The set V of vertices is given by all $(R+1)$-tuples $(t; i_1, \ldots, i_R)$ with $t \in T$ and $r_{i_j} \leq t - 1$ for $j = 1, \ldots, R$. In the definition of the terminal vertex, n must be replaced by $n^* = \max T$. In the definition of successors of some vertex $(t; i_1, \ldots, i_R)$, the first component $t + 1$ must be replaced by the smallest number $s \in T$ which is greater than t.

For the $\sum C_i$-problem the costs are given by (11.1) with $w_i = 1$ for all $i = 1, \ldots, n$.

For the $C_{\max}$-problem, the cost associated with an arc (u, v), where $u = (t; i_1, \ldots, i_R)$ and $v = (s; i_1 + x_1, \ldots, i_R + x_R)$, is equal to zero if $i_\nu = n_\nu$ for $\nu = 1, \ldots, R$. Otherwise the cost is equal to $s - t$.

MPTm | $p_i = 1$ | $\sum w_i U_i$

To solve this problem we need to determine a feasible schedule for the on-time tasks such that the sum of the weights of the late tasks is minimal. Late tasks can be scheduled at the end of the schedule in an arbitrary order. We may assume that an optimal schedule for the on-time tasks exists in which tasks of the same type are finished in order of nondecreasing due dates. Thus, let

$$J_{j_1}, J_{j_2}, \ldots, J_{j_{n_j}}$$

be a sequence of all tasks in I_j ordered according to nondecreasing due dates. We define the network $N = (V, A, l)$ as follows:

- The set V of vertices consists of $(R+1)$-tupels $(t; i_1, \ldots, i_R)$ for $t = 0, \ldots, n$ and $i_j = 0, \ldots, n_j$. A vertex represents a partial schedule in which the first i_j tasks of the set I_j for $j = 1, \ldots, R$ are either scheduled late or in time interval $[0, t]$. We define $(0; \ldots, 0)$ to be the initial vertex and $(n; n_1, \ldots, n_R)$ to be the terminal vertex.

- We have two different types of arcs. Arcs of the first type are between vertices $u = (t; i_1, \ldots, i_R)$ and $v = (t + 1; i_1 + x_1, \ldots, i_R + x_R)$. They are defined as in problem $MPTm \mid p_i = 1 \mid sumw_i C_i$ but under the additional restriction that the scheduled tasks are on time, i.e. $d_{j_{i_j+1}} \geq t + 1$ if $x_j = 1$ for $j = 1, \ldots, R$. These arcs have zero weight since they represent tasks which are on time.

  The arcs of the second type are between vertices belonging to the same time t. They represent the tasks which are scheduled late, i.e. we have arcs from $(t; i_1, \ldots, i_j, \ldots, i_R)$ to $(t; i_1, \ldots, i_j + 1, \ldots, i_R)$ with weight $w_{j_{i_j+1}}$ for all $j = 1, \ldots, R$.

Each schedule in which the on-time tasks of the same type are finished according to nondecreasing due dates corresponds to a path from the starting vertex to the terminal vertex. The length of the path denotes the corresponding objective value. On the other hand, each path defines a feasible schedule for the on-time tasks. Thus, by calculating a shortest path we obtain the optimal objective value and a corresponding schedule in $O(R2^R n^{R+1})$ steps if the feasible tupels $(x_1, \ldots, x_R)$ are calculated in a preprocessing step.

If the number m of processors is small, more efficient algorithms can be given. This is illustrated by the following two examples.

$MPT2 \mid p_i = 1 \mid \sum C_i$ Simple exchange arguments show that an optimal schedule for this problem can be constructed by first scheduling the single processor tasks and then all bi-processor tasks.

MPT2 $\mid$ p$_i$ = 1; r$_i$ $\mid$ C$_{max}$ and MPMPT2 $\mid$ p$_i$ = 1 $\mid$ L$_{max}$

To solve problem $MPT2 \mid p_i = 1; r_i \mid C_{max}$, all bi-processor tasks are first scheduled according to nondecreasing r_i-values. Then, on each processor, we schedule the corresponding single-processor tasks again in an order of nondecreasing r_i-values using the idle time slots left by bi-processor tasks.

Problem $MPT2 \mid p_i = 1 \mid L_{max}$ can be solved similarly.

MPT-Problems with Preemption

Concerning the preemptive case, Kubale [128] has shown that $MPM \mid pmtn \mid C_{\max}$ is strongly $\mathcal{NP}$-hard. On the other hand, $MPTm \mid pmtn \mid C_{\max}$ can be solved polynomially using linear programming (Bianco et al. [24]). For $MPT2 \mid pmtn \mid L_{\max}$ a linear time algorithm exists (Bianco et al. [25]). $MPT2 \mid pmtn \mid \sum C_i$ can be solved by a reduction to the single-machine problem $1 \mid chains \mid \sum C_i$ (Cai et al. [61]). This can be seen as follows.

Let M_1 and M_2 be the two machines. Then we have three types of tasks: M_1-tasks, M_2-tasks, and bi-processor tasks.

Lemma 11.1 An optimal schedule exists with the following properties.

(a) There is no idle time on processor $M_1(M_2)$ before the completion time of the last M_1-task (M_2-task).

(b) The M_1-tasks (M_2-tasks) are sequenced according to the shortest processing time (SPT) rule. The bi-processor tasks are sequenced according to the SPT rule.

(c) None of the bi-processor tasks is preempted by other jobs.

Proof:

(a) If there is idle time on $M_1(M_2)$ before the completion time of the last M_1-task (M_2-task), we shift this task to the left.

(b) If two M_i-tasks are not sequenced according to the SPT rule, eliminate both tasks and reschedule them in the created slot according to the SPT rule.

(c) Apply transformation to bi-processor tasks which is similar to the one described in (b).

None of the transformations described in (a), (b), and (c) increase the $\sum C_i$-value. Thus, there exists an optimal schedule with the described properties. $\square$

Lemma 11.2 In any optimal schedule if a bi-processor task is not the first task, its starting time must be equal to the completion time of some other tasks.

Proof: Assume that some bi-processor task J starts at time t and t is not the finishing time of some task. Then at time t at least one task is preempted and if only one task is preempted on one processor at time t, then the other processor has an idle interval finishing at time t. Moving J slightly to the left will decrease the $\sum C_i$-value. Thus, an optimal schedule has the described properties. □

Due to Lemmas 11.1 and 11.2, an optimal schedule can be constructed by first scheduling the M_1-tasks and M_2-tasks in SPT-order on their corresponding processors. Then we have to insert the bi-processor tasks, again in SPT-order, starting at the finishing times of the single-processor tasks. This insertion problem may be solved by solving a corresponding problem $1 \mid chains \mid \sum C_i$ which is constructed in the following way.

Let $t_1 < t_2 < \ldots < t_q$ be the time instances where a task finishes in the SPT-schedule for the M_1-tasks and M_2-tasks. Define two chains of jobs. The first chain consists of q tasks

$$J_1' \to J_2' \to \ldots \to J_q'$$

where J_i' has the processing time $t_i - t_{i-1}$ and $t_0 = 0$.
The second chain

$$J_1'' \to J_2'' \to \ldots \to J_r''$$

contains the bi-processor tasks ordered according to the SPT-rule. Consider the $1 \mid chains \mid \sum C_i$ problem which is provided by these two chains.

11.2 Shop Problems with *MPT*: Arbitrary Processing Times

In this section we will discuss polynomial algorithms for open shop, flow shop, and job shop problems with multiprocessor tasks with arbitrary processing times.

Open Shop Problems

We will first discuss the complexity of MPT open shop problems with an arbitrary number of machines and $C_{\max}$-criterion. The complexity depends on the compatibility structure of the stages of the problem.

Stage 1:

Stage 2:

Stage 3:

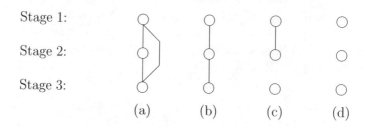

(a)　　　(b)　　　(c)　　　(d)

Figure 11.1: Four types of compatibility graphs.

Stages i and j are called **compatible** if the corresponding machine sets μ_i and μ_j are disjoint. Otherwise they are called **incompatible**. The compatibility structure of a system with r stages can be described by a corresponding **compatibility graph** $G = (V, E)$. G is an undirected graph with the r stages as vertices. There is an edge between two vertices i and j $(i \neq j)$ if and only if the stages i and j are incompatible.

Now consider an open shop problem with two stages. If these two stages are incompatible, then the problem is easy since no tasks can be processed simultaneously. Thus, the tasks can be scheduled one after the other in any order. Otherwise, if the stages are compatible, then the problem reduces to its classical counterpart $O2 \parallel C_{\max}$, which can be solved in $O(n)$ time (see Section 6.2.1). We have the following

Theorem 11.3 $OMPT \mid stages = 2 \mid C_{\max}$ can be solved in $O(n)$ time.

For a system with three stages, we essentially have the four types of compatibility graphs shown in Figure 11.1.

Using these graphs we may formulate the following

Theorem 11.4 $OMPT \mid stages = 3 \mid C_{\max}$ can be solved in $O(n)$ time if its compatibility graph is given by Figure 11.1(a), 11.1(b) or 11.1(c). Otherwise it is $\mathcal{NP}$-hard.

Proof: The problem defined by Figure 11.1(a) is again trivial. Consider the problem of Figure 11.1(b). All tasks of Stage 2 are incompatible with all other tasks. Thus w.l.o.g. they can be processed at the beginning of any feasible schedule. Because the tasks in Stage 1 are compatible with the tasks in Stage 3, the problem reduces to $O2 \parallel C_{\max}$.

For a problem given by Figure 11.1(c) we proceed as follows. We concatenate Stages 1 and 2 to one stage, where the processing time of a job in this stage is given by the sum of its processing times of Stage 1 and Stage 2. Thus, we obtain the classical problem $O2 \parallel C_{\max}$ where, additionally, one special preemption per job is allowed. Since any solution of the problem $O2 \mid pmtn \mid C_{\max}$ can be transformed into one without preemption without increasing the makespan (Gonzalez & Sahni [104]), this additional condition may be dropped.

The classical problem $O3 \parallel C_{\max}$ is represented by the graph in Figure 11.1(d). Thus, this case is $\mathcal{NP}$-hard (Gonzalez & Sahni [104]).   □

A consequence of Theorems 11.3 and 11.4 is that $OMPT2 \parallel C_{\max}$ can be solved in $O(n)$ time. If we have three stages, the compatibility graph is given by Figure 11.1(b) and Theorem 11.4 applies. If there are two stages, Theorem 11.3 applies.

The following problems are $\mathcal{NP}$-hard since the corresponding problems without multiprocessor tasks are $\mathcal{NP}$-hard: $OMPT2 \mid r_i \mid C_{\max}$, $OMPT2 \parallel L_{\max}$, $OMPT3 \parallel C_{\max}$, $OMPT2 \parallel \sum C_i$, $OMPT2 \mid tree \mid C_{\max}$, $OMPT \mid n = 3 \mid C_{\max}$.

If the number of machines is fixed, then the number of possible stages is also fixed. Thus, the general problems $OMPTm \mid n = k; prec; r_i \mid \sum w_i U_i$ and $OMPTm \mid n = k; prec; r_i \mid \sum w_i T_i$ are solvable in constant time.

Flow Shop Problems

Again, we classify MPT flow shop problems according to the compatibility structure of the stages.

Similar to the MPT open shop problem, the MPT flow shop problem with two stages is either trivial or it reduces to problem $F2 \parallel C_{\max}$, which can be solved in $O(n \log n)$ time (see Section 6.3).

Theorem 11.5 $FMPT \mid stages = 2 \mid C_{\max}$ can be solved in $O(n \log n)$ time.

The possible compatibility graphs for MPT flow shop problems with three stages are shown in Figure 11.2.

Obviously, the problems described by Figures 11.2(c) and 11.2(d) (Figures 11.2(e) and 11.2(f)) are symmetric to each other.

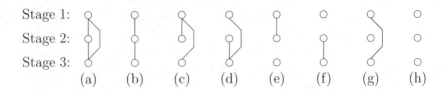

Stage 1:
Stage 2:
Stage 3:
    (a)   (b)   (c)   (d)   (e)   (f)   (g)   (h)

Figure 11.2: Compatibility graphs for MPT flow shop problems with three stages.

Theorem 11.6 $FMPT \mid stages = 3 \mid C_{\max}$ can be solved in $O(n \log n)$ time if its compatibility graph is given by Figure 11.2(a), 11.2(c), 11.2(d), 11.2(e) or 11.2(f). In all other cases the problem is $\mathcal{NP}$-hard.

Proof: The problem defined by Figure 11.2 (a) is again easy and can be solved in linear time.

Similarly, as the problems in Figure 11.2(b) or 11.2(c) reduce to $O2 \parallel C_{\max}$, problems in Figure 11.2(c), 11.2(d), 11.2(e) or 11.2(f) reduce to $F2 \parallel C_{\max}$. Note that for problem $F2 \parallel C_{\max}$, the optimal values for the preemptive and nonpreemptive case are again the same.

Figure 11.2(h) shows the compatibility graph of $F3 \parallel C_{\max}$, which is $\mathcal{NP}$-hard (Garey & Johnson [99]). An $\mathcal{NP}$-hardness proof for the problems given by Figures 11.2(b) and 11.2(g) can be found in Brucker & Krämer [48]. □

Problems $FMPT2 \parallel C_{\max}$ with a compatibility graph given by Figure 11.2(b) are $\mathcal{NP}$-hard, which implies that $FMPT2 \parallel C_{\max}$ is $\mathcal{NP}$-hard. $FMPT2 \parallel \sum C_i$ is $\mathcal{NP}$-hard because $F2 \parallel \sum C_i$ is $\mathcal{NP}$-hard (Garey & Johnson [97]). Finally, $FMPTm \mid n = k; prec; r_i \mid \sum w_i U_i$ and $FMPTm \mid n = k; prec; r_i \mid \sum w_i T_i$ are solvable in constant time.

Job Shop Problems

Problem $JMPT2 \mid p_{ij} = 1 \mid C_{\max}$ is $\mathcal{NP}$-hard (Brucker & Krämer [48]), contrary to the fact that $J2 \mid p_{ij} = 1 \mid C_{\max}$ is polynomially solvable (Timkovsky [198]).

Also, $JMPT3 \mid n = 3 \mid C_{\max}$ and $JMPT3 \mid n = 3 \mid \sum C_i$ are $\mathcal{NP}$-hard because the classical counterparts are $\mathcal{NP}$-hard (Sotskov & Shakhlevich [190]).

However, it is possible to extend the other known polynomial time algorithms for the classical job shop problem to the MPT case.

Theorem 11.7 The following job shop problems with MPT are polynomially solvable:

(a) $JMPT2 \mid n_i \leq 2 \mid C_{\max}$,

(b) $JMPT \mid n = 2 \mid f$ if f is regular, and

(c) $JMPT2 \mid n = k \mid C_{\max}$.

Proof: (a) If the first (last) task of a job requires both processors, it can be moved to the beginning (end) of the schedule without changing the schedule length. Thus, the problem is equivalent to scheduling the single-processor tasks, which is equivalent to the classical problem $J2 \mid n_i \leq 2 \mid C_{\max}$. Because the classical problem can be solved in $O(n \log n)$ time (Jackson [119]), $JMPT2 \mid n_i \leq 2 \mid C_{\max}$ can be solved with the same complexity.

(b) Like the classical problem $J \mid n = 2 \mid f$, problem $JMPT \mid n = 2 \mid f$ can be formulated as a shortest path problem. It can be solved by the methods developed in Section 6.4.2.

(c) As in Section 6.4.3, we reduce $JMPT2 \mid n = k \mid C_{\max}$ to a shortest path problem in an acyclic network $N = (V, A, l)$. The construction of N can be described as follows.

The two processors are denoted by A and B. We consider only active schedules , i.e. schedules in which no task can be started earlier without violating feasibility. Given an active schedule, we have a unique sequence

$$t_0 = 0 < t_1 < t_2 < \ldots < t_q$$

of times at which one of the following conditions holds:

- two single-processor tasks start to be processed jointly on both processors,

- a bi-processor task starts, or

- a single-processor task starts to be processed on one processor and on the other processor an idle period starts (see Figure 11.3).

Figure 11.3: Structure of a $JMPT2 \mid n = k \mid C_{max}$-schedule.

In addition, let t_{q+1} denote the makespan.

We call the set D_μ of tasks scheduled in the interval $[t_\mu, t_{\mu+1}]$ ($\mu = 0, \ldots, q$) a **block**. A block consists either of one bi-processor task or one or more single-processor tasks. $l_\mu = t_{\mu+1} - t_\mu$ is the length of block D_μ. The network $N = (V, A, l)$ is defined by:

- The set V of all index tuples $\boldsymbol{v} = (v(i))_{i=1}^k$ with $0 \leq v(i) \leq n_i$ for $i = 1, \ldots, k$. The vertex $\boldsymbol{s} = (0)_{i=1}^k$ is called the initial vertex. The vertex $\boldsymbol{t} = (n_i)_{i=1}^k$ is called the terminal vertex. Vertices define the end or start of a block.

- $(\boldsymbol{u}, \boldsymbol{v}) \in A$ if and only if $\boldsymbol{u} < \boldsymbol{v}$, where the set of tasks

$$\{O_{i,j(i)} \mid i = 1, \ldots, k; u(i) < j(i) \leq v(i)\}$$

  defines a block.

- For each $(\boldsymbol{u}, \boldsymbol{v}) \in A$, $l(\boldsymbol{u}, \boldsymbol{v})$ is the length of the block corresponding to $(\boldsymbol{u}, \boldsymbol{v})$.

Note that a set of tasks defines a block if the tasks can be scheduled without idle times between the tasks scheduled on each processor and only the first tasks on processor A and B start at the same time.

In N, each $\boldsymbol{s}$-$\boldsymbol{t}$-path corresponds to a feasible schedule. Furthermore, there is an $\boldsymbol{s}$-$\boldsymbol{t}$-path corresponding to an optimal schedule. Thus, to solve the MPT job shop problem we have to find a shortest $\boldsymbol{s}$-$\boldsymbol{t}$-path. The network has $O(r^k)$ vertices, where $r = \max_{i=1}^{k} n_i$. Therefore, an optimal schedule can be found in $O(r^{2k})$ time if the network N is given.

As shown in Section 6.4.3, we need $O(r^{2k})$ time to construct the network. This provides an $O(r^{2k})$-algorithm.   □

11.3 Shop Problems with MPT: Unit Processing Times

Job Shop Problems

We consider a job shop problem with a fixed number of jobs consisting of unit time tasks. The algorithm we will present is a straightforward generalization of an algorithm for the problem without multiprocessor tasks due to Meyer [166]. This algorithm can be applied to the general objective functions $\max f_i$ and $\sum f_i$ where f_i denotes a monotonous nondecreasing function of the completion time of job i. Furthermore, we may have release times and precedence constraints between jobs.

JMPT $| \; p_{ij} = 1; \text{prec}; r_i; n = k \; | \; \max f_i \; (\sum f_i)$

To solve this problem we first determine time slots $t_1, \ldots, t_l \; (l = \sum_{i=1}^{k} n_i)$ which are sufficient for some active schedule for the problem. Then the problem will be formulated as a shortest path problem in a suitable network.

We may assume $r_i < r_j$ whenever i precedes j. If we assume that all tasks must be processed on the same processor, we obtain the time slots $t_1, \ldots, t_l$ by scheduling the k jobs in order of nondecreasing release dates with processing times n_i.

A feasible schedule defines a path in the following network $N = (V, A, d)$ from some initial vertex to a terminal vertex:

- The set V of vertices consists of $(k + 1)$-tupels $(t_j, i_1, \ldots, i_k)$ for $j = 1, \ldots, l$ and $0 \leq i_\nu \leq n_\nu (\nu = 1, \ldots, k)$. Such a vertex represents a partial schedule for the interval $[0, t_j]$ where i_ν indicates the last task of job ν which is already scheduled. Additionally, we have an initial vertex $(t_1 - 1, 0, \ldots, 0)$ and a terminal vertex $(t_l + 1, n_1, \ldots, n_k)$.

- We have arcs between nodes $(t_j, i_1, \ldots, i_k)$ and $(t_{j+1}, i'_1, \ldots, i'_k)$ representing the tasks scheduled in time slot t_{j+1}. There is an arc between two vertices if a k-tupel $(x_1, \ldots, x_k) \in \{0, 1\}^k$ exists with $i'_\nu = i_\nu + x_\nu, \nu = 1, \ldots, k$ such that:

- the tasks of $S = \{O_{\nu,i_\nu+1} \mid x_\nu = 1\}$ can be processed in parallel,

- the release dates are respected, i.e. $O_{\nu,i_\nu+1} \in S$ implies $r_\nu < t_{j+1}$, and

- the precedences are respected, i.e. if job μ precedes job ν and $x_\nu = 1$, then the value of i_μ must equal n_μ.

- The arcs are weighted with the maximum (sum) of all $f_\nu(t_{j+1})$-values of jobs finishing exactly at time t_{j+1}, i.e. jobs ν with $x_\nu = 1$ and $i_\nu + x_\nu = n_\nu$. If no job finishes at time t_{j+1}, the arc weight is set to $-\infty(0)$.

Each feasible schedule corresponds to a path from the initial vertex to the terminal vertex and vice versa. The corresponding objective value is given by the length of the path, where the length of a path is the maximum (sum) of all arc values. Thus, we only need to find a shortest path which takes $O(k2^k m \sum_{i=1}^{k} n_i \prod_{i=1}^{k} n_i)$ time since we have $O(\sum_{i=1}^{k} n_i \prod_{i=1}^{k} n_i)$ vertices, $O(2^k)$ arcs incident at each vertex, and the inspection of an arc takes $O(km)$ time.

Flow Shop Problems

We solve different flow shop problems with multiprocessor unit time tasks and a fixed number of stages.

FMPT | $\mathbf{p_{ij} = 1; stages = r}$ | $\sum \mathbf{w_i C_i}$

We may assume $w_1 \geq w_2 \ldots \geq w_n$. Then there always exists an optimal schedule in which job i finishes before job j if $i < j$.

We define the network as follows:

- The set V of vertices consists of $(r+2)$-tupels $(i, i_0, \ldots, i_r)$ for $i = 1, \ldots, nr$ and $0 \leq i_k \leq n$ ($k = 0, \ldots, r$) with $\sum_{k=0}^{r} i_k = n$. It represents a partial schedule for the interval $[0, i]$ where i_k indicates the number of jobs that are finished up to stage k. Thus, i_r equals the number of jobs that are completely finished. We have an initial vertex $(0, n, 0, \ldots, 0)$. The vertex $(nr, 0, \ldots, 0, n)$ is defined to be the terminal vertex.

- The arcs between vertices $(i, i_0, \ldots, i_r)$ and $(i + 1, i'_0, \ldots, i'_r)$ represent the tasks scheduled in time slot $i + 1$. Hence we have an arc between two nodes if an r-tupel $(x_1, \ldots, x_r) \in \{0, 1\}^r$, representing the stages processed in time slot $i + 1$, exists such that

  - the processor requirements of the stages, i.e. the sets μ_j with $x_j = 1$, are pairwise disjoint,

  - a job is processed in stage k only if at least one job was processed up to stage $k - 1$, i.e. $x_k = 1$ only if $i_{k-1} > 0$, and

  - i'_k equals the sum of the number of jobs already processed up to stage k in $[0, i]$ and the number of jobs which are processed in stage k in $[i, i + 1]$ minus the number of jobs which are processed in stage $k + 1$ in $[i, i + 1]$, i.e. $i'_k = i_k + x_k - x_{k+1}$ for all $k = 1, \ldots, r - 1$, $i'_0 = i_0 - x_1$ and $i'_r = i_r + x_r$.

- The arcs have zero weight if $x_r = 0$. If $x_r = 1$, the weight equals $(i + 1)w_{i_r+1}$ because we may assume that job $i_r + 1$ is now finished.

Each schedule in which the jobs are finished in order of nonincreasing weights corresponds to a path from the initial vertex to the terminal vertex. The objective value is given by the length of the path. Conversely, from each such path, a schedule with objective value equal to the length of the path can be constructed as follows. For each arc $(x_1, \ldots, x_r)$ of the shortest path ending at a node $(i + 1, i'_0, \ldots, i'_r)$, schedule for $x_j = 1$ job $(i'_j + \ldots + i'_r)$ in stage j in time slot $[i, i + 1]$. Note that the resulting schedule is always a permutation flow shop schedule, i.e. a schedule in which the job order for each stage is the same.

In a preprocessing step we calculate all feasible $(x_1, \ldots, x_r)$-tupels in $O(2^r(r + m))$ steps. The network has $O(nrn^r)$ vertices since the value of i_r is uniquely determined by $i_0, \ldots, i_{r-1}$, and hence $O(r2^r n^{r+1})$ arcs. Inspection of an arc takes $O(r)$ steps. Thus, it takes $O(r^2 2^r n^{r+1} + 2^r(r + m))$ time to calculate a shortest path, i.e. an optimal schedule.

Using similar techniques, $FMPT \mid p_{ij} = 1; stages = r \mid \sum T_i$ and $FMPT \mid p_{ij} = 1; stages = r; r_i \mid \sum C_i(C_{max})$ can be solved in $O(r^2 2^r n^{r+1} + 2^r(r + m))$ time. For the latter, we may assume that jobs are processed in order of nondecreasing release dates. Furthermore, time slots are calculated as described for problem $JMPT \mid p_{ij} = 1; prec; r_i; n = k \mid$ $\max f_i$ by computing an earliest possible starting schedule. Then the network can be defined as for problem $FMPT \mid p_{ij} = 1; stages = r \mid \sum w_i C_i$ with the following additional restriction. Arcs with $x_1 = 1$ are only allowed to end at a node $(t_{j+1}, i'_0, \ldots, i'_r)$ if $r_{n-i'_0} \leq t_{j+1} - 1$. Here we assume that $r_1 \leq r_2 \leq \ldots \leq r_n$.

FMPT $\mid$ p$_{ij}$ = 1; stages = r $\mid$ $\sum$ w$_i$U$_i$

We proceed in a similar way as for problem $MPTm \mid p_i = 1 \mid \sum w_i U_i$. We are interested in finding a feasible schedule for the on-time jobs. We assume that $d_1 \leq \ldots \leq d_n$ since the on-time jobs can be finished in order of nondecreasing due dates. The network is defined as follows:

- The set V of vertices consists of $(r + 2)$-tuples $(i, i_0, \ldots, i_r)$ for $i = 1, \ldots, nr$ and $0 \leq i_k \leq n$ $(k = 0, \ldots, r)$ with $\sum_{k=0}^{r} i_k = n$. Furthermore, we have vertices $(0, n - i, 0, \ldots, 0, i)$ for $i = 0, \ldots, n$. A vertex represents a partial schedule for the on-time jobs scheduled in interval $[0, i]$ and the late jobs scheduled in $[d_n, \infty[$. Here i_k $(k = 0, \ldots, r - 1)$ indicates the number of jobs which have been processed up to stage k. The value of i_r indicates the number of jobs which are either finished on time in $[0, i]$ or scheduled late. $(0, n - i, 0, \ldots, 0, i)$ indicates that the first i jobs are scheduled late. The vertex $(0, n, 0, \ldots, 0)$ is defined as the initial vertex while $(nr, 0, \ldots, 0, n)$ is the terminal vertex.

- The arcs are defined as in problem $FMPT \mid p_{ij} = 1; stages = r \mid \sum w_i C_i$ under the restriction that arcs with $x_r = 1$ are only allowed to end at a vertex $(i + 1, i'_0, \ldots, i'_r)$ with $d_{i'_r} \geq i + 1$. These arcs have zero weight since they represent jobs which are on time. Additionally, we have arcs between vertices belonging to the same time slot i. They represent the jobs which are scheduled late, i.e. for $i_0 > 0$ we have arcs from $(i, i_0, \ldots, i_r)$ to $(i, i_0 - 1, \ldots, i_r + 1)$ with weight w_{i_r+1}.

Each schedule in which the on-time jobs are finished according to nondecreasing due dates corresponds to a path from the initial vertex to the terminal vertex. The length of the path denotes the corresponding objective value. On the other hand, each path defines a feasible schedule for the on-time jobs. Thus, by calculating a shortest path we obtain the optimal objective value and a corresponding schedule in $O(r^2 2^r n^{r+1} + 2^r(r+m))$ time.

Recall that a fixed number of processors induces a bounded number of stages of a flow shop problem. Thus, the problems $FMPTm \mid p_{ij} = 1 \mid \sum w_i C_i$, $FMPTm \mid p_{ij} = 1 \mid \sum T_i$, $FMPTm \mid p_{ij} = 1; r_i \mid \sum C_i(C_{max})$, and $FMPTm \mid p_{ij} = 1 \mid \sum w_i U_i$ are also solvable in polynomial time.

Open Shop Problems with Multiprocessor Tasks

In an open shop problem, tasks of a job might be processed in an arbitrary order. By prespecifying for each possible order the number of jobs which have to be processed according to this order, we obtain a scheduling problem which can be solved by generalizations of the approaches for flow shop problems presented in the last section.

OMPT $\mid$ p$_{ij}$ = 1; stages = r $\mid$ $\sum$ w$_i$C$_i$

In this problem each job is processed according to one of the $C = r!$ possible (stage) orders $\pi_1, \ldots, \pi_C$. Thus, each schedule defines a C-tupel $(n_1, \ldots, n_C)$, where n_i denotes the number of jobs which are processed according to π_i. Hence, we have to calculate all different tupels $(n_1, \ldots, n_C)$ with $0 \leq n_i \leq n$ for all $i = 1, \ldots, C$ and $\sum_{i=1}^{C} n_i = n$, and solve the corresponding optimization problem for each such tupel. Then the best schedule of all these subproblems gives the optimal schedule of the open shop problem.

We may assume $w_1 \geq \ldots \geq w_n$. Then an optimal schedule exists with $C_1 \leq \ldots \leq C_n$. We generalize the definition of the network for problem $FMPT \mid p_{ij} = 1; stages = r \mid \sum w_i C_i$ as follows:

- The vertices are $(1 + C(r + 1) + r)$-tupels $(i, i_{1,0}, \ldots, i_{1,r}, i_{2,0}, \ldots, i_{C,r}, j_1, \ldots, j_r)$ for $i = 0, \ldots, nr - 1$, $0 \leq i_{\mu,\nu} \leq n_\mu$ ($\mu = 1, \ldots, C; \nu = 0, \ldots, r$) and $j_k \in \{0, 1\}$ ($k = 1, \ldots, r$). Furthermore, we assume $\sum_{\nu=0}^{r} i_{\mu,\nu} = n_\mu$ for $\mu = 1, \ldots, C$. A vertex represents a partial schedule for the interval $[0, i + 1]$, where $i_{\mu,\nu}$ indicates the number of jobs which have to be scheduled according to π_μ and have been processed up to stage $\pi_\mu(\nu)$. The entry j_k denotes the number of tasks processed in stage k in $[i, i+1]$. The initial vertex is given by $(0, i_{1,0}, \ldots, i_{1,r}, i_{2,0}, \ldots, i_{C,r}, j_1, \ldots, j_r)$ with $j_k = 0$ for $k = 1, \ldots, r$, $i_{\mu,0} = n_\mu$ for $\mu = 1, \ldots, C$, and $i_{\mu,\nu} = 0$ for $\nu \neq 0$. The vertex $(nr, i_{1,0}, \ldots, i_{1,r}, i_{2,0}, \ldots, i_{C,r}, j_1, \ldots, j_r)$ with $j_k = 0$ for $k = 1, \ldots, r$, $i_{\mu,r} = n_\mu$ for $\mu = 1, \ldots, C$, and $i_{\mu,\nu} = 0$ for $\nu \neq r$ is defined as the terminal vertex.

- The set A consists of two different types of arcs. Arcs of the first type are between vertices $(i, \ldots, i_{\mu,\nu}, \ldots, j_1, \ldots, j_r)$ and $(i, \ldots, i'_{\mu,\nu}, \ldots, j'_1, \ldots, j'_r)$ belonging to the same time i. They represent the scheduling of a task in stage $\pi_q(s)$ in $[i, i+1]$. Hence, we have an arc if $i'_{q,s} = i_{q,s} + 1$, $i'_{q,s-1} = i_{q,s-1} - 1$ and $i'_{\mu,\nu} = i_{\mu,\nu}$ otherwise. Furthermore, we have $j'_{\pi_q(s)} = j_{\pi_q(s)} + 1$ and $j'_k = j_k$ otherwise. We must ensure that no processor is required more than once. This check takes $O(r)$ time if we assume a preprocessing as in the flow shop section. These arcs have zero weight if no job is finished, i.e. $s < r$. Otherwise we may assume that jobs $1, 2, \ldots, \sum_{\mu=1}^{C} i_{\mu,r}$ are already finished in $[0, i+1]$. Hence, the job $\sum_{\mu=1}^{C} i_{\mu,r} + 1$ finishes at time $i + 1$ and the weight of the arc equals $(i+1)w_{\sum_{\mu=1}^{C} i_{\mu,r}+1}$. Arcs of the second type are between vertices $(i, \ldots, i_{\mu,\nu}, \ldots, i_{C,r}, j_1, \ldots, j_r)$ and $(i+1, \ldots, i_{\mu,\nu}, \ldots, i_{C,r}, 0, \ldots, 0)$. In this situation no task is scheduled. Thus they have zero weight.

Thus, by calculating a shortest path we get an optimal schedule for the subproblem. All $O(n^{r!})$ subproblems have a total of $O(nrn^{r!r}2^r) = O(r2^r n^{r!r+1})$ nodes. At the most $O(r!r)$ arcs start from each node and the inspection of an arc takes $O(rr!)$ time. As in the flow shop section, we calculate all feasible $(j_1, \ldots, j_r)$-tupels in $O(2^r(r+m))$ time in a preprocessing step. Thus, problem $OMPT \mid p_{ij} = 1; stages = r \mid \sum w_i C_i$ can be solved in $O(r^3(r!)^2 2^r n^{r!r+1} + 2^r(r+m))$ time.

Now observe that the subproblems of the open shop problems with objective function $\sum T_i$, $\sum w_i U_i$ and $\sum C_i(C_{max})$ with release dates can be solved by similar generalizations of the corresponding flow shop problems. Hence, we conclude that $OMPT \mid p_{ij} = 1; stages = r \mid \sum T_i$, $OMPT \mid p_{ij} = 1; stages = r; r_i \mid \sum C_i(C_{max})$ and $OMPT \mid p_{ij} = 1; stages = r \mid \sum w_i U_i$ can also be solved in $O(r^3(r!)^2 2^r n^{r!r+1} + 2^r(r+m))$ time.

Similar to the flow shop situation, we conclude that the problems $OMPTm \mid p_{ij} = 1 \mid \sum w_i C_i$, $OMPTm \mid p_{ij} = 1 \mid \sum T_i$, $OMPTm \mid p_{ij} = 1; r_i \mid \sum C_i(C_{max})$ and $OMPTm \mid p_{ij} = 1 \mid \sum w_i U_i$ are also solvable in polynomial time.

We are interested in classifying shop problems with multiprocessor tasks and unit processing times with respect to their complexity status. Thus, we remark that open shop problems with 2 jobs and unit processing time tasks, i.e. $OMPT \mid p_{ij} = 1; n = 2 \mid C_{max}$, can be reduced to a matching problem in a bipartite graph $G = (V \cup W, A)$ as follows. Each task of job 1 (job 2) corresponds to a vertex of V (W). An edge between a vertex of V and a vertex of W exists if the represented tasks can be processed in parallel. An optimal schedule for the open shop problem corresponds to a maximal matching in the graph G and vice versa. Thus it can be calculated in $O(r^{2.5})$ time (Even & Kariv [88]), where r denotes the number of stages. Note that this approach can be generalized in a straightforward way to solve $OMPT \mid p_{ij} = 1; r_i; n = 2 \mid max f_i (\sum f_i)$ in $O(r^{2.5})$ time if the f_i are monotonic nondecreasing.

11.4 Multi-Mode Multiprocessor-Task Scheduling Problems

In a multi-mode multiprocessor-task scheduling problem ($MMPT$-problem) there is set $\mathcal{A}_i = \{A_i^1, \ldots, A_k^{m_i}\}(\mathcal{A}_{ij} = \{A_{ij}^1, \ldots, A_{ij}^{m_{ij}}\})$ of machine sets $A_i^\nu(A_{ij}^\nu)$ and corresponding processing times $p_i^\nu(p_{ij}^\nu)$ associated with each task i (operation O_{ij}). We have to assign a set $A_i^\nu(A_{ij}^\nu)$ to each task i (operation O_{ij}). If $A_i^\nu(A_{ij}^\nu)$ is assigned to i (O_{ij}), then task i (operation O_{ij}) occupies all processors in the set $A_i^\nu(A_{ij}^\nu)$ for $p_i^\nu(p_{ij}^\nu)$ time units. Thus, after the assignment we have a multiprocessor task problem. The $MMPT$-problem consists of finding an assignment and scheduling the tasks (operations) on the assigned machines such that some objective function is minimized. In the $\alpha|\beta|\gamma$-notation, $MMPT$-problems are characterized by $\alpha_1 \in \{MMPT, MGMPT, MJMPT, MFMPT, MOMPT\}$. The sets $\mathcal{A}_i(\mathcal{A}_{ij})$ may be restricted. For example, we may assume that each task requires a fixed number q of processors. Then $\mathcal{A}_i$ is the set of all subsets of processors of size q. In this case we usually assume that the processing time depends only on this number of processors. To indicate such a model we add "$size_i$" to the β-field. In connection with models for parallel computing other restrictions are possible (see Blazewicz et al. [27]). Next we will briefly discuss known complexity results for $MMPT$-problems.

Problem $MMPT2 \parallel C_{\max}$ is $\mathcal{NP}$-hard because the $\mathcal{NP}$-hard problem $P2 \parallel C_{\max}$ is a special case of this problem. However, it can be solved with complexity $O(nT)$ where $T = \sum_{i=1}^{n} p_{\min}(i)$ is the sum of minimal processing times

$$p_{\min}(i) = \min_{\nu=1}^{m_i} p_i^\nu$$

of tasks i. The special case of $MMPT3 \parallel C_{\max}$ in which only two machines are involved in the bi-machine sets can also be solved pseudopolynomially with complexity $O(nT^2)$ (see Chen & Lee [64]).

In the remaining part of this section we discuss polynomial algorithms for "size$_i$"-problems. Firstly, two-processor problems are considered. In this case we have **1-tasks** and **2-tasks** depending on the number of processors needed. Denote by n_1 and n_2 the number of 1-tasks and 2-tasks, respectively.

MPT2 | r_i; $p_i = p$; size$_i$ | $C_{\max}$

It can be easily shown by exchange arguments that the following algorithm solves this problem.

Algorithm MPT2 | r_i; $p_i = p$; size$_i$ | $C_{\max}$

1. $t := \min_{r=1}^{n} r_\nu$;
2. WHILE not all tasks are scheduled DO
   BEGIN
3.   IF an unscheduled 2-task j with $r_j \leq t$ exists THEN schedule j at time t
4.   ELSE schedule a largest possible number of 1-tasks j with $r_j \leq t$ at time t;
5. $t := \max\{t + p; \min\{r_\nu \mid \nu \text{ is unscheduled }\}$
   END

The multiprocessor tasks problem

MPT2 | $r_i; p_i = 1; size_i | \sum C_i$

can be solved by a similar algorithm. All we have to do is to replace Statements 3 and 4 by the following statement:

If at least two 1-tasks are available at time t, then assign any two such tasks for processing from time t. Otherwise, assign any available 2-task for processing, or, if there is no such 2-task available, assign any available 1-task for processing.

Theorem 11.8 Any schedule constructed by the algorithm above is optimal.

Proof: Let C_j be the completion times in a schedule S constructed by the algorithm above, and let S^* be an optimal schedule. Let t be the first point in time where these two schedules differ. We will show by an interchange argument that in this case S^* can be converted to an optimal schedule $\bar{S}$ that coincides with S at least up to point $t + 1$.

Note that, since S and S^* coincide up to the point t, any task j that is processed in schedule S in the interval $[t, t + 1]$ satisfies

$$r_j \le t \le C_j(S^*).$$

Suppose that according to S two 1-tasks j_1 and j_2 are processed in the interval $[t, t + 1]$. If $C_{j_1}(S^*) = C_{j_2}(S^*)$, then $\bar{S}$ can be obtained by swapping j_1 and j_2 with tasks processed in schedule S^* in the interval $[t, t + 1]$. If $C_{j_1}(S^*) < C_{j_2}(S^*)$, we first swap j_2 with a task processed in parallel with j_1, and then again swap j_1 and j_2 with tasks processed in schedule S^* in the interval $[t, t + 1]$. Suppose that only one task j is processed in schedule S in the interval $[t, t+1]$. Observe that in this case due to the construction of S exactly one task must be processed in this interval in the optimal schedule S^*. Moreover, if $size_j = 1$, then this task is also a 1-task. Hence, $\bar{S}$ can be obtained from S^* by swapping j and the task processed in the interval $[t, t + 1]$. It is easy to see that

$$\sum_{j=1}^{n} C_j(S^*) = \sum_{j=1}^{n} \bar{C}_j(S^*),$$

in each case and the optimality of S follows by a simple inductive argument. $\square$

MPT2 | $p_i = p$; size$_i$ | $\sum U_i$

Task j is early in some schedule S if $C_j(S) \leq d_i$, otherwise this task is late. By simple interchange arguments it is easy to prove the following.

Lemma 11.9 There is an optimal schedule such that

- all late tasks are scheduled (in any order) after all early tasks,

- all early tasks with the same size are scheduled according to non-decreasing due dates and 1-tasks precede 2-tasks with the same due date, and

- if a 1-task j is late, then all 2-tasks with due dates less than or equal to d_j are also late.

The following algorithm constructs an optimal schedule which has the properties of Lemma 11.9.

Algorithm MPT2 | $p_i = p$; size$_i$ | $\sum U_i$

1. Calculate a list L in which the tasks are ordered according to non-decreasing due dates. If 1-tasks and 2-tasks have the same due date then place the 1-tasks before the 2-tasks;
2. WHILE L is not empty DO
   BEGIN
3. Select the first task j in L;
4. IF task j is a 2-task THEN
5.   IF j late if added to the partial schedule of early tasks THEN
       add j to the set of late tasks
       ELSE schedule j;
6. IF task j is a 1-task which can be scheduled on time THEN insert j into the partial schedule of early tasks in the first time slot
   ELSE
7.   IF the partial schedule of early tasks contains a 2-task THEN
       eliminate the 2-task k scheduled last among all 2-tasks, add
       it to the set of late tasks, move all early tasks scheduled after
       k one unit to the left, and schedule task j
       ELSE add j to the set of late tasks
   END

Using two lists (a doubly-linked one for the current partial schedule of early tasks and another list containing the early 2-tasks from right to left) and storing the first free time periods for 1- and 2-tasks in the current partial schedule respectively, the algorithm can be implemented in such a way that it runs in $O(n \log n)$ time. To show that this algorithm provides an optimal schedule, let S be a schedule for early tasks constructed by the algorithm and let S^* be an optimal schedule satisfying Lemma 11.9 which coincides with S in the interval $[0, t]$, where t is maximal. We consider two cases.

Case 1: In S two 1-tasks i and j are scheduled at time t. Then for all 1-tasks l in S^* with starting time greater than or equal to t we must have $\max\{d_i, d_j\} \leq d_l$, since otherwise l must have been scheduled at or before time t in S. If in S^* a 2-task k is scheduled at time t and i or j is scheduled as a late task, then we replace k by i and j and schedule k as a late task. If both i and j are scheduled early, then we may assume that both are scheduled at the same time and we swap i, j and k. After this swap i, j and k will be early in the resulting schedule because $\max\{d_i, d_j\} \leq d_k$ which can be seen as follows. Assume that $d_k < d_i$. Then k must have been deleted from S. Because $d_k < d_i$ all 1-tasks h with starting times $\geq t$ in S must belong to S^* (otherwise we may replace k by h in S^* and we have Case 2 which will be considered later). Let l be the 1-task which eliminates k from S. Then all tasks scheduled before l in S as well as k belong to S^* which contradicts the fact that k is eliminated in S. In each case we have a contradiction to the maximality of t because after these modifications the schedule derived remains optimal. If in S^* one or two 1-tasks are scheduled, then again we can swap tasks such that i and j will be scheduled at time t.

Case 2: In S a 2-task j is scheduled at time t. If in S^* a 2-task k with $d_j \leq d_k$ is scheduled at time t, then j and k can be swapped. If in S^* a 2-task k with $d_k < d_j$ is scheduled, then in S task k must have been eliminated by some 1-task l and as in Case 1 we may assume that all 1-tasks scheduled before l as well as k belong to S^* which again is a contradiction. If in S^* one or two 1-tasks are scheduled at time t and j is scheduled early, then these 1-tasks and j can be swapped. Otherwise, j is scheduled late and we consider the first time $t' > t$ where a 2-task l is scheduled early in S^* (if no such 2-task exists, let t' be the completion time of the last early task in S^*). Let T be the set of tasks scheduled in S^* in the time interval $[t, t']$. If we now eliminate l from S^*, schedule all tasks in T one time unit later, and schedule j at time t, we then get another optimal schedule, because no rescheduled task in T is late. This can be seen as follows. In S, after scheduling the 2-task j, no 1-task will be scheduled late. Because S and S^* coincide up to time t, all tasks in T are scheduled early in S after time $t+1$. Thus, they are also scheduled early in S^* if moved one time unit to the right.

MPT2 | $\mathbf{p_i = p; size_i}$ | $\sum \mathbf{T_i}$

We consider the case $p_i = 1$. Problems with $p_i = p$ are solved similarly. Because the functions $T_i(t) = \max\{0, t - d_j\}$ are non-decreasing, in an optimal schedule all tasks are processed within $[0, C_{\max}]$ where

$$C_{\max} := \left\lceil \frac{n_1}{2} \right\rceil + n_2.$$

Assume that $i_1, \ldots, i_{n_1}$ is a sequence of all 1-tasks and $j_1, \ldots, j_{n_2}$ is a sequence of all 2-tasks, each ordered according to non-decreasing due dates. It can be shown by exchange arguments that in an optimal schedule the 1-tasks and 2-tasks are scheduled in these orders. Thus, we only have to merge these two sequences into a single sequence specifying the order in which the tasks should be allocated for processing. We will show that this can be accomplished by a dynamic programming procedure.

Let $t = C_{j_k}$ the finish time of the 2-task j_k in some optimal schedule S^*. Then $\alpha_k(t) := \min\{2(t-k), n_1\}$ 1-tasks are processed in the interval $[0, t]$. If in S^* task j_{k-1} finishes at time t' and j_k finishes at time $t > t'$ then $\alpha_k(t) - \alpha_{k-1}(t')$ 1-tasks are scheduled in the interval $[t', t]$ in the given order. The corresponding costs for scheduling these 1-tasks are denoted by $\eta_k(t', t)$.

For $t = C_{j_k}$ where $1 \le k \le n_2$ and $k \le t \le C_{\max} - (n_2 - k)$ denote by $F_k(t)$ the minimal costs associated with the tasks processed in the interval $[0, t]$ when 2-task j_k finishes at time t.

All relevant $F_k(t)$-values can be calculated by the following recursion.

Initialization

$$F_1(1) = T_{j_1}(1)$$

$$F_1(t) = T_{j_1}(t) + \sum_{\nu=1}^{\alpha_1(t)} T_{i_\nu} \left(\left\lceil \frac{\nu}{2} \right\rceil \right) \quad \text{for } 1 < t \le C_{\max} - (n_2 - 1)$$

Iteration

$$F_k(t) = \min_{t' < t}\{F_{k-1}(t') + \eta_k(t', t) + T_{j_k}(t)\}$$

$$\text{for } 2 \leq k \leq n_2 \text{ and } k \leq t \leq C_{\max} - (n_2 - k).$$

The optimal solution value is given by

$$\min_{n_2 \leq t \leq C_{\max}} F_{n_2}(t) + \eta_{n_2}(t, C_{\max}).$$

It is easy to see that the computational complexity of the whole procedure is $O(n^3)$.

MPT2 | prec; $p_i = p$; size$_i$ | C$_{\max}$

Lloyd [162] has shown that the procedure for solving the identical parallel machine problem $P2 \mid \text{prec}; p_i = 1 \mid C_{\max}$ can be adapted to solve the corresponding multiprocessor-task scheduling problem with "size"-characteristic.

Finally, we consider problems of type

MPTm | $p_i = p$; size$_i$ | f

with $f \in \{\sum w_i C_i, \sum w_i U_i, \sum T_i\}$. These problems can be reduced to the corresponding multiprocessor task scheduling problems with m dedicated processors as follows. Let n_k be the number of tasks i with $size_i = k \in \{1, \ldots, m\}$. There are $\binom{m}{k}$ possibilities to assign k processors to each of these n_k tasks. Thus, the number of all possible assignments for the set of all tasks i with $size_i = k$ is certainly bounded by $n_k^{\binom{m}{k}}$. This implies that the number of all possible assignments for the set of all tasks $1, \ldots, n$ is bounded by

$$\prod_{k=1}^{m} n_k^{\binom{m}{k}} \leq \prod_{k=1}^{m} n^{\binom{m}{k}} \leq n^{2^m}.$$

Furthermore, the size problem can be solved by solving all these possible multiprocessor task scheduling problems. Due to these observations, problems $MPTm \mid p_i = 1, size_i \mid \gamma$ with $\gamma \in \{\sum w_i C_i, \sum w_i U_i, \sum T_i\}$ are polynomially solvable since the corresponding multiprocessor task problems with dedicated processors are polynomially solvable. Although these problems are polynomially solvable for a fixed number m, the complexity of the corresponding algorithms grows exponentially with m.

11.5   Complexity Results

Tables 11.1 to 11.3 show complexity results for multiprocessor-task scheduling problems with dedicated processors. In Tables 11.1 and 11.2 polynomially solvable and $\mathcal{NP}$-hard problems for single stage problems are listed. Table 11.3 contains multi-stage problems which are polynomially solvable. There is no table for corresponding $\mathcal{NP}$-hard multi-stage problems which are $\mathcal{NP}$-hard because most of these problems can be found in Tables 6.3, 6.5 and 6.8. Additionally, in Krämer [48] it is shown that $FMPT \mid n = 3 \mid C_{\max}$ is $\mathcal{NP}$-hard and proofs that $FMPT2 \parallel C_{\max}$ and $JMPT2 \mid p_{ij} = 1 \mid C_{\max}$ are strongly $\mathcal{NP}$-hard can be found in Brucker & Krämer [48].

Table 11.4 contains multiprocessor-task scheduling problems of type "$size_i$" which are polynomially solvable. Table 11.5 contains corresponding $\mathcal{NP}$-hard problems. $\mathcal{NP}$-hard parallel scheduling problems, i.e. problems with $size_i = 1$ for all jobs i, are not listed in Table 11.5.

$MPT2 \mid C_{max}$ 11.1 Hoogeveen et al. [113]   O(n)

$MPTm \mid r_i; p_i = 1 \mid C_{max}$ 11.1 Brucker & Krämer [49] $O(R2^R n^{R+1})$

$MPTm \mid r_i; p_i = 1 \mid \sum C_i$ 11.1 Brucker & Krämer [49] $O(R2^R n^{R+1})$

$MPTm \mid p_i = 1 \mid \sum w_i C_i$ 11.1 Brucker & Krämer [49] $O(R2^R n^{R+1})$

$MPTm \mid p_i = 1 \mid \sum w_i U_i$ 11.1 Brucker & Krämer [49] $O(R2^R n^{R+1})$

$MPTm \mid p_i = 1 \mid \sum T_i$ 11.1 Brucker & Krämer [49] $O(R2^R n^{R+1})$

$MPT2 \mid pmtn \mid L_{\max}$ Bianco et al. [25] $O(n)$

$MPT2 \mid pmtn \mid \sum C_i$ Cai et al. [61] $O(n \log n)$

$MPTm \mid pmtn \mid C_{\max}$ Bianco et al. [24]   lin. progr.

Table 11.1: Polynomially solvable multiprocessor-tasks problems with dedicated processors.

* $MPT \mid p_i = 1 \mid C_{max}$ Hoogeveen et al. [113]

* $MPT2 \mid chains; p_i = 1 \mid C_{max}$ Blazewicz et al. [28]

* $MPT2 \mid\mid r_i \mid C_{max}$ Hoogeveen et al. [113]

* $MPT3 \mid\mid C_{max}$ Hoogeveen et al. [113]

* $MPT2 \mid\mid L_{max}$ Hoogeveen et al. [113]

* $MPT \mid p_i = 1 \mid\mid \sum C_i$ Hoogeveen et al. [113]

* $MPT2 \mid\mid \sum C_i$ Hoogeveen et al. [113]

* $MPT2 \mid chains; p_i = 1 \mid \sum C_i$ Blazewicz et al. [28]

Table 11.2: $\mathcal{NP}$-hard multiprocessor-tasks problems with dedicated processors.

$FMPTm \mid n = k; prec; r_i \mid \sum w_i U_i$ Krämer [48]

$FMPTm \mid n = k; prec; r_i \mid \sum w_i T_i$ Krämer [48]

$FMPT \mid p_{ij} = 1; stages = r \mid f$ 11.3 Brucker & Krämer [49]
with $f \in \{\sum w_i C_i, \sum T_i, \sum w_i U_i\}$ $O(r^2 2^r n^{r+1} + 2^r(r + m))$

$FMPT \mid p_{ij} = 1; stages = r; r_i \mid f$ 11.3 Brucker & Krämer [49]
with $f \in \{C_{\max}, \sum C_i\}$ $O(r^2 2^r n^{r+1} + 2^r(r + m))$

$JMPT2 \mid n_i \le 2 \mid C_{max}$ 11.2 Brucker & Krämer [48]
                                                      $O(n \log n)$
$JMPT \mid n = 2 \mid f$ 11.2 Brucker & Krämer [48]
with f regular $O(r^2 \log r)$
$JMPT2 \mid n = k \mid C_{max}$ 11.2 Brucker & Krämer [48]
                                                      $O(r^{2k})$
$JMPT \mid p_{ij} = 1; prec; r_i; n = k \mid f$ 11.3 Brucker & Krämer [49]
with $f \in \{\max f_i, \sum f_i\}$ $O\left(k 2^k m \sum_{i=1}^{k} n_i \prod_{i=1}^{k} n_i\right)$

$OMPT2 \parallel C_{max}$ 11.2 Brucker & Krämer [48]
                                                      $O(n)$
$OMPTm \mid n = k; prec; r_i \mid \sum w_i U_i$ Krämer [48]

$OMPTm \mid n = k; prec; r_i \mid \sum w_i T_i$ Krämer [48]

$OMPT \mid p_{ij} = 1; stages = r \mid f$ 11.3 Brucker & Krämer [49]
with $f \in \{\sum w_i C_i, \sum T_i, \sum w_i U_i\}$ $O(r^3 (r!)^2 2^r n^{r!r+1} + 2^r(r + m))$

$OMPT \mid p_{ij} = 1; stages = r; r_i \mid f$ 11.3 Brucker & Krämer [49]
with $f \in \{C_{\max}, \sum C_i\}$ $O(r^3 (r!)^2 2^r n^{r!r+1} + 2^r(r + m))$

$OMPT \mid p_{ij} = 1; r_i; n = 2 \mid f$ 11.3 $O(r^{2.5})$
with $f \in \{\max f_i, \sum f_i\}$ and
with f_i regular

Table 11.3: Polynomially solvable shop scheduling problems with multi-processor-tasks and dedicated processors.

$MPT2 \mid prec; p_i = p; size_i \mid C_{\max}$		Lloyd [162]
		$O(n^{\log 7})$
$MPT2 \mid r_i; p_i = p; size_i \mid C_{\max}$	11.4	Lee & Cai [148]
		$O(n \log n)$
$MPT2 \mid r_i; p_i = 1; size_i \mid \sum C_i$	11.4	Brucker et al. [45]
		$O(n \log n)$
$MPT2 \mid p_i = p; size_i \mid \sum U_i$	11.4	Brucker et al. [45]
		$O(n \log n)$
$MPT2 \mid p_i = p; size_i \mid \sum Ti$	11.4	Brucker et al. [45]
		$O(n^3)$
$MPTm \mid p_i = p; size_i \mid f$		
with $f \in \{\sum w_i C_i, \sum w_i U_i, \sum T_i\}$	11.4	Brucker et al. [45]

Table 11.4: Polynomially solvable multiprocessor-tasks problems of type "$size_i$".

$*\ MPT \mid p_i = 1; size_i \mid C_{max}$		Lloyd [162]
$*\ MPT2 \mid chains; r_i; p_i = 1; size_i \mid C_{max}$		Brucker et al. [45]
$*\ MPT2 \mid r_i; size_i \mid C_{max}$		Lee & Cai [148]
$*\ MPT3 \mid chains; p_i = 1; size_i \mid C_{max}$		Blazewicz & Liu [29]
$*\ MPT5 \mid size_i \mid C_{max}$		Du & Leung [80][1989]
$*\ MPT2 \mid chains; p_i = 1; size_i \mid L_{max}$		Brucker et al. [45]
$*\ MPT2 \mid size_i \mid L_{max}$		Lee & Cai [148]
$MPT2 \mid size_i \mid \sum C_i$		Lee & Cai [148]
$*\ MPT \mid p_i = 1; size_i \mid \sum C_i$		Drozdowski & Dell' Olmo [79]
$*\ MPT2 \mid prec; p_i = 1; size_i \mid \sum C_i$		Brucker et al. [45]
$*\ MPT2 \mid size_i \mid \sum w_i C_i$		Lee & Cai [148]

Table 11.5: $\mathcal{NP}$-hard multiprocessor-tasks scheduling problems of type "$size_i$".

Bibliography

[1] E.H.L. Aarts, P.J.M. van Laarhoven, J.K. Lenstra, and N.L.J. Ulder. A computational study of local search algorithms for job shop scheduling. *ORSA Journal on Computing*, 6(2):118–125, 1994.

[2] J.O. Achugbue and F.Y. Chin. Scheduling the open shop to minimize mean flow time. *SIAM Journal on Computing*, 11:709–720, 1982.

[3] D. Adolphson and T.C. Hu. Optimal linear ordering. *SIAM Journal of Applied Mathematics*, 25:403–423, 1973.

[4] A.V. Aho, J.E. Hopcroft, and J.D. Ullman. *The design and analysis of computer algorithms*. Adisson-Wesley, Reading, Mass., 1974.

[5] R.K. Ahuja, A.V. Goldberg, J.B. Orlin, and R.E. Tarjan. Finding minimum-cost flows by double scaling. *Mathematical Programming, Ser. A*, 53(3):243–266, 1992.

[6] R.K. Ahuja, T.L. Magnanti, and J.B. Orlin. *Network Flows*. Prentice Hall, Englewood Cliffs, 1993.

[7] R.K. Ahuja, J.B. Orlin, and R.E. Tarjan. Improved time bounds for the maximum flow problem. *SIAM Journal on Computing*, 18(5):939–954, 1989.

[8] S.B. Akers and J. Friedman. A non-numerical approach to production scheduling problems. *Operations Research*, 3:429–442, 1955.

[9] S. Albers and P. Brucker. The complexity of one-machine batching problems. *Discrete Applied Mathematics. Combinatorial Algorithms, Optimization and Computer Science*, 47(2):87–107, 1993.

[10] D. Applegate and W. Cook. A computational study of the job-shop scheduling problem. *ORSA Journal on Computing*, 3(2):149–156, 1991.

[11] I. Averbakh, O. Berman, and I. Chernykh. The m machine flowshop problem with unit-time operations and precedence constraints. *Operations Research Letters*, 33(3):263–266, 2005.

[12] K.R. Baker. *Introduction to Sequencing and Scheduling*. John Wiley & Sons, New York, 1974.

[13] K.R. Baker, E.L. Lawler, J.K. Lenstra, and A.H.G. Rinnooy Kan. Preemptive scheduling of a single machine to minimize maximum cost subject to release dates and precedence constraints. *Operations Research*, 31:381–386, 1983.

[14] P. Baptiste. An $0(n^4)$ algorithm for preemptive scheduling of a single machine to minimize the number of late jobs. *Operations Research Letters*, 24:175–180, 1999.

[15] P. Baptiste. Polynomial time algorithms for minimizing the weighted number of late jobs on a single machine with equal processing times. *Journal of Scheduling*, 2:245–252, 1999.

[16] P. Baptiste. Batching identical jobs. *Mathematical Methods of Operations Research*, 53(3):355–367, 2000.

[17] P. Baptiste. Preemptive scheduling of identical machines. Technical Report 2000-314, Universite de Technologie de Compiegne, France, 2000.

[18] P. Baptiste. Scheduling equal-length jobs on identical parallel machines. *Discrete Applied Mathematics*, 103(1):21–32, 2000.

[19] P. Baptiste. On preemption redundancy. *BM research report*, 2002.

[20] P. Baptiste and P. Brucker. Scheduling equal processing time jobs: a survey. In J. Y.-P. Leung, editor, *Handbook of Scheduling*, pages 14.1–14.37. Chapman & Hall/CRC, New York, 2004.

[21] P. Baptiste, P. Brucker, S. Knust, and V.G. Timkovsky. Fourteen notes on equal-processing-times scheduling. OSM Reihe P, Heft 246, Universität Osnabrück, Fachbereich Mathematik/Informatik, 2002.

[22] P. Baptiste, P. Brucker, S. Knust, and V.G. Timkovsky. Ten notes on equal-execution-times scheduling. *4 OR*, 2:111–127, 2004.

[23] P. Baptiste and V.G. Timkovsky. Shortest path to nonpreemptive schedules of unit-time jobs on two identical parallel machines with minimum total completion time. *Math. Methods Oper. Res.*, 60(1):145–153, 2004.

[24] L. Bianco, J. Blazewicz, P. Dell'Olmo, and M. Drozdowski. Scheduling preemptive multiprocessor tasks on dedicated processors. *Performance Evaluation*, 20(4):361–371, 1994.

[25] L. Bianco, J. Blazewicz, P. Dell'Olmo, and M. Drozdowski. Linear algorithms for preemptive scheduling of multiprocessor tasks subject to minimal lateness. *Discrete Applied Mathematics*, 72(1-2):25–46, 1997.

[26] J. Blazewicz and K. Ecker. A linear time algorithm for restricted bin packing and scheduling problems. *Operations Research Letters*, 2:80–83, 1983.

[27] J. Blazewicz, K. H. Ecker, E. Pesch, G. Schmidt, and J. Weglarz. *Scheduling computer and manufacturing processes.* Springer Verlag, Berlin, 1996.

[28] J. Blazewicz, J.K. Lenstra, and A.H.G. Rinnooy Kan. Scheduling subject to resource constraints: classification and complexity. *Discrete Applied Mathematics*, 5(1):11–24, 1983.

[29] J. Blazewicz and Z. Liu. Scheduling multiprocessor tasks with chain constraints. *European Journal of Operational Research*, 94(2):231–241, 1996.

[30] P.V.E. Boas. Preserving order in a forest in less than logarithmic time. In *16th Annual Symposium of Foundations of Computer Science*, pages 75–84, Long Beach, 1978. IEEE Computer Society.

[31] H. Bräsel, D. Kluge, and F. Werner. A polynomial algorithm for the $[n/m/0, t_{ij} = 1, tree/C_{\max}]$ open shop problem. *European Journal of Operational Research*, 72(1):125–134, 1994.

[32] H. Bräsel, D. Kluge, and F. Werner. A polynomial algorithm for an open shop problem with unit processing times and tree constraints. *Discrete Applied Mathematics*, 59(1):11–21, 1995.

[33] P. Brucker. An efficient algorithm for the job-shop problem with two jobs. *Computing*, 40(4):353–359, 1988.

[34] P. Brucker. A polynomial algorithm for the two machine job-shop scheduling problem with a fixed number of jobs. *Operations Research Spektrum*, 16(1):5–7, 1994.

[35] P. Brucker, M.R. Garey, and D.S. Johnson. Scheduling equal-length tasks under treelike precedence constraints to minimize maximum lateness. *Mathematics of Operations Research*, 2(3):275–284, 1977.

[36] P. Brucker, A. Gladky, H. Hoogeveen, M.Y. Kovalyov, C.N. Potts, T. Tautenhahn, and S.L. van de Velde. Scheduling a batching machine. *Journal of Scheduling*, 1(1):31–54, 1998.

[37] P. Brucker, S. Heitmann, and J. Hurink. How useful are preemptive schedules? *Operations Research Letters 31*, 31:129–136, 2003.

[38] P. Brucker, J. Hurink, and S. Knust. A polynomial algorithm for $P|p_j = 1, r_j, outtree| \sum C_j$. *Mathematical Methods of Operations Research*, 56:407–412, 2002.

[39] P. Brucker, J. Hurink, and W. Kubiak. Scheduling identical jobs with chain precedence constraints on two uniform machines. *Mathematical Methods of Operations Research*, 49(2):211–219, 1999.

[40] P. Brucker, B. Jurisch, and M. Jurisch. Open shop problems with unit time operations. *Zeitschrift für Operations Research. Methods and Models of Operations Research*, 37(1):59–73, 1993.

[41] P. Brucker, B. Jurisch, and A. Krämer. The job-shop problem and immediate selection. *Annals of Operations Research*, 50:73–114, 1994.

[42] P. Brucker, B. Jurisch, and A. Krämer. Complexity of scheduling problems with multi-purpose machines. *Annals of Operations Research*, 70:57–73, 1997.

[43] P. Brucker, B. Jurisch, and B. Sievers. A branch and bound algorithm for the job-shop scheduling problem. *Discrete Applied Mathematics*, 49(1-3):107–127, 1994.

[44] P. Brucker and S. Knust. Complexity results for single-machine problems with positive finish-start time-lags. *Computing*, 63:299–316, 1999.

[45] P. Brucker, S. Knust, D. Roper, and Y. Zinder. Scheduling UET task systems with concurrency on two parallel identical processors. *Mathematical Methods of Operations Research*, 53(3):369–387, 2000.

[46] P. Brucker and M.Y. Kovalyov. Single machine batch scheduling to minimize the weighted number of late jobs. *Mathematical Methods of Operations Research*, 43(1):1–8, 1996.

[47] P. Brucker, M.Y. Kovalyov, Y.M. Shafransky, and F. Werner. Batch scheduling with deadlines on parallel machines. *Annals of Operations Research*, 83:23–40, 1998.

[48] P. Brucker and A. Krämer. Shop scheduling problems with multiprocessor tasks on dedicated processors. *Annals of Operations Research*, 57:13–27, 1995.

[49] P. Brucker and A. Krämer. Polynomial algorithms for resource-constrained and multiprocessor task scheduling problems. *European Journal of Operational Research*, 90:214–226, 1996.

[50] P. Brucker and S.A. Kravchenko. Preemption can make parallel machine scheduling problems hard. OSM Reihe P, Heft 211, Universität Osnabrück, Fachbereich Mathematik/Informatik, 1999.

[51] P. Brucker and S.A. Kravchenko. Complexity of mean flow time scheduling problems with release dates. OSM Reihe P, Heft 251, Universität Osnabrück, Fachbereich Mathematik/Informatik, 2004.

[52] P. Brucker and S.A. Kravchenko. Scheduling jobs with equal processing times and time window on identical parallel machine. OSM Reihe P, Heft 257, Universität Osnabrück, Fachbereich Mathematik/Informatik, 2004.

[53] P. Brucker and S.A. Kravchenko. Scheduling jobs with release times on parallel machines to minimize total tardiness. OSM Reihe P, Heft 258, Universität Osnabrück, Fachbereich Mathematik/Informatik, 2005.

[54] P. Brucker, S.A. Kravchenko, and Y.N. Sotskov. On the complexity of two machine job-shop scheduling with regular objective functions. *Operations Research Spektrum*, 19(1):5–10, 1997.

[55] P. Brucker, S.A. Kravchenko, and Y.N. Sotskov. Preemptive job-shop scheduling problems with a fixed number of jobs. *Mathematical Methods of Operations Research*, 49(1):41–76, 1999.

[56] P. Brucker and R. Schlie. Job-shop scheduling with multi-purpose machines. *Computing*, 45(4):369–375, 1990.

[57] P. Brucker and O. Thiele. A branch & bound method for the general-shop problem with sequence dependent setup-times. *Operations Research Spektrum*, 18(3):145–161, 1996.

[58] J. Bruno, E.G. Coffman, Jr., and R. Sethi. Scheduling independent tasks to reduce mean finishing time. *Communications of the ACM*, 17:382–387, 1974.

[59] J. Bruno and P. Downey. Complexity of task sequencing with deadlines, set-up times and changeover costs. *SIAM Journal on Computing*, 7:393–403, 1978.

[60] J. Bruno, J.W. Jones, III, and K. So. Deterministic scheduling with pipelined processors. *IEEE Transactions on Computers*, 29(4):308–316, 1980.

[61] X. Cai, C.-Y. Lee, and C.-L. Li. Minimizing total completion time in two-processor task systems with prespecified processor allocations. *Naval Research Logistics. An International Journal*, 45(2):231–242, 1998.

[62] J. Carlier. The one-machine sequencing problem. *European Journal of Operational Research*, 11:42–47, 1982.

[63] J. Carlier and E. Pinson. An algorithm for solving the job-shop problem. *Management Science*, 35(2):164–176, 1989.

[64] J. Chen and C.-Y. Lee. General multiprocessor task scheduling. *Naval Research Logistics*, 46(1):57–74, 1999.

[65] J. Cheriyan and S.N. Maheshwari. Analysis of preflow push algorithms for maximum network flow. *SIAM Journal on Computing*, 18(6):1057–1086, 1989.

[66] Y. Cho and S. Sahni. Preemptive scheduling of independent jobs with release and due times on open, flow and job shops. *Operations Research*, 29(3):511–522, 1981.

[67] V. Chvatal. *Linear programming*. W. H. Freeman and Company, New York - San Francisco, 1983.

[68] E. G. Coffman, Jr., J. Sethuraman, and V.G. Timkovsky. Ideal preemptive schedules on two processors. Technical report, Columbia University, 2002.

[69] E.G. Coffman, Jr. *Scheduling in Computer and Job Shop Systems*. J.Wiley, New York, 1976.

[70] E.G. Coffman, Jr. and R.L. Graham. Optimal scheduling for two-processor systems. *Acta Informatica*, 1:200–213, 1971/1972.

[71] E.G. Coffman, Jr., M. Yannakakis, M.J. Magazine, and C. Santos. Batch sizing and job sequencing on a single machine. *Annals of Operations Research*, 26(1-4):135–147, 1990.

[72] R.W. Conway, W.L. Maxwell, and L.W. Miller. *Theory of Scheduling*. Addison Wesley, Reading, Mass., USA, 1967.

[73] S.A. Cook. The complexity of theorem-proving procedures. In *Proceedings of the 3rd Annual ACM Symposium on Theory of Computing*, pages 151–158. ACM-Press, 1971.

[74] G.B. Dantzig. Application of the simplex method to a transportation problem. In T.C. Koopmans, editor, *Activity analysis of production and allocation*, pages 359–373. John Wiley & Sons, Inc., 1951.

[75] M. Dell'Amico and M. Trubian. Applying tabu search to the job-shop scheduling problem. *Annals of Operations Research*, 41(1-4):231–252, 1993.

[76] M.I. Dessouky, B.J. Lageweg, J.K. Lenstra, and S.L. van de Velde. Scheduling identical jobs on uniform parallel machines. *Statistica Neerlandica*, 44(3):115–123, 1990.

[77] U. Dorndorf and E. Pesch. Evolution based learning in a job shop scheduling environment. *Computers & Operations Research*, 22(1):25–40, 1995.

[78] M. Dror, W. Kubiak, and P. Dell'Olmo. Strong-weak chain constrained scheduling. *Ricerca Operativa*, 27:35–49, 1998.

[79] M. Drozdowski and P. Dell' Olmo. Scheduling multiprocessor tasks for mean flow time criterion. Technical Report RA-003/98, Institute of Computing Science, Poznan University of Technology, 1998.

[80] J. Du and J.Y.-T. Leung. Complexity of scheduling parallel task systems. *SIAM Journal on Discrete Mathematics*, 2(4):473–487, 1989.

[81] J. Du and J.Y.-T. Leung. Minimizing total tardiness on one machine is NP-hard. *Mathematics of Operations Research*, 15(3):483–495, 1990.

[82] J. Du and J.Y.-T. Leung. Minimizing the number of late jobs on unrelated machines. *Operations Research Letters*, 10(3):153–158, 1991.

[83] J. Du and J.Y.-T. Leung. Minimizing mean flow time in two-machine open shops and flow shops. *Journal of Algorithms*, 14(1):24–44, 1993.

[84] J. Du, J.Y.-T. Leung, and C.S. Wong. Minimizing the number of late jobs with release time constraint. *Journal of Combinatorial Mathematics and Combinatorial Computing*, 11:97–107, 1992.

[85] J. Du, J.Y.-T. Leung, and G.H. Young. Minimizing mean flow time with release time constraint. *Theoretical Computer Science*, 75(3):347–355, 1990.

[86] J. Du, J.Y.-T. Leung, and G.H. Young. Scheduling chain-structured tasks to minimize makespan and mean flow time. *Information and Computation*, 92(2):219–236, 1991.

[87] J. Edmonds and R.M. Karp. Theoretical improvements in algorithmic efficiency for network flow problems. *Journal of the Association for Computing Machinery*, 19:248–264, 1972.

[88] S. Even and O. Kariv. An $o(n^{2.5})$ algorithm for maximum matching in general graphs. In *Proceedings of the 16th Annual Symposium of Foundations of Computer Science*, pages 100–112, Long Beach, 1975. IEEE Computer Society.

[89] A. Federgruen and H. Groenevelt. Preemptive scheduling of uniform machines by ordinary network flow techniques. *Management Science*, 32:341–349, 1986.

[90] M.J. Fischer and A.R. Meyer. Boolean matrix multiplication and transitive closure. In *Proceedings Twelfth Annual Symposium on Switching and Automata Theory*, pages 129–137, East Lansing, Mich., 1971.

[91] L.R.jun. Ford and D.R. Fulkerson. Maximal flow through a network. *Canadian Journal of Mathematics*, 8:399–404, 1956.

[92] G.N. Frederickson. Scheduling unit-time tasks with integer release times and deadlines. *Information Processing Letters*, 16:171–173, 1983.

[93] S. French. *Sequencing and scheduling: an introduction to the mathematics of the job- shop.* Ellis Horwood Limited, New York, 1982.

[94] D.R. Fulkerson. An out-of-kilter method for minimal-cost flow problems. *SIAM Jouranl of Applied Mathematics*, 9:18–27, 1961.

[95] H.N. Gabow and O. Kariv. Algorithms for edge coloring bipartite graphs and multigraphs. *SIAM Journal on Computing*, 11:117–129, 1982.

[96] M.R. Garey and D.S. Johnson. Scheduling tasks with nonuniform deadlines on two processors. *Journal of the Association for Computing Machinery*, 23:461–467, 1976.

[97] M.R. Garey and D.S. Johnson. Two-processor scheduling with start-times and deadlines. *SIAM Journal on Computing*, 6(3):416–426, 1977.

[98] M.R. Garey and D.S. Johnson. "Strong" NP-completeness results: motivation, examples, and implications. *Journal of the Association for Computing Machinery*, 25(3):499–508, 1978.

[99] M.R. Garey and D.S. Johnson. *Computers and intractability. A guide to the theory of NP-completeness*. W. H. Freeman and Company, San Francisco, 1979.

[100] M.R. Garey, D.S. Johnson, and R. Sethi. The complexity of flow-shop and jobshop scheduling. *Mathematics of Operations Research*, 1(2):117–129, 1976.

[101] A.V. Goldberg and R.E. Tarjan. Finding minimum-cost circulations by successive approximation. *Mathematics of Operations Research*, 15(3):430–466, 1990.

[102] T. Gonzalez. A note on open shop preemptive schedules. *IEEE Transactions on Computers C-28*, pages 782–786, 1979.

[103] T. Gonzalez and D.B. Johnson. A new algorithm for preemptive scheduling of trees. *Journal of the Association for Computing Machinery*, 27(2):287–312, 1980.

[104] T. Gonzalez and S. Sahni. Open shop scheduling to minimize finish time. *Journal of the Association for Computing Machinery*, 23(4):665–679, 1976.

[105] T. Gonzalez and S. Sahni. Flowshop and jobshop schedules: complexity and approximation. *Operations Research*, 26(1):36–52, 1978.

[106] T. Gonzalez and S. Sahni. Preemptive scheduling of uniform processor systems. *Journal of the Association for Computing Machinery*, 25:92–101, 1978.

[107] J. Grabowski, E. Nowicki, and S. Zdrzalka. A block approach for single-machine scheduling with release dates and due dates. *European Journal of Operational Research*, 26:278–285, 1986.

[108] R.L. Graham, E.L. Lawler, J.K. Lenstra, and A.H.G. Rinnooy Kan. Optimization and approximation in deterministic sequencing and scheduling: A survey. *Annals of Discrete Mathematics*, 5:287–326, 1979.

[109] N.G. Hall and M.E. Posner. Earliness-tardiness scheduling problems. I: Weighted deviation of completion times about a common due data. *Operations Research*, 39(5):836–846, 1991.

[110] P. Hall. On representatives of subsets. *Journal of the London Mathematical Society*, 10:26–30, 1935.

[111] L.A. Herrbach and J.Y.-T. Leung. Preemptive scheduling of equal length jobs on two machines to minimize mean flow time. *Operations Research*, 38(3):487–494, 1990.

[112] D.S. Hochbaum and D. Landy. Scheduling with batching: minimizing the weighted number of tardy jobs. *Operations Research Letters*, 16(2):79–86, 1994.

[113] J.A. Hoogeveen, S.L. van de Velde, and B. Veltman. Complexity of scheduling multiprocessor tasks with prespecified processor allocations. *Discrete Applied Mathematics. Combinatorial Algorithms, Optimization and Computer Science*, 55(3):259–272, 1994.

[114] J.E. Hopcroft and R.M. Karp. A $n^{5/2}$ algorithm for maximum matchings in bipartite graphs. *SIAM Journal on Computing*, 2:225–231, 1973.

[115] W.A. Horn. Some simple scheduling algorithms. *Naval Research Logistics Quarterly*, 21:177–185, 1974.

[116] T.C. Hu. Parallel sequencing and assembly line problems. *Operations Research*, 9:841–848, 1961.

[117] E. Ignall and L. Schrage. Apllications of the branch and bound technique to some flow-shop scheduling problems. *Operations Research*, 13:400–412, 1965.

[118] J.R. Jackson. Scheduling a production to minimize maximum tardiness. Research Report 43, Management Science Research Project, University of California at Los Angeles, 1955.

[119] J.R. Jackson. An extension of johnson's results on job lot scheduling. *Naval Research Logistic Quaterly*, 3:201–203, 1956.

[120] S.M. Johnson. Optimal two-and-three-stage production schedules with set-up times included. *Naval Research Logistic Quaterly*, 1:61–68, 1954.

[121] B. Jurisch. Lower bounds for the job-shop scheduling problem on multi-purpose machines. *Discrete Applied Mathematics. Combinatorial Algorithms, Optimization and Computer Science*, 58(2):145–156, 1995.

[122] H. Kahlbacher. *Termin- und Ablaufplanung - ein analytischer Zugang*. PhD thesis, University Kaiserslautern, 1992.

[123] J.J. Kanet. Minimizing the average deviation of job completion times about a common due date. *Naval Research Logistic Quaterly*, 28:643–651, 1981.

[124] R.M. Karp. Reducibility among combinatorial problems. In *Complexity of computer computations (Proc. Sympos., IBM Thomas J. Watson Res. Center, Yorktown Heights, N.Y., 1972)*, pages 85–103. Plenum, New York, 1972.

[125] L.G. Khachiyan. A polynomial algorithm in linear programming. *Doklasy Akademii Nauk SSSR*, 244:1093–1096, 1979.

[126] S.A. Kravchenko. Minimizing the number of late jobs for the two-machine unit-time job-shop scheduling problem. *Discrete Applied Mathematics*, 98(3):209–217, 1999.

[127] S.A. Kravchenko. On the complexity of minimizing the number of late jobs in unit time open shops. *Discrete Applied Mathematics*, 100(2):127–132, 1999.

[128] M. Kubale. Preemptive scheduling of two processor tasks on dedicated processors. *Zeszyty Naukowe Politechnik: Ślaskiej, Seria: Automatyka Z. 100*, 1082:145–153, 1990.

[129] W. Kubiak. Exact and approximate algorithms for scheduling unit time tasks with tree-like precedence constraints. In *Abstracts EURO IX - TIMS XXVIII Paris, 195*, 1988.

[130] W. Kubiak, S. Sethi, and C. Sriskandarajah. An efficient algorithm for a job shop problem. *Annals of Operations Research*, 57:203–216, 1995.

[131] W. Kubiak and V.G. Timkovsky. A polynomial-time algorithm for total completion time minimization in two-machine job-shop with unit-time operations. *European Journal of Operational Research*, 94:310–320, 1996.

[132] H.W. Kuhn. The Hungarian method for the assignment problem. *Naval Research Logistics*, 2, 1955.

[133] J. Labetoulle, E.L. Lawler, J.K. Lenstra, and A.H.G. Rinnooy Kan. Preemptive scheduling of uniform machines subject to release dates. In *Progress in combinatorial optimization (Waterloo, Ont., 1982)*, pages 245–261. Academic Press, Toronto, Ont., 1984.

[134] B.J. Lageweg, J.K. Lenstra, E.L. Lawler, and A.H.G. Rinnooy Kan. Computer-aided complexity classification of combinatorial problems. *Communications of the ACM*, 25:817–822, 1982.

[135] E.L. Lawler. Optimal sequencing of a single machine subject to precedence constraints. *Management Science*, 19:544–546, 1973.

[136] E.L. Lawler. A "pseudopolynomial" algorithm for sequencing jobs to minimize total tardiness. *Annals of Discrete Mathematics*, 1:331–342, 1977.

[137] E.L. Lawler. Sequencing jobs to minimize total weighted completion time subject to precedence constraints. *Annals of Discrete Mathematics*, 2:75–90, 1978.

[138] E.L. Lawler. Preemptive scheduling of uniform parallel machines to minimize the weighted number of late jobs. Report BW 105, Centre for Mathematics and Computer Science, Amsterdam, 1979.

[139] E.L. Lawler. Preemptive scheduling of precedence-constrained jobs on parallel machines. In M.A.H. Dempster, J.K. Lenstra, and A.H.G. Rinnooy Kan, editors, *Deterministic and stochastic scheduling, Proceedings of the NATO Advanced Study and Research Institute on Theoretical Approaches to Scheduling Problems held in Durham, July 6–17, 1981*, volume 84 of *NATO Advanced Study Institute Series C: Mathematical and Physical Sciences*, pages 101–123, Dordrecht, 1982. D. Reidel Publishing Co.

[140] E.L. Lawler. Recent results in the theory of machine scheduling. In A. Bachem, M. Groetschel, and B. Korte, editors, *Mathematical programming: the state of the art (Bonn, 1982)*, pages 202–234. Springer, Berlin, 1983.

[141] E.L. Lawler. A dynamic programming algorithm for preemptive scheduling of a single machine to minimize the number of late jobs. *Annals of Operations Research*, 26(1-4):125–133, 1990.

[142] E.L. Lawler and J. Labetoulle. On preemptive scheduling of unrelated parallel processors by linear programming. *Journal of the Association for Computing Machinery*, 25(4):612–619, 1978.

[143] E.L. Lawler, J.K. Lenstra, and A.H.G. Rinnooy Kan. Minimizing maximum lateness in a two-machine open shop. *Mathematics of Operations Research*, 6(1):153–158, 1981.

[144] E.L. Lawler, J.K. Lenstra, and A.H.G. Rinnooy Kan. Erratum: "Minimizing maximum lateness in a two-machine open shop" [Math. Oper. Res. **6** (1981), no. 1, 153-158]. *Mathematics of Operations Research*, 7(4):635, 1982.

[145] E.L. Lawler, J.K. Lenstra, A.H.G. Rinnooy Kan, and D.B. Shmoys. *Sequencing and Scheduling: Algorithmus and Complexity*, volume 4 of *Handbook in Operations Research and Managment Science*. North-Holland, Amsterdam, 1993.

[146] E.L. Lawler and C.U. Martel. Preemptive scheduling of two uniform machines to minimize the number of late jobs. *Operations Research*, 37(2):314–318, 1989.

[147] E.L. Lawler and J.M. Moore. A functional equation and its application to resource allocation and sequencing problems. *Management Science*, 16:77–84, 1969.

[148] C.-Y. Lee and X. Cai. Scheduling one and two-processor tasks on two parallel processors. *IIE Transactions on Scheduling and Logistics*, 31:445–455, 1999.

[149] H.W. Lenstra, Jr. Integer programming with a fixed number of variables. *Mathematics of Operations Research*, 8:538–548, 1983.

[150] J.K. Lenstra. Not published.

[151] J.K. Lenstra. *Sequencing by enumerative methods.* Mathematical Centre Tracts. 69, 1977.

[152] J.K. Lenstra and A.H.G. Rinnooy Kan. Complexity of scheduling under precedence constraints. *Operations Research*, 26(1):22–35, 1978.

[153] J.K. Lenstra and A.H.G. Rinnooy Kan. Computational complexity of discrete optimization problems. *Annals of Discrete Mathematics*, 4:121–140, 1979.

[154] J.K. Lenstra and A.H.G. Rinnooy Kan. Complexity results for scheduling chains on a single machine. *European Journal of Operational Research*, 4(4):270–275, 1980.

[155] J.K. Lenstra, A.H.G. Rinnooy Kan, and P. Brucker. Complexity of machine scheduling problems. *Annals of Discrete Mathematics*, 1:343–362, 1977.

[156] J.Y.-T. Leung, O. Vornberger, and J.D. Witthoff. On some variants of the bandwidth minimization problem. *SIAM Journal on Computing*, 13(3):650–667, 1984.

[157] J.Y.-T. Leung and G.H. Young. Minimizing total tardiness on a single machine with precedence constraints. *ORSA Journal on Computing*, 2(4):346–352, 1990.

[158] J.Y.-T. Leung and G.H. Young. Preemptive scheduling to minimize mean weighted flow time. *Information Processing Letters*, 34(1):47–50, 1990.

[159] L.A. Levin. Universal sorting problems. *Problemy Peredachi Informatsii*, 9:265–266, 1973.

[160] C.Y. Liu and R.L. Bulfin. On the complexity of preemptive open-shop scheduling problems. *Operations Research Letters*, 4(2):71–74, 1985.

[161] C.Y. Liu and R.L. Bulfin. Scheduling open shops with unit execution times to minimize functions of due dates. *Operations Research*, 36(4):553–559, 1988.

[162] E.L. Lloyd. Concurrent task systems. *Operations Research. The Journal of the Operations Research Society of America*, 29(1):189–201, 1981.

[163] I. Lushchakova. Two machine preemptive scheduling problem with release dates, equal processing times and precedence constraints. *European J. Oper. Res.*, 171(1):107–122, 2006.

[164] V.M. Malhotra, M.P. Kumar, and S.N. Maheshwari. An $O(|V|^3)$ algorithm for finding maximum flows in networks. *Information Processing Letters*, 7:277–278, 1978.

[165] R. McNaughton. Scheduling with deadlines and loss functions. *Management Science*, 6:1–12, 1959/1960.

[166] W. Meyer. *Geometrische Methoden zur Lösung von Job-Shop Problemen und deren Verallgemeinerungen.* PhD thesis, Universität Osnabrück, Fachbereich Mathematik/Informatik, 1992.

[167] M. Middendorf and V.G. Timkovsky. Transversal graphs for partially ordered sets: sequencing, merging and scheduling problems. *Journal of Combinatorial Optimization*, 3(4):417–435, 1999.

[168] G.J. Minty. Monotone networks. *Proceedings of the London Mathematical Society*, 257:194–212, 1960.

[169] C.L. Monma. Linear-time algorithms for scheduling on parallel processors. *Operations Research*, 30:116–124, 1982.

[170] C.L. Monma and C.N. Potts. On the complexity of scheduling with batch setup times. *Operations Research*, 37(5):798–804, 1989.

[171] J.M. Moore. An n job, one machine sequencing algorithm for minimizing the number of late jobs. *Management Science*, 15:102–109, 1968.

[172] R.R. Muntz and E.G. Coffman, Jr. Optimal preemptive scheduling on two-processor systems. *IEEE Transactions on Computers*, pages 1014–1020, 1969.

[173] R.R. Muntz and E.G. Coffman, Jr. Preemptive scheduling of real-time tasks on multiprocessor systems. *Journal of the Association for Computing Machinery*, 17:324–338, 1970.

[174] J.F. Muth and G.L. Thompson. *Industrial Scheduling*. Wiley, New York, 1963.

[175] G.L. Nemhauser and L.A. Wolsey. *Integer and combinatorial optimization*. Wiley, New York, 1988.

[176] C.T. Ng, T.C.E. Cheng, and J.J. Yuan. A note on the single machine serial batching scheduling problem to minimize maximum lateness with precedence constraints. *Operations Research Letters*, 30:66–68, 2002.

[177] E. Nowicki and C. Smutnicki. A fast tabu search algorithm for the job shop problem. *Management Science*, 42(6):797–813, 1996.

[178] J.B. Orlin. A faster strongly polynomial minimum cost flow algorithm. *Operations Research*, 41(2):338–350, 1993.

[179] S.S. Panwalkar, M.L. Smith, and A. Seidmann. Common due date assignment to minimize total penalty for the one machine scheduling problem. *Operations Research*, 30:391–399, 1982.

[180] M. Pinedo. *Scheduling: Theory, Algorithms and Systems*. Prentice Hall, Englewood Cliffs N.J., 1995.

[181] A.H.G. Rinnooy Kan. *Machine Scheduling Problems: Classification, Complexity and Computations*. Martinus Nijhoff, The Hague, 1976.

[182] A. Schrijver. *Theory of linear and integer programming*. Wiley, Chichester, 1986.

[183] N.V. Shakhlevich and Yu.N. Sotskov. Scheduling two jobs with fixed and nonfixed routes. *Computing*, 52(1):17–30, 1994.

[184] N.V. Shakhlevich, Yu.N. Sotskov, and F. Werner. Shop scheduling problems with fixed and non-fixed machine orders of jobs. *Annals of Operations Research*, 92:281–304, 1999.

[185] B. Simons. A fast algorithm for single processor scheduling. In *19th Annual Symposium on Foundations of Computer Science (Ann Arbor, Mich., 1978)*, pages 246–252. IEEE, Long Beach, Calif., 1978.

[186] B. Simons. Multiprocessor scheduling of unit-time jobs with arbitrary release times and deadlines. _SIAM Journal on Computing_, 12(2):294–299, 1983.

[187] R.A. Sitters. Two NP-hardness results for preemptive minisum scheduling for unreleated parallel machines. In _Proc. 8th International IPCO Conference_, volume 2081 of _Lecture Notes in Computer Science_, pages 396–405. Springer, 2001.

[188] W.E. Smith. Various optimizers for single-stage production. _Naval Research Logistics Quarterly_, 3:59–66, 1956.

[189] Y.N. Sotskov. The complexity of shop-scheduling problems with two or three jobs. _European Journal of Operational Research_, 53(3):326–336, 1991.

[190] Y.N. Sotskov and N.V. Shakhlevich. NP-hardness of shop-scheduling problems with three jobs. _Discrete Applied Mathematics_, 59(3):237–266, 1995.

[191] C. Sriskandarajah and E. Wagneur. On the complexity of preemptive openshop scheduling problems. _European Journal of Operational Research_, 77(3):404–414, 1994.

[192] V.A. Strusevich. Two-machine super-shop scheduling problem. _Journal of the Operational Research Society_, 42(6):479–492, 1991.

[193] V.S. Tanaev, V.S. Gordon, and Y.M. Shafransky. _Scheduling theory. Single-stage systems. Vol. 1._ Kluwer Academic Publishers., Dordrecht, 1994.

[194] V.S. Tanaev, Y.N. Sotskov, and V.A. Strusevich. _Scheduling theory. Multi-stage systems_, volume 285 of _Mathematics and its Applications_. Kluwer Academic Publishers Group, Dordrecht, 1994. Translated and revised from the 1989 Russian original by the authors.

[195] T. Tautenhahn. _Open-shop-Probleme mit Einheitsbearbeitungszeiten_. PhD thesis, Fakultät für Mathematik, Otto-von-Guericke-Universität Magdeburg, 1993.

[196] T. Tautenhahn and G.J. Woeginger. Minimizing the total completion time in a unit-time open shop with release times. *Operations Research Letters*, 20(5):207–212, 1997.

[197] Z. Tian, C.T. Ng, and T.C.E. Cheng. An $O(n^2)$ algorithm for scheduling equal-length preemptive jobs on a single machine to minimze total tardiness. *Journal of Scheduling*, 9(4):343–364, 2006.

[198] V.G. Timkovsky. On the complexity of scheduling an arbitrary system. *Soviet Journal of Computer and Systems Sciences*, 23(5):46–52, 1985.

[199] V.G. Timkovsky. The complexity of unit-time job-shop scheduling. Technical Report 93-09, Department of Computer Science and Systems, McMaster Univ. Hamilton, 1993.

[200] V.G. Timkovsky. A polynomial-time algorithm for the two-machine unit-time release-date job-shop schedule-length problem. *Discrete Applied Mathematics. Combinatorial Algorithms, Optimization and Computer Science*, 77(2):185–200, 1997.

[201] V.G. Timkovsky. Identical parallel machines vs. unit-time shops, preemptions vs. chains, and other offsets in scheduling complexity. Technical Report, Department of Computer Science and Systems, McMaster Univ. Hamilton, 1998.

[202] V.G. Timkovsky. Is a unit-time job shop not easier than identical parallel machines? *Discrete Applied Mathematics. Combinatorial Algorithms, Optimization and Computer Science*, 85(2):149–162, 1998.

[203] J.D. Ullman. NP-complete scheduling problems. *Journal of Computer and System Sciences*, 10:384–393, 1975.

[204] J.D. Ullman. Complexity of sequencing problems. In J.L. Bruno, E.G. Coffman, Jr., R.L. Graham, W.H. Kohler, R. Sethi, K. Steiglitz, and J.D. Ullman, editors, *Computer and Job/Shop Scheduling Theory*. John Wiley & Sons Inc., New York, 1976.

[205] P.J.M. van Laarhoven and E.H.L. Aarts. *Simulated annealing: theory and applications*. D. Reidel Publishing Company, Dordrecht, 1987.

[206] P.J.M. van Laarhoven, E.H.L. Aarts, and J.K. Lenstra. Job shop scheduling by simulated annealing. *Operations Research*, 40(1):113–125, 1992.

[207] M.A. Yakovleva. A problem on minimum transportation cost. In *Applications of mathematics in economic research*, pages 390–399. Izdat. Social'no - Ekon Lit., Moscow, 1959.

Index

Printing: Krips bv, Meppel
Binding: Stürtz, Würzburg